Images of the Body in India

Images of the Body in India

Editors
Axel Michaels
Christoph Wulf

Routledge
Taylor & Francis Group
LONDON NEW YORK NEW DELHI

The original edition was published under the title
"The Body in India: Ritual, Transgression, Performativity" Paragrana, vol. 18/2009/1

This edition published 2011 in India
by Routledge
912 Tolstoy House, 15–17 Tolstoy Marg, Connaught Place, New Delhi 110 001

Simultaneously published in the UK
by Routledge
2 Park Square, Milton Park, Abingdon, Oxfordshire OX14 4RN

First issued in paperback 2015

Routledge is an imprint of the Taylor & Francis Group, an informa business

Typeset by
Star Compugraphics Private Limited
D-156, Second Floor
Sector 7, Noida 201 301

British Library Cataloguing-in-Publication Data
A catalogue record of this book is available from the British Library

ISBN 13: 978-1-138-66284-1 (pbk)
ISBN 13: 978-0-415-60230-3 (hbk)

Contents

The Body in Visualisations and Images

Axel Michaels and Christoph Wulf

Rethinking the Body: An Introduction

In this book we are pursuing two objectives: on the one hand, and foremost, we want to address and study the concept of the body in India; on the other, we want to show that this analysis takes account of the fact that the human body is understood differently in Western cultures when compared to Indian cultures. The two objectives are inter-linked and represent the specific aim of this volume, namely, what is understood by the body in its cultural context?

The Body in Indian Cultures

Any attempt to put forward a single concept of the body would be falsifying Indian thought which is based on a variety of independent sources, social groups, languages, regions, religions and beliefs, and which therefore cannot be reduced to one, single, uniform world-view. After all, it must not be forgotten that the term 'Hinduism' itself, denoting a monolithic religion, was coined by Muslims to speak of the phenomenon of Indian religious life whereas the so-called 'Hindus' themselves have not tended to regard themselves as a unitary social group or community. Thus, in cases where the Hindu conceptions of the body are spoken of, it is usually either simplistic or reductive or even wrong, tending predominantly to focus on just one corpus — mostly Sanskrit literature — and merely one social group, the Brahmin priests.

From this perspective, various body concepts appear in relation to South Asia, only some of which we focus on: (1) *subtle and gross bodies*; (2) *social bodies*; (3) *the transformation and transgression of the body*; and (4) *the sacrifice as a body and the body as a sacrifice*. Further differentiations include, for example, the tantric, medical, yogic or devotional body (see WUJASTYK forthcoming, BOUILLIER/TARABOUT 2002, HOLDREDGE 2008, MAAS 2007–8). In all these concepts and notions it is clear that, as Veena DAS (1985: 181) aptly remarked, 'the moment we look at the body as a system of meanings rather than as biological substance, it ceases to be merely given. It is, then, culturally created.'

The difference between *subtle and gross bodies* is fundamental to the Indian Hindu context. It concerns the religious outlooks, as well as yogic methods, practised even today. The difference is inconceivable without the classical Sāṃkhya system of philosophy (see LARSON/BHATTACHARYA 1987). In this system, the process of evolution starts with the emerging of intellect (*buddhi*) which, in turn, produces the ego (*ahaṃkāra*). The ego produces the mind (*manas*), the five sense faculties (*buddhi-indriya*: ear, skin, eye, tongue and nose), five corresponding sense organs or action faculties (*karma-indriya*: voice, hand, foot, anus and genitals), and five subtle elements (*tanmātra*: sound, touch, colour, taste and smell) which, in turn, produce the five gross elements (*mahābhūta*: air, wind, fire, water and earth). In this dualistic philosophy, psychic qualities have physical properties by which they can affect other things. Although the *puruṣa*s or individual souls are, in truth, also pure spirit, they are differentiated by a subtle body (*sūkṣmaī-śarīra*) even as the various *puruṣa*s are essentially identical. They are not individuals who migrate through worlds and world ages but individuations of the one and only *Puruṣa* which is in itself eternal, immovable, pure (spiritual) light, and of pure and non-attributive consciousness. It is therefore possible only for the liberated to know the *Puruṣa*; all others are deluded by their thoughts and senses, i.e., by their subtle and gross bodies.

When *prakṛti* or material nature manifests itself in the process of evolution, the *puruṣa*s become a gross body because of the law of *karma*. However, the great *Puruṣa* is only seemingly active because in fact only *prakṛti* is active because its constituents, the *guṇa*s, are imbalanced through intellect, the ego, mind, etc. Those who are liberated know about this erroneous relationship because they do not have consciousness of any thing; they are themselves pure consciousness without any duality any more.

From the conception of body and nature in the Sāṃkhya system, it is clear that salvation or *Puruṣa* is identified with static, immovable, inactive states, whereas suffering is linked with dynamic, active, evolutionary and causal processes, the eternal cycle of ages and rebirth (*saṃsāra*).

A great deal is invested in this system that displays the Indian way of thinking: asceticism, retribution or the Karma system, reincarnation, multi-corporeality, and the spiritual and ritualistic salvation teachings. However, it also shows that the question of dematerialisation of the body is one that has occupied India from early on. It did not focus on the visualisation of the body and the diffusion through image media to the extent that it does in modern times, but rather the inner display of a 'disembodied being' and in this sense the dematerialisation of body action and thinking. This is because, according to the Sāṃkhya system, matter also comprises thought and feeling. This subtle matter is the material from which rebirth (and thus reincarnation) takes place. Only its mental and physical dematerialisation finally leads to disembodiment and, through this, release.

Since the body matter also includes theoretical and mental processes, the body is not, according to the Sāṃkhya system and common opinion a monad that is determined by its physical body limits. In most Indian religions, the body is thought of as a porous structure and concerns not only the individual but also the social group. The body becomes a *social body*. Impure actions and thoughts befall, for example, not only the individuals, but also relatives and family members. Individuality becomes a dividuality (Marriott 1968, 1989); the individual body becomes a social body.

This becomes clear, for example, in the Hindu death ritual (see Michaels 2004b, Gutschow/Michaels 2005), which is, fundamentally, a gradual transformation of the body in which the bereaved play a part. After the gross body of the dead person has been burnt, the deceased remains in a subtle body with a mouth only the size of a pin, which has feelings but no body organs. It is then essentially a kind of hungry pest which oppresses the bereaved who have to take care of it so that it finds its place and union with its ancestors. The bereaved relatives reassemble him in the form of doughboys or balls (*piṇḍa*) in a death ritual in order to finally unite him with the three forefathers (father, grandfather and great-grandfather), who are also present in the form of piṇḍas. The piṇḍa body is a social body, not an individual one. 'Connected through the sacrificial balls' (*sapiṇḍa*) is a description of connection and relatedness which is also considered at various stages in life: birth, endogamy and exogamy conditions and inheritance law — the one allowed to perform the ancestral ritual is a doughboy associate and thus entitled to inherit. *Sāpiṇḍya* relatives form a common body because one is connected through forefathers and foremothers. At the same time, this ritual shows how, in such contexts, an individual body is fragmented into its *membra disiecta* and recomposed.

The social body is also evident in Indian concepts of purity and impurity. To obtain purity or moreover, to maintain it, it is necessary, above all, to avoid forbidden body contact. But here the body not only means the physical body and contact with it or its secretions: glances, gestures or words, for example, are forms of body contact that can contaminate. In this sense, purity is avoidance of impurity, impurity being the loss of purity. According to McKim Marriott (1968, 1989), a definition of purity and impurity that would be binding on all Indian religions is not possible on the basis of the Sāṃkhya system while paying attention to the interactions between individuals and social groups. In order to find out who may touch whom, who may enter whose house, who may eat with whom or who may marry whose daughter, the forms of encounter and exchange matter for the notions of purity and impurity rather than personal antipathies or likings.

The diverse interpretations of the *transformation and transgression of the body* becomes evident when we view it from this perspective. Not only is gender transgressed in a mythological sense, and even partly reversed, the body itself becomes the space for its transgression, the preferred place for realising mythological/ritualistic ideas and concepts. Transformations from God to person, person to animal or person to ancestor or ghost and *vice versa* are often only regarded as different forms of incarnation. Self-deification, as Max Weber described certain forms of asceticism, is also easily possible in India as the incarnation of gods in people.

Also, the important concept of a second birth with the result of a second, holy body, which every male Hindu from the upper classes receives at his initiation (see MICHAELS 2004: 71–110), clarifies how much the natural body can be replaced or complemented by a body constructed during a ritual. These ritualistic body transformations and relations are defined considerably by their public performances: it depends on making the new body created during the ritual visible and official.

In many instances, Hinduism must be understood only from the all-embracing system of sacrifice or its criticism thereof. *Sacrifice as a body* is visible in Vedic religious practices; *the body as a sacrifice* emerges later in the cremation of the dead and in certain ascetic paths. The ancient Vedic sacrifice was largely anthropometrical, corresponding to the body measurements of the organiser of the sacrifice. At the same time, the sacrificer was identified with the sacrifice and thus with its attendant reward of salvation. 'In truth, the sacrifice is the person', is how it is referred to, for example, in the *Śatapatha Brāhmaṇa*, a text from approx. 800 BC on the basis of which several doctrines of salvation have developed, partly ritualistic, and partly of a gnostic/spiritual nature (see MICHAELS 2004: 315–44), whereby the microcosm is equated with the macrocosm or the self with the absolute. While the person and its body can be identified with the whole in this way, the body, especially in tantric forms, is also viewed as the place of the whole world. Thus, individual organs or body limbs are attributed to the gods or various spiritual levels.

Several forms of asceticism with their special body techniques have therefore become accepted (see MICHAELS 2004a): yoga, fasting or mortification, practices which primarily try to control natural bodily comportments like clothing and nakedness, eating and drinking, walking and sitting, sleeping and being awake, talking and remaining silent. But as a result of the humble and devotional surrender to a god, it also leads to ecstatic forms of expression, where the body is predominantly at the fore.

The 'Body' in Humanities and Social Sciences in Western Cultures

Before we continue with our analysis of the body in India, we want to show the different conceptualisation of the body in Western cultures (focusing on Germany) to make the reader aware of the distinctive way in which the body is conceptualised in India. A few decades ago in Germany a distinction was made between 'Körper' and 'Leib', where 'Körper' referred to the physical body and 'Leib' to the animated body, a difference Germans no longer consider meaningful. This difference established a dualism which, on the basis of new research in the natural and social sciences and humanities as well as textual and visual material from non-Western cultures, is now considered outmoded. Instead, one assumes a multidimensional understanding of the body where the specific aspects of a given culture need to be specified. Thus, as we will see later, the degree of difference between a dualistic European and a monistic Indian understanding of the body is inadequate, and too narrowly analysed. A context-related examination of differences — such as those between spirit and body, consciousness and soul, purity and impurity, nature and culture seems more useful and enriching. Our thoughts and considerations on this matter are further specified below. But first, we take a look at discussions on the body currently taking place in Germany before returning to tackle the concepts of the body of India.

Since the beginning of the 1980s, the body has become an important topic of academic debate in humanities and social sciences in Germany (see KAMPER/WULF 1982; FEHER 1989), and now constitutes one of the main topics in cultural studies research in Germany and other European countries (see ANDRIEU 2006; MARZANO 2007). In view of the variety and richness of the research that has now become available — especially on the human body — it is possible to say that there is currently some agreement on the central meaning of body-images and body-concepts as cultural forms of identity and self-interpretation in European academia. The origin of the modern body in the West with its concomitant processes of distancing and disciplining, visualisation of the inner self and self-observation, and keenness for knowledge and power has been explored in several ways, and have brought to the fore questions of dematerialisation, technologisation, fragmentation, sexuality and the performativity of the body.

Electronic media is playing an effective role in the *dematerialisation* of the body, body perceptions and experiences. The origins of this process may be traced back to when people in society became literate and developed writing skills as a result of the introduction of printing and the implementation of general compulsory education. Following from that, but moving fast forward to the present, the presence of a physical body is no longer essential; instead, the presence of a text detached from its author is sufficient. To be understood a text no longer has to be read by a person who is present in the physical sense. In fact, individual silent reading of the text is enough. With the spread of image-media has come an increase in the dematerialisation of the body as one without a physical presence but into an image. This transformation — where the world becomes image — is characterised by Heidegger as follows (albeit in the context of 'modernity'): the important change is not that the image of the world changes in the transition from the middle ages to modernity, but that in modern times the world is perceived as an image (HEIDEGGER 1980: 88). This is transformed into an image in the media, giving it a worldwide ubiquity and simultaneity of human body images leading to a dematerialisation of the body. This inflation of image over person/body and the new forms of idolatry it has engendered appear as irrefutable results of this development (HUPPAUF/WULF 2009).

In this process of abstraction, the *technologisation* of living and world conditions plays an important role: the processes of the body's assimilation to machines that are important, if not decisive, for future development is a mark of this category. The aim of the technologies of the living is an ever-increasing displacement of the interface between body and machine into the body interior. With increasingly extensive, complex and miniaturised prostheses, the age- or illness-related disabilities of the body can be alleviated to a great extent. And the development is continuing — in the long term life technologies, particularly genetic engineering and reproductive technology, have and will further transform the human body and our understanding of it with lasting effect. Virtual technologies are opening up further new perspectives.

These processes are accompanied by the *fragmentation* of the human body, which is driven by (among other things) the portrayal of bodies and body parts in the media, for example in advertisements on TV. Here the body — in parts — becomes the subject for historical/anthropological research. For example, the fragmentation process, religious and ritualistic practices with body parts, dismemberment of body parts and violence, gender-specific fetishes and the eroticisation of individual body parts become multiple foci of interest. Body parts are examined as *pars pro toto* for the entire person; it is about the relationship of the medium of embodiment and body, expression and incorporation (BENTHIEN/WULF 2001; BÖHME 2006).

The differentiation between 'sex' and 'gender' and the problematisation of this difference in feminist and queer theory (BUTLER 1997) show that the development of human *sexuality* is not natural but, like language and imagination, evolved in a historical/cultural context. From the beginning, the human body is connected to sexual discourse; however, it does not construct it. It is not a passive matrix for cultural processes; its sexuality originates in an active process, which results in the materialisation of the sexual body. The body appears as a result of eliminations on the basis of sexual difference and social adjustments.

Finally, the question today of *performativity* of the human body and the performative dimensions of cultural productions is central. Here the performative character of the social practice and the staging of social activities are examined. People physically enact in situations and social arrangements how they perceive their relationship to other people and the world, and what implicit knowledge guides them. The interest is in the performative, the staging and playful character of the social activity. Contingencies and continuities play a significant role here. What are the bases of the performatives and how are they shown in language, power and action? It is here that the centrality of rituals becomes evident: they are one of the most important forms of social activity that create communities using performances. With the help of ethnographical methods, the constitution, aesthetic form and changes in rituals can be mapped and analysed, and its pivotal role and protean performative element in upbringing, education and socialisation becomes apparent. The performative character of social activities also plays an important role in social organisations and institutions (see GEBAUER/WULF 1995; WULF 2002, 2005; WULF/ZIRFAS 2004, 2007 MICHAELS 2007).

Content and Perspectives

In India, as in Europe, when one talks about the body there is not only a perception of the body but there are also many conflicting body images and body concepts. Considerable differences appear depending on the historical and cultural context, religious orientation and classes or castes. The diversity of the body images is visible amongst individuals and communities, as well as between geographical regions and social contexts. The variation is also expressed in religious and philosophical texts, narratives, rituals and gestures, as well as visualisations and images, e.g. in movies and advertisements. It is depicted in the daily lives of people in villages, towns and large modern urban centres. Overlaps with globalised body images in Europe are visible particularly in writings where body images in contemporary Indian society are being examined. Capturing, commenting on or analysing all of them is not possible in a single volume; here we concentrate on three points. In Part 1 we examine the role of the body in religious and philosophical texts. Different historical and anthropological approaches are discussed, and then (in Part 2) the various contributions explore the role of the body in narratives and ritual performances. Here important narratives containing body images will be consulted. Using predominantly ethnographical studies, the articles establish which body images are expressed in rituals and body performances. The performative character of the ritualistic arrangements plays a central role here. Finally, Part 3 examines the contribution of imaginations of the body in images. The modern educational processes of individual and collective imaginaries, which stem from the influence of new media, are analysed.

We assume that the body is the result of a design across cultures, including the religious and philosophical texts of India. Over the last 150 years, there have been two important yet different phases in the understanding of the Hindu body. In the first phase, which stretches from 1860 to 1920, Hindu intellectuals referred to the body with nationalistic motives within the context of a newly constituted 'Hindu science' of the living body. In the second phase, between 1920–1970, a militant Orientalism from a 'mixture of cultural relativism, the craze for Hindu spirituality and the political counter-culture movement' (ZIMMERMANN) led to a new understanding of the body. In this phase, emphasis was placed on the fluidity of Indian body perceptions when compared to the rigidity of European perceptions. At the same time, it became clear that body perceptions also readjust to modern notions stemming from newer demands of knowledge and control. Foucault's 'technologies of the self' relates to the task of 'mobilis[ing] the governmentality of individuals'.

Moreover, with reference to traditional medical knowledge, the Orientalists designed the body as a real object, which was consequently shaped and modernised with the help of colonial strategies. In the process, they overlooked the fact that the body as a real body is a design which, within the framework of Hindu science, was strengthened using Ayurvedic theories and Sanskrit canonical references in such a way that its fictional character was no longer visible. The aim of these efforts was to establish a connection between Indian traditions and science in Indian public opinion and thereby unite traditional beliefs with modern knowledge. With the emergence of new cultural areas and the development of a counter-culture in the 1970s, concepts of the body changed. Medical anthropology and the efforts to conceptualise 'another body' became particularly important. The dialectics between the spiritual image of India created by the nationalists and Western materialism played a central role here, the two being conflictual to the understanding of the body and body images up to the present day.

Once a reference framework for the current understanding of important aspects of the human body was set up, there was a step backwards once again into the history of Indian body-thoughts. Here, initially the limits of the body in Brahmanism were elaborated upon: spirit and heart were recognised as decisive powers which created the body, making it possible for the person to procreate. Particularly important was the skin which created the surface of the body, the *tanu*, giving the body its identity. It was the nakedness of the skin that was considered as a differentiating characteristic of the person. With the help of the sacrifice, during which the person is like a foetus, it is born with a new body. 'In the Vedas, man transforms the nakedness imposed on him into a mode of regulating, or rather modulating, his relations with the other elements of the sacrificial world of which he is the centre' (MALAMOUD).

In various philosophical Sanskrit texts the body of God plays an important role, primarily in connection with the creation of the universe. Here there is a mutual relationship between the existence of God, its body and its image. In Sanskrit texts there is a devotional, ritualistic and epistemic approach to this. In the devotional approach, there is a fusion of God, its body and its image. God enters the world of the people with the help of his body. In the ritualistic approach, there is a difference between the deity, its body and its image. 'The image is transformed into a living body of God which is able to receive material homage, in the form of food, flowers, scents, etc.'). The focus here is on the discussion about God's existence, its body and its image in the texts of the Nyāyā-Vaiseśika school between the first and eleventh century (COLAS).

A particular aspect of the Indian understanding of the body is represented in the practices of Yogis, which have also influenced the philosophical, medical, ritualistic and mythological traditions of Hinduism. Self-externalisation in rituals, narratives and philosophy lies at the centre of these practices. It takes place by entering the sun's rays or penetrating into the body of another being, often another person. For instance, the penetration of the Yogi into the body of King Janaka helps him to learn the esoteric teachings and forms the model for his later tantric initiation. In the 11th century, a commentary described 'a Yogi's gradual reduction of the sense, cognition, and action capacities of another person's self to a fluid amalgam, which he then incorporates into his own self....' (WHITE). While the ordinary person's mind leaves his body first upon death, it is different in the case of the Yogi, whose spirit/body connection has already been released through initiation, practices, etc.

In tantrism, the body is the place of a spiritual experience. The question that arises is how to understand the relationship between the experience in the lived body and the system of representation and symbols that are expressed in sacred texts. This relationship between body and symbolic representation is mimetic: the body is understood as a symbolic system with whose help the position of the person in the cosmos is determined; at the same time, it is the location of the subjective experience of the Yogi which is, for instance, expressed in the breathing practices, discussed by Flood in this volume. The body as a symbolic system and as lived body are connected and cannot be separated. Thus, for instance, in the *Netratantra*, a tantric text from Kashmir, ritual practices for cleansing the body, deification of the body through mantras, and worshipping have their place. The body is an extensive symbolic system in which meanings are assigned to its individual parts. Here 'the primacy of the body as pre-cognitive experience, the existential possibility of culture in contrast to the body and world as pre-given semiotic system' (FLOOD) are important. We have the world in and with the body; as the lived being, the body becomes a symbolic system within a culture. The breath links the lived body experience with the symbolic system of the body. The Yogi moves in mimetic processes between its body and the symbolic system, which opens an 'as if' world.

Another perspective of the body can be seen when one considers the humorous and satirical work of Sanskrit. Here 'blatant rather than subtle indications as to the character's status in life, their profession, attitude to life and general proclivities' (BALDISSERA) are presented. The narratives report of grotesque bodies, which are ugly and unsightly, lewdly drunk, and have no clear sexual identity disrupt the established order and attributions, and play eagerly with ambiguity.

These representations of the body are closely connected with body differences; for this reason, the history of the body can be written only as one of entanglements. This is shown, for example, in Unani medicine, which has its origins in Greece; it spread to India where it is used even today among Muslims. According to this system, the human body consists of four humours defined by their mixture of cold, hot, moist and dry elements. Their varied composition serves to explain the diversity of the human character. Illnesses are caused by disturbances to the balance. 'Europe, the Arab world, and India had known an entangled history of medical knowledge, based on a common perception or humoral pathology' (PERNAU), which essentially defined the understanding of the body. The individual body is seen in close relation to the social and cosmic order; health is more than a balanced relationship of juices. This understanding of the body changes the moment it is seen as subjective and autonomous. Furthermore, the knowledge necessary for health preservation is considered to be a combination of medicine, morale and religion.

Perceptions to recognise the human body as a clear, vast and open body constitute an important part of Indian thoughts on the body. On the one hand, the body is a local unit; on the other, a manifestation of a *worldwide plane* takes place in it. People can travel into infinity on the body's astral rays and experience this world for themselves. The astral body experiences infinity; it is open for the ceaselessness of these regions. In this experience, a substantial externalisation of the body takes place. This happens because the body is not an isolated separate being, but a spatially extended being. There is a performative aspect in the fragmentation of the body: 'because, directing the *radiation* of a body toward the realm of the vast openness that envelops all other cosmic regions actually takes place as the performance of a caesura that marks *a radical change of the entire quality, the material world as such is corporally experienced*' (BÖHLER).

After central body concepts from religious and philosophical texts are reconstructed in the first part, the second part will explore body perceptions in narratives and rituals. How 'bodies of knowledge simultaneously disclose a knowledge of the body, one that is deployed by Teyyam performers of formerly untouchable castes to mount an explicit critique of the spiritual, and hence, moral illegitimacy of caste' (FREEMAN) is examined in the first article. The untouchable body becomes the space where a higher spiritual ethic is displayed. During ritualistic ceremonies, when the obsessed dancers from the lowest caste invoke the gods with their bodies and interact with the gathered devotees of all castes, the question that arises is whether they possess the bodies of untouchables at that moment or not; if not, then what bodies do they have at that moment, and to what extent are those bodies culturally shaped. The ritual, practical and instrumental knowledge that is necessary for the production of this body and performance are properties of the untouchable caste, which through this obtains new possible courses of action in religious contexts. A transformation takes place in the ritual, which changes the body of the untouchable. There is a flow of conscious energy in general and individuated forms between all beings which transcends the separative limits. One conclusion that may be drawn from it is that personhood in India is considered more permeable than the unitary self in Western culture.

The perceptions of God's body developed in a culture plays an important role: how the body is conceptualised essentially determines how the human body is conceived. 'In the numerous religions that make up what we call "Hinduism", god is frequently embodied, or, to put it more precisely, the numerous gods, goddesses, and demons of the Hindu pantheon have a startling variety of embodied forms, ranging from the zoomorphic (Vishnu's fish, turtle, and boar incarnations; the 'monkey-god' Hanuman), to the anthropo-zoomorphic (Narasimha, the 'man-lion;' Ganesha, with his human body and elephant's head) to the human (Rama, Sita, Krishna), and the hyper-human (Durga with her eight arms, Brahma with his three heads, Ravana with his ten heads)' (SAX). Using the example of popular myths about the Hindu god Bhairav, Sax examines his contribution to the performance of ritual healings. For this purpose, his appearance as a saviour is depicted, followed by an iconography of Bhairav and a description of its production and performance in rituals whose effects are particularly lasting because they are not only performed with language but also with the entire body.

The gods manifest their energy not only in healing rituals but also in dance. This is illustrated using the example of Odissi dance; a field study in Orissa is the basis of the analysis of body perceptions in this dance form. Taking into consideration the historical dimension as well as its aesthetic quality, the central elements of understanding the body are defined, which includes the behaviour of the *bhakta* which determines the movements of the body in the dance, the 'love and surrender' in which the dancer devotes himself to the divine. Using the example of several well-known dancers (gurus), the significance of the master for learning the practical basic body movements for dance is identified. In contrast to many Western dance theories, 'the body [is] not only expressive, it is also impressive, i.e. it is a medium into which something enters ... the body of the Odissi dancer is a receptacle for deities and divine energy' (SCHNEPEL).

To become competent in a dance form or to perform a ritual is the result of a multi-dimensional embodiment process. The case study of a ritual at a temple near Chennai shows that many priests are unable to read the sacred texts that form the basis of the ritual, but are, however, in a position to produce and perform the ritual on the basis of a bodily knowledge incorporated into mimetic processes. The analysis also reveals that the sacred texts often contain no information on the practical knowledge that is required for the performance of the ritual. The focus is mainly on basic questions such as those regarding a person's eligibility. For this reason, the prospective priests require practical training that qualifies them to perform rituals. 'A great deal of priestly competence is achieved through watching, "being with elders", but also by playing priest, and imitating their ritual actions' (HÜSKEN).

The embodiments that take place in rituals are, due to their effect, of central importance. This is shown in three further case studies of ritual celebration in

Tamil Nadu which deal with rituals of Periandavar worship, performed by the Kaniyan community and Hook- swinging rituals. These analyses attempt to established how the human body is shaped through social power structures and relations, through political, economic, social and cultural conditions and how it undergoes consistent change. In the rituals analysed, the effort to satisfy the gods in order to preserve health and prosperity takes centre stage. The rituals show 'how the human "body" and "self" [are] submitted to the divine spirit and get purified by the shaman. The body of the shaman is considered sacred. During his spirit possession, his body is the medium for the divine spirit' (JOHN). The divine status of the body, which serves as a religious vehicle, is depicted in the rituals.

Visualisation processes of the body are examined in the third part of this volume. The focus is predominantly on developments in the modern and contemporary periods, where the relationship of body and mediumistic visualisation achieve a new quality. As a result of globalisation, there are many similarities in this area between the Indian experience to those in Europe and the USA, without losing sight of the heterogeneity of Indian body images.

The first contribution by Juneja shows how the body was used in visual practices at the Mughal court to communicate ethical conceptions of the polity. Harnessing the body as a medium also meant making the body the subject of visual representations. For this, important texts in multiple regimes of visuality were translated. In one set of manuscript illustrations, there were juxtaposed images where to some extent the images followed another dynamic than the texts. In the majority of court histories and manuscripts, text and image were connected in an overall view. 'Visibility, vision and visuality — all formed channels through which ritual practice, bodily experience and images interposed on and codified each other' (JUNEJA). The task of the court painter was to transform the body of the king into an image and to render it tangible as an 'instrument of the soul'. 'The variety of pictorial experiments to create images that worked as both *of* the body and those which stand *for* the body, had the power that could generate cohesion among multi-ethnic and pluri-religious imperial elites in north India during the 16th and 17th centuries and could equally be reappropriated by these to define anew the boundaries between the empire and the regions' (*ibid.*).

Using the example of the multiple bodies of the bride, the concurrence of heterogeneous body images and body conceptions is explored by Brosius. Here, overlaps between traditional Indian and globalised Western body images can be identified: 'the bridal body patrols and transgresses borders between tradition and modernity, taste and vulgarity, global and local flows. The performative concepts of ritual, heritage, leisure and exhibition are important to understand the complexity of lifestyle politics in neoliberal India' (BROSIUS). As marriage is regarded as the chief celebration to take place in people's lives in India, a 'marriage industry' has emerged, which the new middle and upper classes use to stage and show off their social status, purchasing power, ethnic identity, as well as gender and family relationships. These celebrations are an integral part of the many, to some extent disputed, discussions on romantic love and family obligations, as well as national identity in transnational contexts. The bride's body becomes a 'tradeable item of "world class" and national taste'. The overlap of the 'ethnic' and 'cultured' bodies are of particular interest. To give expression to the ethnic character of the bride's body, clothing and posture serve as symbols, which are used to express cultural diversity and 'ethnic chic'. In a traditional marriage, the bride's body serves as a ritual gift helping to unite two families; the virginal purity of the woman's body thus plays an important role. In marriages of the upper middle-class and upper class, new perceptions being publicised in lifestyle magazines — of the beautiful, seductive female body and a romantic love based thereon — add to this perception. The bride should also be a virgin and not defile the reputation of the family she is marrying into. Wedding videos serve to put the bride's body on stage and celebrate its beauty. An increasing emphasis on the bride's sensuality and sexual desires is adding to this, as is the associated responsibility to maintain a healthy married life. Many, to some extent contradictory, desires and requests blend together the body of the bride and the imaginary place occupied by her, which allow the body to be seen as an image of insatiable desire.

Lasting changes to body images and their associated individual and collective identities occur within the framework of the increasingly expansive information technology. For example, the documentary 'John and Jane' by Ashim AHLUWALIA (2005) about working in a Call Centre shows how globalisation and new media can lead to distorted and restructured identities. In these transitional spaces three dimensions of constructing meaning are particularly important: 1) time: here, Indian employees work in Call Centres at night-time when it is daytime in America; 2) space: the Call Centre is an 'in-between space' between the USA and India. 'On the one side the image of a systematic, well-organised, rich, modern, clean and beautiful place called America, reproduced in the Call Centre reality, and on the other side the "hassle dazzle" of India' (CLEMENS); and 3) social: in order to be able to perform their tasks, Indian employees must become mentally American. The language spoken by them plays a significant role here; a new identity is produced through Americanised English. 'English started coming into me, an American feeling that I started to have. That culture has gone into me' (*ibid.*). The agents in the Call Centre must therefore develop a transitional identity without which they are unable to fulfil the duties of their work. During their work hours they must transform a virtual world into a real one. 'Naomi', one of the protagonists in this film, also shows this identity change through her body: she has dyed her hair blonde and speaks and dresses like an American to the extent that she is often asked where she comes from. She has found a new identity. Finally, it shows how the development of person, body and consciousness interact to create new forms of identity.

Conclusion

Dematerialisation, technologisation, fragmentation, sexuality and *performativity* are interlinked processes that are becoming increasingly important for understanding the body and perceptions of the body in Western, and partly in non-Western, societies. *Subtle and gross bodies, social bodies, the transformation and transgression of the body* and *the sacrifice as a body and the body as a sacrifice* are particularly representative of India. The discussion on these dimensions already clarifies this. The human body has become more than ever the problem, and once hard-and-fast conceptions of the human body have softened up considerably. *Of which body are we speaking when we talk about the body* is the decisive question today? The human body, whose 'naturalness' is so often sworn against social institutions and necessities, is never 'natural'. Even there, where its 'naturalness' is asserted, it deals with a historical/cultural concept with whose help it is 'forgotten' that each form of 'naturalness' of the body is an historical/cultural design of 'nature' and in most cases serves to show certain casts and mouldings of the body as unquestionable, unchangeable, and beyond criticism. The reference to the 'naturalness' of the body has the function of concealing social power relations and not letting them enter into the consciousness. In the traditional understanding of the female and male body, the connection is obvious between body conception and social power relations. Even if we nowadays understand the difference between 'sex' and 'gender' as a historical/cultural construction, it gives rise to the possibility of understanding the body in new light. This understanding encounters the limits imposed by language, which often has inadequate concepts for new differentiations. It is therefore even more important to understand the concepts, as understanding the body from a precise knowledge of different cultures and languages. This volume is an attempt to do so in the context of Indian cultures.

In view of its complexity, the human body eludes, time and time again, the acknowledgement that there is no end in sight to its anthropological research. In the course of this development, it is necessary to assume a *corpus absconditum*. This means that one consciously renounces the necessary reductionist attempt of constructing a closed 'body concept' consistent in itself. As God and person are not completely recognisable and identifiable, the complexity of the body remains incomprehensible. Only the recognition of different aspects of the body depending on questions and approaches is possible. As no academic or scientific discipline alone is responsible for the body, research on the body is an area of inter- and transdisciplinary, as well as inter- and transnational, research which is increasingly becoming a focal point of research studies.

If today, more than before, the question of the performativity of the human body is interesting and explored as a social practice and materialisation of the in-scene composition of possibilities, this process will also be understood as a medium of corporal self-assurance in space, time and society. In this respect, human bodies are appearing less as a result but more as a process, and less closed, rather more open and manageable for future developments.

References

Andrieu, B. (Ed.) (2006): Le dictionaire du corps en science humaines et sociales. – Paris.

Benthien, C./Wulf, C. (Eds.) (2001): Körperteile: Eine kulturelle Anatomie. – Reinbek.

Böhme, H. (2006): Fetischismus und Kultur. – Reinbek.

Bouillier, V./Tarabout, G. (Eds.) (2002): Images du corps dans le monde hindou. – Paris.

Butler, J. (1997): Excitable Speech: A Politics of the Performative. – New York.

Das, V. (1985): Paradigms of Body Symbolism: An Analysis of Selected Themes in Hindu Culture. In: Burghart, R./Cantlie, A. (Eds.): Indian Religion. – London, pp. 180–207.

Feher, M. (Ed.) (1989): Fragments for a History of the Human Body, 3 Vols. – New York.

Gebauer, G./Wulf, C. (1995): Mimesis: Culture, Art, Society. – Berkeley/Los Angeles.

Gutschow, N./Michaels, A. (2005): Handling Death: The Dynamics of Death and Ancestor Rituals Among the Newars of Bhaktapur, Nepal. – Wiesbaden.

Heidegger, M. (1980): Die Zeit des Weltbildes (1938). In: Heidegger, M.: Holzwege. – 6th ed. – Frankfurt/M., pp. 73–110.

Holdredge, B. A. (2008): Body. In: Mittal, S./Thursby, G. (Eds.): Studying Hinduism: Key Concepts and Methods. – London/New York, pp. 19–40.

Huppauf, B./Wulf, C. (Eds.) (2009): Dynamics and Performativity of Imagination: The Image between the Visible and the Invisible. – London/New York.

Kamper, D./Wulf, C. (Eds.) (1982): Die Wiederkehr des Körpers. – 2nd ed. – Frankfurt/M.

Larson, G. J./Bhattacharya, R. S. (Eds.) (1987): Encyclopedia of Indian Philosophies. Vol. IV: Sāṃkhya: A Dualist Tradition in Indian Philosophy. – Delhi.

Maas, P. A. (2007/2008): The Concepts of the Human Body and Disease in Classical Yoga and Āyurveda. In: Wiener Zeitschrift für die Kunde Südasiens, 51 (2007–2008), pp. 125–162.

Marriott, M. (1968): Caste Rankings and Food Transactions. In: Singer, M./Cohn, B. S. (Eds.): Structure and Change in Indian Society. – Chicago, pp. 133–171.

Marriott, M. (1989): Constructing an Indian Ethnosociology. In: Contributions to Indian Sociology (n.s.), Vol. 23, No.1, pp. 1–39.

Marzano, M. (Ed.) (2007): Dictionaire du corps. – Paris.

Michaels, A. (2004): Hinduism: Past and Present. – Princeton/Oxford. (German Original: Der Hinduismus: Geschichte und Gegenwart, 2nd ed., Munich, 2006)

Michaels, A. (2004a): Die Kunst des einfachen Lebens: Eine Kulturgeschichte der Askese. – Munich.

Michaels, A. (2004b): Wohin mit den Ahnen? Totenritual und Erlösung in indischen Religionen. In: Graf, F. W./Meier, H. (Eds.): Der Tod im Leben. – Munich, pp. 269–92.

Michaels, A. (Ed.) (2007): Die neue Kraft der Rituale. – Heidelberg.

Ramaswamy, S. (2002): Visualising India's Geo-Body: Globes, Maps, Bodyscapes. In: Contributions to Indian Sociology (n.s.), Vol. 36, No. 1–2, pp. 151–182.

WUJASTYK, D. (forthcoming): Interpreting the Image of the Human Body in Pre-Modern India. In: International Journal of Hindu Studies. (Revised version of his article in BOUILLIER/TARABOUT 2002, pp. 71–99)

WULF, C. (2002): Anthropology of Education. – Münster.

WULF, C. (2005): Zur Genese des Sozialen: Mimesis, Ritual, Performativität. – Bielefeld. (French edition 2008)

WULF, C./KAMPER, D. (Eds.) (2002): Logik und Leidenschaft: Erträge Historischer Anthropologie. – Berlin.

WULF, C. *et al.* (2010): Rituals in the Lives of Young People. – London. (German edition 2001, French edition 2004)

WULF, C./ZIRFAS, J. (Eds.) (2004): Die Kultur des Rituals. – München.

WULF, C./ZIRFAS, J. (Eds.) (2007): Pädagogik des Performativen: Theorien, Methoden, Perspektiven. – Weinheim.

The Body in Religious and Philosophical Texts

Francis Zimmermann

A Hindu to His Body: The Reinscription of Traditional Representations*

Although the following pages fall into the field of classical Indian studies and the author has access to Sanskrit sources, they are not directly concerned with Hindu representations of the body as developed before the days of British colonialism. This is an attempt to put into a historical perspective the knowledge gathered over two centuries, *a construction of the knowledge about* the representations of the body in the Hindu world. In view of the critical history of Orientalist disciplines that has developed over the last few years we make a clear distinction between two periods in the construction of this knowledge. The representations of the body that emerged from reading, translating and interpreting classical writings of Hindu India, became the subject of two successive reinscriptions beginning in the second half of the nineteenth century. Our analysis of these reinscriptions is presented below.

This analysis is firmly rooted in the modern age. Drawing on the work of historians of Indian nationalism, we will retrace how a "Hindu science" of the body emerged for the first time at the end of the nineteenth century, followed, at a later period, by the reception of the representations of Hinduism in the West. One might say that there have been two successive phases or two directions in the modern craze for the wisdom of Hinduism. *Phase One*: engendered by the writings of Indian intellectuals themselves, the birth of an indigenous Orientalism, nationalist in its inspiration, which brought the subject of the existence of a "Hindu science" into the public arena of colonial India (1860-1920). Thus, in the midst of other domains of the senses was born a Hindu science of the living body (animal and human), appearing as an ideological construction, constitutive of an exotic world and a sharing of reality between them (the Hindus) and us (the moderns). *Phase Two:* almost a century later came a new militant Orientalism, this time created in the West, governed by an ideology which was a mixture of cultural relativism, the craze for Hindu spirituality and the political counter-culture movement (1970–1980). These two phases can be interpreted, retrospectively, as two rewritings

* The original French version of this article was first published under the title "Ce qu'un hindou dit à son corps. La réécriture des répresentations traditionnelles" in: Bouillier, Véronique and Angot, Michel (Eds.): *Images du corps dans le monde hindou* (CNRS Éditions, Paris, 2002), pp. 49-69, in the series *Monde indien. Sciences sociales 15e-20e siècle* and is reproduced here with the kind permission of CNRS Éditions.

of traditional Hindu representations which were influenced by the West. In both cases, Orientalism was the instrument of a construction of ideological realities which were highly imbued with subjectivity. Tangible reality, aspects of the body such as moods and illnesses, food and gestures, were constructed and presented culturally as particular to India, essentially Hindu.

As a European studying Sanskrit texts, I would classify myself as having, of necessity, been part of this second phase. Therefore I bring an introspective, critical approach to bear on this retrospective view of the contemporary rewriting of Hindu representations. How can we speak of India without appearing presumptuous in speaking for other people? For some years now our Indian colleagues have been engaged in writing the history of the construction of colonial knowledge and Orientalism in nineteenth century Anglo-India. About fifteen years ago, they dismissed the afore-mentioned militant Orientalist phase, denouncing it as being "postcolonial," i.e., an extension of Europe's exoticising projections on to India. They then put forward a different approach to Indian studies—i.e. creating an archaeology of knowledge about India. I would also like to take up this criticism, drawing on a recent work by Gyan PRAKASH (2000)[1] which expands and refurbishes the theories of *Subaltern Studies* (a school of historiography which came into being in India during the state of emergency in the nineteen seventies and pursued the objective of giving a voice to the natives), in the History of Science, basing its analyses of the relationship between erudite knowledge and political power on Michel Foucault.

The seventies was the time when, promoted by the enormous popularity of alternative medicine, a certain image of the Hindu body became widespread. It was seen as functioning on the basis of unctuousness and fluidity and characterised by the dialectic of fire and water (the coction of the humours), by a fluidity as opposed to the rigidity of the western body. This was a body image that differed from ours in the West, which functioned as a *critical theory* establishing the legitimacy of the alternative therapies which were inspired by this image—"critical" in the sense that it ran counter to western biomedicine. It assumed a metonymy between the body (the humours) and the plant kingdom (saps), an image a body in symbiosis with nature which established the legitimacy of practices imported from India by the counter-culture movement—non violence, i.e. vegetarianism. The work done by Indologists on this subject during the seventies implicitly fulfilled the moral, political and existential expectations of the enlightened American and European public of the time. My hypothesis in what follows, however, is that this image of the Hindu body developed by Indologists was originally constructed by Hindu nationalists at the end of the nineteenth century. I find Gyan Prakash's interpretation convincing and draw upon it in my detached

[1] Gyan Prakash is Professor of History at Princeton.

reflections on the subject of "representations in the Hindu world," an area that can only be considered within the ideological framework of the Hindu nationalism that has now been in existence for a hundred years.

However, I propose to go still further and dissect the mechanism behind Prakash's genealogical explanation. He contextualises the representations of India in the West, showing that they were initially reinscriptions of traditions, traditions that have been reappropriated by politics. This explanation applies not only to the representations of the body in the work of subalternist historians (even though the Body is a strategic theme), because they were profoundly influenced by Foucault's critical philosophy of biopower and the governing of human bodies; Prakash's explanatory mechanism is valid for all sorts of Indian matters, and in particular for all the moral, political and aesthetic issues which are widespread in contemporary Indian-language literature: the theme of the little village community, for example, or the theme of kinship which gives structure to traditional Hindu society, etc. I will therefore attempt to describe the approach and critical position of a scholar such as Gyan Prakash within the field of "Indian Studies" (a field whose legitimacy he contests, although he does not say so explicitly).

The governing of human bodies in colonial India

I turn first to Gyan Prakash's excellent chapter on "Body and Governmentality," (cf. Prakash 2000, ch. 5) which takes from Foucault the analysis of a genealogy of the modern mutation, the procedure which, in simple terms, has brought about the evolution of the European state from wielding legal power to wielding bio-power. Initially a purely political, administrative authority, the state has come to represent power over biological life and power over the body, an authority that controls the population, establishing law and order through the knowledge and practices of public sanitation.

To govern the modern subject is to inculcate in him or her methods of knowing and controlling his or her own body. Governmentality is a complex of procedures proposed or prescribed to individuals to establish, maintain or transform their identities through self-mastery or self-knowledge. Governmentality is an internalisation of the government within the spirit of each citizen. According to Foucault, all societies have technologies which permit individuals to perform a certain number of operations on their bodies, souls, thoughts and behaviour in order to improve themselves and attain a certain state of happiness, purity or supernatural power. To a cynical observer it appears as an *internalisation* of disciplines of government through which the state benefits from the appropriation of individual strategies. Prakash applies this concept of the hold of political power over private life to colonial India, and within this concept, in India, Hindu representations of the body have historically always played a role.

In modern India (during the colonial period), Hindu representations of the body were *technologies of the self* as conceptualised by Foucault, that is, the relays of social control in every individual subject's cultural baggage, (native) disciplines, reappropriated by the state to ensure the self-fabrication of the bodies of the natives through good public health policies (which the English called sanitation). From the perspective of the subject, technologies of the self, which embrace technologies of the body (and particularly technologies of care or the control over vital fluids) are nothing other than correlates of the technologies of social domination. To mobilise these technologies of the self or disciplines of the self, as was done in India, is to mobilise the "governmentality" of individuals in such a way that they assume the responsibility for their own discipline.

"What was colonial about the colonization of the body [by the British authorities in India]?" asks Gyan PRAKASH (2000, p. 127). How did the British colonial authorities, who at the outset had only Western knowledge of medicine and psychology to apply to matters of the body and sanitation, succeed in governing the Indians as if they were modern subjects—in other words making colonial knowledge function as technologies of the self? They did it by reappropriating the Hindu representations of the body. They managed to reappropriate the representations of the body in the local culture by eliminating all compromise between modern science and Ayurveda and the traditional therapies.

In the early nineteenth century the British treated the Indians as part of the scenery, as products of the soil, of drainage, water, climate and illnesses, whom they counted and classified according to distinct medical-topographical regions. Confident In the belief that India represented uncharted territory, the colonial medical authorities concentrated on identifying different regimens of health and illness. Thus it was that the effort to control, regulate and reform *the tropics*, where climatic fevers combined with the irrationality of the inhabitants to cause violent epidemics, resulted in new knowledge based on grand administrative surveys. From this medical geography there emerged an image of the body in the tropics, a kind of basic personality of the human body in an Indian environment, made up, in the eyes of the European observers, of unsanitary habits and superstitious beliefs, to which it was necessary to apply modern science and sanitation to reform and restore its health and well-being.

Initially, but for quite a short period, culminating in 1835[2], native medicine and pharmaceutics were integrated into medical knowledge as inferior but

[2] This period of integration of Hinduism and its traditional sciences, such as Ayurveda, comes about in 1835, publication date of Macaulay's famous *Minute*, which marks the victory of the Anglicists over the Orientalists.

useful complements to Western medicine. Since the end of the eighteenth century British Orientalists had been translating classical texts and gathering details of native medical practices. Without ever putting them on an equal footing with Western medicine, the British believed that making inventories of native medical ideas and local practices and remedies which would be controlled by their enlightened vision would provide useful supplements to a therapeutic system adapted to India. While it might be a collection of erroneous and non-scientific beliefs, it was one whose distortions concealed a Body different from the European body in other words a kind of basic personality of the human body specific to India.

Thus the Orientalists read native medicine as a conglomeration of erroneous, imprecise signs of the presence, the existence, of the body as a real object, and this understanding of the tradition justified the application of scientific and administrative research strategies which conceptualised the body in India as an a priori object, as an entity whose existence preceded the discourse and research connected with it; the body, in its local specificity, as material placed at the disposal of medical examinations and sanitation measures; the body as the object of knowledge and technologies of governing which must take account of its indigenous nature. In their research and colonial practices at the end of the nineteenth century, what the British scholars and doctors noted, therefore, was more than simply Hindu representations of the body that would (as additions whose scientific standards were dubious but which were useful nonetheless) allow them to adapt Western representations of the body to the tropical context. They noted the existence of a specifically Hindu body. Native beliefs and practices were one element taken into account in the colonial sciences, but as an ethnographic object (per se) and not as a native science of this object. In other words the representations of the body found in classical writings and Hindu traditions were no longer considered in terms of knowledge of this object, the body, but in terms of the beliefs and practices that constituted this object, which meant that they themselves became an object of knowledge—ethnography as an administrative science.

At the time, classical Indology was adopting the same approach, i.e. one which made India into an object of knowledge for the Europeans. This project obscured the colonial link that made it possible. In their naiveté, the Sanskritists were unable to see that the production of knowledge about India and colonisation were linked, although this was what made their research possible in the first place. This is why, despite the fact that the division between East and West had been created by the very process of colonisation, at the time of the triumph of Orientalism everything took place as though this twofold opposition between Orient (mystical mind, unctuous body) and Occident (rational mind, bony body) pre-dated colonisation, as though it was in the nature of things, a justification of colonisation even (the weakness of the one calling for the domination of the other). The Indologists, believing the writings to contain this dichotomy, created the cliché of the mystical, unctuous Hindu as a foil to the matter-of-fact, rational Briton and presented this dichotomy as an explanation for the British conquest (cf. PRAKASH 1992, p. 355).

Hindu science

Such was the colonial order that the Hindu nationalists were to subvert by their reinscription of Hindu representations of the body in the annals of science. I would like now to turn to the periodisation proposed by David ARNOLD (1999) in an article which draws attention to the striking importance of history in science in India during the period from 1860 to 1920. Indian scientists of the time sought systematically to relate their research to the mythical view of a "Hindu" past in science. No doubt they were vying with Western science, which also presented itself as the heir of a long tradition. However they were also drawing on the view of the Hindu tradition suggested by the Orientalists, the Golden Age of Antiquity followed by a long period of decadence caused by Muslim invasions which was fortunately interrupted by British colonisation.

This construction of a Hindu past was dealt with at length in the writings and discourses of the small group of philosophers and scholars who were the driving force of the Indian scientific renaissance in Bengal at the end of the nineteenth and beginning of the twentieth century. In the Hindu world, these representations of the body, known to us through the work of the Orientalists and in particular through Ayurvedic theories, and supported by many quotations in Sanskrit, were to be reintegrated in a scientific and even *positivist* discourse and find themselves endowed with a new epistemological status. The physiological doctrines of Ayurveda (a "medicine") and Samkhya ("physics"), etc. were no longer something to be studied for their own sake, but rather instruments of knowledge. Gyan PRAKASH (2000, p. 147) interprets this reversal of perspective as a political re-appropriation, "the reinscription of colonial governmentality."

The following is an example of this type of reinscription applied to a Sanskrit text, taken from Brajendranath SEAL (1985), a Bengali philosopher who was a member of Brahmo Sanmaj's reformist movement and in 1915, influenced by his reading of Auguste Comte, published a work entitled *The Positive Sciences of the Ancient Hindus*. We will take a detail of Ayurvedic doctrine—the list of the seven tissues of the body: chyle, blood, flesh, fat, bone, marrow, semen—which are transformed into each other through a series of successive sublimations or "cookings." A final coction produces a sublimate of semen, ojas in Sanskrit, an imaginary vital fluid which represents the quintessence of all organic fluids. Medical works use the image of a wheel to describe this continuous transformation of the tissues of the body: "The transformation (*parivṛtti*) of the nutritive tissues by a series of coctions is continuous, like [the movement of] a wheel.[3]" Seal updates the Sanskrit text some fifteen to twenty centuries later by translating this *image*, the wheel, as though it were a *concept*—metabolism:

> The semen, or rather all the elements, in their finer essence, give off *ojas*, which returns to the heart, the receptacle of chyle and blood, and again floods the body and sustains the tissues, thus completing the wheel or self-returning circle of metabolism (*parivṛttis tu cakravat*, cf. Charaka and Vagbhata) (SEAL 1985, p. 205).

From a strictly logical point of view this process of *reinscription* transforms an image (the perpetual movement of a wheel) into a concept (the metabolism of tissues in the organic physiology of the nineteenth century).

The ambition of nationalist Hindu intellectuals was to reconcile India and science *in the imaginary* of the Indian public. It was a matter of breaking the bond of subordination that made an object of science out of Hindu culture. Let us no longer speak of "representations of Hindu bodies" as an object of Orientalist or ethnographic study; rather let us rehabilitate "the Hindu science of the Body." From the perspective of the British colonialists things Indian were the subject of administrative knowledge. For the Hindu elites it was a question of repatriating and indigenising this knowledge, of returning the colonial sciences (sanitation, for instance) to the bosom of Hindu culture, of subordinating the state (the colonial government) to the nation (native values). The dialectic between incorporating and being incorporated sheds light on this question. Reinscription, in the sense used by Gyan Prakash, involves turning on its head the relationship between them and us; colonial science, which incorporated Orientalism, is henceforth itself incorporated (as one representation among others) in the system of local representations, and within this system, because we are in India, the Hindu representations of the body are the incorporators.

In this nationalist policy of the reinscription of representations, India, as a homogenous cultural area, plays a decisive role. Colonial knowledge is no longer imported from Europe and applied to India as an object, the Hindu body-object. Medicine (tropical medicine) is, if not integrated, at least combined with traditional knowledge such as Ayurveda. Now the relationship of the (Hindu) representations of the body to the Body (of the colonised Indians) as an objective reality is turned on its head; there is a return to the view that prevailed before 1835. There is no longer a particular *object*, the *tropical object-body*, which is the object of knowledge in universal medicine. There are "knowledges" in the plural, among which there are the different forms of Hindu knowledge of the body in its specific ecological context and in its specifically Hindu subjectivity. In his reinscription of representations, Gyan Prakash advocates a return to subjectivity.

---

[3] Vahata, *Astangahrdayasamhita, Sarirasthana* III, 66: "...*pakakramadibhih santata bhojyadhatunam parivrttis tu cakravat.*"

In creating the idea of a national medicine, a modern Hindu medicine that would be suited to an independent India, the authors of a great number of treatises on Ayurvedic medicine published in Sanskrit, Bengali and English during the first half of the twentieth century always took care to follow in the wake of colonial medicine. According to Gyan Prakash, the concept of a national medicine was born under the shadow of colonial medicine, ostensibly taking cover under its authority, and it sought to act upon a native body the reality of which had been revealed by the colonial sciences themselves. This reinscription, which transformed the science of the body into national medicine—and transformed the science of the body in the tropics into a science of the bodies of the natives—was not an act of rejection but of reclaiming or reappropriating[4]. At the same time these scholars emphasised the presence of subjectivity in the Hindu *image of the body*. For just one among many other possible quotations, see Kaviraj Nagendranath Sengupta, *The Ayurvedic System of Medicine*, 3rd edition, translated from Bengali and published in Calcutta, 1919.

> *Special practices for different individuals.* These practices laid down for the different seasons should be varied according to the constitution [sanskrit *prakrti*] and idiosyncracy [sanskrit *satmya*] of each person (Sengupta 1995, Vol. 1, p. 13).

In the years following independence, the rehabilitation of Ayurveda took the form of a policy of supporting an *integrated system* in which anatomy and other disciplines of modern medicine were taught to future practitioners of Hindu medicine. We see that the roots of this syncretism went back a long way and that it translated this idea of a national medicine that had been a dream since the beginning of the century.

Prakash reminds us that all kinds of alternative therapies flourished in British India—chromopathy, mesmerism, hypnotism, mechanotherapy and homeopathy, which is more fashionable than ever in independent India. This selection met the ideological expectations of the native elite, to whom Prakash refers as "the urban middle class," who were obsessed by the wish to define which therapeutics were appropriate for the Hindu Body[5]. This interpretation,

---

[4] "The concept of a national medicine, however, emerged under the shadow of colonial medicine's authority, and it sought to act upon a body brought to the surface by the knowledges and practices of colonial governmentality. For this reason, it operated as a strategy of reinscription, not rejection, of colonial therapeutics." (Prakash 2000, pp. 146f.)

[5] "The efficacy of different patent medicines were items of urban middle-class conversations. Such discussions were not always systematic and learned, and they did not seriously threaten the dominance of Western medicine. But they were important for an elite obsessed with defining an appropriate therapeutics for India. For at issue in this definition was the body materialized by state institutions. Insofar as the body was produced as an effect of knowledges and tactics, attempts to reinscribe colonial therapeutics were efforts to intervene in the relationship between the state and the population" (Prakash 2000, p. 150).

which is Marxist in origin, is perhaps somewhat confusing in that it links, within one and the same blanket term, the idea of social class, urbanisation and the reappropriation of Hinduism by Indian intellectuals in the years 1860–1920. I consider it more pertinent to remember that it was precisely at this time that the administrative geography—the completion of the Survey of India—and the political decisions establishing the external borders of British India quite literally set nationalism in stone and allowed the native elite from then on to think of "India" as a unity, contained within its natural borders (mountains and oceans). The Hindu Body is a specific reality, if one subscribes to the ideology which was developed during those years, because India has a natural unity written into its geography.

Cultural areas

The Indologists of my generation have inherited this ideology. Of course, at the time when we were /pursuing our studies, knowledge of things Indian was naturally centred on "India," in its essence, and we never questioned this orientation until thirty or even forty years after Independence. In 1947, Indian Studies in the West were confronted with "decolonization, anticolonial sentiments and upsurges against neocolonialism."[6] This intellectual climate favoured the emergence of a new Indianism that revolved around the "cultural area" where Hindu civilisation ruled. In the 1950s conditions were created for a symbolic anthropology based on studies of texts and (a) productive collaboration between classical Indology and the social sciences, mainly in the United States and to a lesser degree in England and France. For political reasons arising from the Second World War[7], vast surveys, richly endowed with funds from the big American foundations, were begun in India on the subject of *karma*, retribution for acts perpetrated in previous lives, which, rightly or wrongly, seemed to get right to the roots of the Hindu personality.

They were, in fact, centred on the notion of the Person in which the representations of the Body, on the one hand, and a worldview on the other were crystallised. The text specialists were the first to be called upon in these surveys because they had access to the religious dogmas, which, following the

[6] "Nationalist historiography [had] made histories centred on India the norm. Postwar decolonization, anticolonial sentiments, and upsurges against neo-colonialism also created a congenial political and intellectual climate for an orientation based on India. This orientation was institutionalized in the United States by the establishment of South Asia area studies programs in the 1950s." (Prakash 1992, p. 362). The creation of the Centre d'ètudes indiennes de sciences sociales by Louis Dumont at the Ècole pratique des hautes études in 1957 was inspired by this orientation.

[7] Area studies took the form of applied research, designed to serve the needs of diplomacy, on the "basic personalities" of the Japanese, Hindus, etc.

dominant "holistic"[8] paradigm, constituted the basis of the specific Hindu worldview. The ethnologists, on the other hand, had the task of identifying in each individual case the elements of the scholarly traditions actually taught and observed in local practices. There was a growing awareness of the inevitably syncretist nature of the scholarly traditions. To quote Charles Keyes, one of the driving forces of this project: "There is no single integrated textual tradition based on a 'canon' to the exclusion of all other texts." (KEYES 1983, p. 271).[9] Thus it was necessary to construct what was later known as *a pragmatics* of the scientific, philosophical and religious texts of Hinduism. For example, the academic descriptions of the body that we find in Sanskrit texts only come alive and take on meaning in the practices, institutions and rites of a local community that concretises them. Keyes promulgated this principle, which was characteristic of the holism of the 1960s, with the remark that "Textual constructions of religious ideas serve to formulate dogma for a community of people only if these constructions fit into a total religious field of meaning." (KEYES 1983, p. 271). If we substitute medical for religious, this statement still remains valid. In the collective imaginary, the Ayurvedic texts only live to the extent that they are integrated in the syncretist practices of the Hinduism of today and in local beliefs.

The renaissance of Ayurvedic studies took place within the context of holism. Thus the medical doctrines presented in the Sanscrit texts were subjected to a reinscription—to use Gyan Prakash's term—to a reinterpretation, i.e. an updating or reappropriation which, by virtue of the assumed unity of Hindu civilisation, accentuates their philosophical and religious connotations. I have purposely selected the following noteworthy example so as to be able to compare it to the passage by Brandraneath Seal that I quoted earlier.

The place occupied by the imaginary theories and descriptions of embryogenesis in the Ayurvedic texts and, particularly, in the section of the medical collections on the *Elements of the Human Body*[10] is important enough to suggest that this is the expression of a fundamental *schema* of collective thinking. Indologists who were trained in the sixties or seventies were searching for these schemas, which Margaret TRAWICK (1995, p. 289) called "basic cultural templates," the basic images of a culture. Genesis by sublimation, by means

[8] We are presuming that the reader is aware of the implicit reciprocal link that was made in social anthropology at the time, i.e. between the definition of the field of enquiry as the homogenous "cultural area" and the "holistic" method of interpretation (Louis Dumont) which makes sense of the elements observed by relating them to the total social fact.

[9] See KEYES/DANIEL 1983. This classical work, which I believe to be the best introduction to this American literature on the Hindu personality, was resulted from various interdisciplinary workshops that met between 1976 and 1978.

[10] *Śārīrasthāna*, lit.: "Place [book] where one treats the Things [Elements] of the body" (In view of the elongation of the first syllable in *śārīra* it must be translated like this.)

of which a physical element liberates a quintessence—the soul which is transmitted to the embryo, in the case of procreation—, is, in effect, one of these schemas of the imagination that one can find traces of in all sorts of medical, philosophical and religious doctrines. It thus guides our reading of the text on the transformation of the seven tissues into each other proposed by Margaret Trawick:

> From the food in the stomach, blood is derived, with faeces as a waste product. From blood, flesh is derived, with urine as a waste product. From flesh, fat is derived, with perspiration as a waste product. From fat, bone is derived; from bone, marrow is derived; and from marrow, semen is derived. At each derivation, a waste product is emitted, and each derivative substance is considered purer and "harder" than its precursor. Thus through seven generations or derivations, the seven constructive substances of the body are formed. Once again, as with the liberation of the soul from the body, we find the derivation of a pure male essence from its mixed female substrate. The root metaphor of birth and the associated interest in origins, generations, derivations, and purifications may be found not only in the Ayurvedic texts but also in Dharmashastra, the texts describing ideas of human society and behaviour that were compiled in northern India around the same time the Ayurdvedic texts were compiled (Trawick 1995, p. 293).

So here we have an *imagery* which, in the original texts, was, unambiguously of a purely physiological nature. There is talk of coction, and of sublimation, in the sense in which this word is used in cookery or pharmacy, of the filtering of liquids and excretion of residues. However, the interpreter projects on to this imagery philosophical and religious *doctrines* which come from other domains of Hindu tradition. The distinction between the "feminine substrate" and "masculine essence," introduced here to explain the production of sperm, comes from the Sāmkhya philosophical system. From a culinary image (cooking as sublimation) we slip into to a religious image when the word *purifications* is introduced. The amalgamation of the different domains of the Hindu tradition—medicine, religion and law (the Dharma texts)—is explicitly accomplished as the text continues, which reduces the legal *concept* of *jāti*, "caste" to the level of *images*, under the pretext that etymologically, *jāti* means "birth." This is, purely and simply, a play on images and this is what constitutes, in the interpretation of procreation as sublimation, as a "basic metaphor," an ideological reinscription of the Hindu Body which is hardly more faithful to the original texts than that of Brajendranath Seal. Positivism imposed upon Seal the image of metabolism, while holism imposed upon Trawick the image of sublimation. He drew the Ayurvedic representations in the direction of modern science, while she drew them towards the religious polarity of pure and impure.

These schemas (*templates*) or "root metaphors" are tantamount to philosophical ideas used by historians of Ayurvedic medicine and ethnologists studying the representations of the body to structure their receptions of the classical texts (on the one hand) and the surveys they conduct in the field (on the other). Indian studies of the "cultural area" type and medical anthropology, at the time when this discipline was established at the turn of the seventies, shared the same constructivist method to the extent that they used *categories of thought and language* to structure their subject matter.[11] Using a category borrowed from philosophical thought—be it Western or exotic—as a principle to structure one's field of enquiry is one possible constructivist technique in the humanities and social sciences.

This was the theoretical background to Charles Leslie's launch of an ambitious comparative project in 1971 which completely revolutionised our knowledge of Asian traditional medicines.[12] The pivotal decision in Leslie's initiative was to professionalise research and clearly separate the study of observed tradition (a task for ethnographers) and the interpretation of doctrine in the texts (a task for historians, philologists and philosophers). This contrasted with the dilettantism that had prevailed in the work of Orientalists[13] up to that time, who prided themselves on making the occasional field observation. Thereafter, this requirement of having a clearly defined division of labour subsequently made it possible both for historians and ethnologists to collaborate with each other and also to have intellectual exchanges with the Indian practitioners.

Thus, Leslie distinguishes between classical (canonical) texts of the scholarly (syncretist) tradition of the Hindu (Ayurdevic system) and Muslim medicines (Yunani system), the beliefs and practice of which today in India make up the concrete and social life of the texts.[14] The practitioners who cultivate a scholarly version of traditional medicine interpret the original texts in the light of the more recent commentaries and teachings conveyed by the

---

[11] I prefer to speak of a "constructivist" history rather than of a "foundational history," as G. Prakash (1992, p. 365) does, but I mean the same thing. Prakash postulates the existence of root metaphors —he calls them *posited essences*, on the same page— on which he bases the specificity of the culture under study.

[12] 1971 was the year in which Charles Leslie organised the Burg Wartenstein symposium. The lectures given at this symposium were published five years later in Leslie 1976a. This was a major turning point in the field of research with which we are concerned here, in so far as it coincides with the birth of "medical anthropology," since the first articles by Horacio Fabrega and Arthur Kleinman, which founded this discipline, were published in 1972 and 1973. References in Zimmermann 1995, p. 5ff.

[13] See, for example, the observations on current Ayurveda practices (pp. xx-xxv) by means of which Jean Filliozat (1979) brings out what he calls the validity or the value of the teachings of a classical text, in his edition of *Yogasataka*.

[14] "The point I want to make is that by the 19th and 20th centuries, the traditional beliefs and practices of Ayurvedic physicians were radically different from the classic texts, and were deeply influenced by Yunani medicine" (Leslie 1976b, p. 356).

word of a master, irrespective of their own knowledge of them. To follow their teaching, as some of us tried to do in the seventies, was to work at the interface the texts and practices, semantics and pragmatics, Orientalism and the social sciences, without departing from the methodological framework of the cultural areas.

The counter-culture

During the first few years of the seventies a new discipline, medical anthropology, was established on the basis of a new working hypothesis, i.e. that the clinical practice of medicine, the sick body and the experience of disease were cultural constructs. Starting from research on new illnesses and syndromes specific to a particular culture, there was a marked increase in the number of dissertations by American medical anthropologists on selected *concepts* (illness, emotion, suffering and the narrativity of symptoms), as if they were referring to observable realities, despite the fact that they were not given, but reconstructed by the observer.

Chronology is meaningful provided that we attempt to define the transitions as exactly as possible. For the last few years I have set my self the task of contextualising the research carried out by the Sanskritists and medical historians during those years by reading the classical texts of Hinduism—the large medical collections of Suśruta, Caraka and Vāgbhata. To begin with I limited myself to France. I tried to pinpoint the moment at which, between 1976 and 1980, the body as healer (interest in the idea that the patient is his own best healer) first appeared and when the ideology of "wisdom of the patient" was at its peak, and then twelve to fifteen years later, the point at which (1992) the body became a legal entity, when the courts enforced the right of each subject to construct him- or herself (the issue of transsexuals), and then the point at which the body became a legal category (in the laws passed in 1994 that were said to be bioethical). The popularity of alternative therapies accompanied the increasing influence of the ideology of the "wisdom of the patient" and, in particular, the importing into the West of traditional Indian and Chinese schools of medicine. They came to support the assumption of control of the body by the legal system, by popularising an image of the *holistic* world in which nature itself was traditionally instituted as a legal subject.

The seventies were also the era in which the existentialist political movement that became known as the "counter-culture"[15] was at the peak of its influence and led to a passionate interest in all things Indian in young students at Western universities. In order to research this aspect further, I then shifted the focus of my investigation to North America. Basing my account on a

[15] The chronology, actors and issues of this cultural movement are excellently described by Christiane Saint-Jean-Paulin (1997).

critical reception of American texts on bioethics and medical anthropology I attempted to describe the progress made within the social sciences (the culture and personality school, the development of area studies and the short-lived synthesis (1971-1985) between Orientalism and anthropology), in conjunction with the history of American counter-culture, the emergence of bio-ethics in the United States and the rediscovery of medical cosmologies in Asia. I shall now give a brief summary of my findings.

There are two sides to the history of the medical practices in the West in the last thirty years. On the one hand there was an inexorable increase in the recourse to legal intervention in medicine (associated with a biologisation of law). This was the emergence, followed by the rule, of bioethics. And on the other hand, we had the explosion of alternative medicines on to the healthcare market beginning in the seventies. On one side we have all that belongs to biological and medical science in our society and on the other the alternative medicines. The "advances" of biological and medical science led to the emergence of a cluster of institutions, bodies of knowledge and practices dedicated to the *government of the body*, to the most *objective* realities—be they legal or biological—of the field of medicine. At the opposite pole to this legal and scientific objectivity, the only chance we have of assigning the alternative (in the full sense of the word) medicines to their rightful place without seeing them as belonging to the sects or psychotherapies, is not to ensure that their content of "objective" knowledge is not revealed (which is what the pharmaceutical companies and the health economists would want), but to study them from the point of view of the patient's subjectivity.

Excluded from the field of bioethics, subjectivity is making its return in alternative medicines. They have flourished in the philosophical context of the counter-culture, whose issues have simultaneously influenced certain currents of the nascent bioethics sector and, in particular, the "procedural" current: a dialectic between the principle of autonomy (the patient's informed consent) and the principle of beneficence (the compassion of the physician for all manifestations of life). One of these issues is, for example, that of the continuity between the plant kingdom and the human body, which is clearly expressed in the poem by Ramanujam cited below. In terms of alternative medicine this is the body being infused with all the saps of the plant world, which ensures its unctuousness and its fluidity. In bioethical terms, we are living in a world in which all living beings (the trees…) have a personality and rights. These two perspectives, alternative medicine(s) and bioethics, are two sides of the same coin—one cannot exist without the other. It was in this historical context that Charles Leslie made a breakthrough, both in the colloquia that he organised between 1971 and 1985 and in the collections of papers that resulted from these colloquia, which brought anthropologists, historians and philologists together) in the study of the medical traditions of Asia. Today we would merely be revealing our naiveté were we simply to present a description of a medical "doctrine" or a "cosmology," as we did in the seventies, be it the exotic example of Ayurveda or within the context of reflections (en vogue at the time) on the rights of all beings in Nature to our compassion. We must reinstate these representations (of the Body and Nature) that we have adopted at least partly from Hinduism, to their rightful place in the history of medicine and bioethics in contemporary Western culture.

For a time the way in which the Orientalists presented the medical traditions of Asia in Europe and the United States made it seem to be a critical theory—an "other" body, an "other" medicine, an "other" subjectivity. However, this critical dimension of Asian medicines lost its edge at the end of the eighties; they have gone out of fashion. Orientalism was disqualified and new cultural and political issues took over this role of *critical theory* in the field of medical anthropology, which was no longer directed at the misdeeds of Western medicine and biology in themselves, but at the medicalisation of "social suffering." Since then, linguistic anthropologists have created other concepts which are different from those that were used to describe the medical cosmologies and the body image at that time, in particular the concept of "indexicals" (the contextual parameters of the speech act, the anchor points of subjectivity in speech), which would be relevant for the analysis of the place of subjectivity in the clinical encounter, the religious ceremony and, more generally, the expression of the emotions in acts of speech. A contemporary ethnologist working on the Body in India—i.e. body images and the expression of the emotions, medical ideologies, religious representations, the performing arts—locates himself within the context of situations where people speak to each other. He describes how distinctions are made, explicitly and implicitly, between "the" body and its ownership ("your" body) in this or that local language, in medical consultations, rituals and the performing arts. Ultimately, these distinctions shape our representations of subjectivity.

Reinscriptions

Let us conclude this sketch of a periodisation of the history of the representations of the constructed Body in Hinduism by briefly returning to the analytic tool that we borrowed from Gyan Prakash. Can we schematise this ideological process that he termed *reinscription*? It seems to me that wherever we find this reinscription, a dialectic between the sphere of private life and the sphere of public life comes into play. We can thus resume our analysis of the period between 1860 and 1920 by saying that for Prakash, the native elites reinscribed the values of the private sphere in the public sphere, thus creating, with the aid of the Orientalists, a positivist version of Hinduism. Prakash adopted this notion of a division between the inner and outer spheres from Partha Chatterjee (1993). The nationalists constructed a spiritualist image of Hinduism that they located within the private sphere, the *inner sphere of family, women, tradition, and spirituality* (cf. Prakash 2000, p. 158),[16] while at the same time situating it in the shadow of the Western materialism imported by the coloniser into the public sphere of British India. The reinscription of Hindu tradition, penned by the Hindu nationalist writers, was a political strategy whose aim was to topple Ayurveda and other *private* disciplines of self control in the public arena, even if this meant making them into instruments of social control since they would be integrated into the modern instruments of governmentality.

Prakash very briefly outlines two other issues which he considers to have been affected by this dialectic between Eastern spirituality and Western technology in the nascent imaginary of India, i.e. the elementary structures of kinship and the village community ("*the bonds of community*"). To reinscribe these in the language of modernity is to transpose them from the spiritual domain into the political sphere:

> For, the nationalist imagination operated as a form of reinscription. Its ambition was to rewrite India and Indian interests scripted by colonial governmentality, to domesticate and bring within the domain of the nation the space constituted by technics and its political imperative—the state …
>
> The "inner" sphere of the nation—defined by the nationalists as its essential, spiritual domain that the West was to be kept out of—could not be insulated from the inessential "outer" sphere of modern science and technology in which the West was dominant. Nationalism could never concede that the nation existed only in its "inner" recesses, because that would cede the sphere of politics and economics to colonialism altogether. Colonial subjugation drove anticolonial nationalism in a more ambitious direction as it simultaneously drew upon and transgressed the inner/outer dichotomy, distinguishing community from the state while seeking to realize the former in the latter. Nationalism spoke in both languages of kinship and statecraft, it invoked the bonds of community and mobilized for state power (Prakash 2000, p. 179).

Later Prakash was to say that village communities ("*the little village community*"), which were compared to little republics, "aped" the modern state, while simultaneously expressing in the public sphere a reality that was of a spiritual nature—the organic solidarity that bound together the village community—which (in the imaginary of the nationalist writers, of course) had been inscribed in national Hindu culture from time immemorial (cf. Prakash 2000, p. 186).

This attempt at a retrospective analysis of the history of the representations of the body in India in the colonial and contemporary eras is based on the same principle. I have borrowed from Prakash the idea of a dialectic between disciplines of the self in the private domain and the government of the body in the public sphere. It is my impression that we have seen this dialectic operate twice. The first time was between 1860 and 1920, which permitted me to outline and explain its second appearance between 1970 and 1980. Only this

[16] See Chatterjee 1993, index s.v. "spiritual (domain)," "inside," etc.

second appearance is of any real interest to me, as will be clear, since the approach that I have taken is essentially reflective and intended to put my Orientalist work in perspective.

The Orientalist reconstruction of the Hindu representations of the Body, as it was received within the counter-culture, combined two principles, one of which was physiological or geographical and had to do with ecology, the humours, trees and the jungle, while the other was psychological and moral, situated in the realm of discourse, wisdom, self-discipline and subjectivity. What Prakash has to say only has relevance for the second of these two principles. To take the first into account and restore the physiological, geographical and ecological dimension to the representations of the body which come to us from Hinduism, would it not be fitting to take the (discerning, convincing) deconstruction of the "national medicine" proposed by Prakash and add to it a return to the land with its geographical roots—to move from the ears to the eyes, from discourse to the look, contextualising, returning to the landscapes of the tropics? The representations of the body are inseparable from the representations of the physical environment.

One might object that this is to fall back into the ideology of the sixties when Ramanujan fulfilled the expectations of the children of the counter-culture by publishing the poem that inspired the title of this essay, from which I would also like to quote an excerpt in conclusion.

A Hindu to His Body

Dear pursuing presence,
dear body: you brought me
curled in womb and memory
[…]
You brought me: do not leave me
behind. When you leave all else,
my garrulous face, my unkissed
alien mind, when you muffle
and put away my pulse
to rise in the sap of trees
let me go with you and feel the weight
of honey-hives, in my branching
and the burlap-weave of weaver birds
in my hair.

Attipat K. Ramanujan[17]

[17] First published in *the Striders* (1966), cited here from Ramanujan 1995. I have omitted half of the poem. In fact, it is essentially the last verse that interests us here, since it identifies the humours of the body with the saps that circulate in the plant kingdom. A.K. Ramanujan (1929–1993), who was a professor of linguistics at the University of Chicago, an inspired translator and wrote poetry in English, was speaking "in the name of India," so to speak, in the West in the sixties.

A vitalist and cosmic, vegan and supremely New Age reinscription of the representations of the Hindu Body, this poem only makes sense if seen in the context of the theory of the humours and the definition of death in Hindu medicine. As sentient beings animals die when the contact between the soul, the sensorimotor organs and the tangible world that is sustained by the inner being (*manas*) is broken. *My unkissed alien mind* is an image of this detachment of the inner being when deprived of the kiss of the body. The humours of the animal body are merely one avatar among others of the vital fluids that course through Nature. The humours of the body are no different from the vegetable saps. Where we say that a dead person has returned to the earth, Ramanujan sees his body, reduced to the essential—the nourishing saps—, dissolve into the plant kingdom and live on in the branches, the honey and the birds' nests.

References

Arnold, D. (1999): A Time for Science: Past and Present in the Reconstruction of Hindu Science, 1860-1920. In: Ali, D. (Ed.): Invoking the Past: The Uses of History in South Asia. – New Delhi, pp. 156-177.

Chatterjee, P. (1993): The Nation and Its Fragments: Colonial and Postcolonial Histories. – Princeton.

Keyes, C. F. (1983): Merit-Transference in the Kammic Theory of Popular Theravada Buddhism. In: Keyes, C. F./Daniel, E. V. (Eds.): Karma: An Anthropological Inquiry. – Berkeley, pp. 261-286.

Keyes, C. F./Daniel, E. V. (Eds.) (1983): Karma: An Anthropological Inquiry. – Berkeley.

Leslie, C. (Ed.) (1976a): Asian Medical Systems: A Comparative Study. – Berkeley.

Leslie, C. (1976b): The Ambiguities of Medical Revivalism in Modern India. In: Asian Medical Systems: A Comparative Study. – Berkeley, pp. 365-367.

Prakash, G. (1992): Writing Post-Orientalist Histories of the Third World. In: Dirks, N. B. (Ed.): Colonialism and Culture. – Ann Arbor.

Prakash, G. (2000): Another Reason: Science and the Imagination of Modern India. – 1st edition 1999. – New Delhi.

Ramanujan, A. K. (1995): The Collected Poems. – New Delhi.

Saint-Jean-Paulin, C. (1997): La Contre-culture: Etats-Unis, années 60: la naissance de nouvelles utopies. – Paris.

Seal, B. (1985): Positive Sciences of the Ancient Hindus. – 1st edition 1915. – Delhi.

Sengupta, K., S. (1995): The Ayurvedic System of Medicine. – 3rd edition. – 1st edition 1919. – Trivandrum.

Trawick, M. (1995): Writing the Body and Ruling the Land: Western Reflections on Chinese and Indian Medicine. In: Bates, D. (Ed.): Knowledge and the Scholarly Medical Traditions. – Cambridge.

Aṣṭāṅgahṛdayasaṃhitā of Vahata = Kunte, A. M. *et al.* (Ed.) (1939): Astangahrdayasamhita. – 6th ed. – Bombay.

Yogaśataka of Nāgārjuna = Filliozat, J. (Ed.) (1979): Yogasataka: texte médical attribué à Nagarjuna, textes sanskrit et tibétain. – Pondicherry. (Publications de l'Institut Français d'Indologie Vol. 62)

Zimmermann, F. (1995): Généalogie des médecines douces. – Paris.

Charles Malamoud

The Skin and the Self: A Note on the Limits of the Body in Brahmanic India

"Give me a spirit, a heart, that I might have a body, a skin, a son, a grandson." This prayer is said by the officiant called *adhvaryu*, on behalf of the person making the sacrifice as he watches the smoke rising from the fire as it consumes the entrails of the victim.[1] The immolated animal disintegrates and its constituent elements are scattered across the cosmos. The person making the sacrifice wishes to differentiate himself from the victim, with which he is partially identified, and strives to preserve or rather establish the integrity and fullness of his being. He will find continuation in his descendants, but he must first reassure himself of his own body, *tanu*. What delimits the body and at the same time creates a whole out of its parts is its covering of skin, *tvac*. While in India, as elsewhere, the skin, like the eye and the ear, is a sense organ (*indriya*),[2] it is interesting that in this context only the skin is mentioned. It is more than simply the organ of touch—it is the surface of the *tanu* which gives the body its identity.[3]

> In humans this membrane of identity certainly also serves to protect, but this protection is inadequate. This inadequacy is a characteristic of the species.

---

[1] TSI 3, 11, 1: *mano me hārdi yaccha tanūṃ tvacaṃ putraṃ naptāram aśīye*. For details of ritual, see TS VI 4, 1, 1ff. and ŚB III 8, 4, 8.

[2] From the Atharva-veda (AS XIX 9, 5) we have the doctrine of the five senses of perception and their corresponding organs, with *manas*, the "spirit" and organ of coordination, as a sixth sense. The skin is also listed as one of the bodily substances of the man-sacrificer, the other elements being the bones, flesh, tendons and nerves (*snāvan*), marrow (TB I 5, 9, man being expressly defined as "fivefold") or the hair, blood, flesh, bones and marrow (TS VII 4, 9, 1).

3 Amongst the terms for "body" in Sanskrit, *tanu* is peculiar in that it can, at least in the oldest texts, be used as a synonym for *ātman*, "soul" or "self," a term which is also used as a reflexive pronoun. Conversely, *ātman* is also frequently used in the sense of "body," and refers to the trunk, in particular, as opposed to the limbs, head or tail end. What is of great interest, and worthy of special study, is the *absence* of the skin and touch in the lists of the functions and organs which are arranged around the breath, the main subject of ŚāṅkhĀ.

In fact, in a hymn of the Atharvaveda we read: "This (naked skin) among the hides is born upon man (alone), all other animals are not naked."[4] These words accompany the sacrificer's gesture when he gives one of the officiants upon whose services he calls, a piece of clothing by way of payment for performing the ritual *dakṣiṇā*). We learn from the Kauśikasūtra that a certain amount of gold should be added to the garment.[5] The gold and the garment are invited to clothe the body (the *ātman*) of the Brahman to whom these gifts are made. Furthermore on this occasion rice porridge (*brahmaudana*) is prepared, on which a skin forms that is said to be "a homespun garment," in other words one that has been produced spontaneously by the rice from its own substance. Therefore if "all the other animals" (at least all the *paśu*, animals likely to be sacrificial victims[6]) are "not naked," man has need of an additional skin to cover his natural nakedness. The garment is an artefact that permits him to bridge the gap between his own natural state and the natural state of animals.[7] Whether the garment is an extra skin for man or whether naked skin is inadequate as a garment, this is what is clearly shown in the text which teaches that when the sacrificer gives the officiant a garment he is saving his own skin.[8]

Human individuals are naked from birth. While still a foetus we are wrapped in amniotic membranes which clothe us. To find ourselves stripped of these membranes is part of the great shock of the "wind of birth" which pushes the foetus out of the womb against its will, causing it also to forget the memory of all that preceded its entry into the world (cf. MALAMOUD 2004). One area of the human body is more hairless even than the others: the palms. This is due to the fact that the creator god Prajāpati, exhausted from bringing forth the creatures and terrified by his own weakness, rubbed his hands, a gesture expressing his anxiety (in English we talk of wringing our hands),

[4] AS XII 3, 51: *eṣā tvacāṃ puruṣe saṃ babhūva*
anagnāḥ sarve paśavo ye anye
kṣatreṇātmānampari dhāpayātho
'motaṃ vāso mukham odanasya

The second half of this verse is obscure. Cf. Bloomfield's translation: "Clothe yourselves, (ye Brahmans), in sheltering garments: (even) the face of the porridge is a homespun garment!" (BLOOMFIELD 1897, SBE XLII, p. 192 and p. 654).

[5] Kauś LXII 23.

[6] We are reminded of the definition in ŚB VII 5, 2, 23: *paśūnāṃ puruṣa eva yajate* "of all the animals suited to be sacrificial victims, man alone is (also) a sacrificer." For this definition and other characterisations/of the human being in the Veda cf. MALAMOUD 2005, pp.187–204.

[7] Man is *atvac*, "without skin," which is to say lacking the thick skin of animals. Likewise the *yūpa* "sacrificial post" is also said to be "without skin" (ŚB V 2, 1,6). See note 21 below.

[8] ŚB IV 3, 4, 26. In VS VII 47, the priest addresses the garment with which he has been presented: "Be a skin for the one who gives, a solace for me who receives."

and the hairs that had grown on his palms came off. Thus the human species acquired, as a hereditary characteristic, a trait that afflicted the Creator after he had brought forth the creatures.[9] (Let us remind ourselves that at this stage of mythology, the cosmogonic god is anthropomorphic: of all created beings man is the one that most resembles Prajāpati).

Now man, at least if he belongs to one of the three higher classes of society, experiences in the later course of his life other births after this initial birth.[10] In fact, each time he undertakes to offer a sacrifice he has to submit to a series of preliminary rites that make up the *dīkṣā*, a "consecration." By means of a highly complex series of ascetic observances, the person making the sacrifice is supposed to form a new body that is capable of taking part in the actual sacrifice. The *dīkṣā* is like a period of gestation. During this period the person making the sacrifice is like a foetus (cf. Lévi 2003, pp. 103ff.), and he therefore wraps himself in clothes that perform the same function for him as the membranes do for the actual foetus. At the end of this period of gestation he is born with his new body and casts aside his membrane-clothes. In the case of a sacrifice whose main offering is *soma*, this birth takes place at the moment at which the purchase of this plant is concluded. It is from the plant that the juice, a drink of immortality for the gods, will be extracted.[11] If he were to unclothe himself earlier, foetuses would run the risk of being born prematurely and there would be miscarriages. The mimed, symbolic gestation in the sacrificial space has direct effects on real gestations in the world outside it.

During the whole ritual one of the officiants, the *adhvaryu*, also has to hold, or have within reach, the skin of a black antelope (*kṛṣṇājina*). This is the symbol (one of the symbols) of the sacrifice.[12] Detached from the body it clothed, this dead skin is an example of what in Sanskrit is termed *carman*, a neuter word, whereas the feminine word *tvac* is used to designate the living skin (both the thick hairy skin of animals as well as the thin hairless skin of humans). However this division is not rigid, and in many passages of the Vedas, both hymns and prose texts, *tvac* is used to designate what in fact is a

[9] ŚB II 2, 4, 4; BĀU I 4, 6. Cf. Minard 1949, §50b.

[10] First of all the initiation ceremony of apprenticeship to Veda, in the course of which a young boy becomes a "twice-born," *dvija*. However in JB I 259, we also learn that "the sacrificer is born twice: once following the coupling of his parents and once out of the sacrifice. From the coupling of his parents he is born for this world, while from the sacrifice he is born for the other world …, the heavenly world."

[11] TS VI 1, 3, 2 ff. and also ŚB III 1, 1, 6–3, 24.

[12] At the very moment when the sacrificer is completely absorbed in his sacrificial tasks, he surrounds himself by objects which, in addition to their individual functions, are destined to represent either the sacrifice as a whole or the person of the sacrificer himself, as if it were necessary for him constantly to have before his eyes a sign or a memento of the whole in which the parts of the ritual have their place (ŚB VI 4,1, 6).

carman[13]. The most common explanation for this is that the dead skin acts as a living skin, but for a different organism from the one from which it was taken. This is the case here. When he picks up the black antelope skin and shakes it to drive out the demons who want to impede the sacrifice, the *adhvaryu* says to the skin: *śarmāsi* "you are a protection"—among humans this skin is known as *carman,* but among gods the name for it is *śarman.*[14] However, in the following stage this same skin (cf. HILLEBRANDT 1879, p. 3) is described as *tvac*, living skin. It is spread on the ground, with the neck pointing towards the west, with the words, "You are the skin (*tvac*) of Aditi ... Aditi is the earth."[15] The earth has a body, the female body of the goddess Aditi. Just like the bodies of men, Aditi's body is given a skin as a protective covering. However, unlike the clothing of man, the skin with which one covers the earth, being the hide of an animal, must be accepted, or, to be more precise, recognised by the organism that receives it. There must be an affinity between the being to be clothed and the garment-skin with which it is covered, a kind of homogeneity perceived as the condition of "accord." "May Aditi recognise

---

[13] The cast of the snake, when shed from the body, is usually referred to as *tvac*. It is seen as being in the state that it is in the process of leaving and not in the state that is about to enter. In the same way, the human's hair and beard (*keśaśmaśru*), which have to be shaved, and the nails (*nakhāni*) which have to be cut to enter into the sacrifice are seen as a kind of skin, a *tvac*, but are already dead and thus impure (*mṛtā vā eṣā tvag amedhyā*), whereas these excrescences/outgrowths do not become waste material until they have been separated from the body from which they stemmed (TS VI 1, 1, 2; JB I 345). The elements that make up this "dead skin" are rejected but not always eliminated. They can be buried at the foot of a tree, in particular when rites are performed in honour of ancestors, with the idea that they will be reintegrated in to the cycles of life. Cf. KRICK 1982, p. 89, note 226.

[14] ŚB I 1, 4, 4: *athā kṛṣṇājinam ādatte/śarmāsīti carma vā etat kṛṣṇasya tad asya tan mānuṣaṃ śarma devatra tasmād āha śarmāsīti tad avadhunoty avadhūtaṃ rakṣo' vadhūtā arātaya iti/tan nāṣṭrā evaitad rakṣāṃsy ato'pahanti*. "Then he takes the skin of the black antelope. 'You are *śarma,*' he says. For among men this black antelope skin is *carma*. For the gods it is *Śarma.* This is why he says, 'You are *śarma.*' He shakes it (saying), 'Shaken is the demon, shaken are the hostile forces.' This is how the harmful spirits, the demons, are driven out." The vocabulary of gods and that of men complement each other harmoniously. It is true that *carman* and *śarman* have different roots, but here, as in numerous other passages the authors of the Brāhmaṇa take advantage of a similarity of form between two words to claim or suggest that one of them, i.e. the one used by the gods, is the etymon of the other, that is accepted among men. The term used by the gods focuses on the virtue of the object, while the term used by humans is quite simply the name by which this object is known. In the ritual words, the sacrificer, a human, does not hesitate to use the form used by the gods. In numerous other passages of the Brāhmaṇa, the relationship between the language of the gods and the language of men is much more problematical. An alteration of the etymological form results from the gods' loving mysteries and loving to create mysteries.

[15] ŚB I 1, 4, 5: *tat pratīcīnagrīvam upastṛṇāti. adityās tvag asi ... iyaṃvai pṛthivy aditis.* Also TS I 1, 5, 2; TB III 2, 5, 5.

you. One recognises and receives what belongs to one. He uses this incantation of 'accord' to address the skin, thinking, 'May they not harm each other.'"[16]

The body metaphor is applied in a more detailed manner to the piece of land that constitutes the sacrificial area. To be more precise, Prajāpati, wanting to give man a "point of support" (*pratiṣṭhā*), created woman, but it seems that this woman is more of a companion to this male, Prajāpati himself, who is the divine creator but also the personified sacrifice, since the parts of the female body are none other than the constitutive elements of the sacrificial area: "her lap (*upastha*) is the altar (*vedi*), her hair the strewn grass (*barhis*), her skin (*carman*, thus rather a skin that clothes her?) the two parts of the *soma* press (*adhiṣavaṇe*), and the two lips of her vulva (*muṣkau*) the lighted fire in the centre (*samiddho madhyatas*)."[17] If the use of the word *carman* is surprising here, as is also the analogy drawn between this skin and the instrument thought to correspond to it, the construction is clear in the following example, (which shows what constitutes the body of the sacrifice. "The chariot that carries the oblations (*havirdhānam*) is the head (*śiras*) of the sacrifice, the sound holes (*uparavāḥ*) are the breaths (*prāṇāḥ*), the two pieces of the soma press (*adhiṣavaṇe*) its two jaws (*hanū*), the skin (*carma*) (on to which the juice of the *soma* runs), its tongue (*jihvā*), the stones of the press (*grāvāṇaḥ*) its teeth (*dantāḥ*), the fire of the offertory (*āhavanīyaḥ*) its mouth (*mukham*), the superior altar (*uttaravediḥ*) its nostril (*nāsikā*) and the shed (*sadas*) its belly (*udaram*)."[18]

Is nakedness simply a form of physical inferiority? Do we find in these texts, which are an exegesis of the Brahmanic rites, the idea that the natural nakedness of human beings can be immodest? The *vedi*, this altar which, as we have just seen, is compared to the lap of the female body and which, in other passages, is also by itself the image of the female body in its entirety (its form and proportions[19]), may not be revealed naked to the gaze of the gods or the Brahman scholars who are sitting around her. This is why it is covered with a thick covering of strewn grass, the *barhis*.[20] Another ritual

---

[16] ŚB I 1, 4, 5: *prati tvāditir vettu ... prati hi svaḥ saṃ jānīte tat samjñām evaitat kṛṣṇāya ca vadati ned anyo 'nyaṃ hinasāta*. On the notion of *samjñā*, "accord" and the vocabulary and grammatical usages of this term, see Condotti 2006, passim (pp. 46–50 for references to non-technical uses).

[17] BĀU VI 4, 3.

[18] TS VI 2, 11, 4.

[19] The *vedi* must be drawn in such a way that its contours are suggestive of a woman's shoulders, waist and hips, ŚB I 2, 5, 15–16.

[20] ŚB I 3,3,8: *anagnā* to make the *vedi* is not naked, *anagnatā*, to work on its non-nakedness. Similarly, to avoid exposing the sacrificial cake that he has just cooked naked (*nagna*) and hairless (*muṣita*) to the gazes of the demons, the *adhvaryu* covers and dresses (*abhivāsayati*) it with ashes (ŚB I 2, 2, 16). Prior to doing so he has recited an incantation intended to protect the skin (*tvac*) of this cake from being harmed by the fire.

object, this time a masculine one, must not be clothed: this is the sacrificial post (*yūpa*) which has to be encircled with a cord made of grass (*kuśa*), up to the level of the navel of the person making the sacrifice, since it is here that the man girds his loins with a cloth which covers the lower part of his body.[21] Since nakedness was prescribed for the execution of certain magical rites (cf. KEITH 1925, p. 388), it may be supposed that it was forbidden otherwise, but we do not know exactly which parts of the body had to be covered under all circumstances, apart from the sexual organs, of course. The prostitute known as *mahānagnī*, "the great naked one," was distinguished by nakedness, a certain nakedness. In a mythical narrative Speech was described as follows:[22] the Gandharvas, who are celestial musicians, have the *soma* that the gods covet. The gods agree to buy it from the Gandharvas. The goddess Speech offers herself as the price for this sale: "the Gandharvas like women, Speech is a woman." She becomes the "great naked one" that the gods surrender to the Gandharvas in return for the *soma*.

Human beings also have another reason for clothing themselves: not to scare others. We are covered with a skin which leaves us naked, but it has not always been so. We learn that in the beginning we had a true skin which afforded good protection and served as clothing. It was the cows that were naked. The gods took pity on the cows. "In truth, it is on the cows that all depends here on Earth. Let us put this skin that man has on the cows; then they will be better able to withstand the rain, the winter cold and the summer heat. They skinned man and put his skin on the cows ... Man is a creature that has been denuded. This is why he bleeds every time he is scratched by a blade of grass or some other object. They put this (other) skin, clothing, on him. That is why only man wears clothes. It is the skin that the gods gave him. It is also why man has to take care to be well-dressed, well-provided with this skin which belongs to him. One likes to see a well-dressed man, even if he has no

---

[21] ŚB III 7, 1, 19. Like humans, as represented by the person making the sacrifice, the sacrificial post is *a-tvac*, "without skin." This must be understood as deprived of the really protective skin that animals have (ŚB V 2, 1, 6; but the tree out of which the post will be made is, of course, "non-naked" if its trunk is covered with branches, KauṣB X 2). This is one example of the homology between the body of the person making the sacrifice and the sacrificial device which is considered to be a body, both as a whole and in its different constituent parts.

[22] AB I 27. For a more detailed and florid description see ŚB III 2, 4, 1–6: the *soma* in the possession the Gandharvas because one of them intercepted it when it was on its way to the gods, carried by a bird. Speech returns to the gods with the *soma*. The Gandharvas resign themselves to losing the *soma*, but they are so infatuated with Speech that they want to conquer her anew with their singing. They compete with the gods to seduce her. For further details of the ancient form of the myth of the stolen *soma* see SCHNEIDER 1971. For more information on the goddess Speech, seductress and seduced, see MALAMOUD 1989, pp. 175ff.

grace, since he is thus well-provided with the skin that is his. He should not stand naked before a cow, since the cow knows that it is wearing the skin of man. It trembles, fearing that he will take it back. This is why cows also only approach man when he is properly dressed."[23] In post-Vedic India, not to scare others and yet to be able to imagine the fear that one can inspire, i.e. to put oneself in another's shoes, was to become a refined complement of the wish not to make others suffer.

This myth or pseudo-myth—or legend—throws light on a fundamental characteristic. It introduces the idea that human nakedness was not among the primary characteristics of the species, but that it is acquired. This, of course, is reminiscent of the story in Genesis. In the Vedas (to stay with the narrative that I have just summarised) humans become naked because the gods decide to remove their skins. This is in no way a punishment or a misfortune, but rather an inconvenience that needs to be remedied. In contrast, Adam and Eve become naked because they perceive that they are naked and know immediately that that is shameful. This realisation is both the consequence and the proof of the transgression that they have just committed. They become aware of both their lack and their guilt simultaneously. This is the work of the serpent.[24] The Fall condemns humans to live on earth with Paradise behind them, but the gaze of God upon them and the need to cover their nakedness. It is the beginning of an existence consisting in differences between oneself and others and dedicated to the production of artefacts. In the Vedas, man transforms the nakedness imposed on him into a mode of regulating, or rather modulating, his relations with the other elements of the sacrificial world of which he is the centre. He finds companions in his nakedness, i.e. creatures

---

[23] ŚB III 1, 2, 13–16. JB II 182 gives a different version: in the beginning (*agre*), the skin that man possesses belonged to the animals (*paśu*) and the animals' skins belonged to man. Not being able to withstand the rain and the heat, the animals suggested to man that they should exchange skins. Man asked, "What advantage shall I have?" The animals replied, "We will be food for you (*ādyā* [*sic* in the version edited by Lokeś Candra] *te syāma iti*). And here is clothing for you." They held out to him a red cow's skin (*rohiṇīṃ chavim*). He must cover himself with it during the ritual known as *viśvajit*. This skin is both the mark of man's affinity with cows and an object, a form that belongs to him. Because he is covered with this skin the animals that he eats in this world do not avenge themselves in the other world by eating him in turn (*tathā hainam amuṣmin loke paśavo nādanti*). "This is why man, too, may not appear naked in front of a cow — the cow might run away from him, conscious of the fact that it is wearing his skin."

[24] *Sitôt pétris, sitôt soufflés,*
Maître Serpent les a sifflés,
Les beaux enfants que Vous créâtes !
Holà ! dit-il, nouveaux venus !
Vous êtes des hommes tout nus,
O bêtes blanches et béates ! (Paul Valéry, *Ebauche d'un serpent*)

to be provided with a garment that is supposed to be a skin and with a skin intended as a garment. It masks the laceration, the essential violence of the sacrifice, without ever making it disappear. It continuously knits together again what has been torn and reunites the objects which man initially had to separate in order to dispose of them, constantly projecting into beings from which he makes either replicas of or substitutes for himself.

References

Bloomfield, M. (1897): Hymns of the Atharvaveda: together with Extracts from the Ritual Books and the Commentaries – Oxford. (The Sacred Books of the East Vol. 42)

Condotti, M. P. (2006): Interprétations du discours métalinguistique. – Florence.

Hillebrandt, A. (1879): Das altindische Neu- und Vollmondsopfer. – Jena.

Keith, A. B. (1925): The Religion and Philosophy of the Veda and the Upanishads. – Cambridge, Mas.

Krick, H. (1982): Das Ritual der Feuergründung (Agnyādheya). – Vienna. (Sitzungsbericht der Österreichischen Akademie der Wissenschaften, Philosophisch-Historische Klasse, Vol. 399)

Lévi, S. (2003): La doctrine du sacrifice dans les Brâhmaṇas. – 3rd edition. – With preface by L. Renou and postscript by Ch. Malamoud. – Paris.

Malamoud, C. (1989): Cuire le monde. – Paris.

Malamoud, C. (2004): Un vent violent m'a séparé de moi". In: L'inactuel, new series, 10, January 2004, pp. 9–18.

Malamoud, C. (2005): Féminité de la parole. – Paris.

Minard, A. (1949): Trois énigmes sur les cent chemins, Vol. 1. – Paris.

Schneider, U. (1971): Der Somaraub des Manu. – Wiesbaden. (Freiburger Beiträge zur Indologie Vol. 4)

Abbreviations

AB	Aitareyabrāhmaṇa
AS	Atharvasaṃhitā (Śaunaka)
BĀU	Bṛhadāraṇyaka Upaniṣad
JB	Jaiminīyabrāhmaṇa
Kauś	Kauśikasūtra of the Atharvaveda
Śaṅkh Ā	Śāṅkhāyana Āraṃyaka
ŚB	Śatapathabrāhmaṇa (Mādhyaṃdina)
TB	Taittirīyabrāhmaṇa
TS	Taittirīyasaṃhitā
SBE	Sacred Books of the East

Gérard Colas

God's Body: Epistemic and Ritual Conceptions from Sanskrit Texts of Logic

This paper deals with the notions of the body of God as found in several Sanskrit philosophical works. In most of them, discussions on God's body are incidental to the topic of the creation of the universe. Consequently, they are intimately connected with the arguments for or against the existence of a God-creator. This will lead us to an interesting conception of the image of God in an 11th century work, the *Nyāyakusumāñjali*. This paper is divided into three parts: God's existence, his body and his image, each notion dependent on the previous one; if God does not exist, his body and image do not exist; if his body does not exist, there cannot be any image of it.

One may distinguish at least three different approaches in Sanskrit texts with regard to the relation between the notions of God, his body and his image. We may name them: devotional, ritualistic and epistemic. While the first two approaches are clearly associated with religion, this is not the case with the epistemic approach, although the main and original aim of one of the epistemic systems, that of Mīmāṃsā, was to explain the Vedic ritual corpus.

Here the expression devotional approach refers to the common religious attitude. It is characterized by immediacy between the devotee and the divine representation, concrete statue etc. or mystical, mental image, diagrams etc. In this approach there is a spontaneous and non-rational fusion between God, his body and his image. This fusion may concern only God and his body, as in the notion of *avatāra*, "divine descent,"[1] and not his image. The deity is said to come into the world of human beings by taking a body. But the fusion may concern the three notions, God, his body and his image, as illustrated by the notion of *arcāvatāra*, i.e. "divine descent as an image of worship." The image of God is considered as God himself and honoured with various offerings. Although the expression *arcāvatāra* may not be used in the works of the Tamil Āḻvārs (composed probably from 6th to 10th century), where the poet-devotees express different sentiments towards divine Vaiṣṇava images, it usually underlies them.[2] Another expression of the devotional approach is the

[1] See Hacker 1960 and Couture 2001 for this notion.

[2] It appears in Piḷḷai Lokācārya's *Śrīvacanabhūṣaṇa* (verses 34–35, 39, 196–197). See also Hardy 1983, pp. 261–269, 468 fn. For the identification of God, his body and his image, see Hardy 1983, pp. 288–302. Another early textual evidence of this identifying attitude could be the *Vaikhānasasmārtasūtra*, which may be situated between the 4th and, perhaps, the 6th century (see Colas 1996, pp. 22f., 49, 38).

notion of "self-manifested" divine image (*svayaṃvyakta*), where the deity is believed to manifest itself as an object or image with which it is consubstantial. Thus in the devotional attitude no distinction is made between the three concepts, namely God, his body and his image.

The ritualistic approach, on the other hand, distinguishes between the deity, its body and its image. The image is transformed into a living body of God which is able to receive material homage, in the form of food, flowers, scents, etc. The process of installation, consisting of successive stages of technical, ritual and mystical actions, insures the presence of God in the image. The *Baudhāyanagṛhyapariśiṣṭasūtra* and the *Vaikhānasāsmartasūtra* are early texts describing this ceremony (cf. Colas 1994). The earliest precisely datable ceremony of installation is found in the *Bṛhatsaṃhitā*, a 6th-century text. Later, temple-priest manuals of around the 10th century considerably expanded the ceremony. Patrons, astrologers, artists, priests and others work to achieve the final product, namely a concrete god-cum-image which, receptacle of the power of God, is considered as imbibed with divine presence and thus fit for devotion. However, the presence of God in the installed image remains volatile, because it is believed that god could leave. When daily obligatory rites are discontinued or when the image is damaged or touched by unqualified people, God is said to be unhappy or angry and to depart from the image.[3]

The third approach, which I call "epistemic," is that which is found in philosophical texts, sometimes wrongly qualified as "theological." Here, we take epistemic to mean relating to an organized system based on rational investigation. As we shall see, the ancient works of schools like Nyāya[4] and Sāṃkhya have little to do with theism. They clearly distinguish between God, his body and his image. Although their discussions on these notions are incidental to their main preoccupations, which are metaphysical and physical, they are nevertheless significant. One must wait until the 12th century to see a philosophical system, that of Viśiṣṭādvaita, synthesize the notions of God, his body and his image in a rational manner. This paper will concentrate on the third approach, that is, discussions of God's existence, his body and his image in philosophical texts, especially those of the Nyāya-Vaiśeṣika school from the 1st century up to the 11th century.[5]

[3] For more details on the installation ceremony, see Colas 1989; 1996, pp. 308–214; Einoo/Takashima 2005.

[4] To simplify the discussion, I shall take Nyāya and Vaiśeṣika to form a single school here.

[5] For a historical résumé, see Potter 1977a, pp. 1–7, esp. 3f. (beginnings of the school); for a brief recent attempt towards historical dating of the beginning of the school, see Bronkhorst 2006, p. 289.

1. God's existence

1.1. Global indifference about the question of God in the earlier period

Up until around the 11th century, most of the Indian epistemic systems were agnostic. They were not interested in the question of God, but were concerned with physics, rational evolution of natural principles and epistemology. The ancient form of Sāṃkhya, known from the 4th century *Saṃkhyakārikā*, is clearly not concerned by the question of the existence or role of God. Vācaspati Miśra's major reformulation of the Sāṃkhya school in the 9th or 10th century did not change the doctrine in this matter.[6] In spite of the introduction of the concept of God as the creator of the universe by the 16th-century Vijñānabhikṣu (cf. LARSON 1987, p. 37), God remained a secondary notion in this school. Patañjali's *Yogasūtras* admitted the existence of God, but simply as a particular sort of *puruṣa* ("man"), not as a creator of the universe. In Mīmāṃsā, the great advocate of Vedic religion, the notion of god was accessory and remained so throughout the evolution of that system. Gods were considered as mere linguistic entities. There is no such a thing as a creator of the universe and of the Veda, for Veda is eternal and the structure of the universe is held to be unchangeable in order to safeguard the eternity of Veda. The Buddhist and Jain systems can also be said to have been atheistic or agnostic, even though they integrated practices which we would call religious today. Gods are mortal and have no role in creation in Buddhism and Jainism (cf. WARDER 2004, p. 148; DUNDAS 2002, p. 90). They are subject to suffering decay and death in Buddhism, though they are relatively privileged and powerful beings (cf. CONZE 1995, pp. 57f.; GOMBRICH 1994, pp. 23f.; WARDER 2004, pp. 148f.). According to Jainism, they take birth spontaneously, possess senses and are subject to death and rebirth, even though they enjoy such privileges as changing their physical appearance (cf. JAINI 1998, pp. 110, 129; DUNDAS 2002, p. 90).[7]

1.2. The absence of interest for God in the ancient Nyāya school

The question of the existence of God does not appear or is at best secondary in the early Nyāya speculations. Issues related to the existence of God only gained importance in the 11th century, probably due to religious influence, especially as a means of taking a stand vis-à-vis notions such as the revelation of the Veda at each creation. The *Vaiśeṣikasūtras*, which probably existed in

---

[6] However, in his *Tattvavaiśāradī* on Vyāsa's *Bhāṣya*, he argued that "the Lord is not only eternal, but also responsible for the creation and dossolution of manifestation" (FEUERSTEIN 1987, p. 388).

[7] It should be noted that Purāṇic Hinduism occasionally mentions the death of divine incarnations, for instance that of Kṛṣṇa described at the end of the *Mahābhārata*.

the first centuries of our era, and the early Vaiśeṣika author Candramati (probably 5th century), do not refer to God. The *Vaiśeṣikasūtras* are concerned with physical laws, including the laws of merits and demerits of the selves. The notion of God does appear but only secondarily and casually in the *Nyāyasūtras*, which probably existed in the first three centuries of our era. The *sūtra* 4.1.19 refers to a thesis according to which God is the cause of the universe, and the two following *sūtras* discuss it. But this thesis was most probably not that of the author of the *Nyāyasūtras*. The ancient Naiyāyika authors probably accepted the belief in gods, but did not give them any special place in their system. The first extant commentary of the *Nyāyasūtras*, i.e. the *Bhāṣya*, by Vātsyāyana, which perhaps dates from the 5th century, seems to agree with the thesis of 4.1.19, but not so explicitly.

1.3. The progressive introduction of God in Nyāya

The situation evolved in the 6th century with Praśastapāda and Uddyotakara who clearly endorse the notion of a God creator in their commentaries on the *sūtras*. In Praśastapāda's *Padārthadharmasaṃgraha* (pp. 48f., commenting on the *Vaiśeṣikasūtras*), God (Maheśvara) periodically dissolves the universe to give rest to souls, and recreates it to allow souls to exhaust their *karman* through experience in the created world. However, his function in the creation and destruction of the universe is limited. Firstly, because he has to operate according to the time cycles of destruction and creation as well as the individual *karman* of the souls. Secondly, because he delegates Brahmā, another god, to create the material universe. According to Uddyotakara, commenting on the *Nyāyasūtras* (pp. 949f.), the activity of creation is in God's nature, but is strictly limited. God cannot continuously create the universe, but has to consider such causes as the maturation of *dharma* and *adharma*. Uddyotakara rejects Puranic and religious concepts of a god who acts and creates by mere fantasy or free will.

The situation changed dramatically in the Nyāya school of the 11th century with the theocentric position of Udayana, known especially from his *Nyāyakusumāñjali*. The main aim of this text was to establish the existence of God through reasoning. Since that had already been established by his Naiyāyika predecessors, we may suppose that the Udayana's specifically theological effort was probably due to an external factor, either ideological or religious.

2. God's body

2.1. Introduction

As I have already mentioned, discussions on God's body and images were not a major subject for the pre-12th century stage of Indian philosophical systems, although they were mentioned. I shall concentrate on two systems: Mīmāṃsā and Nyāya.[8] These two schools deal with the question of God's body in two very different perspectives and at different periods. The earliest discussion in Mīmāṃsā dates from around the 4th-5th century. The earliest available Nyāya reference to the question is found in a 9th century text—the *Nyāyamañjarī*—, that is, at least three centuries later (cf. Potter 1977b, p. 342). This time difference is in itself interesting. The motivations of Mīmāṃsā in relation to these topics are ritualistic and social, while those of Nyāya are more "philosophical," being connected with the definitions of God and of body, even though the Nyāya point of view reflects a progressively growing pressure from religion.

2.2. Mīmāṃsā perspective

Śabara's commentary (4th-5th century) on the *Mīmāṃsāsūtras* attacks the thesis that deities have bodies and even consume food and other offerings. In the same passage he criticizes the notion that deities possess villages and territories, which in reality are owned by temple priests. The rejection of these two points arises from the pro-Vedic and ritualistic attitude of Mīmāṃsā, according to which sacrifice is self-sufficient with regard to its results. Vedic sacrifice is thus independent of gods, who have only a secondary role to play (cf. Colas 2004, pp. 151–155). The period when Śabara lived saw the development of the *pūjā* type of image worship with offerings of food to religious images. Contemporary inscriptions record that the temple image worship was associated with donations of villages and lands to Hindu and Buddhist images. That religious images were held to be landowners was probably not unknown to Śabara. The Mīmāṃsā conception of sacrifice was naturally opposed to such *pūjā* worship of gods and to the notion of God's body associated with it (cf. Colas 2006, pp. 370ff.; 2009, pp. 106ff.).

The question of God's body also appears to have been a crucial question for Mīmāṃsā from a social point of view. Vedic priests increasingly turned towards image worship during that period. The boundaries between Vedic rites and image worship had become permeable since several centuries (cf. von Stietencron 1977, pp. 128f.; Colas 2006, pp. 360–370). Financing the production of religious statues, perpetuating image worship, building temples,

[8] According to R. Sharma *et al.* (1987, p. 255) the *Yuktidīpikā* (680–700?) asserts the notion of body of God. According to Dasgupta (1975, p. 153) Yāmunācārya (probably 11th century, "1010 ?" according to Potter 1983, p. 216), one of the founders of Viśiṣṭādvaita, "follows the method of the *Nyāya*" and asserts that the "intelligent person" who produced the universe "has no body, but still He carries on the functioning of His desires by His *manas*." This seems to allude to a passage of the *Īśvarasiddhi* section of the *Siddhitraya* (p. 96), which represents the Naiyāyika, but not necessarily Yāmuna's point of view.

etc. engulfed a growing part of the religious budget of the wealthy and powerful. It was probably important for the Vedic revivalists of Śabara's period to clearly redefine the profession of Vedic priests vis-à-vis that of temple priests. All notion of representing gods and creating their images was consequently to be banned in the context of a Vedic ritual. The denial of God's body by Śabara reflects this concern.

2.3. Nyāya perspective

Nyāya too was reluctant to admit the possession of a body by God, but for reasons different from those of the Mīmāṃsā. The earliest discussions I could find on the question of God's body in Nyāya are from two 9th-century works, Bhāsarvajña's *Nyāyabhūṣaṇa* and Jayanta Bhaṭṭa's *Nyāyamañjarī*. Both the works reject the notion of God's body. Bhāsarvajña denies that God the creator has a body (pp. 453, 465f.) and he refutes the Mīmāṃsā charge that a body is necessary for God to create the universe (p. 448). Jayanta Bhaṭṭa's work (see pp. 175–188, particularly 185–188) also denies the possession of a body by God. The opposing argument is that a god cannot create without possessing a body and that the possession of a body by God entails logical contradictions. For example, God's body is neither perceivable nor inferable. If God had a body like a potter, it would mean that like a potter, he would lack omniscience, suffer, etc. Moreover, if God had a body, it would require a creator of that body, resulting in logical infinite regress. Jayanta answers this criticism by proving that the creation of the universe by God is not connected with his possession of a body. However, he accepts, in a brief statement, the possibility of God taking a body in view of emitting the Veda (p. 218). These are some of the arguments which Udayana later developed in the 11th century.

Thus both these 9th-century authors are very careful to separate the issue of creatorship from that of the possession of a body, because the admission of body for God would raise theoretical problems difficult to overcome by mere reasoning. It may be pointed out that both authors were closely linked with so-called "Tantric" traditions. Bhāsarvajña was a follower of the Pāśupata tradition (cf. Potter 1977c, p. 399) and Jayanta Bhaṭṭa defended the authority of Śaivāgama (cf. Potter 1977b, p. 342). It could signify that intellectually important 9th-century Tantric authorities denied that God has a body and perhaps did not subscribe to such religious beliefs as those of *avatāra* and similar. One may wonder whether it means that "Tantric" erudites (or, more precisely, erudites of certain "Tantric" traditions) isolated their reasoning from the main non-scholarly stream of "Tantric" beliefs or whether "Tantrism" in general or several particular "Tantric" traditions were simply not adhering to common Purāṇic religion.

Two centuries later, Udayana developed these questions in his different works. He was the first Naiyāyika to give central importance to the notion of

God and discuss the subject of his body (cf. CHEMPARATHY 1972, pp. 140–7, 152f., 171). According to him, the possession of a body by God depends on the functions he assumes: cognition, creation and instruction. God as an omniscient knower does not have a body. As a creator he is held not to have a body, but, as we will see, Udayana accommodates a religious belief in this matter. Finally God takes a body to instruct Veda.

Udayana states that the omniscience of God contradicts his possession of a body, for if he had one, it would give rise to limited knowledge, as is seen in ordinary beings. The author points out further contradictions to the notion of God's body. For instance, God's body does not exist, since it is not perceived; even if it did exist, it could not be of atomic size, because it would then not be the substrate of senses, etc., as a body is required to be according to the Naiyāyika definition of body.

Udayana states that God does not need a body to be a creator. In response to the argument that all agents possess a body, and that God as creator of the universe should also have one, Udayana shows how God can be an agent without having a body. However, he does make two concessions. He believes that in a way, the atoms that constitute the universe can be said to form his body, but they cannot be considered as the substratum of senses, since God does not require senses; atoms cannot be considered as the locus of God's experience, since He does not experience pleasure or pain. Udayana makes another concession, while commenting on the belief that God uses the service of the secondary God Brahmā to create the material world. According to Udayana, this can be interpreted in two different ways. The first interpretation is that God is the co-creator, and that Brahmā is in charge of the practical aspect of the creation. The second is that God himself assumes the form of Brahmā for the sake of creation.

While Udayana rejects the possession of a body by God as creator, he admits the necessity for him to assume specific bodies to perform specific actions such as instructing the Veda. These are called "bodies of manifestation" (*nirmāṇakāya*), an expression which is also found in Buddhism (cf. KAVIRAJ 1922). They are also called an "instrumental body" (*upakaraṇaśarīra*). As it is neither a support of senses nor a substratum of pleasure and pain, this body of manifestation of God is not an ordinary body. Unlike the Mīmāṃsakas who believe that Veda is eternal, Udayana, like all Naiyāyikas, holds that Veda is instructed by God on each creation and that God requires organs of speech and a body in order to speak.

The reason why Udayana is reluctant to speak of a body in the case of God is not hard to find. The *Nyāyasūtras*, the ultimate authority in matters of Nyāya doctrine, defines body as "the substratum of actions, of sense-organs and of experience" (*ceṣṭendriyārthāśrayaḥ śarīram*) (1.1.11). Vātsyāyana, the first known commentator on the *Nyāyasūtras*, explains that the body is the receptacle where pleasure and pain appear. According to another *Nyāyasūtra*, "a body and its connection with a soul are caused by the karman of the soul" (*śarīrotpattinimittavatsaṃyogotpattinimittaṃ karma*) (3.2.66). Vātsyāyana further explains that the diversity in the physical and social conditions of individuals is explainable only by karman (on 3.2.67). Thus the connection of the souls with specific bodies is due to their past deeds.

Udayana cannot contradict or alter the definition of body laid down by the basic texts of Nyāya, and this definition certainly cannot apply to the body of God, if he has one. However, the 6th-century Nyāya-Vaiśeṣika author Praśastapāda admits that God experiences various kinds of feelings. According to this author the desire of God to destroy and recreate the universe arises from his compassion for the souls (cf. Chemparathy 1968, p. 75). Udayana shares the same conception (cf. Chemparathy 1972, p. 145). Although the notion that God has feelings implies that he has a body, it cannot be accepted that his body is produced by *karman*, or that he experiences pain and pleasure in it as human beings do. Udayana gets round this difficulty by admitting the possibility of a "body of manifestation" for particular actions. He specifies that this kind of body is neither substratum of senses nor field of experience.

3. God's image

To the best of my knowledge the question of religious images is not examined in ancient Naiyāyika texts. I shall limit my investigations to Udayana's statements in his *Nyāyakusumāñjali* (*kārikās* 8, 11 and 12 with his autocommentary). In fact, Udayana's reflections on the divine image are completely disconnected from the question of God's body, for they arise during his discussion on the functioning of rituals. They answer contemporary criticisms, which he reports, that rituals are fraudulent or used as means to obtain social prestige. They concern deities rather than the supreme God who creates the universe.

We may recall that according to the manuals of the temple-priests from the end of the first millenium, a major action in the ritual installation of an image consists in introducing divine power (*śakti*) into that image.[9] The image is thus imbibed with divine power and the presence of the deity activated in it. At about the same time as these manuals, Udayana expounded another view. He states that the only transformation produced by rites takes place in the performer of the rite. He rejects the idea that an object which has undergone a particular ritual treatment could have any kind of efficiency. According to him, the rite does not instill the image with a divine presence or power; it only gives rise to a conscious reflection by deities contemplating themselves in the image. That is to say, there is no real entering of the deity into the image, but

[9] See the publications referred to in the introduction to this paper.

an act of consciousness of the deity towards the image. Udayana explains that it is like a king who becomes aware of his resemblance with his image painted by an artist. Thus, although Udayana denies, on rational grounds, the claims of the priestly class that their ritual actions imbibe the religious image with divine power, he legitimates the ritual worthiness of the religious image (cf. COLAS 2004, pp. 159–164).

Conclusion

The notion of God is central to Udayana's works, but neither the notion of God's body nor that of God's image fit within the Nyāya framework. Udayana defends rituals connected with divine images, but his line of reasoning cannot operate the conjunction between God, his body and his image, which the temple priests and devotees achieve through ritual and devotion respectively. Udayana pushes to a maximum the boundaries of his rational legacy with regard to religion and devotion. But crossing these boundaries would have required the integration of non-rational elements foreign to the system.

No major epistemic system up to the 11th century fully integrates the notions of God's body and his image into their doctrinal reflections. God in the systems discussed so far appears to be a mere causal necessity for the creation of the universe. Even in Śaṅkara's works in the 8th century, God, much inferior to the supreme being (the Brahman), only satisfies the religious need at a mundane level. It was Rāmānuja, the main historical founder of Viśiṣṭādvaita who radically reversed the perspective, in the 12th century. According to him, the existence of God is known only through scriptures, not through reasoning. He placed a god possessing infinite auspicious qualities at the centre of his epistemic system. He asserted that the animate and inanimate world forms the body of God (cf. DASGUPTA 1975, pp. 298ff.; SRINIVASACHARI 1970, pp. 221–250). The possession of body by God, his descent as an *avatāra* and as a divine image became metaphysically and theoretically feasible. Viśiṣṭādvaita is the first major epistemic system, in which equal importance is attached to reason and devotion, which can be qualified as theological. It paved the way for later theological doctrines developed by Nimbārka, Vallabha and others. The episode in Vallabha's hagiography in which he identifies an image of Kṛṣṇa as God himself is a culminating point in the synthesis of the notions of God, his body and his image.

References

Sanskrit texts

Nyāyabhūṣaṇa = YOGĪNDRĀNANDA, S. (Ed.) (1968): Nyāyabhūṣaṇa by Bhāsarvajña. – Vārāṇasī.

Nyāyamañjarī = ŚUKLA, Ś. (Ed.) (1936): Nyāyamañjarī by Jayanta Bhaṭṭa. – Benares.

Nyāyasūtras = Taranatha/Amarendramohan (Eds.) (2003): Nyāyadarśana with Vātsyāyana's Bhāṣya, Uddyotakara's Vārttika, Vācaspati Miśra's Tātparyaṭīkā, and Viśvanātha's Vṛtti. – Reprint of the 1st edition: Calcutta, 1936–1944. – Delhi.
Praśastapādabhāṣya = Dvivedin, V. (Ed.) (1895): The Bhāshya of Praśastapāda together with the Nyāyakandalī of Śrīdhara. – Benares.
Siddhitraya = Viraraghavacharya, U. T. (Ed.) (1972): Sri Yamunacharya's Siddhitraya with a Sanskrit Commentary (Goodha Prakasa) by [...] U.T. Viraraghavacharya and with [...] Translation in English by R. Ramanujachari & [...] K. Srinivasacharya. – Madras.

Secondary sources

Bronkhorst, J. (2006): Systematic Philosophy between the Empires. Some Determining Features. In: Olivelle, P. (Ed.): Between the Empires: Society in India 300 BCE to 400 CE. – Oxford, pp. 287–313.
Chemparathy, G. (1968): The Īśvara doctrine of Praśastapāda. In: Vishvesharanand Indological Journal, 6, pp. 65–87.
Chemparathy, G. (1972): An Indian Rational Theology: Introduction to Udayana's Nyāyakusumāñjali. – Vienna.
Colas, G. (1989): L'instauration de la puissance divine dans l'image de temple en Inde du Sud. In: Revue de l'Histoire des Religions, 206, pp. 129–150.
Colas, G. (1994): On the Baudhāyanagṛhyapariśiṣṭasūtra and the Vaiṣṇavāgamas. In: Filliozat, P.-S./Narang, S. P./Bhatta, C. P. (Eds.): Pandit N.R. Bhatt Felicitation Volume. – Delhi, pp. 511–525.
Colas, G. (1996): Viṣṇu, ses images et ses feux : Les métamorphoses du dieu chez les vaikhānasa. – Paris.
Colas, G. (2004): The Competing Hermeneutics of Image Worship in Hinduism (Fifth to Eleventh Century AD). In: Granoff, P./Shinohara, K. (Eds.): Images in Asian Religions: Texts and Contexts. – Vancouver/Toronto, pp. 149–179.
Colas, G. (2006): Jalons pour une histoire des conceptions indiennes de yajña. In: Colas, G./Tarabout, G. (Eds): Rites hindous, transferts et transformations. – Paris, pp. 343–387.
Colas, G. (2009): Images and Territory of Gods: From Precepts to Epigraphs. In: Berti, D./Tarabout, G. (Eds.): Territory, Soil and Society in South Asia. – New Delhi, pp. 99–139.
Conze, E. (1995): Le bouddhisme dans son essence et son développement. – 1st English ed. 1951. – Paris.
Couture, A. (2001): From Viṣṇu's Deeds to Viṣṇu's Play or Observations on the Word avatāra as a Designation for the Manifestations of Viṣṇu. In: Journal of Indian Philosophy, Vol. 29, No. 3, pp. 313–326.
Dasgupta, S. (1975): A History of Indian Philosophy. Vol. III, – 1st ed. 1922. – Delhi.
Dundas, P. (2002): The Jains. – 2nd ed., 1st ed. 1992. – London.
Einoo, S./Takashima, J. (Eds.) (2005): From Material to Deity: Indian Rituals of Consecration. – New Delhi.
Feuerstein, G. (1987): The Concept of God (Īśvara) in Classical Yoga. In: Journal of Indian Philosophy, Vol. 15, No. 4, pp. 385–397.
Gombrich, R. (1994): Theravāda Buddhism: A Social History from Ancient Benares to Modern Colombo. – 1st ed. 1988. – London.
Hacker, P. (1960): Zur Entwicklung der Avatāralehre. In: Wiener Zeitschrift für die Kunde Süd- und Ostasiens und Archiv für indische Philosophie, 4, pp. 47–70.

Hardy, F. (1983): Virahabhakti: The Early History of Kṛṣṇa Devotion in South India. – Delhi.

Jaini, P. S. (1998): The Jaina Path of Purification. – 1st ed. 1979. – Delhi.

Kaviraj, G. (1922): Nirmāṇakāya. In: Jha, G. (Ed.): The Princess of Wales Saraswati Bhavana Studies, 1, pp. 47–58.

Larson, G. J. (1987): Introduction to the Philosophy of Sāṃkhya. In: Larson, G. J./ Bhattacharya, R. S. (Eds.): Encyclopedia of Indian Philosophies. Vol. IV: Sāṃkhya: A Dualist Tradition in Indian Philosophy. – Delhi, pp. 3–103.

Larson, G. J./Bhattacharya, R. S. (Eds.) (1987): Encyclopedia of Indian Philosophies. Vol. IV: Sāṃkhya: A Dualist Tradition in Indian Philosophy. – Delhi.

Potter, K. H. (1977a): Introduction to the Philosophy of Nyāya-Vaiśeṣika. In: Potter, K. H. (Ed.): Encyclopedia of Indian Philosophies. Vol. II: Indian Metaphysics and Epistemology: The Tradition of Nyāya-Vaiśeṣika up to Gaṅgeśa. – Delhi, pp. 1–208.

Potter, K. H. (1977b): Jayanta Bhaṭṭa. In: Potter, K. H. (Ed.): Encyclopedia of Indian Philosophies. Vol. II: Indian Metaphysics and Epistemology: The Tradition of Nyāya-Vaiśeṣika up to Gaṅgeśa. – Delhi, pp. 341–343.

Potter, K. H. (1977c): Bhāsarvajña. In: Potter, K. H. (Ed.): Encyclopedia of Indian Philosophies. Vol. II: Indian Metaphysics and Epistemology: The Tradition of Nyāya-Vaiśeṣika up to Gaṅgeśa. – Delhi, pp. 398–400.

Potter, K. H. (1983): Encyclopedia of Indian Philosophies. Vol. I: Bibliography. – 2nd revised ed.; 1st ed. 1970. – Delhi.

Sharma, R. et al. 1987 = Sharma, R./Bhargava, D./Sharma, S. K. (1987): Yuktidīpikā. In: Larson, G. J./Bhattacharya, R. S. (Eds.) (1987): Encyclopedia of Indian Philosophies. Vol. IV: Sāṃkhya: A Dualist Tradition in Indian Philosophy. – Delhi, pp. 227–269.

Srinivasachari, P. N. (1970): The Philosophy of Viśiṣṭādvaita. – 1st ed. 1943. – Madras.

von Stietencron, H. (1977): Orthodox Attitudes towards Temple Service and Image Worship in Ancient India. In: Central Asiatic Journal, Vol. 21, No. 2, pp. 126–138.

Warder, A. K. (2004): Indian Buddhism. – Reprint of the 3rd revised ed.; 1st ed. 1970. – Delhi.

David Gordon White

Yogic Rays: The Self-Externalization of the Yogi in Ritual, Narrative and Philosophy

While most Indian and western commentators and scholars, following the ca. third-century CE *Yogasūtras* (YS) of Patañjali, have assumed the Hindu yogic body to be a closed, self-contained system, a significant volume of data from a variety of sources—ranging from the classical Upaniṣads down through the Tantras (and including passages from the *Yogasūtra*s themselves)—indicate that an "open" model of the yogic body has also been operative in Hindu philosophical, medical, ritual and mythological traditions. In these open models, the mind-body complex is linked, often via "solar rays," to the sun of the macrocosm, as well as to other mind-body complexes, which Yogis are capable of entering through their practice.

As Peter Schreiner (1999) has noted, the term *yoga* appears nearly 900 times in the *Mahābhārata* (MBh), of which well over 250 in the didactic teachings of the "Mokṣadharma" section of its twelfth book, and over 100 in the *Bhagavadgītā* alone. When, however, one focuses on the term *yogi* in the epic, one finds fewer than a hundred occurrences; and when one looks for *narrative* descriptions of the practice of yoga there, that number dwindles to twelve. One finds a remarkable uniformity among these narratives, which portray the practitioner of yoga as either entering into the sun or penetrating the body of another being. Six of these narratives concern *kṣatriyas* or warriors (Bhīṣma, MBh 13.154.3–6; Balarāma, MBh 16.5.11–15; Kṛṣṇa, MBh 16.5.18–25; the five Pāṇḍavas and Draupadī, MBh 17.1.28, 44; 17.2.1; Bhūriśravas, MBh 7.118.16b, 17a–18b; and Droṇa, MBh 7.165.35b–42b) who, "yoked to yoga" (*yoga-yukta*), usually on the battlefield, are described as going to the sun. One concerns a hermit (Śuka, MBh 12.318.53–12.320.3[1]), who goes to the sun. The remaining five concern hermits of one sort or another (Bharadvāja, MBh 13.31.29–30; Vipula, Sulabhā, Vidura, and Kāvya Uśanas) who enter into the bodies of other beings, usually humans. Most of these accounts are found in late portions of the MBh, the great majority figuring in the epic's twelfth and thirteenth books.

---

[1] Discussed in Hiltebeitel 2001, pp. 301f. Portions of this chapter have appeared in David Gordon White, *Sinister Yogis* (Chicago: University of Chicago Press, 2009). They are reproduced here with permission from the University of Chicago Press.

The best-known epic narrativization of yoga involving the penetration of another person's body concerns the Pāṇḍava king Yudhiṣthira and his Kaurava uncle Vidura, both of whom are incarnations of the god Dharma. After the final battle has been won, Yudhiṣthira withdraws to a hermitage, in the vicinity of which he comes upon Vidura alone in the forest. Yudhiṣthira announces himself, at which point Vidura

> . . . fully fixed his gaze upon the king, having conjoined with his faculty of sight (*dṛṣṭi*) the faculty of sight in him. And the wise Vidura, who was fixing his breaths in his breaths and his senses in his senses, also verily entered [Yudhiṣthira's] limbs with [his own] limbs. Applying his power of yoga (*yogabalam*), Vidura, who was seemingly set ablaze with fiery splendor, entered into the body of the king. Then the king likewise saw that [that] body of Vidura, whose eyes were dull and glassy, and which was propped up against a tree, was devoid of consciousness. He then felt himself to be several times stronger [than before], and the righteous king of great splendor recalled his entire past and . . . the practice of yoga (*yogadharma*) as it had been recounted [to him] by Vyāsa. (MBh 15.33.24–29)

In this case, the yogic transfer is final: Vidura has left his now dead body behind to permanently cohabit the body of Yudhiṣthira. Other epic accounts of less permanent yogic transfers explicitly designate rays (*raśmi*) as transfer media. So, for example, an account from the Mokṣadharma sub-parvan of the epic's twelfth book describes a Buddhist nun (*bhikṣuki*) named Sulabhā who, giving up her former body through yoga (*yogatas*), has taken on the appearance of a beautiful woman to appear before King Janaka of Mithila (MBh 12.308.7b, 10a, 12ab).[2] Thereafter, she instructs him on the nature of liberation after first entering his body:

> That connoisseur of yoga entered (*praviveśa*) into the king, having conjoined (*saṃyojya*) his consciousness with [her] consciousness, [his] eyes with [her] eyes, and [his] rays (*raśmīn*) with [her] rays (*raśmibhiḥ*). With the bonds of yoga did she bind him . . .(MBh 12.308.16b–17b)

Then, at the conclusion of a 160-verse "inner dialogue" that takes place inside the king's heart, Sulabhā states: "Just as a solitary mendicant would dwell for one night in a an empty citadel, so indeed do I dwell tonight in this body of yours." (MBh 12.308.190ab). The use of the term "citadel," for the body or the heart that encloses the self or person within,[3] is one that extends from the ca. fifth-century BCE *Bṛhadāraṇyaka Upaniṣad* (BṛU) (BṛU 2.1.17–19) forward into the Tantras.[4]

---

[2] For a discussion, see Fitzgerald 2002, pp. 641–77.

[3] Here, I am following Smith's (2006, p. 21 and passim) astute translation of the term *puruṣa* as "person," and *ātman* as "self."

[4] See below, fn. 55.

Sulabhā's yogic penetration of king Janaka for the purpose of schooling him in esoteric teachings becomes, I would argue, the model for later tantric initiation. Such an initiation also appears to be implied in the language of the account of a Bhargava seer (*ṛṣi*) named Bharadvāja, in whose hermitage Divodāsa, the king of Kāśī, has taken refuge after having lost his entire lineage, army and kingdom to the sons of a rival king named Vītahavya. The seer produces a fully-formed thirteen year-old child named Pratardana from his sacrificial fire. Then "yogically co-penetrated (*yogena . . . samāviṣṭa*) by the wise Bharadvāja, and taking on a splendor (*tejas*) that suffused the entire world, he [Pratardana] co-penetrated (*samāviśat*) [Bharadvāja] in that place. And so, with his armor, bow, and arrow, he blazed like a fire." (MBh 13.31.27–31). Not only does the verbal form *sam-ā-viś* appear in the classical terminology of tantric initiation, but the multiple references to (a ray of) light (*tejas*) are of a piece with the many explicit solar associations found in early accounts of yoga.

The epic account of Droṇa's battlefield apotheosis provides a brilliant illustration of this type of imagery. Upon hearing the announcement of the death of his son, Droṇa "yokes himself to yoga" (MBh 7.165.35b):

> Practicing yoga, that great ascetic who had become a luminous being (*jyotirbhūto*), that teacher, advanced (*ākrāmat*) toward heaven, to which advance is difficult (*durākramam*) even by the good and the true. And when he was gone [toward heaven], the impression arose that there were two suns seemingly [merged] into a single point, and the sky was filled with luminaries. Then [he] entered into the moon, which was shining like the sun, and in a twinkling, his light disappeared . . . With Droṇa now gone to the World of Brahman . . . five humans saw that great self who was yoked to yoga as he went to the highest path (*paramāṃ gatim*). (MBh 7.165.39a-41a, 41c-42b)

A number of non-critical recensions of the MBh evoke the piercing of the solar orb, and link said piercing to the practice of yoga in the following aphorism: "Two penetrate the orb of the sun: the recluse (*parivrāḍ*) and the hero who, yoked to yoga (*yogayukta*) has lain down his life on the battlefield."(MBh 5.33.52).[5] This same aphorism is found in the first- to sixth-century CE *Pañcatantra* (1.333), a tenth-century Nyāya-Vaiśeṣika philosophical commentary,[6] and on medieval hero stones in Karnataka (cf. SETTAR/SONTHEIMER 1982, p. 274).

Returning to epic accounts that portray the yogic penetration of one being by another, for the good of the latter (but without the initiatory overtones),

5 *178 in the critical edition, following 5.33.52 in the K2.4.5; D8.10; K1; and D2.7 manuscripts: *dvāv imau puruṣau loke sūryamaṇḍala bhedinau/parivrāḍyogabhuktaśca raṇe cābhimukho hatah//.*

6 *Vyomavatī* (no verse numbering), in SASTRI's 1983 ed., Vol. 1, p. 4.

I now turn to the story of Vipula, a young Bhargava hermit who protects his guru's wife Ruci from the advances of the lascivious god Indra.

> Hereupon, Vipula, through yoga, indeed entered Ruci in that [place], [in order] to protect his preceptor's wife from the multiformed . . .[Indra].[7] With [his] two eyes [engaged] in her two eyes, having conjoined [her] rays with his rays, Vipula entered into [her] body like wind into the sky . . . (MBh 13.40.56–57) and he bound all of her sense organs with the bonds of yoga (*yoga-bandhanaiḥ*) . . . [such that] she was immobilized by his power of yoga (*yoga-bala-mohitā*) (MBh 13.41.11ab, 12b).

A final epic narrative portraying the yogic penetration of a foreign body—this time, however, in a hostile or predatory mode—is the account of Kāvya Uśanas who is, exceptionally for the epic, termed both a Yogi and a Mahāyogi (*mahāyogin*), as is Śiva, his divine rival in the myth. Kāvya Uśanas has yogically entered into the body of Kubera and stolen his wealth. A disconsolate Kubera appeals to the Great Yogi Maheśvara (i.e. Śiva), saying "Now that I have been besieged by the yogic person (*yogātmakena*) Uśanas, my wealth is gone, and that great ascetic has slipped away, on a path of his own yogic making." (MBh 12.278.12). Śiva spears Kāvya Uśanas on the tip of his pike, swallows him, and eventually ejaculates him, whence his well-known sobriquet Śukra, "Semen" (but also "Shiny," a reference to the planet Venus, with which he is also identified) (MBh 12.278.13–32).[8]

A cursory examination of the language of these narratives reveals that, in addition to their explicit mentions of yoga or Yogis, many refer to solar luminescence and rays of light (*raśmi, tejas*) as media for the penetration of one being by another. These elements of yogic practice are expressed doctrinally in the "Yogavida*ḥ*" chapter of the epic's same Mokṣadharma sub-parvan:

> [P]ractitioners of Yoga who are without restraints [and] endowed with the power of yoga (*yogabalānvitāḥ*) are [so many] masters (*īśvarāḥ*), who enter into [the bodies of] the Prajāpatis, the sages, the gods, and the great beings. Yama, angry Antaka, and death of terrible prowess: none of these masters (*īśate*) the practitioner of yoga, who is possessed of immeasurable splendor . . . A practitioner of yoga can lay hold of several thousand selves, and having obtained [yogic] power, he can walk the earth with all of them. He can obtain [for himself] the sense objects. On the other hand, he can undertake terrible austerities, or, again, he can draw those [sense objects] back together [into himself], like the sun [does] its rays of light. (MBh 12.289.24–25)

---

[7] This verse is an insertion following MBh 13.40.55, found in only four Devanagari manuscripts.

[8] In fact, this entire account is narrated in answer to the question (12.278.4) of how Kāvya Uśanas became Śukra.

The principal revealed sources for the metaphysical assumptions undergirding these epic transformations are *Upaniṣadic*, the best-known of these being the circa fifth-century BCE *Chāndogya* (ChU), which postulates that the solar rays that creep into the channels of the individual subtle body also constitute the path taken by the dead:

> The channels (*nāḍīs*) of the heart are made of a fine essence that is tawny, white, blue, yellow and red. Verily, the sun on high is tawny, it is white, it is blue, it is yellow, it is red. Like a road between two villages goes from one to the other, so too the solar rays go to two worlds, this world below and the world above . . . But when he is departing from this body, then he advances upward along these very rays (*raśmibhiḥ*) . . . No sooner does he cast his mind to it, than does he go to the sun. That indeed is the door of the world (*lokadvāram*), an entrance for those who know . . . On that subject, this verse: "There are a hundred and one channels of the heart. One of these passes up to the crown of the head. Going by that one, one goes to immortality . . ." (ChU 8.6.1–2, 5–6)

The third- to first-century BCE *Kaṭha Upaniṣad* (KU) reproduces the same passage, and links it directly to the practice of yoga.[9] The circa third-century CE sixth book of the *Maitri* Upaniṣad (MU) calls the channel that leads to immortality the *suṣumnā*, along which one may advance upward (MU 6.21). This same channel, "transpiercing the solar orb, advances beyond [the sun] to the World of Brahman. They [the dead] go by it to the highest path (*parāṃ gatim*)." (MU 6.30). These statements in fact frame the MU's narrative account of a sage named Śākāyanya, who initiates a king named Bṛhadratha, and thereby empowers him to rise, via the channels of the heart, to the world of *brahman*, at which point the king's name is changed to Marut, "He who Shines" (MU 6.27–28).

Another relatively late Upaniṣad, the *Praśna* (PU), explains that the sun gathers all living beings (or life-breaths, *prāṇān*) into its rays (*raśmiṣu*) as it moves across the sky (PU 1.6). In fact, the radiant sun appears to be the divine prototype for all of the epic practitioners who either rise via its rays to their apotheosis or who channel themselves through rays to enter into other people's bodies. As both epic and, in particular, Ayurvedic sources clearly state, the solar and lunar rays are concrete channels linking those heavenly bodies' heating or cooling properties to the bodily humors of individuals. Here, the medical literature divides the year into six seasons, even as it structures the same into a bipolar system in which the relative influences of the sun and moon directly generate balances or imbalances of heat, moisture, and wind in the ecocosm, which in turn indirectly provoke discontinuities (*doṣa*s), within the bodily microcosm, of the three humors: bile, phlegm, and wind. In

---

[9] KU 6.16, which is framed by 6.11, which "defines" yoga, and 6.18, the final verse of the Upaniṣad, which alludes to the "entire set of yogic rules taught by Death."

these descriptions, the term *yoga* ("junction," or *saṃyoga*, "conjunction") is employed, together with a variety of prefixes, to denote particular seasonal conjunctions between the outer world of the ecocosm and the inner world of the human organism.[10] Throughout the ayurvedic year, it is the extreme effects of the sun and moon—and to a lesser extent, wind—on the ecocosm, that must be moderated within the body through special diets, regimens and behaviors; and it is the task of the physician to effect a "balanced junction" (*saṃayoga*) when confronted with humoral imbalances provoked by an "excessive junction of time" (*kālātiyoga*), a "deficient" or "non-junction of time" (*kālāyoga*) or a "disjunction of time" (*kālamithyāyoga*) (CS 1.11.42–43).[11] Time here refers to seasonal climatic tendencies, in which heat and moisture are transferred, between sun, moon, and the bodies of creatures, via rays. So, according to the *Carakasaṃhitā* (CS), the winter "moon, filling the world with its cool rays, causes it to swell," (CS 1.6.5) while "in the hot season, the sun intensively drinks up (*pepīyate*) the world's moisture."(CS 1.6.27a; cf. *Suśrūtasaṃhitā* (SS) 1.6.8a) These principles receive a mythological treatment in the third book of the MBh, in which Yudhiṣṭhira is exhorted to pray to the sun in order to procure food for his family and followers during his twelve-year forest exile:

> In the beginning, the emitted beings were greatly afflicted with hunger. Then Savitṛ [i.e., the sun], out of compassion, [acted] like their own father. Having gone to its northern course, [and] drawing the resins of effulgence (*tejorasān*) [of earth] upward with [its] rays, the sun, [having now] returned to its southern course, entered into the earth . . . Sprinkled with the resins of effulgence of the moon, the sun that had gone into the earth was reborn as the nourishing plants . . . That [sun] is the food of living creatures on earth . . . the father of all beings . . . (MBh 3.3.5–9)

Taken together, these references illustrate what Francis ZIMMERMAN (1975, p. 94) has termed "a vast metabolism of foods and fluids," through which beings are yoked to the sun through networks of rays. Early Upaniṣads like the BṛU (4.3.6) intimate that the inner self (*ātman*) likewise is a luminous entity whose light radiates outward (through the eyes, in the case of vision) to illuminate the objective world, even in the absence of sun, moon, and fire.[12] This, in fact, becomes the foundation for classical Indian theories of perception (*pratyakṣa*), as found in the 2nd century BCE to 2nd century CE Nyāya and Vaiśeṣika *sūtra* literature. Mīmāṃsaka, Sāṃkhya, Vedānta, and Nyāya-Vaiśeṣika theories of perception all portray the sense organs as *prāpyakāri*, i.e., as directly efffecting sense perception when they come into contact with

[10] An important study of this terminology is ZIMMERMANN 1975.

[11] For a discussion, see ZIMMERMANN 1975, p. 92.

[12] *ātmaivāsya jyotirbhavati* (BṛU 4.3.6), cited in KING 1999, p. 147.

their objects (cf. KING 1999, p. 148).[13] Thus, the Nyāya-Vaiśeṣika school holds that while seat of the visual organ is the eyeball in its socket or the pupil of the eye, visual perception in fact occurs when a ray of light (*tejas*) emitted by the pupil, comes into direct contact, even con-forms, with its object, from a distance (SINHA 1986, Vol. 1, p. 21). Whence the *Nyāyasūtra*'s (NS) terse formulation: "Perception is the consequence of contact between a ray and an object."[14] This core foundational concept of Nyāya philosophy's "direct realism" (MATILAL 1986, p. 224) is reiterated and expanded upon in myriad ways throughout the Nyāya-Vaiśeṣika corpus. However, ordinary (ocular) perception only reaches the "surface" of things, and in this, the perceiving mind or sense organ differs from the sun, whose rays actually penetrate the earth or the bodies of living beings to infuse them with its vivifying energy or to definitively reabsorb their life breaths at death.

Did the philosophical schools know of a form of perception that more closely approximated the divine model of the radiant sun? The answer is yes, with *yogi-pratyakṣa* (Yogi perception) being the name given to extraordinary powers of vision. The issue is introduced in the *Vaiśeṣikasūtra*s' (VS) discussion of the proposition that, because they are not substances, the self and mind are imperceptible through the senses. However, the author Kaṇāda stipulates, the perception of such imperceptibles can arise—unlike normal perception, which is the result of a fourfold contact (*catuṣṭaya-sannikarṣa*) between the self, the mind, a sense organ, and an object (PADhs)[15]—through a "special" (*viśeṣa*) and direct conjunction (*saṃyoga*) between a mind and its object. This becomes the point of departure for a series of discussions by later commentators, beginning with the 450–550 CE *Padārthadharmasaṃgraha* (PADhS) of Praśastapāda. In his commentary on Kaṇāda's aphorisms, this author explains what makes that contact special, and in the process introduces the concept of an enhanced form of perception exclusive to Yogis (albeit without employing the term "Yogi perception"):

> In the case of those who are different than ourselves, that is, of Yogis who are "yoked" (*yogināṃ yuktānām*), it is by virtue of a mind [whose power has been] enhanced through yoga-generated disciplined practice that there arises the vision of the true form[s] (*svarūpa*) of their own self as well as [the selves] of others, the quarters of space, time, atoms, wind, [and] mind . . . Then again, in the case of those [Yogis] who are "unyoked" (*viyuktānām*), direct perception into to subtle, hidden and distant objects arises through a fourfold contact that has been enhanced

---

[13] The term is used and discussed, for example, by Bhāsarvajña in his *Nyāyasāra* and *Nyāyabhūṣaṇam* auto-commentary (in Yogindrananda's edition, 1968, p. 94).

[14] NS 3.1.35: *raśmyarthasannikarṣaviśeṣāt grahaṇam*.

[15] Glossed in NK 166 as: *ātmano manasā saṃyogo manasa indriyeṇa indriyasyārthena* (in JHA 1977, pp. 443f.; and JETLY/PARIKH 1991, pp. 436f.).

> through yoga-generated disciplined practice. (PADhS 99 in Jha 1997, pp. 464f. and Jetly/Parikh 1991, p. 455)

What is it in normal perception that is rectified or enhanced by yoga-generated discipline (*yogajadharma*)? Here, the 991 CE *Nyāyakandalī* (NK) of Śrīdhara, an important sub-commentary on the PADhS, provides the conceptual bridge between normal perception, Yogi perception, and the power—shared by the sun and by hermit Yogis in epic narratives—of entering into another body:

> [The perception on the part] "of those who are different than ourselves" means "Yogi perception" (*yogi-pratyakṣam*) . . . The innate (*svabhāvikam*) true form of the self is beheld by Yogis . . . When, however, out of a desire to know them, he directs his continuous train of thought toward another [person's] self . . . then he augments [his] disciplined practice to an inconceivable degree . . . and by virtue of that power (*balāt*) his inner organ (*antaḥkaraṇa*), going out from his body, is yoked to those of other selves, etc. (NK 172 in Jha 1997, pp. 464ff. and Jetly/Parikh 1991, pp. 455ff.)

We have already seen that this power—of the mind or self (*antaḥkaraṇa* may be translated either way) of a Yogi to enter into another person's body and come into direct contact with that person's self—had been theorized and mythologized several centuries earlier. The circa 3rd century CE YS used the term *citta* ("mind-stuff") to denote that portion of a Yogi's mind-body complex that entered into the body of another being in the supernatural power of *paraśarīrāveśa* (cf. YS 3.38).The "Yogakathana" chapter of the MBh's twelfth book described the process by simply referring to the person of the Yogi as penetrating other bodies—which is precisely what figures like Vidura, Vipula, Sulabhā, and Kāvya Uśanas did in their epic myths. What is new in the NK is its attention to the mechanics of these penetrations. Yogi perception occurs when one's own self or mind is yoked, via a ray of perception, to another being's self inside that other being's body. This opens the way to a variety of ritual techniques that become commonplace in medieval religious practice, most especially 1) tantric initiation through the "binding of the channels" (*nāḍī-saṃdhāna*), by means of which a guru enters into the body of an initiate via their yoked channels, to change the latter's caste and effect other ontological transformations in him in preparation for his penetration by the deity himself (cf. SvT 3.49–53; 4.65–67, etc.); and 2) *prāṇa-pratiṣṭhā*, a practitioner's installation of the breaths into a worship image via the same sorts of linkages (cf. Smith 2006, pp. 388ff.; 411, n. 66).

Now, Śrīdhara, who was a late-tenth century theorizer of the yogic penetration of one person by another, was born in Bengal but was also well read in western India. However, well over a century before his time, and well to the north, in Kashmir, an unknown hand had actually described the mechanics of such penetration: this is the early ninth-century *Netratantra*'s (NT) discussion of "subtle yoga." Following a brief synopsis of the practice (20.28a-29a), the text provides the following detailed instructions:

> Having advanced (*ākramya*), via the upper or lower entrance [of his subtle body], into that [other person's self] which is situated in his heart, and having attacked its cohesiveness, [the Yogi] should go to work on [that self's] equanimity [and then], attaching [himself] to its prime mover [i.e. the ego], he should go to work on its autonomy. With his own all-pervasive Energy, he should smash . . . encapsulate . . . and annihilate its Energy. Thereupon . . . the connoisseur of yoga . . . should heat up [the other self] with . . . with the solar nature of his mind-stuff (*citsūryatvena*). Situated in the other [person's heart], it can melt away [the other self's] rays in the same way as the sun, with [its] rays, [melts away the rays of the moon]. He should then yoke, in the [other person's] heart, all of the action organs, beginning with the organ of speech . . . [and he should yoke] from every side the [organs' associated] elements, [which have become] liquified . . . [And then], having laid hold of those piled up debris of [the other person's] inner organ (*antaḥkaraṇa*) with his own consciousness, the Yogi should then enter [that body with his self], advancing upon (*ākramya*) that body-citadel from every side. He should quickly bring all of that which has been melted down and seized into his own place [i.e. his body or heart]. At that very moment, he [also] brings the [other body's] self [into his heart], through the yokings of seals and spells. (NT 20.29b-36a)

This process, of a Yogi's gradual reduction of the sense-, cognition- and action-capacities of another person's self to a fluid amalgam, which he then incorporates into his own self, is explicated by the Kashmiri Kṣemarāja's helpful commentary, which, written in the first half of the eleventh century, is at least fifty years later than the NK passage quoted above. In it, Kṣemarāja summarizes a lost work, entitled the *Tattvārthacintāmaṇi*, a text attributed to Kallaṭabhaṭṭa, who was a late ninth-century disciple of Vasugupta, the author of the *Spandakārika*s (Dwivedi 1985, p. 9).[16] Here, in a description of "globule practice" (*golakābhyāsa*), Kṣemarāja writes that the Yogi can reduce himself to the size of a globule, and through breath control, enter into the body of another person. He remains there for a period of one hundred morae, and then mounts an assault on that "city of eight (*puryaṣṭakam*) with his own city of eight, by means of his breath, whose energy-based power has been projectively expanded." (Kṣemarāja ad NT 20.28°–29a, in Shastri 1939, pp. 226f.).[17]

---

[16] It is probable that Kṣemarāja's Kallaṭa was the same as the eponymous disciple of Vasugupta, because Kṣemarāja followed him in writing a commentary on the same *Spandakarika*s.

[17] Cf. SvT 11.85, on the *puryāṣṭakam* (that which is comprised of eight fortresses, i.e. the eight constituents of the subtle body: the five subtle elements plus the mind, intellect and ego faculty), which Goudriaan (1992, p. 175, n. 34) relates to the "fortress" of the Upaniṣads.

Later in his interpretation, Kṣemarāja quotes an unnamed source, which states that "He becomes a Yogi, whose activities result in [control over] the movement of every limb of the person [whose body has been] invaded [by him], whenever [that person] eats, drinks, moves, stands, or sleeps. After that, he may use him, cast him off, immobilize him, make him open [his eyes], make him complete, or cause him to reach the most excellent (*viśiṣṭa*) abode." (Kṣemarāja ad NT 20.30, in Shastri 1939, p. 227). Finally, referring to the NT's use of the language of solar rays, Kṣemarāja comments:

> With the rays that originate from his own enflamed eyes,[18] [the Yogi] who is situated there in that other body melts the rays coming from that person's eyes, like the [rays of] the sun [melt] the rays of the moon. (Kṣemarāja ad NT 20.32b-33a, in Shastri 1939, p. 229)

So here we see that, even in a situation in which the physical eyes set in his eye sockets are no longer operative, the Yogi's eyes as disembodied sense organs capable of perceiving and even penetrating other bodies and selves via their rays continue to function as they would have when still embodied. In this respect, Kṣemarāja's commentary neatly synthesizes all of the partially adumbrated models of Yogi perception and penetration found in the epic, *Upaniṣadic*, Ayurvedic, Nyāya-Vaiśeṣika, and Tantric sources that precede him. Now, as B. K. Matilal has shown, many of the Nyāya-Vaiśeṣika commentators were, from as early as the fifth century, influenced by if not adherents of such Śaiva religious orders as the Pāśupatas and Māheśvaras (cf. Matilal 1977, p. 85), so we should not be surprised to find such syntheses, between myth, theory, and practice, appearing among these groups in the medieval period.

What of the past one thousand years, the time since Kṣemarāja wrote his commentary? Have Yogis' special powers of perception and penetration continued to receive mention in later medieval or modern traditions? In fact, it was in the Kashmir of Kṣemarāja's time that the great anthologies of Indian fantasy and adventure literature begin to appear, anthologies in which the stock villain was, precisely, a Yogi who abused his powers in order to take over other people's bodies. That tradition continues down to the present day, where in rural South Asia, naughty children continue to be threatened by exasperated parents with the phrase: "If you're not good, the Yogi will come and take you away." Closer to home, George W. Bush announced a few years ago that he had looked into Vladimir Putin's eyes and seen into his soul, proof that in this field, as in every other, this American president was a failure.

---

[18] One may read *cakṣurādiraśmi* either as "a ray originating from the eye" or "a ray of the eye, etc." In the latter case, "etcetera" would refer to the fact that every one of the five sense organs perceives through the contact of a ray and its object.

I will conclude with one final voice in the rich history of this tradition. The Bengali pundit Gopīnāth Kavirāj (1887–1976) was one of the last great Tantric scholar-practitioners of South Asia. After a brilliant career as a Sanskritist and university president at the Government Sanskrit College in Benares, Kavirāj retired from his academic duties in 1937 to devote his life to personal practice. He was initiated by Swāmī Viśuddhānanda, a tantric Yogi of Benares who had gained fabulous magical powers under a mysterious Tibetan master. Another influence was the Bengali Shobharānī Raha, whom he queried, on the occasion of their very first meeting in 1938, about Yogi perception (cf. Clémentin-Ojha 1990, pp. 87–90).

In 1964, Kaviraj published a chapter entitled "Parakāyapraveśa," in which he synthesized both his intellectual and experiential knowledge of this supernatural power (Kaviraj 1964, pp. 25–32). In it, he wrote:

> Concentration (*dhāraṇā*) normally implies a bodily support, but for Yogis, disembodied (*videha*) concentration is also a necessity. By disembodied concentration, I mean that the mind-stuff (*citta*) located inside the body can be sent outside of the body to some desired place . . . In the same way that the unified rays of the eye leave the eye and, becoming yoked (*yukt*) to the external object to be perceived, are conformed (*pariṇat*) to its form, just so rays emanating from the mind-stuff as well act upon their external objects . . . An ordinary person's mind does not leave his body until the time of death; this is not so for the Yogi, whose mind-body connection has been loosened through initiation, practice, etc. . . . The body contains multiple "mind-bearing" channels (*manovāha nāḍī*) . . . It is not the case that the channels that are inside the body are only inside the body. They also fan out from the body into the wide world (*virāṭ viśva*). By means of this net of channels (*nāḍījāl*) every man is [joined] together with every [other] man. Why is this so? Because everything is connected to everything else.
>
> . . . It is necessary that the Yogi maintain a separation in his field of vision between the body he has entered (and of which he has become the experiencing subject [*bhoktārūp*]), and the channel through which his yoking [of that body] with his own was established . . . This is because he will depend on that path [of the channel] for leaving that body [to return to his own] . . . Having gained this sort of ability, a Yogi becomes empowered to undertake the practice . . . known as mega-disembodied (*mahā-videha*) concentration. It is this that makes entering into another person's body possible. A Yogi's "root mind" (*mūl man*) remains in the body while a separate mind voluntarily inhabits another body, and is yoked to that body. But . . . both remain joined by a luminous threadlike substance . . .
>
> [Then, linking the yogic entering of other people's bodies to Tantric initiation, Kaviraj continues]. When a Yogi's mind has co-penetrated (*samāviṣṭ*) another body, and then returns to its own place [i.e., his own body], it takes a portion of the mind that it has separated off from the other body, and brings it back with it . . . In addition, a portion of guru's mind is left behind in the body of his disciple, where it remains for a long time, even until disciple's death . . . [Thus] the disciple's mind becomes dependent . . . upon that of his guru . . . At the time of a disciple's death,

> the [portion of the] guru's mind [that had remained with his disciple], drawing out the disciple's mind, returns to his own body . . . When his [the disciple's] mind merges with the guru's mind, having come to the guru's place in the guru's body, he attains a plane of existence commensurate with that of the guru . . . Upon arriving at that place (i.e. upon attaining that plane of existence within the guru's body), he enters into an unaging and immortal state of being, and is saved from the world of death . . . The more people's bodies a Yogi is able to make his own through *kāyapraveś*, the greater the number [of bodies] will be pervaded by his mind, and the more he will be able to use his own action-energy (*kriyā-śakti*) for the general welfare (*viśva-kalyāṇ karne meṃ*), in his all-pervasive form (*vyāpak rūp meṃ*).

In many ways, these data speak for themselves. To begin, they explain, in concrete terms, why gurus are venerated as gods (because they have the power of salvation). More importantly, they explode our received notions of the limits of the subtle body, which goes far beyond a Buddha's cranial protuberance (*uṣṇīṣa*)—which also emits rays into multiple Buddha universes (cf. Mus 1968, pp. 561ff.)—or the subtle "end of the twelve" (*dvādaśānta*) that rises above a practitioner's cranial suture.[19] Rather than being unidirectional in its extension beyond its visible physical contours, the human body bristles with openings and extensions that are nothing other than the rays of perception that flow out of every sense organ to "touch and take the measure of every being at every level in the hierarchy of transmigrations," (Mus 1968, p. 562) and in the case of the sun, Yogis, Buddhas and gods, to penetrate those beings and transform them as they please. Lastly, and most importantly, these emic accounts of the body's extensions buttress McKim Marriott's theories of Indian transactions in substance-code, according to which "pervasive boundary overflows" are the rule in a system in which "dividual" or "divisible" persons are constantly absorbing and diffusing particles of their own "coded substances" (Marriott 1976, p. 111). Before it became closed off from the world to ensure the splendid isolation (*kaivalyam*) of Puruṣa from Prakṛti, the yogic body was, and remains, an open system, capable of transacting with every other body—human, divine, and celestial—in the universe.

References

Bṛhadāraṇyaka Upaniṣad. In: Limaye, V. P./Vadekar, R. D. (Eds.) (1958): Eighteen Principal Upaniṣads (Upaniṣadic Text with Parallels from extant Vedic Literature, Exegetical and Grammatical Notes). – Poona.

Carakasaṃhitā = Acarya, J. T. (Ed.) (1992): Caraka Saṃhitā, with the commentary of Cakrapāṇidatta. – Reprint. – Benares.

Chāndogya Upaniṣad. In: Limaye, V. P./Vadekar, R. D. (Eds.) (1958): Eighteen Principal Upaniṣads (Upaniṣadic Text with Parallels from extant Vedic Literature, Exegetical and Grammatical Notes). – Poona.

[19] Or the upper jaw (Mus 1968, p. 549).

Clémentin-Ojha, C. (1990) : La divinité conquise: Carrière d'une sainte. – Nanterre.

Dwivedi, V. (1985): Introduction. In: Dwivedi, V. (Ed.): Netratantram [Mṛtyuñjaya Bhaṭṭāraka] with the Commentary Udyota of Kṣemarājācārya. – Delhi.

Fitzgerald, J. L. (2002): Nun Befuddles King, Shows "Karmayoga" Does Not Work: Sulabhā's Refutation of King Janaka at MBh 12.308. In: Journal of Indian Philosophy, Vol. 30, No. 6, pp. 641–77.

Goudriaan, T. (1992): The Pluriform ṛtman from the Upaniṣads to the Svacchanda Tantra. In: Wiener Zeitschrift für die Kunde Südasiens 36, pp. 163–86.

Hiltebeitel, A. (2001): Rethinking the Mahābhārata: A Reader's Guide to the Education of the Dharma King. – Chicago.

Kaṭha Upaniṣad. In: Limaye, V. P./Vadekar, R. D. (Eds.) (1958): Eighteen Principal Upaniṣads (Upaniṣadic Text with Parallels from extant Vedic Literature, Exegetical and Grammatical Notes). – Poona.

Kaviraj, G. (1962). Bhāratīy Saṃskṛti aur Sādhanā, Vol. 1. – Patna.

Kaviraj, G. (1964). Bhāratīy Saṃskṛti aur Sādhanā, Vol. 2. – Patna.

King, R. (1999). Indian philosophy: an Introduction to Hindu and Buddhist Thought. – Washington, D.C.

Limaye, V. P/Vadekar, R. D. (Eds.) (1958): Eighteen Principal Upaniṣads (Upaniṣadic Text with Parallels from extant Vedic Literature, Exegetical and Grammatical Notes). – Poona.

Mahābhārata = Sukthankar, V. S. et al. (Eds.) (1933–1960): Mahābhārata, 21 Vols. – Poona.

Maitri Upaniṣad. In: Limaye, V. P./Vadekar, R. D. (Eds.) (1958): Eighteen Principal Upaniṣads (Upaniṣadic Text with Parallels from extant Vedic Literature, Exegetical and Grammatical Notes). – Poona.

Marriott, M. (1976): Hindu Transactions: Diversity Without Duality. In: Kapferer, B. (Ed.): Transaction and Meaning. Directions in the Anthropology of Exchange and Symbolic Behavior. – Philadelphia.

Matilal, B. K. (1977): Nyāya-Vaiśeṣika. A History of Indian Literature, Col. 6, Fasc. 2. – Wiesbaden.

Matilal, B. K. (1986): Perception, An Essay on Classical Indian Theories of Knowledge. – Oxford.

Mus, P. (1968) : Où finit Puruṣa? In: Charles Malamoud (Ed.) : Mélanges d'Indianisme à la mémoire de Louis Renou. – Paris, pp. 539–63.

Netratantra = Shastri, M. K. (Ed.) (1926, 1939): The Netra Tantram with commentary by Kshemaraja, 2 Vols. – Bombay. (Kashmir Series of Texts and Studies, Nos. 46 and 61)

Netratantra = Dwivedi, V. (Ed.) (1985): Netratantram [Mṛtyuñjaya Bhaṭṭāraka] with the Commentary Udyota of Kṣemarājācārya. – Delhi.

Nyāyasūtra of Gautama Akṣapada = Ghosh, R. (Ed.) (2003): Nyāyadarśana of Gotama [With Sanskrit Text, Vātsyāyana Bhāṣya, Sanskrit Commentary, English Summary and English Translation]. – Tr. by S. C. Vidyabhusana. – Delhi.

Nyāyabhūṣaṇam of Bhāsarvajña = Yogindrananda, S. (Ed.) (1968): Śrīmadācāryabhāsarvajñapraṇītasya nyāyasārasya svopajñaṃ vyākhyānaṃ Nyāyabhūṣaṇam. – Benares.

Nyāyakandali = Jetly, J. S./Parikh, V. G. (Eds.) (1991): Praśastapādabhāṣya, with three sub-commentaries. – Baroda. (Gaekwad's Oriental Series, No. 174)

Padārthadharmasaṃgraha of Praśastapāda = Jha, D. (Ed.) (1997): Praśastapādabhāṣyam (Padārthadharmasaṃgraha) of Praśastapādācārya with the Commentary Nyāyakandalī by Śrīdhara Bhaṭṭa along with Hindi Translation. – Varanasi. (Ganganathajaha-Granthamala, Vol. 1)

PraśnaUpaniṣad. In: Limaye, V. P./Vadekar, R. D. (Eds.) (1958): Eighteen Principal Upaniṣads (Upaniṣadic Text with Parallels from extant Vedic Literature, Exegetical and Grammatical Notes). – Poona.

SCHREINER, Peter (1999): What Comes First (in the Mahābhārata): Sāṃkhya or Yoga? In: Asiatische Studien/Etudes Asiatiques, Vol. 53, No. 3, pp. 755–77.

SETTAR, S./SONTHEIMER, G. (1982): Memorial Stones. A study of their origin, significance and variety. – Heidelberg.

SINHA, J. (1986): Indian Psychology, 3 Vols. – Delhi.

SMITH, F. M. (2006): The Self Possessed: Deity and Spirit Possession in South Asian Literature and Civilization. – New York.

Suśrutasaṃhitā = GHANEKAR, B. G. (Ed.) (1980): Suśruta Saṃhitā, with the commentary of Atrideva. – 5th ed. – Delhi.

Svacchandatantra = DWIVEDI, V. (Ed.) (1985): The Svacchandatantram with commentary "udyota" of Kṣemarājā, 2 Vols. – Delhi.

Vyomavatī of Vyomaśiva = SHASTRI, G. (Ed.) (1983, 1984): Vyomavatī of Vyomaśivācārya, 2 Vols. – Benares. (M. M. Sivakumarasastri Granthamala, No. 6)

Yogasūtras of Patañjali = ARANYA, S. H. (Ed.) (1981): Yoga Philosophy of Patañjali Containing his Yoga aphorisms with the commentary of Vyāsa in the original Sanskrit, and annotations thereon with copious hints on the practice of Yoga. – Tr. by Swami Hariharananda ARANYA. – Calcutta.

ZIMMERMANN, F. (1975): Ṛtu-Sātmya: Le Cycle des saisons et le principe d'appropriation. In: Purusartha 2, pp. 87–105.

Abbreviations

BṛU	Bṛhadāraṇyaka Upaniṣad
ChU	Chāndogya Upaniṣad
CS	Carakasaṃhitā
KU	Kaṭha Upaniṣad
MBh	Mahābhārata
MU	Maitri Upaniṣad
NK	Nyāyakandalī of Śrīdhara
NS	Nyāyasūtra of Gautama Akṣapada
NT	Netratantra
PADhS	Padārthadharmasaṃgraha of Praśastapāda
PU	Praśna Upaniṣad
SS	Suśrūtasaṃhitā
SvT	Svacchandatantra
VS	Vaiśeṣikasūtra of Kaṇāda
YS	Yogasūtras of Patañjali

Gavin Flood

Body, Breath and Representation in Śaiva Tantrism[1]

Many tantric texts present ornate and complex accounts of the body and its relation to the wider cosmos and for many texts which claim to convey a transcendent message, the body is the locus of spiritual experience. One of the problems, not only of tantric traditions but of religion in general, is the relationship between experience in the lived body and the system of representation or symbolic system expressed in texts of revelation. That is, to what extent do the texts represent events and experiences of human beings in the world and to what extent do the experiences of human beings conform to the symbolic systems of texts? What are the mechanisms of mimesis whereby experience is mapped on to representation and vice versa? In this paper I wish to develop two interwoven lines of argumentation, one which develops the idea that there is a symbiotic relationship between lived body and symbolic representation which we can see particularly in relation to the breath, the other which argues that the textual source that bears witness to event or experience becomes integrated into a broader narrative of tradition and interpreted in particular, ideologically lead ways. That is, the text that bears witness to event becomes part of a narrative account or explanation which is, in fact, the object of the historian's focus. The body is central to this process in being the location of experience and in bearing witness to history, in being integral to the way tradition measures itself and integrates the body into its narrative accounts, and is also central to "scientific" historical concerns. I intend to ground these rather abstract ideas in a study of a particular text, chapter seven of the *Netratantra* and to show how in that text the body is understood as a symbolic system for mapping the cosmos and human beings' place within it. Yet we also have the body as the locus of subjective, yogic experience, especially seen in the breath. These two analytically distinct realms—the body as symbolic system and lived body—are inseparably interconnected, each reflecting the other. This relationship is furthermore embedded within a historical process in which the text that bears witness to the human body becomes integrated into the narrative of the tradition.

[1] My thanks to Emma Kwan for discussion about the topic of this paper.

The *Netratantra*

In the medieval period in South Asia when what might generally be called the tantric traditions dominated, a discourse developed about ritual practice concerned with both personal salvation (*mokṣaḥ*) and worldly prosperity (*arthaḥ*). By the tenth century different philosophical traditions were mutually aware and there was rigorous debate between them along with different salvational systems vying with each for dominance and royal patronage (cf. SANDERSON 1985, p. 190). By the early medieval period traditions had developed, especially those focused on the god Śiva, that revered a body of texts called Tantras or Āgamas that were regarded as the fulfilment and transcendence of earlier scriptural revelation both primary (*śruti*) and secondary (*smṛti*).[2] Sanderson observes that from the 6th century AD Śaivism became the "principle faith of the elites in large parts of the Indian subcontinent and in both mainland and insular Southeast Asia" (SANDERSON 2004, p. 231). Kings were legitimated by power, not only sovereign power but power gained through religious authority and through the support of religious groups (cf. MICHAELS 2004, pp. 276–279) and the *Netratantra* must be understood in this context. The *Netratantra* was a text that occupied a place between the orthoprax, vedic oriented Śaiva traditions and the extreme Kaula cults that consciously flouted vedic purity rules in order to transcend the limiting prohibition and injunction (*vidhi*) of those earlier systems which they read as inhibition (*śaṅka*) to achieve liberating experience.[3]

There is a pioneering paper outlining the text by Hélène BRUNNER (1974), an important paper by SANDERSON (2004), and PADOUX (2002), VASUDEVA (2004) and WHITE (2003) have published work on the text. Sanderson dates the text from between c. 700–850 AD and shows how it must be understood in the context of Śaiva officiants operating in the realm of the king's chaplain, a role traditionally held by the Atharvavedin *purohita*. Thus, while it is concerned with esoteric visualisations, its context is nevertheless political and points to an understanding of governance that is very different from more recent conceptualisations which separate the esoteric from the political. The body of the king becomes divine through ritual construction in ways specific to particular systems and texts which parallels the divinisation of a temple icon. The king in the palace becomes the analogue of the deity in the temple (cf. FLOOD 2006, p. 74).

---

[2] Alexis Sanderson in a number of publications has mapped out these traditions. See, for example, SANDERSON 2007.

[3] M. S. Kaul (Ed.): *The Netratantra with uddyota by Kṣemarāja*, 2 Vols. (Srinagar: Kashmir Series of Texts and Studies, 46 and 61, 1926 and 1927). These are based on Kashmiri manuscripts with Kṣemarāja's commentary. There is also a manuscript from Nepal from the Nepal-German Manuscript library (*Amṛteśvaratantram*, 285, reel B25).

The *Netratantra* is focussed on the worship and propitiation of Amṛteśvara also known as Mṛtuñjaya, Mṛtjujit, and Netranātha along with his consort Amṛteśvarī called Śrī or Lakṣmī in the text. Sanderson shows how the *Netra's* remit of operation is the royal family and all rites described are for their protection, including the subtle forms of worship in chapters seven and eight. The text describes how the mantra of Netranātha (*oṃ juṃ saḥ* in the short version) protects the king from waking to sleeping and that, in Sanderson's terms, the Śaiva officiants were active "in almost all the areas of observance assigned by the Atharvavedic tradition to the brahmanical royal chaplain…" (SANDERSON 2004, pp. 74).

Within this concern for royalty, the *Netra* assumes the ritual practices characteristic of tantric traditions, namely the regular ritual practices that involved the purification of the body (*bhūtaśuddhiḥ*), the divinization of the body through imposing mantras upon it (*nyāsaḥ*), inner (*antara/mānasa-*), and external worship (*bahir-yāgaḥ*). One of the features shared by all of these traditions is the divinisation of the body and the idea that only a god can worship a god or becoming Śiva one can then worship Śiva (cf. FLOOD 2006, p. 11). This does not necessarily reflect a monistic ontology as the Śaiva Siddhānta texts and others are dualistic or, more accurately, pluralistic in assuming three ontologically distinct realities of soul (*paśuḥ*), universe (*pāśaḥ*), and Lord (*patiḥ*). The *Netratantra* shares this ritual world and the practitioner should visualise Amṛteśvara as part of his practice and symbolically become one with him so that one day he will existentially realise this truth in his own person. Here we have a text composed within a courtly milieu and yet whose concerns are with esoteric matters such as meditation and supernatural power and which is open to the non-dualistic interpretation given to it by Kṣemarāja (c. 1000–1050 AD).

The Representation of the Subtle Body

The *Netratantra* presents the body as a symbolic system which comprises three forms, gross or physical (*sthūla-*), subtle (*sūkṣma-*) and supreme (*para-*). The description of these three levels is also a description of practices, thereby locating the symbolic representation in the lived body. Chapters six and eight are concerned with the visualisation of Amṛteśvara in his gross and supreme forms whereas chapter seven is concerned with the subtle visualisation (*sūkṣma-dhyānam*) that occurs during mental worship. In this visualisation the practitioner identifies himself with the subtle body of the Lord which the text describes. As is common in this material we have a number of different systems overlaid on each other so that rich connections are made between the body and metaphysical categories[4]; a tradition that goes back many

[4] For an excellent account of these homologies see PADOUX 2002.

hundreds of years before the tantric texts to vedic times and the connections (*bandhaḥ*) between the cosmos and the sacrifice. The body is arranged along a vertical axis which is also the vertical axis of the cosmos with various centres located along it.[5] Through the practice of mantra and breath control the yogi symbolically journeys up the body to the goal of liberation at or above the crown of the head. In the opening verses Amṛteśa addresses the Goddess:

> Now I will declare the highest, subtle visualisation which comprises six circles, seven supports, three objects, five spaces, twelve knots, three powers, and three astral spendours (*dhāman*, sun, moon, fire). One knows this body, O one with beautiful hips, pervaded by three, ten, seventy two thousand, then thirty five million channels (to which one must add) pollution and disease. With the supreme nectar produced by the subtle meditation, the yogi acheives fullness in himself and for others. He becomes a divine body (*divya-dehaḥ*) bereft of all affliction.[6]

Here we have an account of the structure of the subtle body which is familiar to other important related texts such as the *Mālinīvijayottaratantra*,[7] the *Kubjikāmatatantra*[8] and the later *haṭha yoga* tradition: a list of locations along the central axis or "vein" of the body known as the *suṣumnā* located between the right and left channels, the *īḍā* and *piṅgalā* respectively. Indeed, the terms *cakra, ādhāra, lakṣya,* and *vyoma* or *ākāśa* are found in the *Mālinī* and more clearly used in the later thirteenth century text, the *Siddhasiddhāntapaddhati* attributed to Gorakhnāth.[9] The idea is clear that the structure of the subtle body contains innumerable channels that convey the breath or life force (*prāṇaḥ*) to the centres. Kṣemarāja's commentary tells us that by the "seasons" is meant the six locations (*sthānāni*) of the "place of birth" (*janma-*), navel (*nābhi-*), heart (*hṛt-*), palate (*tālu*), "drop" (*bindu-*) between the eyes, and place of resonance (*nāda-*) in the head. As Padoux has

---

[5] For an excellent account of the *cakras* and their occurrence in the history of Sanskrit texts see WHITE 2003, pp. 220–234.

[6] *Netratantra* 7.1–5:

ataḥ paraṃ pravakṣyāmi dhyānaṁ sūkṣmam anuttamam |
ṛtucakraṁ svarādhāraṃ trilakṣyaṃ vyomapañcakam ||1||
granthidvādaśasaṃyuktaṁ śaktitrayasamanvitam |
dhāmatrayapathākrantaṃ nāḍitrayasamanvitam ||2||
jñātvā śarīraṃ suśroṇi daśanāḍipathāvṛtam |
dvāsaptatyā sahasrais tu sārdhakoṭitrayeha ca ||3||
nāḍivṛndiḥ samākrāntaṁ malinaṁ vyādhibhir vṛtam |
sūkṣmadhyānāmṛtenaiva pareṇaivoditena tu ||4||
āpyāyaṃ kurute yogī ātmano vā parasya ca |
divyadehaḥ sa bhavati sarvavyādhivivarjitaḥ ||5||

[7] See Vasudeva 2004.

[8] See Heilijgers-Seelen 1994.

[9] See Banerjea 1962, p. 30.

observed, the text does not explicitly mention the thousand petalled lotus of later yogic traditions (cf. Padoux 2002, p. 174), although it does mention the *dvādaśānta*, the point twelve fingers above the crown of the head (although sometimes identified with the aperture at the crown). These six centres or "circles" (*cakrāṇi*) are associated with twelve "knots" (*granthayaḥ*) and sixteen vowels (*svarāḥ*) which Kṣemarāja links to the "supports" (*ādhārāḥ*) of the soul (*jīvaḥ*), namely the big toe, ankle, knee, generative organ, anus, the "bulb" (*kanda-*), the "channel" (*nāḍī-*), stomach, heart, "tortoise channel" (*kūrmanāḍī-*), throat, palate, eye centre, forehead, aperture of Brahmā, and the place of "twelve fingers."[10] The three astral spheres (*dhāmānaḥ*), fire, sun and moon known to later yogic texts indicating inner, cosmological visions, are also the names of the three channels; sun being linked with the *piṅgalā*, moon with the *iḍā* and fire with the *suṣumnā* are associated with this structure. The precise locations in the body that some of these names refer to, namely *nāḍi* and *kanda* is somewhat obscure. The *kanda* in later tradition is a "bulb" located "in the middle between the navel and the penis,"[11] and the *nāḍi* might here refer to a region in the same location which the later *Khecarīvidyā* refers to as the "bamboo staff" (*veṇudaṇḍaḥ*) (*Khecarividyā* 3.43), but this is mere speculation. The general point, however, is that the subtle body is visualised as a vertical axis along which are located various centres linked by channels.

Kṣemarāja's commentary refers to this subtle visualisation as the procedure according to the standard system or revelation (*tantra-prakriyā*) and contrasts it with an alternative, esoteric system of visualisation, the procedure according to the esoteric tantric, "family" tradition (*kula-prakriyā*). He quotes an unknown and unnamed source describing this alternative visualisation, as the Śaiva doctrine (*nayaḥ*) permits all (cf *Netratantra* comm., p. 147). Indeed, this is the only surviving text where this system is described.[12] This is the text Kṣemarāja quotes:

> The Kula (system) is to be known from the base of the penis (ascending) through the middle (channel) known as "poison" (*viṣa-*). At the root (centre) the powerful one (*śāktaḥ*) is declared, which sets in motion the sound of awakening.
>
> Then (the centre) called "fire," four fingers (length) above (the penis) below the navel and in the navel the support of the vital breath called "the pot" (*ghaṭābhidhaḥ*). In the path between the navel and heart there is (the support) known as "desire for all" (*sarvakāma-*). The (support) known as "the animating one" (*saṃjīvani*) is located between the lotus of the heart and the belly. The tortoise (*kūrmaḥ*) is

---

[10] *Netratantra*, p. 148: *aṅguṣṭha-gulpha-jānu-meḍhra-pāyu-kanda-nāḍi-jaṭhara-hṛt-kūrmanāḍī-kaṇṭha-tālu-bhrūmadhya-lalāṭa-brahmarandhra-dvādaśānta*. For a useful diagram see Brunner 1974, note 1, p. 142.

[11] *Haṭhayogapradīpikā* 3.113, commentary by Brahmānanda, *nābhimeḍhrayor madhye*.

[12] Information supplied by Dr Somadeva Vasudeva, Autumn 2006.

situated in the place of the chest (and) the (support known as the) tongue (*lolā*) is known in the throat. The place of the "finder" (*lambhakaḥ*), the support of nectar (*sudhādhāraḥ*) whose nature is ease (*sudhātmakaḥ*), is above (that). The gentle one (*saumyaḥ*), covered by the power of the moon, is located within the root (*mūla-*) of that (*lambhakaḥ*). The (support) known as the lotus of wisdom (*vidyākamala-*) is in the pleasure of the sky between the eyebrows. The fierce one (*raudraḥ*) is the support on the surface of the palate, established by the power of Rudra. The (support) known as the wish-fulfilling gem (*cintāmaṇi*) is situated at the crossroads. In the middle of the aperture of the absolute (*brahmarandhraḥ*) in the head is the support (called) the fourth (*turyādhāraḥ*) and the support (called) the channel (*nāḍyādhāraḥ*). These are the supreme and subtle awakening which is all pervading and solid. Thus the sixteen supports are told about... [13]

This text presents a slightly different description of the subtle body although the same principle is adhered to, that various centres are linked along a vertical axis. The central channel is referred to here as "poison" (*viṣam*) although in later haṭha yoga texts "poison" is associated with the sun or the *piṅgalā* channel and "nectar" (*amṛtam*) with the moon or *iḍā* channel (cf. *Khecarividyā* 2.46–49. In later texts, the dormant Kuṇḍalinī is associated with poison and the active with nectar (cf. WHITE 1996, p. 221). We also have the idea, developed in later yogic tradition,[14] of the "sound of awakening" (*bodhanādaḥ*), set in motion by divine power (*śaktiḥ*).

What Kṣemtarāja seems to be doing in quoting this alternative system is to bring the *Netratantra* more clearly within his hierarchical system of realization, identifying the tantra prakrīyā with the gross (*sthūla-*) realization in contrast to the subtle realization of the kula. There is generally a fluidity in the visualization of the subtle body which is not thought to be fixed or reified

---

[13] *Netratantra*, p. 147:
meḍhrasyādhaḥ kulo jñeyo madhye tu viṣasaṁjñitaḥ |
mūle tu śākaḥ kathito bodhanādapravartakaḥ ||
agnisaṁjñastataś co rdhvam aṅgulānāṁ catuṣṭaye |
nābhyadhaḥ pavanādhāre nābhāveva ghaṭābhidhaḥ ||
nābhihṛnmadhyamārge tu sarvakāmābhidho mataḥ |
saṃjīvanyabhidhānākhyo hṛtpadmodaramadhyagaḥ ||
vakṣaḥsthale sthitaḥ kūrmo gale lolābhidhaḥ smṛtaḥ |
lambhakasya sthitaścordhve sudhādhāraḥ sudhātmakaḥ ||
tasyaiva mulamāśritya saumyaḥ somakalāvṛtaḥ |
bhrūmadhye gaganābhoge vidyākamalasaṃjñitaḥ ||
raudrastālutalādhāro rudraśaktyā tvadhiṣṭhataḥ |
cintāmaṇyabhidhānākhyaścatuśpathathanivāsi yat ||
brahmarandhrasya madhye tu turyādhārastu mastake |
nāḍyādhāraḥ paraḥ sūkśmo ghanavyāptiprabodhakaḥ ||
ity uktāḥ ṣoḍaśādhārā ....||

[14] E.g. *Haṭhayogapradīpikā* 4.67–106.

but is nevertheless determined by tradition. Although, as Kṣemarāja says, all systems are open to the Śaiva, we also have the idea that the practitioner should not mix systems from different texts but stick to one. The *Rauravāgama* of the Śaiva Siddhānta, for example, says that rites prescribed in one Tantra should not be mixed with another (cf. *Rauravāgama* Vol. 3, supplement 63.18–33).[15] Yet while the tantra and kula systems differ in detail, the general idea that energy or power arises within the body and that this power has soteriological consequences is shared across these systems.

The basic practice of the *tantra-prakrīyā* is that the yogi should lead the supreme power of consciousness (*tāṃ parāṃ citiśaktim ... vahet*) as the middle breath into the central channel from the root centre, where it is called the arising breath (*udāna-*) which is a sacred (*prāṇabrahmani*),[16] between in inhaled and exhaled breath (*prāṇaḥ* and *apānaḥ*). He identifies or binds (*niyojayet*) his own sense of self-worth or pride (*abhimānam*, which Kṣemarāja glosses as one's own energy comprising a particular wondrous experience)[17] with this energy in the root centre (*mūlādharaḥ*). This energy in the form of mantra rises up the central channel, piercing the sixteen "supports" and twelve "knots." Having pierced these centres, the yogi enters the highest, firm place called the *dvādaśānta*,[18] where he experiences supreme detachment (*paratyāgaḥ*) from bondage. This is to become one with the unique nature of the supreme Śiva and to experience the eternal identification or "sameness of flavour" with the supreme Śakti (*nityoditaparāśakti-samarasaḥ*). In his imagination the yogi then descends from the *dvādaśānta* to the heart, entering which he is filled with nectar (*rasāyanam*) whose nature is supreme joy (*paramānandarūpam*) and his body is filled with this, to the pores of the skin. The yogi thus achieves the conquest of death and goes beyond dying and ageing (*ajāramaraḥ*) attaining the state of Mṛyjujit.[19]

The second method according to the kula prakrīyā is, to quote Brunner, "particularly obscure," (BRUNNER 1974, p. 144) but follows the same pattern. The text begins with the meditation on the "place of birth" (*janmasthāna*) which, Kṣemarāja tells us in his commentary, in the Kula system refers to the base centre. Indeed, Vasudeva identifies the *janmsthāna* with the anus (cf. VASUDEVA 2004, p. 271). This would seem to be in line with the Kaula scripture that Kṣemarāja quotes. The text tells us that the yogi should focus (*samāśrayet*) on the deity Kālāgni in the big toe and he should deposit his

15 There are other sources, however, that allow the mixing of texts. See GRANOFF 2000.

16 *Netratantra* p. 153: … *madhyaprāṇe suṣumnākhyodānākhyaprāṇabrahmaṇi* ...

17 *Netratantra* p. 154: *tad asāmānyacamatkāramayaṃ svaṃ vīryam.*

18 *Netratantra* p. 154: *paramaṃ dhruvaṃ dvādaśāntadhāma vedhayedāviśet.*

19 *Netratantra*, p. 155: *yogī tadāsau ajarāmaro bhūtvā kṣipraṃ siddhyati mṛtyujiḍbhāṭṭārakāmāpnoti.* "Then the yogi, being beyond old age and death, succeds immediately and attains the condition of the immortal Lord."

energy there.[20] His energy then moves up to the root centre and thence up the middle channel through the Kaula cosmology and piercing the twelve knots he enters the "supreme place" (*param padam*),[21] which is the abode of the supreme Śiva where the yogi "should become completely filled with nectar from the central channel"[22] which flows to the pores of the skin. This journey through the body is a journey through the levels of the cosmos and the text identifies knots located at different levels of the body with "places" governed by their causes (*kāraṇāni*) called by the same names, and different "circles." That is, there is a complex mapping of five "voids" (*vyomā/kham*), the first at the anus, the second at the navel, the third at the heart, the fourth at the drop (*bindu-*) between the eyes, and the fifth at the place of resonance (*nāda-*) in the forehead, with six "circles" (*cakra-*), twelve "knots"(*granthi-*), and seven "places" (*sthāna-*) and their sovereign "causes" (*kāraṇa-*, namely various deities) onto the vertical axis of the body (cf. *Netratantra* 7.26–29). The yogi should achieve this through visualizing a "trident of knowledge" (*jñānaśūlaḥ*) piercing the knots which Kṣemarāja glosses as vibrating consciousness transformed into the energy of mantra (*mantravīrya-bhūtacitsphurattā*) (cf. *Netratantra* 7.30ab comm., p. 164) rising up the body from the root centre. In what I take to be a reference to yogic technique, the yogi should squeeze or press the root centre or *janmādhāra* (with his heels?) in order to awaken divine power (*śaktiunmeṣam ... pīḍayet*) (cf. *Netratantra* 7.30 and comm.). In his commentary Kṣemarāja cites the *Mālinīvijayotaratantra* describing how the yogi should sit in the lotus posture and guide his mind into the navel region, so impelling it through the voids to achieve the "going in the void" (*khe gatim*) (cf. *Netratantra* 7.39 comm., p. 169).[23] The voids are known to other texts as described by Vasudeva (2004, pp. 270–273).

There is also reference to the *khecarīmudrā*, "the seal of the sky-goer," which in *haṭha yoga* refers to the practice of rolling the tongue back and up into the nasal cavity so preventing the nectar of immortality (*amṛtam*) escaping as it drips down from the crown of the head.[24] It is not clear, however, that this is the practice intended here. The text says that the yogi acquires the "seal (*mudrā*) known as *khecara*" in that place and once the soul is truly "sealed" by

---

[20] *Netratantra* 7.17d. *vīryaṃ tatraiva nikṣipet.*

[21] *Netratantra* 7. 25: *granthidvādaśakaṃ bhittvā praviśet parame pade.*

[22] *Netratantra* 7.47ab. *suṣumāmṛtenakhilaṃ paripurṇaṃ vibhāvayet.*

[23] Vasudeva translates the passage from the *Mālinī*: "Assuming the lotus-posture, the yogin should guide the mind into the navel [-region]. In the form of a staff he should lead it up to the three voids in the head. After restraining it there he should rapidly force it through the three voids [above the head]. By assuming this [attitude] the great hero achieves motion in the void" (Vasudeva 2004, p. 266). The text Kṣemarāja cites is slightly different to the published edition of the *Mālinī*, replacing "mahāyogī" for "mahāvīra."

[24] For this practice see Mallinson 2007.

mudrā then it gradually flows upwards as consciousness to the higher place. Once here, the yogi attains the "sameness of flavor" (*samarasaḥ*) with the absolute which is the attaining of undivided being (*niṣkalaṃ bhavam*), all-pervasiveness, the supreme Śiva.[25] It seems that in the *Netra, khecarīmudrā* refers to an attainment rather than a specific, bodily practice. In his commentary Kṣemarāja writes that the yogi attains that which is called *khecara* due to his moving in the sky of awakening (*bodhagaganam*) which is the void.[26] He also glosses "the supreme place" (*param sthānam*) as the *dvādaśānta* which points to a more metaphysical understanding of *khecarī* although this does not, of course, exclude the possibility that it is also a physical practice.

Having reached the supreme place of Śiva at the *dvādaśanta*, the yogi manifests Śakti in the form of the three human faculties of will, cognition and action (*icchā-jñāna-kriyā-*) (cf. *Netratantra* 7.36 comm, p. 168). The last verses recap how the yogi has achieved the supreme state which is unparalleled nectar (*anaupamyāmṛtam*) where he sees the (inner) rising moon (which contains the nectar of immortality), he knows the endless mass of trembling nectar (cf. *Netratantra* 7. 42cd), and he should become completely filled by it, filling the body internally through the channels and at the same time externally through the pores of the skin. In becoming bathed in nectar he knows in his own experience (*svānubhūtiḥ*) that he has achieved a state of health (*nirāmayam*) and has become the conqueror of time (*kālajit*) and of death (*mṛtyujit*) (cf. *Netratantra* 7. 47).

The theme exemplified above of the universe contained within the body and specifically mapped onto the body is pervasive in tantric texts. We might even say that the subtle body is the map of the cosmos imposed upon the physical body. A text closely related to the *Netratantra*, the *Svacchandatantra* which similarly occupies a middle ground between the extreme tantric sects and the orthodox, brahmanical tradition of the Śaiva Siddhānta, presents the Śaiva cosmology of the thirty six categories (*tattvāni*) which are mapped onto the body. In his commentary on this text, Kṣemarāja says that "as in the body so externally (in the universe the categories) are established" (*yathā dehe yathāca bahiḥ sthitam*) (cf. *Svacchandatantra* 12.4 com, p. 2). The subtle body here has a different structure to that of the *Netratantra* but the principles are fundamentally the same.

With the *Netratantra*, as in many other texts, we are dealing with systems or representations of metaphysics and cosmology mapped onto the body which is divided into different levels. Here the visualization of the subtle body has

[25] *Netratantra* 7.32cd-35ab: *tatsthānaṃ vai khecarākhyāṃ tu mudraṃvindeta yogavit //32// mudrayā tu tayā devi ātmā vai mudiro yadā / tadā cordhvaṃ tu visared vijñanenordhvataḥ kramāt //33// bhindyādibhindyātparaṃ sthānaṃ yāvatsvaravarārcite / tatsthānaṃ caiva saṃprāpya yogī samaraso bhavet //34// niṣkalaṃ bhāvamāpanno vyāpakaḥ paramaḥ śivaḥ*

[26] *Netratantra* p. 166: *khe bodhagagane caraṇāt khecaryākhyāṃ yogī labhet.*

been systematized into two basic traditions of the tantra and kula, the latter being more esoteric, "higher" and closer to the absolute truth than the former in the Kashmiri commentator's hierarchy of traditions. Both the tantra and kula systems visualize the subtle body as a vertical structure with centres and "knots" located along its axis which need to be broken or pierced by the power of consciousness which rises up this vertical axis. This power is also the Goddess and, which is of particular interest here, the "breath" (*prāṇa*). A text of the non-Saiddhāntika tradition, the *Vijñānabhairava*, identifies the arising of energy in the body with *prāṇa* (cf. *Vijñānabhairava* 24) and the Trika tradition identifies *praṇa* with *prāṇa-kuṇḍalinī* (cf. Silburn 1983, p. 84). While the primary designation of the term *prāṇa* is breath, its semantic field is wider to include subtle energy and life-force. The inhaled breath (*prāṇaḥ*) and exhaled breath (*apānaḥ*) are united in the central breath (*udānaḥ*). Behind our text is the much older, classical categorization of the breath or "winds" (*vāyu, vāta*) as being of five kinds: *prāṇa, apāna, vyāna, samāna,* and *udāna* (cf. *Jaiminiya Upaniṣad Brahmaṇa* 4.22–26 quoted in Padoux 2002, p. 165). The *vyāna* breath circulates through the body while the *samāna* breath circulates around the navel and is the power of digestion.

The Lived Body

Having now presented an account of the subtle body as a system of visualization, I wish to move on to a more theoretical consideration of how we can understand this material. The *Netratantra* bears witness to a complex process in the relationship between lived body and the human experience of life and textual representation or symbolic system. We have a problem here that relates to a broader philosophical issue concerning the primacy of the body as pre-cognitive experience, the existential possibility of culture, in contrast to the body and world as pre-given semiotic systems (which might also be seen as the predominance of either phenomenology or semiotics).[27] On the one hand we have the idea presented in the work of Phenomenologists such as Merleau-Ponty that the body and perception operate at a level below cognition and conscious awareness. The lived-body needs to be understood in this way in a pre-objective realm, through stripping back layers superimposed on it through the phenomenological process. The body is "our general medium for having a world" which posits different worlds of significance (Merleau Ponty 1962, p. 169). On the other hand, we have the constructivist idea presented by a number of cultural theorists that the lived body can only be understood within a symbolic system, within a culture, and that the raw experience of the body is always culturally mediated and the body, indeed, socially and politically

[27] For an interesting overview see Csordas 1994.

constructed. Ricoeur might be seen as a refined exemplum of this position in that the body and human action are set within a narrative frame. "If, in fact, human action can be narrated, it is because it is always already articulated by signs, rules and norms. It is always already symbolically mediated" (RICOEUR 1984, p. 57). This is not the place to attempt to resolve this dilemma but it is useful for us in understanding the representation of the subtle body in our text.

Clearly the *Netratantra* presents a complex system which integrates and maps onto the body a number of terms and clearly the text presents the idea that the structures it describes are experiental realities. The text and Kṣemarāja's commentary indicate this. For example, the yogi should "touch" (*vimṛśet*) the supreme Śakti becoming immersed in the ingoing and outgoing breaths (cf. *Netratantra*, p. 153). The breathing is central to the practice and the realization of the power within the body. Thus we have the living body with its breath, an experienced body, becoming the locus for an ornate, cultural overcoding in terms of the symbolic structures in the system.

Mimesis

We might say, therefore, that the breath links the lived experience of the body with the symbolic system of the body. That is, the complex representation of the subtle body in the *Netratantra* and other texts which reflects cosmology and metaphysics and reflects the perception of the soteriological path to liberation, is performed and expressed in the lived body of the yogi. Conversely the lived body of the yogi reflects and enacts the symbolic system; the yogi's body becomes entextualised. There is a process of interaction between lived experience, the lived body through time, and the symbolic representation or construction in the tantric systems. Indeed, the texts themselves seem to be aware of this and the structure of the subtle body is primarily for visualization purposes and not intended to be reified. The visualization of the subtle body is not a medical treatise about the physical body. In spite of modern attempts to locate and identify the *cakras* with the physical body,[28] they cannot actually be located in this objectified way. The structure of the subtle body is a representation that interacts with the lived body or rather that the yogi enacts in his lived body, but they are not part of the objectified body of modern discourse. There is a phenomenology of the subtle body in which the yogic practice centered on the breath is an existential reality. The yogi practices breath control in association with this visualization. Thus a physical practice is simultaneously accompanied by the formation of the body in a cultural imagination that projects onto the experienced body the structures of the system. The world of the yogi is formed through this interaction of lived body and symbolic system.

[28] For an example of an attempt to merge western medicine with the traditional yogic view see WUJASTYK 2002.

We have then an interaction between the world of the text and the lived world of experience. At one level, the text bears witness to the human event or experience which becomes testimony articulated in a source.[29] To understand the mechanism of this relationship we need to turn to the idea of mimesis, not in the sense of mere repetition but in the sense of a dynamic cultural mechanism. Gebauer and Wulff describe this as an "active process" that designates "not a passive process of reproduction but the process of creation, representation, or enactment" (GEBAUER/WULFF 1992, p. 119). This active process represents the subtle body as an imitation of experience, the representation of a course of action, and that experience in turn imitates the structure of the body textually presented. The symbolic system opens up a world of "as if…" to use Ricoeur's phrase. The text presents an account, we might call it a narration, which is both a description and an invitation to follow its description and reproduce its experience in oneself. Using Ricoeur's analysis of mimesis into three modes, we might say that the text implies a pre-understanding of action as a mimesis of the living, experiencing body (mimesis 1), it has an "emplotment" in the sense that the text opens up a world of "as if" for the reader to enter (mimesis 2) and lastly there is a relationship between the text and the world (mimesis 3) (cf. RICOEUR 1984, pp. 52–87). The *Netratantra* assumes a pre-understanding of the yogi's goal and experience, it represents a structure of experience, and it meets world in that the text is a formula for practice. In some ways we might even say that the text shows us the mechanisms involved by which human experience in enmeshed in a symbolic, ideological system. With the *Netratantra* we have an elaborate symbolic system and the body constructed in text-specific ways. The text is imposed upon the body and we have, as it were, an elaborate entextualisation of the body. Such an entextualisation is in the service of a "spiritual" ideology which gives liberation and power as its goal.

But the text must also be understood in the "political" ideology of early medieval courtly life and sovereignty. The text, including the subtle body visualization, is for the king and the king's family, as Sanderson shows, and is part of the mechanism which legitimates and reinforces power within the kingdom. The "as if…" kingdom of the text meets the world through being internalized by the yogi and inscribed, as it were, on the body. With the *Netratantra* we have the subjective or inner life of the yogi becoming integrated into the larger narrative of tradition. This integration is also making the subjective orientation of the yogi towards power and liberation, part of the external, political life of the court. The text can be read purely as a visualization text for the yogi but the broader context shows us that it must also be understood as a political and politicized text as well. The corporeal

[29] For a discussion of this mechanism see RICOEUR 2004, part II.

experience of the body or the corporeal exploring of the tradition enacts that tradition, especially through the breath, and the tradition in turn presents an account of the world to be explored. In the *Netratantra* body, breath and text are brought together in a complex and textured way that is so representative of this period in the history of Indian religions.

Appendix

The Visualisation of the Subtle Body in the Tantra and Kula Systems

ādhāra	vyoman	cakra	granthi	sthāna/kārana
dvādaśānta				
brahmarandhra				Śiva-
			Śakti-	Śakti-
			Nāda-	
			Baindava-	
			Dīpikā-	
			Indhikā-	
lalāṭa	nāda-	śānta-	Sadāśiva-	Sadāśiva-
bindu	4th	dīpti-	Īśvara-	Īśvara-
tālu		bhedana-	Rudra-	Rudra-
kaṇṭha			Viṣṇu-	Viṣṇu-
(kurma)				
hṛt	3rd	yogi-	Brahmā-	Brahmā-
nābhi	2nd	māyā		
(nāḍi)				
(kanda)				
(pāyu)				
meḍhra	janma-	nāḍi-	pāśava-	
			māyā-	
jānu				
gulpha				
aṅguṣṭha				

References

BANERJEA, A. K. (1962): The Philosophy of Gorakhnath. – Ripon.

BRUNNER, H. (1974): Un tantra du nord, le netra tantra. In: Bulletin de l'Ecole Française d'extrême orient, Vol. 61, pp. 125–97.

CSORDAS, T. J. (1994): Introduction. In: CSORDAS, T. J. (Ed.): Embodiment and Experience: The Existential Ground of Culture and Self. – Cambridge, pp. 1–24.

FLOOD, G. (2006): The Tantric Body. – London.

GEBAUER, G./WULF, C. (1992): Mimesis: Culture, Art, Society. – Transl. by Don RENEAN. – Berkeley/Los Angeles/London.

GRANOFF, P. (2000): Other People's Rituals: Ritual Eclectism in Early Medieval Indian Religious [sic]. In: Journal of Indian Philosophy, Vol. 28, No. 4, pp. 399–424.

Haṭhayogapradīpikā of Svatamrama = Haṭhayogapradīpikā with the commentary Jyotsnā of Brahmānanda and English translation (1972). – Madras. (The Adyar Library, General Series No. 4)

Heilijgers-Seelen, D. (1994): The System of Five Cakras in the Kubjikāmatatantra 14–16. – Groningen.

Khecarīvidyā of Ādīnātha = Mallinson, J. (2007): The Khecarīvidyā of Ādīnātha: A Critical Edition and Annotated Translation of an Early Text of Haṭhayoga. – London.

Mallinson, J. (2007): The Khecarīvidyā of Ādīnātha: A Critical Edition and Annotated Translation of an Early Text of Haṭhayoga. – London.

Michaels, A. (2004): Hinduism: Past and Present. – Princeton, N.J.

Merleau Ponty, M. (1962): Phenomenology of Perception. – Trsl. by Colin Smith. – London/New York.

Netratantra = Kaul, M. S. (Ed.) (1926, 1927): Netra-tantra with uddyota by Kṣemarāja, 2 Vols. – Srinagar. (Kashmir Series of Texts and Studies, 46 and 61)

Padoux, A. (2002): Corpse et Cosmos: L'image du corps du yogin tantrique. In: Boullier, V./ Tarabout, G. (Eds.): Images du corps dans le monde hindou. – Paris, pp. 163–87.

Rauravāgama = Bhatt, N. R. (Ed.) (1983): Rauravottarāgama: edition critique, introduction et notes. –Pondichery, Vol. 3. (Publications de l'institut français d'indologie Vol. 66)

Ricoeur, P. (1984): Time and Narrative, Vol. 1. – Transl. by Kathleen McLaughlin and David Pellauer. – Chicago.

Ricoeur, P. (2004): Memory, History, Forgetting. – Transl. by Kathleen Blamey and David Pellauer. – Chicago.

Sanderson, A. (1985): Purity and Power among the Brahmans of Kashmir In: Carrithers, M. et al. (Eds.): The Category of the Person. – Cambridge, pp. 190–216.

Sanderson, A. (2007): The Śaiva Exegesis of Kashmir. In: Goodall, D./Padoux, A. (Eds.) Mélanges tantriques à la mémoire s'Hélène Brunner. – Pondichery, pp. 231–442. (Collection Indologie Vol. 106)

Sanderson, A. (2004): Religion and the State: Śaiva Officiants in the Territory of the King's Brahmanical Chaplain. In: Indo-Iranian Journal, Vol. 47, No. 3–4, pp. 229–300.

Silburn, L. (1961): Le Vijñānabhairava: texte traduit et commenté par Lillian Silburn. – Paris. (Publications de l'Institute de Civilisation Indienne, Série in-8o, fascicule 15)

Silburn, L. (1983): La Kuṇḍalnī ou l'énergie des profondeurs. – Paris.

Svacchandatantra = Sastri, M. K. (Ed.) (1927): The Svacchanda-tantra: With Commentary by Kshemaraja. – Bombay. (Kashmir Series of Texts and Studies Vol. 48)

Vasudeva, S. (2004): The Yoga of the Mālinīviyaottaratantram: Chapters 1–4, 7, 11–17: Critical Edition, Translation and Notes. – Pondichéry. (Collection Indologie Vol. 97)

Vijñanabhairava = Sastri, M. K. (Ed.) (1918): The *Vijñanabhairava* with Commentary by Kṣemarāja and Śivopādhyāya. – Srinagar. (Kashmir Series of Texts and Studies Vol. 8).

White, D. (2003): The Kiss of the Yogin: Tantric Sex in its South Asian Context. – Chicago.

Wujastyk, D. (2002): Interpréter l'image du corps humain dans l'inde pré-moderne. In: Boullier, V./Tarabout, G. (Eds.): Images du corps dans le monde hindou. – Paris, pp. 71–99.

Fabrizia Baldissera

Telling Bodies

Sanskrit humorous and satirical works display a large gallery of interesting bodies—both human, symbolic and divine—caught in the most diversified activities.

The episodes chosen to illustrate some of these motifs come from two of the ancient *bhāṇas* (monologue plays) of the *Caturbhāṇī* collection, the *Pādatāḍitaka* of Śyāmilaka and the *Ubhāyābhisārikā* of Vararuci, both probably composed around the sixth century C.E. Then from a more recent one, the *Śāradātilaka* of some Śaṅkara, possibly belonging to the period between the fourteenth and the sixteenth century. And finally from some satires of Kṣemendra, the polymath of the eleventh century (*Narmamālā, Deśopadeśa, Samayamātṛkā*). Portions of hymns from the *Ṛgveda* and *Atharvaveda* collections are also quoted.

The *bhāṇas* are dramatic works meant to be enacted on the scene, and as such in performance would display different types of *abhinaya*, "mode of recitation." One of these is the *aṇgikābhinaya*, "bodily recitation," that employs stylized postures and gestures, including in some cases a strictly codified alphabet of hand signs. The most interesting type of recitation however is called *sattvikābhinaya*, "true recitation," that should convey the emotions experienced by the actors not in a denotative manner, but through suggestion, i.e. through the expert portrayal of the spontaneous bodily reactions caused by an emotion. The actor's body here is equally involved in the *aṇgikābhinaya* mode, because he employs the same stylized procedures of communication, but in a manner which should be perceived as "spontaneous," where he or she has to resort to the ingenuity of a long dramatic practice and to some measure of improvisation. In the conventions of Sanskrit dramatic literature, which gradually spread to reach all literary genres, the outward manifestations of the emotions in fact could need, for instance, the appearance of sudden pallor or redness, the tremor of some part of the body or of the entire frame, or crying, laughing or fainting, perspiring, the raising of body hair through shivering in pleasure or in fear, or the knitting of the eyebrows. In poetic texts indications of transitory emotional states could be traced down to some almost imperceptible movements, like the suggested involuntary flutter of eyelids, or the contraction of the toes. Great Sanskrit *kāvya* (fictional literature) in verse and prose has mastered the particular art of evoking emotions in this manner, without actually stating them. In the humorous literature, and particularly in the monologue plays of the *bhāṇa* type, such connotation still exists, but has to be somehow more explicitly hinted at or described both by gesticulation and in words by the only actor on the scene, who by convention pretends to meet different characters just behind an unseen street corner, and to hold conversations with them. He actually enacts all of their roles by miming them as he describes their aspect and attitudes, and pretends to "repeat" their replies to his questions.

Kṣemendra's satires, on the other hand, are not meant to be dramatically performed, but were most probably read aloud to a learned meeting of friends who could share the fun.

Given these conventions, the bodies described in Sanskrit satirical literature give blatant rather than subtle indications as to the characters' status in life, their profession, attitudes to life and general proclivities.

Among the numerous bodies portrayed in *bhāṇas* and satires some divine ones are also included, as for instance in the opening verse of the *bhāṇa Pādatāḍitaka*. This stanza introduces an amorous mood and at the same time testifies to the great importance attributed to bodies in humorous literature, while highlighting also the dangerous qualities of divine ones.

Here two unique divine bodies are mentioned: the first belongs to Kāma, the love god, once beautiful but now utterly destroyed, so that he came to be called Anaṅga, "the Bodiless One;" the second is the peculiar body of the great ascetic god Śiva (here called by his epithet Śambhu), of whom only the powerful third eye is recalled, capable of fulgurating and reducing to ashes anybody:

> May Kāma protect you, he who propitiated the wrath of Śambhu by allowing his own body to burn in the fire of his [third] eye, Kāma whose orders are carried on their heads, as if a garland, by the gods led by Indra, Kāma whose bow is the elongated corner of the eye of graceful women, while his arrows, the objects of the senses, pierce and break the hearts of the ascetics who keep the vow of silence. (1)

In the myth referred to, the frightful burning of Kāma's body resulted in making him even more subtly dangerous: as the Bodiless One he became truly invincible, as from then on he could insinuate himself, unperceived, in the hearts of all beings. The stanza moreover, with its mention of the *muni*, the silent ascetic, contains a clever joke: Kāma was burnt to ashes after he tried to pierce Śiva with his arrows in order to make him fall in love. He had failed then, but immediately later, in his new subtler form, he had invaded and vanquished the heart of the strenuous ascetic god.

As regards human bodies, in this literature their main divide is age and gender, while lesser divisions involve their eventual state of intoxication, induced by passion or liquor, and the attitudes in which they are portrayed, with their relative appropriateness to the external circumstances they find themselves in. As it is to be expected, young bodies are usually seen as graceful—perhaps with the grotesque exception of the child courtesan who fills her bodice with false breasts to seduce older men in Kṣemendra's *Samayamātṛkā*—while old ones are usually depicted in a sorry state—again, with some nuances. In these works in fact both old women and old men are shown as they try to improve their appearance with ointments and dyes. The action often takes place in the red light district, and descriptions of women bodies predominate. In this verse of the *Śāradātilaka* for instance the courtesans return home exhausted after a night's work, and their bodies tell a very explicit story:

> The edges of their bodices are sticking to the fresh nail scratches [inflicted] on the circle of their breasts;
> the upper part of their cheeks kissed by lovers is sealed by a shining mark of betel;
> their feet are slowed down by the burden of love sports;
> their sleepy eyes strain to keep open: the prostitutes advance with limbs in which passion is revealed by amorous gestures. (20)

There is also mention of a "third gender" (*tṛtiyā prakṛti*) in an amusing passage of *Ubhāyabhisārikā*, as well as of several males. Here men generally figure as the occasional customers, rich or poor or recently impoverished thanks to the courtesans' wiles. The most important male character in *bhāṇas* is the *viṭa*, "man about town" or "parasite," usually an elderly libertine who has squandered his wealth and now ekes out a living as a parasite and a go-between. As the sole protagonist of *bhāṇa* plays, it is he who describes others.

Satirical writing specializes in exposing people's faults, and especially hypocritical behaviour, not only by describing the context of their deeds, but also in a large way from their appearance, as by convention it was understood that an ungainly body could only house an unworthy being.

In the satire *Narmamālā* there is a sort of symbolism of the body of the protagonist, the notorious *kāyastha*, the "bureaucrat," "official clerk," a term which literally means "who (or "which") stays in the body," and as such could be interpreted in various ways. The body (*kāya*) in a bureaucratic sense could be "the body[politics]," and denote therefore government functionaries. Taken in a mystical sense, it could be the epithet of an esoteric form of Śiva "[the deity] who resides in the body," and the earlier stanzas play with this double etymology (I. 7–9) in punning language that both exalts the god and demeans the functionary. Later (I. 25) another set of rather vulgar metaphors illustrate how despicable a character this particular bureaucrat is. Kṣemendra pretends that his story begins in the mythical past (vv. 20–25), when a demon vanquished by Viṣṇu managed to send his descendants to earth in order to destroy it.

> When the earth with its cities,
> villages, towns and suburbs
> was thoroughly occupied by his descendants—
> who were very cruel

and deprived the people of all means of sustenance,
who were harsh, friends to no one, evil
and stole everything,
Who resembled universal destruction
as they destroyed both movable
and immovable creatio1n (or "properties") everywhere,
And looked as if embraced by Kāla
because their entire bodies
were besmeared by black ink—

Kāyasthas

who were harmful,
for, like constipated stools,
as long as they were in a low position
were very humble,
but in a matter of seconds,
as soon as they rose up,
acted arrogantly,

Kāyasthas

who caused a number of illnesses,
for, like constipated stools,
as long as they were in a low position
were very soft,
but in a matter of seconds,
as soon as they rose up,
became hard. (20–25)

In a literary convention where bodies declare their possessors' worth or unworth through their appearance, it is easy to ridicule people who are often thought to be charlatans by using their body as a metaphor. In the same satire the ugly body and the utterly revolting bodily postures of a despicable *śaiva* guru mirror his ignominy:

With a sheaf of flowers and leaves
and vermilion powder for worship
placed on his head,
with his pot-like large forehead
always moist with big and small round sectarian marks, (II. 104)
He had little hair
matted and bound in a tuft
that only reached
his ear lobes
which were decorated with saffron.
He was glass-eyed,
had a large jaw, (II. 105)
And was bald with a patchy beard,
slow speaking
but still tripping over his mistakes [in Sanskrit];
he had a face (or "he had a mouth")
that looked like the vulva
of an old she-buffalo. (II. 106)
As he could drink in a second
a pitcher of liquor,
while making gurgling noises—

what could compare with the breadth
of his sewer-like throat? (II. 107)
Looking like a *rākṣasa* (demon),
with a heavy-breasted chest,
he wore a meditation belt
which was stained
and stank of wine and meat. (II. 108)
He was adorned
with a deep chasm for a navel,
full of red lead powder,
and had a large belly
filled with a mixture
of fish, rice cakes and sweetmeats. (II. 109)
As from an overburdened cloud,
the sound *gaḍa* rumbled out of him
in steamy eructations,
that were unbearable
with the fresh stench of indigestion
induced through meat and liquor. (II. 110)
The guru,
with his mind completely blinded
by arrogance (or "lust"),
by drunkenness, by unmentionable things,
and by the most profound ignorance,
appeared as if he were
the very embodiment of egotism. (II. 111)
Superior in his bulk (or "Heavy in his bulk"),
in his voice, in stupidity and indolence,
supreme in his penis (or "extraordinarily cock-heavy"),
heavy in his buttocks, his jowls,
his beard and his nostrils,
supreme in cheating (or "heavy in cheating")
prostitutes and officers
and empty of good conduct,
Strange!
This guru, always weighty in everything
is always light
in the great teachings uttered by Śiva. (II. 112)

Other characters who by convention are usually portrayed as both ugly and evil are bawds, the scourge of lovers. *Śāradātilaka* 69–71 offers a rather graphic depiction of a running old maitresse:

Biting her lower lip in great anger and waving away the flies with her hand,
with her tattered garment slipping off
because of her hurried gait

and her shrunken breasts looking like ripe fruits that roll up and down,
with a hump like a camel and just one bad eye,
carrying in her hand half a winnowing basket
and bearing a terrifying aspect,
just like Śūrpanakhā,
the stupid woman keeps growling. (69)
She has dishevelled hair that touches the tip of her ears,
a dirty body which exhales a bad smell,
and a yellow discharge in her eyes.
Stretching out both her arms and walking in quick steps,
this night of final destruction (Kālarātri) for lovers makes a terrific sound. (70)
In her harsh voice she surpasses a female donkey,
in her body she surpasses a plough,
in her belly she surpasses a she wolf,
and in her complexion she surpasses black kohl. (71)

In *Pādatāḍitaka* the *viṭa* seems to show some understanding towards the aged courtesan Dharaṇiguptā, who moves about gracefully and still manages to entice lovers, but the episode suddenly takes a different turn. (Prose passage just before v. 41):

Here is another mobile, ancient pleasure park of the *viṭas*! … In truth even now the remains of her coquetry speak of the long past charms of her youth. In fact,
Both her flabby breasts
are encircled by the white scars of nail marks,
her lower lip, previously sucked dry,
is swollen in the middle and loose at the corners,
and still today, thanks to her [long] practice,
she manifests the correct answer
through the knitting of her eyebrows.
Old age has violently ravaged her beauty,
but has not taken away her coquetry! (41)

Unfortunately the laws of the body do not allow her any respite. Dharaṇiguptā indeed manages to attract a lover, but his fondness for kissing obtains a peculiar reward:

While passionately
kissing her
he coughed up and spat out her tooth which, touched by the tip of his tongue,
had its root shaken into his mouth. (43)

An abundance of coquettish gesture is the special province of the transvestite, the exaggerated parody of a woman, found in conversation with the *viṭa* in *Ubhāyābhisārikā* (prose passage after v. 21). The *viṭa* sees "her" walking towards him: "It is that *kali*[*yuga*] of the street, Sukumarikā, the third gender!"

Sukumarikā looks and acts like a coquettish woman, but tells him that she has been supplanted in her lover's heart by a female slave, so the *viṭa* sympathizes and says that her lover has made a real mistake, because in her case he could embrace her tightly in love-making, without the impediment of a bosom; he could enjoy her continuously, without having to stop due to her menses; and no pregnancy could ever spoil her beauty!

In these works male bodies obtain a fair share of attention especially when it is the matter of ridiculing the strutting allure of the pompous, or a sleeping posture at the time when action would be required, or to show the contrast between an ugly old husband and a beautiful young wife. But sometimes they are very attractive, like in this description of the harmonious gait of a good looking man, who was formerly a chief but had lost his position, and therefore qualified to the status of *viṭa* (*Pādatāḍitaka*, prose passage after v. 41, line 31):

> This is indeed Bhaṭṭi who comes here, adorning the inner part of his house
> by gingerly steps that look like those of a bull
> who lifts up his feet when he is in deep sand.
> Oh, what a good exercise in playful motions!
> It is true that the courtesans' quarter is coquettish play!
> In fact,
> Without the lute (*vīṇā*) and without drums (*mṛdaṅga*) he acts out a one-man show
> as he enters the king's palace with slow strides, advancing with his arms balanced to and fro,
> with his beautiful strong shoulders and breast, sending now and again oblique glances
> while expertly knitting his brows in a coquettish way. (42)

This fellow is mildly ridiculed for his staged allure, but others fare much worse, like the pompous Brahmin brat who displays a misplaced, terrible fit of anger. Tauṇḍikoki Viṣṇunāga is a young Brahmin full of himself, inordinately proud of his function as the royal edict framer. The naïve man did not know that the playful kick he received on his head from his favourite courtesan was a great mark of favour in the game of love. His anger, then, when he took it as a polluting insult, managed to eclipse for a while the lustre of the young courtesan's body. The descriptions of the spontaneous emotional reactions of man and woman are very telling (*Pādatāḍitaka*, prose passage, line 9–10 after v. 8, and vv. 9–10):

> …his eyes turned red, full of anger. With his forehead distorted through the knitting and twitching of his eyebrows, shaking his head, biting his lips and hitting one of his hands with the other, he sighed deeply…
> He then proceeds to abuse the young woman, who gets terribly frightened, as shown in her instant bodily reaction:
> Spoken to in this manner [Madanasenikā] paled like
> the night changes colour when the red twilight [of dawn] wanes.

Lifting her lustreless face, like the moon at the approach of daylight, (9)
with the red glow of passion vanished
due to that uncourteous treatment,
her delicate body bathed in perspiration,
in despair she was asking herself "what is this?",
while her beauty disappeared out of fear, with her head that had lost its flower diadem she touched his feet,
saying "This shall never [happen] again." (10)

If the lovers of courtesans are often young and silly, husbands in these satirical writings are usually portrayed as old and ugly, utterly undesirable. In *Narmamālā* II. 10–11 the *kāyastha* is described as the ugly old husband by a group of young libertines who are secretly plotting to seduce his wife:

One libertine then said:
"She is an easy catch, no doubt;
for how could she endure her husband,
who is old, bald and pot-bellied, (II. 10)
Always absent from home,
lustful and jealous
though incapable of giving sexual pleasure,
with the intense fragrance of a he-goat in rut,
as well as being a slobbering cheat?" (II. 11)

Finally, some of these works present peculiar scenes of dance, very different from those we find in other Sanskrit texts. Here the dance of intoxicated men is seen as particularly ludicrous, and their revolving naked or half naked bodies contribute to create uncanny, grotesque images.

In *Pādatāḍitaka* (line 7 after v. 30) for instance a certain drunk called Baṣpa ("tear"), dances inebriated and his disarranged clothes reveal parts of his body usually hidden:

Who is this man, who is serenaded with warlike (*yaudheyaka*) songs by Rohitaka drummers who have also brass instruments and flutes, while his diadem of amaranth flowers hangs over one of his ears?
As he throws together with a circular motion from left to right his upper garment, whose ends are disordered and have come loose, he exposes now and again one of his buttocks. He is raising the wine cup in his left hand and his dancing causes the [entire] pavilion of the drinking party to laugh. (Describing [him]). Oh, I recognize him! He is that fellow, the son of a Bactrian, Baṣpa, the cock of the courtesans, who has become the unique butt of the jokes of all the rogues! In truth I have never seen him unless intoxicated or drunk, and all the same his hand is not adorned with even half a tiny bean [of gold]. How can this turn out for him? (Upon consideration). Here, I have it. He is very forward, a real pain to everybody, because of his pretending to be on intimate terms with everyone.

> Carrying a handful of spices Baṣpa enters in the middle of the drinkers who have formed a circle of male and female dancers, slaves and stable boys.
> How knowledgeable he is in getting [free] drinks! (31)

Similar dances of drunks are found also in Kṣemendra's *Narmamālā* I. 136–8 and in the description of the "trance" dance of the drunken *śaiva* guru and of his disciples during a *kaula* ritual, (III. 77–80, 82). The first instance describes a functionary, *divira*, who drinks while copying documents:

> Reeling from the wine,
> he trembled as if a ghoul
> had possessed him:
> bracelets of sandalwood
> mixed with sandal marks
> rode along his garlanded arms. (I. 136)
> He was enthralled by the music
> of the loud *phaḍat* sound
> produced by his thick bark ledgers,
> while both his testicles
> leaped around
> as they protruded from the gaps
> in his loin cloth. (I. 137)
> The drunken *divira* danced naked,
> breaking his seat and his jar,
> his body spattered by [black] dollops
> from his rolling, full inkpot. (I. 138)
> Dusty,
> his limbs besmeared with dirt,
> he resembled an erect goblin
> overflowing with intoxication, (or: "with pride")
> and exulting in having
> deprived people of their lives. (I. 139)

In the third chapter the dance of the notorious guru takes place during a *kaula* ritual of sacrifice where all the participants, starting with the guru, get drunk by drinking from the guru's cup:

> Then, after paying homage to [his] leavings,
> all the women of the officer
> with his friends and relatives
> drank repeatedly from the skull cups. (III. 77)
> Whereupon one started to sing,
> another wept loudly,
> one whirled about,
> and another hopped around
> spurred by the sound *śūt*. (III. 78)
> Another enacted the total confusion

arising from his devotion
by remaining motionless for a long time,
as if he had become a corpse. (III. 79)
Yet another,
decorated with a wavering wreath
and completely drunk,
kissed even the wives of the [other] men
(or "kissed even the tongues of the men")
while clasping their necks. (III. 80)
Then out of bliss
the guru raised an arm by the hand,
and getting up slowly from his seat
danced with both [arms]. (III. 82)

Satirical works share the interest shown in the preservation or restoration of men's virility since Vedic times, and ridicule in particular old men who presume to marry young girls. In the *Narmamālā* moreover sexual potency and impotence are used symbolically in the case of the fallen evil *kāyastha* to connote the difference between his prior hubris as an all powerful government officer and his servile abasement when he has lost his exalted position (III. 97):

The functionary,
[once] erect and stiff like a lingam,
(or "[once] haughty and proud like a lingam")
with his loss of power
is [now] reduced
to the condition of an old testicle. (III. 97)

In *Ṛgveda* X. 86 there is a funny contrast between Indra's spouse Indrāṇī and the monkey Vṛṣākapi, whom she describes as "one whose penis remains pendulous between his thighs," while Indra is said to be "the one in front of whom the hairy vulva opens up wide."

Atharvaveda Book 4. 4, quoted in *Kauśikasūtra* 40,14 is both a hymn and an incantation in praise of a plant said to have been used by the *gandharva* (celestial singers, famed to have insatiable lust, whose features are half human and half equine) to restore the lost virility of the god Varuṇa. The plant is excavated because, verse 1, it is "capable of making the phallus stand up" (*śepaharṣaṇī*). The name of such herb (*oṣadhi*) is given in verse 3 as *uchusma* (*mucuna pruritus*), while the *Kauśikasūtra* 40,14–18 quotes both this one and another plant, the *parivyadha* (*calamus reticulatus*), and prescribes to drink two infusions of the plants with warm milk, after putting on one's breast a bow with the string outstretched.

In verse 5 four deities are called upon—Agni, Savitar, Sarasvatī and Brahmaṇaspati—so that they may "stretch his penis (*pasas*) like a bow." And again, verse 7 says: "I stretch (tense) your penis like the string in the bow." Finally in verse 8 god Indra, known as the most virile of the gods, here called "he who has power over the body," *tanūvaśin*, is requested to place in the supplicant the combined strengths of the horse, the mule, the ram, the he-goat, and the bull.

The despicable *śaiva* guru of *Narmamālā* (eleventh century) in III. 64–68 is asked to provide special medicine to one of his rich old devotees who has married a young beauty, and now desires an aphrodisiac, *vajikaraṇa*, strengthened with incantations. Here though rich, the merchant undergoes penury (*daridryā*) in sexual might. Later on it appears that the remedy has dangerous side effects, and that some substances he applies harm even his wife (III. 70):

> And this one
> is a very rich old merchant
> who has a young wife.
> He desires an aphrodisiac
> because he is poor in potency
> during sexual intercourse. (III. 64)
> How could the young woman
> feel any pleasure
> with that drooling old man
> who has runny eyes,
> wheezes and coughs with asthma,
> and sports a pendulous, flaccid penis? (III. 65)
> Even though he has mounted her
> with great effort in love play
> his penis falls down
> as soon as it is up.
> The old merchant cannot sleep
> like a poor man
> brooding on his debts. (III. 66)
> Eager to make love
> even though his penis
> looks like squashed entrails,
> the old man
> places his hand on her vulva,
> and guards it like a treasure. (III. 67)
> After eating meat, milk dishes and ghee
> in the hope of sexual intercourse,
> the old man vomits everything at night
> or gets diarrhoea. (III. 68)
> His wife is always tortured
> as if burnt by the old merchant,
> whose penis is anointed with substances
> recommended by old libertines. (III. 70)

A similar situation is portrayed also in *Deśopadeśa*, section VII, while *Pādatāḍitaka* vv. 71–76 offers an amusing instance of the unwelcome side effects of a medicament taken for a thinning diet by a would be lover: the man after taking bdellium (*guggulum*) loses some of his fat and actually becomes more attractive, but utterly useless in love games, "as enjoyable for women as a *yakṣa* (supernatural beings sometimes believed to be very handsome) [drawn] in a picture" (v. 76). A courtesan who has fallen in love with him spends a whole night trying to excite him, but to no avail!

Apparently men go through all this trouble because of women, whose bodies are considered to be always eager for sex. This is an old tradition, that from the Ṛgveda on (hymn of Yama and Yamī) maintains that women, both human and celestial, tend to distract men from their religious practice because they love being in love and trying to entice them. This is illustrated for instance by the randy young *raṇḍā* (widow) of *Narmamālā*, so difficult to please (III. 31–34):

> Recalling the joys of lovemaking,
> the widow, with her plump thighs and breasts,
> kneads her vulva by night, panting all the while. (III. 31)
> Bending slightly
> the widow gazes
> at her handsome young lover
> oozing juice in streams,
> as a cow gushes milk. (III. 32)
> The golden, plump pussy of the widow,
> shorn of hair, could be confused
> with the gilded slopes of mount Meru,
> whose grass was grazed
> by the horses of the sun. (III. 33)
> If a man had a long and erect penis
> which he had begged and obtained from a horse
> then he might be able
> to satisfy the widow.
> Or perhaps not! (III. 34)

If women seem hard to satisfy sexually, in these texts most men seem really far from desirable, and their bodies, like that of the guru, are the embodiment of greed, cruelty and egotism.

This short gallery of rather grotesque types shows the centrality of the notion of the body in satirical writings. It is often a disfigured body, spoken of in very vulgar terms, that in their authors' words are justified by their edifying purpose. If their public is revolted by these characters and their outer appearance, or finds them laughable, one could hope that they shall strive to avoid following in their footsteps.

References

Atharvaveda = Roth, R./Whitney, W. D. (Eds.) (1856): Atharvavedasaṃhitā. – Berlin.
Ṛgveda = Müller, F. M. (Ed.) (1965): Hymns of the Rig-veda in the Samhita and Pada Texts, 2 Vols. – 3rd ed. – Varanasi.
Deśopadeśa of Kṣemendra = Shastri, M. K. (Ed.) (1923): The Deśopadeśa and Narmamālā of Kṣemendra. – Poona. (Kashmir Series of Texts and Studies No. 40)
Narmamālā of Kṣemendra = Baldissera, F. (Ed.) (2005): The Narmamālā of Kṣemendra: Critical Edition, Study and Translation. – Würzburg. (Beiträge zur Südasienforschung Vol. 197)
Samayamātṛkā of Kṣemendra = Sharma, A./Raghavacharya, E. V. V./Padhye, D. G. (Eds.) (1967): Minor Works of Kṣemendra. – Hyderabad. (Sanskrit Academy Series No. 7)
Śāradātilaka of Śaṅkara = Baldissera, F. (Ed.) (1980): The Śāradātilaka of Śaṅkara. – Poona. (Bhandarkar Oriental Series No. 14)
Pādatāḍitaka of Śyāmilaka = Schokker, G. H. (Ed.) (1966): The Pādatāḍitaka of Śyāmilaka. Part 1: A Text-Critical Edition. – The Hague/ Paris.
Ubhāyābhisārikā of Vararuci = Ramakrishnakavi, M./Ramanatha, S. K. (Ed.) (1922): Caturbhāṇī: Editio Princeps. – Trichur.

Margrit Pernau

The Indian Body and Unani Medicine: Body History as Entangled History

Bodies are described differently by different people, living at different places—this is by no means a new insight. British travellers, traders and colonial officers in India encountered this difference on a daily basis. Doctors and scientists in London and Edinburgh tried to make sense of the descriptions brought back by their colleagues, texts translated from Sanskrit, Arabic, Persian and the vernaculars engaging the attention of medical practitioners no less than of natural scientists. Whether they explained these differences, as in the 18th century, by adaptation processes of a basically similar body to different ecological conditions, or ascribed them, as became prevalent in the 19th century, by racial differences: it were the differences in the bodies themselves, which were thought to induce the difference in description (cf. ARNOLD 2000; HARRISON 1999; PATI/HARRISON 2001).

It is only fairly recently that scholars have started exploring the opposite trajectory. Shifting the starting point from medicine to culture, the attention now focuses on the ways that different cultural representations of the body might be at the origin of bodily differences. Ways of seeing are intimately linked to ways of thinking, to the process of naming and classifying. What is known about the body not only influences the possibilities of medical intervention, but even the experience of illness and of health, the way people relate to their own body.[1]

However, the body is not only a cultural product, but like any other cultural product, it has a history. So while it is of supreme importance for scholars to look at cultural specificities and above all to avoid transplanting notions from one culture to the other, it should not be forgotten that historical actors, and notably medical practitioners, have at all times been doing just that: travelling, borrowing and importing *materia medica* from other places, experimenting with new cures and engaging in a dialogue across cultural boundaries. Cultures, and especially medical cultures, did not develop in isolation from one another, indebted only to their own dynamics, but in constant interchange. A history of the body hence can only be written, this would be my central thesis, as a history of entanglements.

---

[1] See the excellent study of Shigehisa KURIYAMA 2002.

In the following, this thesis shall be elaborated with reference to Unani medicine, a cluster of medical systems still today widely in use among the Muslims (and a good number of Hindus) of South Asia. As its name already indicated, Unani (Ionian) has its origins in Greek medical knowledge, according to which the human body was made up of a combination of four humours, defined by their mixture of cold, hot, moist and dry elements. While each temperament inclined towards a certain humour, their imbalance brought about illness—the same ideal of a balanced condition informing not only medicine, but also justice and state philosophy. The medical specialist's task consisted in linking symptoms to their basis cause, diagnosing what had brought about the imbalance and to remedy it by curbing the excessive humour and adding to the weakened one.

The Greek texts, notable the works of Hippocrates and Galen, were translated into Arabic starting from the 8th and 9th century as part of the integration of Greek philosophy into Islamic thought under the Abbasids. They were developed in the works of ar Razi (864–925) and Ibn Sina (980–1037), through which they influenced not only Arabic, but also European medicine, based on the same Greek heritage. At the same time, Arabic medicine entered into a dialogue with Ayurveda, notably in the field of the exchange of information on medical plants and remedies (cf. Ullmann 1978; Rahman 1987; Klein-Francke 1982). Already long before the period which usually gets focused on by global historians, Europe, the Arab world and India had known an entangled history of medical knowledge, based on a common perception of humoral pathology. However, common roots and encounters notwithstanding, each region knew developments of its own, influenced, among other factors, by local and popular medical knowledge. Therefore, this entanglement neither presupposes the existence of medical "systems" which then entered into contact with each other, nor does it imply the eradication of difference between them. We still know too little about the processes of exchange and notably about the role of actors and groups of actors, who travelled from one region to the other and worked as transmitters and translators of knowledge, which then would permit us to gauge how the remaining differences in the perception and representations of the body were negotiated between the different regions and languages (cf. Attewell 2003).

While the initial phase of Graeco-Arabic medicine, apostrophised as it "golden age," has brought forth a number of studies and the research into the works of ar Razi and Galen fills entire libraries, the challenge from "Prophetic medicine," the attempt to follow the example of the Prophet Muhammad also with regard to the minute advice he has given in matters of health, medicine and diet, has largely been interpreted as a period of decline, in which theology replaced scientific inquiry, and hence lacking in academic interest. However, while the work of Ibn Jawziya (1292–1350) emphasised the need to distinguish medicine from Greek cosmology and to integrate it firmly within an

Islamic frame of thought, he does not seem to have challenged the current perception of the body to the extent hitherto thought (cf. Attewell 2003).[2]

Unani medicine arrived in India during the time of the Delhi sultanate, but it was during the Mughal empire that it saw its greatest expansion. Although there exists a wealth of information on medical practitioners of former periods, written mainly in Urdu, most of them take the shape of biographical compendia which do not aim at showing the historical evolution of the medicine and the processes through which it integrated into a new surrounding, but on the contrary, portray continuity and the unchanging and hence uncorrupted transmission of knowledge. It is only through reading these texts against the grain and following the indications to the largely unpublished sources they provide that they start revealing the extraordinary complexity and the historical variation of what has hitherto been grouped together under the label of Unani medicine (cf. Alavi 2008; Alavi 2007; Liebeskind 1995; Pernau forthcoming).

Included herein are first of all the specialists of the Graeco-Islamic tradition of medicine, those persons who have been trained in the Arabic and Persian versions of the classical texts. These scholars may have been medical practitioners, but knowledge of the classical medical texts also formed a part of the traditional syllabus, as it was taught at the Madrasas. Medicine had multiple links to theology, but also to the teachings of moral and even of politics and cosmology (see below). At least a basic knowledge of the theoretical foundations of medicine could thus be expected from any cultivated gentleman.

In spite of the canonization process, which had set in quite early, these texts were by no means immutable, but underwent constant reinterpretation by means of glosses and commentaries and through their translation first into Persian, then to the vernaculars and their parallel re-Arabicization from the 18th century onward (cf. Alavi 2007, pp. 30–100). Working within the same elite tradition were the Hakims, medical practitioners, who combined textual knowledge with understanding and experience of diagnosis (notably by taking the pulse and examining urine) and remedies. While the theoretical medical texts were in the public domain, this practical knowledge was transmitted only within the families or to select pupils and formed the basis of the prestige and wealth of the urban Hakims. Unlike for the canonical texts, here the boundaries between different medical traditions seem to have been much more fluid, allowing for processes of encounter and mutual borrowing with Ayurveda. While this dialogue was certainly facilitated by a common grounding in

---

[2] See the English translation of his main work, *At-Tibb al-Nabawiya*: Ibn Qayyam al Jawziyya, *Medicine of the Prophet*, transl. Penelope Johnston, Islamic Texts Society 1998. For an edition of the slightly later texts of al Suyuti and Mahmud bin Mohamed al Chaghhayni see Elgood 1962.

humoral pathology (the four humours of Unani being matched by Ayurveda's five), while they classified the properties of remedies in similar ways, the importance of remaining differences, such as the role of the pulse, which was central in Unani and absent in Ayurveda, has not yet been researched. Again, it is only the detailed investigation of the historically changing ways of conceiving the body and its illnesses, which will allow for a more definite answer of how these encounters proceeded and to which extend boundaries remained stable or were renegotiated.

The difference between the learned elite physicians and the local practitioners and Sufi healers, which was drawn sharply in the 19th century attempts at the professionalization of the Hakims, seems to have been more fuzzy before that time, knowledge at a local level being drawn from a variety of sources, medical as well as religious. These different approaches were linked on the one hand by common perceptions of the body and its functioning: for the Sufis too, the four elements and the four humours marked their basic understanding of the material body. Knowledge about how the body worked, how temperaments differed and how certain organs influenced mental and emotional states were considered important not only for healing people, who came to the shrines in search for help, but also was central to Sufi teaching on how to advance on the way leading to the final reunion with God.[3] Qualifying this approach as holistic, as bridging the difference between the body and the soul, may be too simple. Sufis did draw boundaries, but they may not have been where we have been schooled to see them. *Nafs*, the soul, was not some metaphysical reality, but the seat of animal passions and as such closely related to and influenced by the body. *Qalb*, the heart, on the other hand—which would be classified as an organ in modern allopathic medicine—was seen as the centre of the life force, but also as the store-house of divine attributes and as such superior to the *nafs* (cf. Chishti 1991, pp. 12ff., 25ff.). As research into other aspects of Sufism has brought to light the complexity of interaction between Sufis and Yogis, it can reasonably be presumed that in the field of medicine, too, an entangled history of approaches to the body can be uncovered.[4]

On the other hand, even the most learned Hakims did not perceive the body as separated from the soul and the mind and would rarely, if ever, have denied God to be the fountain spring of all healing. For them, as well as for the Sufis, prayer, spiritual healing, the use of herbal medicine, scents and advice on

[3] For an excellent introduction from the view point of a practitioner see Chishti 1991. See also the study of Fabrizio Speziale 2002.

[4] Notably bodily practices in the field of meditation might provide an entry point for this investigation. For the dialogue of the Chishti saint Shah Kalimullah with contemporary Yogis see Rizvi 1992, pp. 296–304; for the engagement of the reformist Naqshbandi Mirza Jan-e Janan with Hindu traditions see Dahnhardt 2002.

diet, fasting and comportment formed no opposition, even if they prob-ably used them to different extents. We simply do not know enough about the pre-colonial practices of healing to be able to venture more definite assertions as to the extent in which Sufis, at least the learned Sufis at the more famous shrines, had knowledge about the classical medical texts and developed medical remedies and cures of their own—which would then permit to infer their perceptions of the body as an object of medical knowledge with more detail and to compare it to the perceptions of the Hakims.

For a long time the assumption that historical change in medical perceptions was first introduced by the British has held sway. However, the present debate on periodization and its link to colonialism has its repercussions in the field of medical history as well.[5] At least in North India, the reconfiguration of Unani medicine started well before the advent of the British. Many of the leading Hakim families were closely linked to the Islamic reformist movement from the 18th century onward. For one this accounted for their distancing themselves from the world of the court and the nobility and its Persianate culture. The importance of Unani was now seen less in its being a part of the general canon of learning which defined the intellectual and social elite, conferring a gentlemanly status to those who adhered to its rules of deportment. Instead it functioned as the specialized knowledge of an elite, qualified for healing illnesses. To this corresponded the shift in language from widely known Persian to Arabic, limited to a circle of insiders (cf. Alavi 2007, pp. 33–46). The use of Arabic also points to their close intellectual relation to the Islamic reform movement, with which they shared a drive towards the systematization of knowledge and also the distancing from Sufi practices considered superstitious,[6] like healing through amulets, the symbolism of numbers and the rituals based on the belief that the healing power of sacred persons, spaces or texts could be transferred through material means (dust of the grave of a saint, verses of the Qoran diluted in water etc.).

It was this movement which was reinforced by the colonial power from the first decades of the 19th century. While medical practitioners in the early phase of the East India Company had still shared basic humoral assumptions with their Indian counterparts, which in turn had enabled a dialogue on appropriate ways of curing tropical diseases, but also on the proprieties of medical plants and herbs, this common tradition came increasingly under attack from the 1830s onwards. Two developments came together for this: in European medicine, illnesses were increasingly ascribed no longer to humoral imbalances or to miasmatic influences, but to germs, giving a new direction to research on medication. Parallel to this, the importance of the study of anatomy increased in the West, where it led to new developments in the field of

[5] With forceful arguments for the revisionist position: Alavi 2007.

[6] For the case of the Sharif Khani family of Delhi see Pernau 2008, pp. 88–91.

invasive surgery (cf. Grmek 1999). The self-confidence which characterised this new generation of doctors, who described their field no longer as an art, but as a science, matched well with the general feeling of superiority evinced by the Anglicists and led to the establishment of a number of schools teaching Western medicine and to the foundation of the Indian Medical Service. State patronage thus shifted from Hakims to Western trained doctors, at least for the higher ranks and for a majority of the Provinces (cf. Kumar 1998; Kumar 1992).[7] Unani medicine, in the eyes of the colonial power, had become just another instance of Indian superstitions, which should and would wither in the light of the supremacy of Western knowledge. The differences may however not have been so clearly cut out as the contemporary images of light and darkness seem to suggest nor the impact of this policy so immediate. Encounters more probably tended to produce plural medicines rather than simply replacing one homogeneous system by another (cf. Ernst 2002; Alavi 2008).

The strategies developed by the Hakims to answer colonial influence went into two directions. The first can be summed up as strategies of professionalization. For the Hakims, defending their ground against allopathy meant sharply demarcating themselves from superstition and quacks without a proper training. Thus, Western influence took up and exacerbated the differentiations among the Indian practitioners, which had already been started earlier. The sifting and classification of knowledge, which had started in the 18th century, were pushed further; simultaneously, training young doctors for the first time no longer took place in a guild-like manner within the traditional families, but led to the establishment of school, in which education could be imparted in a systematic way, examinations constituting the basis for certificates and guaranteeing a uniform standard.[8] The second strategy led to a selective adaptation to Western knowledge. Notably at the Delhi Tibbi College, this implied the integration of anatomy and surgery and partly also chemistry into the curriculum. While this is well known and pointed out in every medical history, the question has hardly been asked, how (and whether!) these different traditions were integrated or whether they were only juxtaposed without an adaptation of the basic assumptions on the perception of the body (cf. Liebeskind 2002).

Anything which can be said on body perceptions in Unani medicine therefore has to take account of a threefold dynamic, working against the possibility of arriving at definite conclusions. First, Unani was at no point a homogeneous system, but a cluster of approaches, whose basic assumptions are not uniform, but which neither are clearly demarcated from each other either. Second, though many of the canonical texts remain the same from the

[7] For a different development in the Panjab see Hume (1977).

[8] For the Takmil ut-Tibb at Lakhnau see Alavi 2007, chapter 7; for the Madrasa Tibbia and the Tibbi College at Delhi see Pernau 2008, pp. 251–60, and Nizami 1988.

time of the Abbasid caliphs to the present, Unani was by no means a static and unchanging system, but shows a marked historical evolution. Third, at no point in history did Unani exist in isolation from other schools of medical thought. This is specially true for India, both in the pre-colonial and in the colonial period. Entanglement can lead to the questioning and subsequent harmonizing of contradictory basic assumptions, however this need not happen: tensions, inconsistencies and even outright contradictions can well survive over long periods of time without calling for a resolution.

These caveats in mind, we can still identify some basic themes, each of which however calls for much more detailed research. While present-day Western medicine and culture tends to take the separation between each individual body and its surrounding—the skin being the palpable limit—as an unquestionable reality, this dividing line is much less pronounced in Unani. The elements which constitute the human body, phlegm, blood, yellow and black bile, are made up of the same oppositions between hot and cold, moist and dry, which also bring forth the natural elements, earth, fire, wind and water. The mixture of the elements, which dominates the environment a person lived in, acts on the state of his bodily elements as well and has to be taken into account in medical diagnosis (cf. Liebeskind 1995). This correspondence between the inner and the outer state was not limited to the immediate environment, but extended even further, to the moon and the stars—hence the traditionally close link between medicine and astronomy.[9] The microcosm and the macrocosm not only reflected each other and obeyed the same laws, they also interacted constantly. Unlike the body perceived through the lenses of germ theory, which is a basically closed and autonomous body, whose invasion by germs constitutes an violation of its natural boundaries and hence a lesion, the body of Unani medicine is open towards its environment, both in health and in illness.[10]

The central concept governing the body and the universe is the idea of balance. Balance of the elements in the body constitutes health, in nature it brings forth the fertility of the fields and livestock, in society it is the basis of justice. All these forms of balance in turn are linked to the cosmic order. Striving for health thus presupposes a bodily regime, diet and exercises and the avoidance of excesses, but also living in harmony with the divine law governing the universe. A medical practitioner attempting to heal illnesses,

---

[9] See for instance the horoscopes calculated for the Mughal emperor at the festival of Nauroz, which drew the correspondences between the position of the planets, the prevalent atmosphere and epidemics for the year to come. See Pernau/Jaffery 2008, p. 200. For the relation between medicine, astrology and alchemy in the classical Arabic medicine see Klein-Francke 1982, pp. 53–64.

[10] The changes from an open body concept to a closed body in colonial perception are brilliantly drawn out in Collingham 2001.

i.e. imbalances of the elements of the body, brought forth by internal or external causes, would take into account the individual temperament, but also the environment of the patient and strive to restore the equilibrium, either by removing the causes of the imbalance, or by supplementing the weakened elements through medication (cf. Bürger 1976).

The intimate correspondence of the individual body and the social and cosmic order, however, also implied that bodily health is more than just keeping the elements balanced, or rather, that this balance of the bodily elements can not be achieved by physical means and remedies only. Medicine, morality and religion thus formed fields of knowledge, which knew different emphases, but within a common framework. Not only the overall temperament of a person, his tendency to sanguinity and rapid flare up of anger or his leaning towards a phlegmatic life-style and dejection, was a result of the mixture of his bodily elements. Different passions and emotions, too, were seen as seated in different bodily organs. Unani medicine's conception of the links of the heart, the liver, the intestines and the brain to emotions and the possibility of their control is at present hardly explored.[11]

Civility, the ability to control certain socially disruptive emotions and to polish others, thus was not only taught in the volumes on *Tahzib ul akhlaq*, on the polishing of the manners, on way of acquiring a certain deportment, of speaking and moving correctly in polite society and of cultivating the refinement which demarcated the respectable strata of society from the common men. It also had a definite and identifiable substratum in the body and its working. Striving for a balance of the elements and humours was necessary not only for the respectable person's health, but also for his virtue. Knowledge of morality hence had to be supplemented by medical knowledge. This relationship, however, did not work as a one-way street. If gaining control of the body was central to morality (and also, at another level, for the ability to proceed on the religious path), the balancing and refining of emotions also had their repercussions on the body and thus could be perceived as preconditions for true and lasting health.

As Seema Alavi has convincingly shown, this common framework of ethics and medicine on the basis of Persianate courtly culture came under attack in the 18th century and was increasingly replaced by recourse to Arabic texts, lacking the "Persian comportment frills" (Alavi 2007, p. 60), a development which was then taken up and pushed further by the East India Company. These changes she ascribes to a reconfiguration of the patronage structure for Unani doctors, who could no longer solely rely on the nobility and the

[11] For the possibilities of such an approach see the work of Guy Attewell (2007, pp. 197–234), who explores Unani practitioners' conceptualization of the interface between the female womb, the tendency towards hysterical fits and standards of moderation and piety.

court but had to reach out to a wider public, interested less in being taught virtue than having its illnesses cured. Doctors thus had at the same time to restrict access to their knowledge and make it more "user-friendly by their concentration on disease, symptoms and medication" (Al avi 2007, p. 60). Professional strategies of the Hakims were an important factor in transforming the agenda of Unani medicine. How did these then link up with a transformation of the perception of the body? As mentioned above, there seems to have existed relations between the reforming Hakims and the Islamic reformist since the second half of the 18th century, on a personal, but also on an intellectual level. Both groups were part of the same movement striving for the rationalization of everyday behaviour. Both aimed at the collection, classification and systematization of their respective knowledge, which thus became not only more complex and refined, but also more clearly differentiated from one another. The distinction between a man's body and his virtue led to the difference between medicine and moral, which were then allotted to two different kinds of increasingly professionalized specialists, the doctor and the religious scholar. The body was not yet completely divided from its environment, but its links to the macrocosm had become much weakened. My hypothesis would be that this new perception of the body as an entity in itself, though in exchange with its surrounding, can also be linked to new notions of subject-hood and a new emphasis on the autonomous individual, who was seen as obliged and able to take responsibility for himself and for the fate of his community, religious or national.

The individualization man gained through emancipation from his social and physical environment, however, he lost again—though at another level—through the standardization processes of the medical system. As indicated above, traditional Unani diagnosis and therapy had always taken into consideration the patient's temperament, his environment and the circumstances under which he was living. In the second half of the 19th century the new professionalization strategies of the Hakims led to the expansion Unani's influence through print media and the commercialization of medicine (cf. Attewell 2007, pp. 238–276). Advice and remedies thus became easily available for a mass public, at the cost however of linking them no longer to the individual, but to classified and generalized symptoms of an illness. A body, in turn, which was held to react in a uniform way to medicine, which was reproducible on a mass scale, could no longer be seen as open even to his physical environment: the standardized body had to be a closed body.

Together with the new pragmatism which marked the generation of medical practitioners at the turn of the century, this development opened up new venues for the encounter with colonial medicine. Less interested in the metaphysical foundation of illness and a consistent perception of the body than in practical results, these Hakims strove to supplement what they saw as the deficiencies in traditional Unani, notably in the field of anatomy, surgery and chemistry, through integrating allopathic knowledge. Once again, professional strategies and changes in perceptions of the body are closely intertwined. What was at stake was not just the introduction of new way of healing, but also the looming introduction of an act limiting government recognition to allopathic doctors only. Thus, the Tibbia College at Delhi, founded by Hakim Ajmal Khan just before the First World War, not only aimed at a common teaching of Unani Tibb and Ayurveda, but also provided for the possibility of the students to take classes in the Government hospital, thus simultaneously grouping forces and challenging the assumption that indigenous systems of medicine were refusing the introduction of change and improvement where necessary (cf. Nizami 1988; Habib 2000).

Together with the rising opposition to British practices of public health administration, notably during epidemics (cf. Arnold 1993), it was this movement which gave a lasting impetus to the reinterpretation of Unani and Ayurveda as Indian (as opposed to universal) medicine, a tendency which partly went against the imagination of all bodies as similar. European medicine might provide excellent results for Europeans, the defenders of the Indian medical systems held, for Indians however, plants and herbs growing locally were not only cheaper, but also better adapted to their bodies.[12] With the same move, the local, the surroundings traditionally held to influence a persons body and health, became the national. The water and air, which through the mixture of their elements impacted the elements composing the human body, were no longer specific to the hills, plains or rivers constituting the natural environment of this body, but to the geographical boundaries of India. Medical thinking was reinterpreted as a part of the Indian culture which had become threatened by colonial innovations and which had to be defended, if body and mind were not to succumb to Western domination (cf. Alavi 2007, pp. 270–278; Alavi 2002; Attewell 2007, pp. 148–191).

However, this belief in an unchanging Indian way of relating to the body, both at the level of theoretical conceptualization and of practical healing, can itself be analysed as the outcome of very specific historical circumstances. As we have shown, Unani has never been a homogeneous medical system nor unchanging through time and space. On the contrary, from its very start, it was the product of multiple entanglements. These entanglements have shaped the boundaries of Unani medicine, in turn including or excluding other systems of knowledge, but they have also shaped the medical practitioners' perception of the genealogy of their knowledge and their sense of belonging. The belief in a unique and different Indian body, which required a national medicine, was but one possibility among many others.

[12] As one example among many see the lecture, the famous writer Nazir Ahmad (1919) delivered at one of the yearly functions at the Madrasa Tibbia in Delhi.

References

AHMAD, N. (1919): Lecturon ka majmua, Vol. 1. – Agra.

ALAVI, S. (2002): A National Medicine in Colonial India? The Muslim Physicians and the Takmil ut-Tibb college at Lucknow. – Lecture held at the Max Mueller Bhavan (04.04.2002). – New Delhi.

ALAVI, S. (2007): Islam and Healing: Loss and Recovery of an Indo-Muslim Medical Tradition 1600–1900. – Delhi.

ALAVI, S. (2008): Medical Culture in Transition: Mughal Gentlemen Physician and the Native Doctor in Early Colonial India. In: Modern Asian Studies, Vol. 42, Issue 5, pp. 853–897.

ARNOLD, D. (1993): Colonizing the Body: State Medicine and Epidemic Disease in Nineteenth Century India. – Berkeley.

ARNOLD, D. (2000): Science, Technology and Medicine in Colonial India. – Cambridge. (New Cambridge History of India III.5)

ATTEWELL, G. (2003): Islamic Medicines: Perspectives on the Greek Legacy in the History of Islamic Medical Traditions in West-Asia. In: SELIN, H. (Ed.): Medicine across Cultures: History and Practice in Non-Western Cultures. – Boston.

ATTEWELL, G. (2007): Refiguring Unani Tibb: Plural Healing in Late Colonial India. – Hyderabad.

At-Tibb al-Nabawiya of Ibn Qayyam al Jawziyya = Medicine of the Prophet (1998). – Transl. by P. JOHNSTON. – Cambridge.

BÜRGER, J. C. (1976): The Practice of Medicine in Ancient and Medieval India. In: LESLIE, C. (Ed.): Asian Medical Systems: A Comparative Study. – Berkeley.

CHISHTI, S. H. M. (1991): The Book of Sufi Healing. – Rochester.

COLLINGHAM, E. (2001): Imperial Bodies: The Physical Experience of the Raj. – Oxford.

DAHNHARDT, T. (2002): Change and Continuity in Indian Sufism. – Delhi.

ELGOOD, C. (1962): Tibb-ul-Nabi or Medicine of the Prophet". In: Osiris, 14, pp. 33–192.

ERNST, W. (Ed.) (2002): Plural Medicine, Tradition and Modernity, 1800–2000. – London.

GRMEK, M. D. (1999): Histoire de la pensée médicale en Occident. Du romantisme à la science moderne. – Paris.

HABIB, I. S. (2000): Delhi Tibbiya College and Hakim Ajmal Khan's Crusade for Indigenous Medicine Systems in Late 19th and Early 20th century India. In: IHSANOGLU, F./GUNERGUN, F. (Eds.): Science in Islamic Civilisation. – Istambul.

HARRISON, M./PATI, B. (Eds.) (2001): Health, Medicine and Empire: Perspectives on Colonial India. – Hyderabad.

HARRISON, M. (1999): Climates and Constitution: Health, Race, Environment and British Imperialism in India 1600–1830. – Delhi.

HUME, J. C. (1977): Rival Traditions and Yunan-i Tibb in the Punjab, 1849–1889. In: Bulletin of the History of Medicine, 51.2, pp. 215–231.

KLEIN-FRANCKE, F. (1982): Vorlesungen über die Medizin im Islam. – Wiesbaden.

KUMAR, A. (1998): Medicine and the Raj: British Medical Policy in India 1835–1911. – Delhi.

KUMAR, D. (1992): Unequal Contenders, Uneven Ground: Medical Encounters in British India, 1820–1920. In: CUNNINGHAM, A./ANDREWS, B. (Eds.): Western Medicine as Contested Knowledge. – Manchester, pp. 172–190.

KURIYAMA, S. (2002): The Expressiveness of the Body and the Divergence of Greek and Chinese Medicine. – New York.

LIEBESKIND, C. (1995): Unani Medicine of the Subcontinent. In: van ALPEN, J./ARIS, A. (Eds.): Oriental Medicine: An Illustrated Guide to the Asian Arts of Healing. – London, pp. 39–63.
LIEBESKIND, C. (2002): Arguing Science: Unani "tibb," hakims and biomedicine in India, 1900–50. In: ERNST, W. (Ed.): Plural Medicine, Tradition and Modernity, 1800–2000. – London, pp. 58–75.
METCALF, B. (1986): Hakim Ajmal Khan: Rais of Delhi and Muslim Leader. In: FRYKENBERG, R. (Ed.): Delhi through the Ages: Essays in Urban History, Culture and Society. – Delhi, pp. 299–316.
NIZAMI, Z. A. (1988): Hakim Ajmal Khan. – Delhi.
PERNAU, M./JAFFERY, Y. (Eds.) (2008): Information and Public Sphere: Persian Newsletters from Mughal Delhi. – Delhi.
PERNAU, M. (2008): Bürger mit Turban: Muslime in Delhi im 19. Jahrhundert. – Göttingen.
PERNAU, M. (forthcoming): Unani Medicine: Health for the Body and Moral Advice. In: Indian Economic and Social History Review.
QAISAR, N. (2001): Unani's Debate with Doctory. In: HARRISON, M./PATI, B. (Eds.): Health, Medicine and Empire: Perspectives on Colonial India. – Hyderabad, pp. 317–356.
RAHMAN, F. (1987): Health and Medicine in the Islamic Tradition: Change and Identity. – New York.
RIZVI, S. A. A. (1992): History of Sufism in India, Vol. 2. – New Delhi.
SPEZIALE, F. S. (2002): Soufism et sciences medicales en Inde. – Paris.
ULLMANN, M. (1978): Islamic Medicine. – Edinburgh.

Arno Böhler

Open Bodies

Macrocosms within microcosms

Following Patañjali's definition of yoga in Yogasūtra 1.2 *yogaś citta vṛtti nirodhaḥ*, yoga usually has been interpreted as a practice to calm down (*nirodhaḥ*) the restless agitations (*vṛtti*) of our embodied minds (*citta*) during their entanglement with the material world (*prakṛti*). On the basis of this classic definition a *yoginī* [practitioner of yoga] has to turn her senses away from the outside world in order to unite herself with the absolute that dwells *in* all of us.

In his article "'Open' and 'Closed' Models of the Human Body in Indian Medical and Yogic Traditions" David G. White (2006) suggested to call such an orthodox picture of the Indian body its *closed* model. "As is well known, Patañjali's principal emphasis is not on the *vibhutis* or the power of leaving an 'open' yogic body, but rather in the total isolation (*kaivalyam*) of the transcendent self through total yogic integration (*samādhi*), based on a 'closed' model of the same" (White 2006, pp. 10f.). Although this closed model became the most prominent one in the course of time, there did exist a wide range of significant alternatives in ancient times as well (cf. White 2006, p. 2).

It will be a main goal of this text to offer such an alternative reading of the Indian body as an "open system." It is constitutive for such a view of the body to understand it as an entity, always already "ex-posed, substantially," toward the world it is surrounded by, so that it is impossible for a body to hide itself from the environment it is embedded in and affected by.

In the final part of this text I will compare this ancient Indian concept of an "open model of bodies" with contemporary efforts of Jean-Luc Nancy to induce such a concept in the West by interpreting bodies as a form of a "world-wide being-with."

> Bodies are never a complete entity, no fulfilled space (space is everywhere fulfilled), but an open space, rather a spatial space than an occupied space, they are what we call a site. Bodies are sites of existence and there is no existence that can take place without a site, a being-here, without a "here," without a "look here" for "this here." (Nancy 2003, p. 18) [English translations of German or French books quoted in this article are made by myself. The page numbers refer to the German editions.]

According to Nancy so far there has not yet been any thoughtful investigation into the ontology of bodies because ontology *as such* has never been considered *as* the ontology *of bodies*; *as states of existences*, or more precisely, as states of a *world-wide local* existence. (cf. NANCY 2003, p. 19)

The local body as the seat of cosmic planes

> Om. Dawn is the head of the horse sacrificial. The sun is his eye, his breath is the wind, his wide open mouth is Fire, the master might universal ...; the stars are his bones and the sky is the flesh of his body. (Bṛhadāraṇyaka Upaniṣad 1.1. in AUROBINDO 1981, p. 327)

Like in many early haṭha yogic, tantric and alchemistic traditions (cf. ELIADE 1969, p. 235), the *Bṛhadāraṇyaka Upaniṣad* too draws a *macrocosmic* picture of our human bodies with the sun as its eyes, the wind as its breath etc. According to this text a body is not merely a three dimensional corporal thing located at a certain place (*loka*), but rather the local seat of cosmic regions. As far as these regions literarily *take place* in the birth of a body only—"dawn is the head of the horse sacrificial" says the *Bṛhadāraṇyaka Upaniṣad*—they are not only *external* to the place a body is corporally located at, but dwell *in* the body as well, insofar as it *is* the local seat of *their* world-wide existence (cf. AUROBINDO 1971, p. 275).

> As is well known, both ayurvedic and haṭha yogic traditions conceive of the human body as a microcosmic replica of the universal macrocosm, whence the following two aphorisms, found in the *Caraka Saṃhitā*: "Earth is that which is solid in man, water is that which is moist, fire is that which heats up, air is breath, ether the empty spaces, *brāhman* is the inner self (*ātman*);" (*Caraka Saṃhitā* 4.5.5) and "Indeed, this world is the measure (*sammita*) of the man. However much there is in man, that much there is in the world" (*Caraka Saṃhitā* 4.4.13) (WHITE 2006, p. 3).

The spatiality of a body apparently has been interpreted in these ancient texts in a *twofold sense*. On the one hand they do denote bodies as *local entities* corporally appearing at a certain place in space and time, on the other they take them as the corporal manifestation of a *world-wide plane*, of an open, broad and luminous *field [loka]*, often characterized by the Sanskrit word *bṛhat*. *Bṛhat* is usually attributed to a vast, shining, bright, luminous entity. In matters pertaining to bodies it indicates their full-grown vastness, luminosity and brightness.[1]

[1] *Bṛhat* etymologically means bright in Middle English, from Old English *beorht*; akin to Old High German *beraht* bright, Sanskrit *bhrājate* [*bhrajāka*] it shines. "... Mahas, the great world, is the Truth of things, identical with the Vedic *ṛtam* which is the principle of *bṛhat*, the Vast" (AUROBINDO 1971, p. 43).

As far as the *spatiality* of a body is a twofold thing *in-itself*, the first two limbs (*aṅga*) mentioned in Patañjali's Yogasūtra 2.29 *yama* and *niyama* are twofold too in regard to their spatial characteristics. *Yama* is a practice determined to improve the relation of a *yoginī* towards its environment, where *niyama* indicates the relation of a *yoginī* toward her own *local* body. (cf. Yogasūtras 2.30–2.45)

Since in ancient times *improving* one's existence meant to make it vaster, wider, broader, more luminous and shining (*bṛhat)*, in addition to these first two *aṅgas* Patañjali also proposes to *stretch* the corporal flexibility of a body while practicing *asanas* (third *aṅga)* and to *stretch* the brightness of one's breath by practicing *prāṇājāma* (fourth *aṅga*) in accordance with the very first and most fundamental aspect of yama, *ahiṃsā*: the yogic imperative not to harm any living being despite one intends to widen, stretch, broaden, extend, spread out the dominion of one's existence [all over the world] while practicing yoga.

Given that *every* local body is the local site of world-wide planes inhabiting a body, bodies do never merely exist at a stable, solid place within space and time. Rather they do *exist*—in the literal meaning of the word "*ek*-sistence"—as an *out-standing* entity, a priori in touch with the environment they are surrounded by.

God of Vastness (Varuṇa)

The field, the local appearance of a body is *surrounded by* has often been identified with the God *Varuṇa* in old Vedic times. The root of the word *Varuṇa* comes from *vāra*, "environing," "enclosing," "surrounding," "pervading" something. It indicates the circumference a body is locally embedded in and in touch with (cf. Aurobindo 1971, p. 447).[2]

[2] The proper position (*sva-rūpe*) of a body is one in which it is ultimately stretched all over the world while being directed toward the Vast as the ultimate Void that surrounds all other planes and local forms of existence. (cf. Yogasūtras 1.3., pp. 9f.). In Aurobindo's (Aurobindo 1971) reading of the Veda, *Varuṇa* plays a significant role. As a leading spiritual poet in 20th century history Aurobindo re-emphasized the necessity of the idea of a possible evolutionary divinization of our bodies in order to avoid the rejection of the material world. (cf. Böhler 1996) *Varuṇa* has often been related to the Greek Uranus and has been identified with the King of "the highest covering ether and all oceans. All expanses are *Varuṇa*'s; every infinity is his property and estate" (Aurobindo 1971, p. 448). All Vedic rivers are streaming from *his* ocean that surrounds all other realms and beings but is not surrounded by them. "[T]he Veda tells us that this King has in his service a thousand physicians; it is by their healing of our mental and moral infirmities that we get a secure foundation in *Varuṇa*'s wide and deep right-mindedness. (I. 24.9. *Viśvāyu* (IV. 42.1)" (Aurobindo 1971, p. 453). *He* release us from ignorance (*avidyā*), narrowness, heaviness and egoism. Because he, together with Mitra is in possession of the truth of infinity, this

On the basis of this fact, the *Ṛgveda* called *Varuṇa* the One of whom wideness is the habitation (AUROBINDO 1971, p. 453). Being the One who surrounds all planes of existence without being surrounded by them, he is the God who dwells in the utmost heaven: *bṛhad dyau.*

> Varuṇa is this highest heaven, this soul-surrounding ocean, this ethereal possession and infinite pervasion … surrounding us with light his possession reveals that dark, *Vṛtra*'s obsession had withheld and obscured. His godhead is the form or spiritual image of an embracing and illuminating Infinity. (AUROBINDO 1971, p. 447f.)

Varuṇa is the One who inhabits the *infinite* void that envelops all finite realms of existence. Therefore he is simply called the God of vastness (cf. AUROBINDO 1971, p. 473 fn. 5)

Insofar as human beings are capable to travel toward this realm of infinity via the astral rays of their bodies, they are able to experience this utmost world *themselves* that surrounds the entire cosmos at its outmost periphery.

Considering this all, it obviously would be a great misunderstanding to misinterpret the *macrocosmic* picture of the human body drawn in these ancient texts merely as a *metaphorical* description of our corporal being in a poetic language. Rather it is the other way round. Many of these texts—like the *Bṛhadāraṇyaka Upaniṣad* quoted above—try to reveal the *macrocosmic* dimensions, always already *embodied* in the local site of a body in order to reveal that bodies do "ek-sist" as *outstanding* entities, constantly *dislocating* themselves in the literary meaning of the Greek word *meta-phero (transfer)* while corporally sensing the environment they are located in. Such a *cosmic*, to wit *world-wide* picture of the body has to be called an open one since it honors the fact that bodies are a priori exposed toward the vast openness of the world they are surrounded by as soon as they appear in space and time.

On the world-wide existence of a bṛhaccharīra

Some*body* who possesses a bright, vast and luminous body therefore has simply been called a *bṛhaccharīra* in *Ṛgvedic times*. The body of a *bṛhaccharīra* is *bṛhat*, broad, wide, shiny, brilliant and glamorous, because the *deha* (body) of such a *dehin* [one who possesses such a body] penetrates all three cosmic dimensions distinguished by the sages (*ṛṣis*) of that times: Earth (1), the

extraordinary couple leads us "to the vastness of that Truth … As lords of that powerful impulsion they bring down the heavens in a luminous rain upon the mortal and take possession of the vast as a home" (AUROBINDO 1971, p. 481). His water thus releases us from sin and destruction. "In sum then, *Varuṇa* is the ethereal, oceanic, infinite King of wide being, wide knowledge and wide might … earth and heaven and every world are only his provinces" (AUROBINDO 1971, p. 455).

antarikṣa or middle region (2) and heaven (*dyau*) (3), the third cosmic region of the universe.

> The *ṛṣis* [sages] speak of three cosmic divisions, Earth, the *antarikṣa* or middle region and Heaven (*dyau*); but there is also a greater Heaven (*bṛhad dyau*) called also the Wide World, the Vast (*bṛhat*), and typified sometimes as the Great Water, *maho arṇaḥ*. This *bṛhat* is again described as *ṛtam bṛhat* or in a triple term *satyam ṛtaṁ bṛhat*. (Aurobindo 1971, p. 42)

An early hymn, devoted to Mitra-Varuṇa explicitly utters the yearning of the *ṛṣis* to reach this utmost heaven that envelops all other beings, *bṛhad dyau,* for the sake of their happiness. "[B]ring to us, O *Varuṇa*, the might and the vastness; form in us the wide world for the conquest of our plenitude, for bliss, for our soul's happiness." (Ṛgveda V.64.6. in Aurobindo 1971, p. 472)

The *body* of a *bṛhaccharīra* obviously has to become vast and luminous (*bṛhat*) because the radiation of such a *dehin* is determined *to reach* the utmost heaven with its rays, *bṛhad dyau*, the seat of Lord *Varuṇa,* called the king of all kingdoms, the Lord of all divine and mortal beings in old Vedic times. (cf. Aurobindo 1971, p. 455)

Since a devotee of *Varuṇa* therefore exposes the most far-reaching and outstanding *mode of existence possible at all*, the entire body of a *bṛhaccharīra* starts to shine bright and luminous. The *astral* body (soul), because it has learned to stay in touch with the realm of infinity (heaven) and therefore "ek-sists" "infinitely stretched," as well as the *solid* body whose local appearance shines bright, precisely because the local existence of such a *dehin* ecstatically experiences the vastness of its world-wide "ek-sistence." Being sensitively in contact with the vast openness that envelops all other cosmic regions a *bṛhaccharīra* is in the delightful position to discover the cosmic aspect of corporal beings. Literarily "ek-sisting" as the local site of somebody whose astral body has corporally reached the realm *of* infinity, it is important to notice that in ancient times the *local* body of a *bṛhaccharīra* is not only intentionally, but *corporally* in touch with the realm of infinity. Having grown brighter and vaster in the course of time, the full-grown body of a *bṛhaccharīra* ultimately has *physically* entered the vast void, *Varuṇa* inhabits, via the rays the local body of such a *dehin* sends out toward infinity. This realm of infinite, an infinitely bright body is in touch with, has later been identified with the World of Brahman.

> The *Maitri Upaniṣad* calls the channel that leads to immortality the *suṣumnā*, along with, through the junction (*yukti*) of breath, the syllable *oṃ*, and the mind, one may progress aloft (*utkramet*). (*Maitri Upaniṣad* 6.21) This same channel, "piercing through the solar orb, progresses beyond (*atikramya*) [the sun] to the World of Brahman (*Maitri Upaniṣad* 6.30)" (White 2006, p. 7).

As far as human bodies, at least in principle, can enter this *suṣumnā* channel that a priori yokes the solid body of a human being with the World of Brahman, the outstanding journey of such a trip toward infinity, in itself stretches the astral body of a *bṛhaccharīra* infinitely and thereby makes it the proper place of a local existence that shines crystal clear, like a diamond, capable to absorb and reflect everything the way it enters the realm of such a brilliant body (*siddhi-deha*).

Thus it becomes clear why yoga has prominently been described as a method that enables us "to reach a point one could not reach before" (DESIKACHAR 1980, p. 2). Since a *yogini* is ecstatically directed toward *bṛhad dyau*—not only mentally but *physically* as well—the body of a *yoginī* is in the brilliant position to overcome, successively, the ignorant status of a body; its stubborn narrowness, in which it falsely identifies itself with the *local* space it inhabits only rather than with the vast and open plane of its macrocosmic existence. To conquer this ordinary heaviness, dullness and ignorance (*tamas*) of vulgar bodies, a *yoginī* has to stretch her body in order to get rid of the stiffness and narrowness of her embodied mind (*citta*).

According to Yogasutra 2.30, the body of a *bṛhaccharīra,* or, expressed in later terms used by Patañjali himself, the body of a *brahmacarya*[3] who has learned to stay in contact with the World of Brahman finally will realize the utmost *yama* possible at all *aparigraha.*[4] "The last *yama* is *aparigraha. Aparigraha* means 'hands off,' 'not to grasp.' *Parigraha* is the opposite of the word *dana*, which means 'to give.' In the way we use *aparigraha* it means 'to receive exactly what is appropriate'" (DESIKACHAR 1980, p. 108).

Once somebody is infinitely stretched toward infinity and henceforth stays in touch with the endless void that comprises all finite beings, one has reached the ultimate quality one can desire and long for: not to demand anything else and nothing more than that, one already possesses.

Aparigraha, being satisfied with what one *is* and what one *has* is the Indian idea of *amor fati.* It is generally known that this concept has strongly been reaffirmed in the West by Friedrich Nietzsche and poststructuralist readers of his work (cf. DERRIDA 1988).

Accomplishing *aparigraha, amor fati*, a *brahmacarya* has finally mastered the ultimate aspect of *yama*; not because he became an ascetic, but because

---

[3] Later on, in yoga terminology, somebody who is sensitively aware of the utmost region enveloping all other regions is called a *brahmacarya*. "The word *brahmacarya* is composed of the root *car*, meaning 'to move' and *brahma* meaning *truth*. Brahmacarya is 'to move in the direction of truth'" (DESIKACHAR 1980, p. 109). Patañjali calls *brahmacarya* a religious scholar continuously directed toward the ultimate reality (cf. Yogasūtras 2.30, 2.38).

[4] The five *yamas* mentioned from Patañjali in Yogasūtra 2.30 are: *ahiṃsā* (not harming anybody), *satya* (speaking the truth), *asteya* (not stealing), *brahmacarya* (moving toward the World of Brahman), *aparigraha* ("re-signing" what is given to one).

he has learned to affirm, enjoy and embrace his world-wide existence entirely in an *ecstatic* way.

Substantial externalization of a body

On the following pages I will provide some more arguments that this *outstanding* performance of a body, in which it spreads the presence of its local being all over the world, has been understood as a *corporal* procedure and not a sheer *mental* one in ancient times.

According to this claim one has to assume that a body, every time it turns itself toward its environment, *in fact does emit parts of its bodily substance* into the world that surrounds it. An outstanding performance that allows a body henceforth to sense and experience even the space *external* to its massy form. Literarily a *fragile* procedure, because as soon as a body *physically* transgresses its solid form *by the radiation of the particles* it has started to emit the body involved in this act actually splits in two parts: On one side it still exists in a solid form at a certain place, but on the other it began to *"ek-sist," at least partially,* in a second (astral) body that has left its solid form in all directions on its world-wide journey through space and time—an illuminative moment in the life of a body, because it enlightens the environment *of* a body *with* the light of its own corporal radiation. *Physically* stepping outward itself, *any* body that *shines* consequently posses a second, luminous "ek-sistence" *outside* the length, bright and depth of its solid appearance according to this ancient doctrine.

> The rays (*raśmi*) of the sun, moon, or any body possessed of radiance or splendor are the means by which [a] body externalizes its innate powers or qualities. Without its rays the sun cannot shine. In the same way, individuals externalize their innate sense capacities by 'beaming' them outside of themselves, when they perceive objects. The beam or ray is what connects the perceiver with the object of perception. Like the sun, the perceiver externalizes a portion of himself, in the form of a ray of perception, without losing himself in that ray or in the perceived object that is the endpoint of that ray. … In this special case, as in the general case of perception, the concrete channel through which one eternalizes oneself remains a solar ray (*raśmi*) which, as was already indicated in the early *Chāndogya Upaniṣ ad*, is concretely linked to the internal channels (*nāḍis*) of the subtle body. (White 2004, pp. 617f.)

Via the sun-like rays, which bodies automatically emit by virtue of their very nature of being a *corporal, hence spatially extended* being, each singular body is never an isolated thing-in-itself, but rather the singular of a plurality, always already in touch with other bodies it is surrounded by (cf. Tholen 2002, Nancy 2004).

Once a body starts to radiate and shine, the radiation of the body obviously has to *penetrate* the local *surface* of a body in order to get out of the finite boarders of its massy appearance. It is important to recognize that a body, while actually *perforating* the surface of its local form by pouring some of its *soma* out into the peripheral world thereby creates a porosity *at* the surface of its corporal being that henceforth enables it to sense and experience *both* somatic dimensions of its world-wide existence *at once*. Its local, solid site as well as the site of its astral "ek-sistence" within the macro-cosmic dimensions of the radiation it has rolled out during its luminous appearance. Existing *partially* in a solid body, *partially* in an astral body, the subject involved in such a procedure has finally acquired *a skin like surface* by virtue of which it is able to *sense* its environment *directly on the periphery of its bodily surface*.

Though *every* body that radiates exists in this multi-dimensional sense within in space and time "[y]ogis can, however, through their 'out of body concentration' (*videha-dhāraṇā*), greatly augment this process, and externalize far more powerful components of themselves (their breath, energy, mind, intellect, consciousness etc.) in order to leave their bodies behind … " (White 2004, p. 618). Intentionally *pouring out* (*visarga*) some of their soma into the outer world to ultimately connect their astral rays with the highest heaven, *bṛhad dyau*, the *deha* of a *yoginī* finally starts to shine vast and bright, like the sun.

In many Hindu traditions the channel that combines the local body of a *yoginī* with the cosmic realm of the infinite void is signified as *dvādaśānta*, the "end of twelve," because it was perceived to be a located twelve fingerbreadths above the fontanel (cf. White 2006, p. 11).

Once a *yoginī* is able to open this yoke (*cakra*) so close to the solid form of her body, a passage opens that directly connects her local form of her being with the utmost cosmic sphere of the universe, the World of Brahman.

Changing the quality of matter: a corporal trope

It is important to realize the *performative* aspect involved in this fragmentation of a body. Because, directing the *radiation* of a *body* toward the realm of the vast openness that envelops all other cosmic regions actually takes place as the performance of a caesura that marks *a radical change of the entire quality, the material world as such is corporally experienced*.

Whereas ordinary bodies usually experience the *prakṛti* aspect of the material world, in which our corporal existence appears as a narrow, heavy and painful reality (*tamas*) that imprisons the cosmic regions of our mind, the *body of* a *yoginī*, in touch with the World of Brahman, acquires a *śakti* quality: the quality of the feminine aspect of the divine Lord (Īśvara).

According to Eliade's thoughtful investigations on the relation of Yoga, Tantrism and Alchemy, this transformation of *the way, how* we corporally experience the quality of matter in our own bodily existences has been an important aspect of many tantric yoga traditions, especially in regard to their sexualized ritual performances. (cf. White 2003, p. 1–26)

> Every naked woman incarnates *prakṛti*. Hence she is to be looked upon with the same adoration and the same detachment that one exercises in pondering the unfathomable secret of nature, its limitless capacity to create. … The second stage consists in the transformation of the woman-*prakṛti* into an incarnation of the Śakti; the partner in the rite becomes a goddess, as the yogin must incarnate the god (ELIADE 1969, p. 259).

Wherever such a tantric ritual is accomplished successfully, the body of the ritual performers acquired a *sattva* quality by virtue they are able henceforth to mirror and reflect the true positions of things. Having implemented the form of vastness *into* the realm of matter through the ritual adoration and detachment of corporal enjoyments, earth itself has become a "divine" place, in which plenitude, bliss and bodily happiness flourishes (cf. ELIADE 1969, p. 259).

> The ceremonial union between the *brahmacārin* (lit., "chaste young man") and the *puṃścalī* (lit. "prostitute") may well express a desire to effect the *coincidentia oppositorum*, the reintegration of polarities, for we find the same motif in the mythologies and the iconographic symbolism of many archaic cults. (ELIADE 1969, p. 256f.)

The ritual coitus *(maithuna)* between a "chaste young man" and a "prostitute" is primordially determined to induce the rhythmic concentration of the bodies involved in the tantric rite in order to merge their polarities, so that the performers *corporally* start to sense the brightness of their earthly existences and the gayness of their corporal beings.

Matter, in Indian philosophies, therefore essentially can possess both qualities. It *can* appear as a prison for any body prominently experiencing the *prakṛti* aspect of it. On the other hand, once this dull aspect of matter has been mastered, matter can *expose* its divine qualities (*śakti)*.

In alchemist traditions this *śakti* aspect of matter has been carried to its extreme in assuming that our ordinary body can even be transformed by the successful accomplishment of adequate rites into an *extraordinary body* (*siddhi-deha, divya-deha*)[5] that has become "incorruptible" through drinking the soma wine of immortality.

> The body thus built up in the course of time by the Haṭha yogins, tantrists, and alchemists corresponded in some measure to the body of a "man-god"—a concept that, we know, has a long pre-history, both Indo-Āryan and pre-Āryan. The tantric theandry was only a new variant of the Vedic macranthropy. The point of

[5] Some schools distinguish two forms of "incorruptible bodies": *siddhi-deha* and *divya-deha*. The former is the body of somebody liberated *in* life (*jīvan-mukta*), the later the one of a *para-mukta*, a wholly spiritual body (*cinmaya*), possessing infinite knowledge (*jñāna-deha)* as far as such a divine body is no longer at all bound to matter.

> departure for all these formulas was of course the transformation of the human body into a microcosmos, an archaic theory and practice, examples of which have been found almost all over the world and which, in Āryan India, had already found expression from Vedic times. The "breaths," as we have seen, were identified with the cosmic winds and with the cardinal points. Air "weaves" the universe, and breath "weaves" man … (ELIADE 1969, p. 235).

Driven by the vital force to manifest the "man-god" form of a body here on Earth,[6] one could say that the ancient Indian concept of the human body was a *hybrid one* since it assumed that the quality of matter permanently oscillates between the *pakṛti* and *śakti* aspect of the material world, at least in a human life.

The Dawn

In order to actually *posses* such a diamond body (*vajrayāna*) — a *yoginī* has to direct the vital forces of her horses (*aśva)* toward infinity in order to induce the factual birth of such a lumionous body. "Om. Dawn is the head of the horse sacrificial," says the *Bṛhadāraṇyaka Upaniṣad* (1.1. in AUROBINDO 1981). "There are so many dawns that have not yet glowed"[7] Nietzsche quotes from the Ṛgveda as the motto of his book *Morgenröthe* (*Dawn*).[8]

Both texts force the *asvas,*[9] the vital forces of our corporal existence to look ahead in order to prepare the arrival of a new mode of existence, in which a

[6] Aurobindo has re-established this ancient goal of Indian spirituality in 20th century India, posing that a "divine life in a divine body is the formula of the ideal" that he envisages. (AUROBINDO 1989, p. 20)

[7] "Es giebt so viele Morgenröthen, die noch nicht geleuchtet haben." (NIETZSCHE 1980, p. 9) On the significance of the sun in Nietzsche's *Thus Spoke Zarathustra* (cf. NEHAMAS 2000, pp. 165–190).

[8] This book explicitly ends with aphorism Nr. 575, in which Nietzsche quotes India as the site of a culture we intentionally try to reach with our boats, but probably will fail to arrive, because, driving from Europe in a westward direction, we are in danger to go astray on our "Indian" journey toward infinity. "*Wir Luft-Schifffahrer des Geistes!* — Alle diese kühnen Vögel, die in's Weite, Weiteste hinausfliegen … Wird man vielleicht uns einstmals nachsagen, dass auch wir, nach *Westen steiernd, ein Indien zu erreichen hofften*, — dass aber unser Loos war, an der Unendlichkeit zu scheitern? Oder, meine Brüder? Oder? —" (NIETZSCHE 1980, p. 331)

[9] In its chronological gallop the horses manifest things in time and space. Their gallop is the quality of time, in which it actually takes place while generating things during the dawn of their birth. According to ancient times this race of time does not *produce* the things that are successively revealed during the course of time, but merely *let them appear*. "All things exist already in Parabrahman, but all are not here manifest. They are already there in Being, not in Time." (AUROBINDO 1981, p. 342) So long as the horse of time keeps on running, all different kinds of things will *enter* being according to the swift movements of the horses of time. Each thing that appears during the act of its spatio-temporal genesis is a certain type of rider of such a horse of time.

living being has actually learned to affirm the vastness of its bodily existence as a mode of being-in-the-world rather than being-in-itself.

> "Dawn," says the ṛṣi, "is the head of the Horse sacrificial." Now the head is the front, the part of us that faces and looks upon our world,—and Dawn is that part to the Horse of the Worlds … it is the Being's movement forward, it is its impulse to look out at the universe in which it finds itself and looking toward it, to yearn, to desire to enter upon possessions of a world which looks so bright because of the brightness of the gaze that is turned upon it. The word *Uṣas* means etymologically coming into manifested being; and it could mean also desire or yearning (Aurobindo 1981, pp. 337f.).

Corpus (Jean-Luc Nancy)

So far I have considered *ancient Indian* concepts of a *bright, vast and open body*. I would like to continue my considerations with some remarks on Jean-Luc Nancy's remarkable text *Corpus*, in which he actually offers us an extraordinary concept of the body.

Assuming that one has to acknowledge that "'[t]he whole philosophy of nature' has to be revised, once 'nature' is thought of as the exposition of bodies" (Nancy 2003, p. 35), Nancy argues that a body can never be a *thing-in-itself precisely* because the *surface* of a body functions like a *skin* (cf. Nancy, pp 18f.)

A skin, however, does not merely *cover* a body at the margins of its corporal surface; despite the function of enveloping a body it also *opens* it while making its surface porous. This sensible act, in which a body actually realizes that it *already "ek-sists" in a world*, surrounded and affected by, radically changes the whole spatial situation of a body. Because recognizing the world-wide openness of its position, a body reveals the *exposedness of its* local appearance. A priori thrown *into* a world that surrounds it, a body no more appears to be a thing-*in*-itself, but rather an *extraverted* being—a mode of "partes *extra* partes" (Nancy 2003, p. 29), since it can never take place *without* a world, *in* which it appears.

Realizing *its ecstatic* nature as a mode of *being-in-the-world*, bodies "are not merely in a space, but space in the bodies as well" (Nancy 2003, p. 29). In touch with the vast openness of the world that surrounds it, it is part of a wider, vaster, broader space always. Appearing *within* an outside that exceeds its local appearance, a body is already *in distance* with itself. Constantly distancing itself from itself it actually *ex*-poses that a body is "infinitely more than a primordial (finite) being only" (Nancy 2003, p. 29).

Leaving the home of its "proper place" to extend the presence of its corporal appearance upon the world external to it, this act of widening and transgressing itself is nothing alien to a body, no inappropriate operation against its very own nature, but rather the *proper, authentic way* in which a body follows its very own nature: to continuously stretch the inner-worldly extensions of its world-wide existence.

The operation of a body, in which it *breaks-away-from-itself*, flees, and thereby fragments itself, is finally nothing else than very essence *exposed* in the lifelong performance of a body. Since the *aseity* of a body essentially consists in the movement, in which a body *transgresses* its local form of being, it follows, that the *proper* place of a body can never be fixed by measuring the spatial extensions of its local appearance. On the contrary;—driven by its very nature to widen the realm of its luminous appearance, "a body is that which pushes the margins of its existence to the utmost extreme by padding in the dark, grasping, hence touching" (Nancy 2003, p. 124).

One does not have to *push* a body to flee its proper place, since bodies do follow this move automatically. According to their very nature they long to encounter, grasp and touch *other* bodies.

Extension

"The soul is extended, but does not know it" (Nancy 2003, p. 23). This note from Freud, published posthumously, summarizes the central endeavor of Nancy's book *Corpus*. One should forget to think of souls as immaterial entities, because they are, according to this line, rather the (in)*tensional* aspect of corporal extensions. "The soul is extension or the extensional aspect of a body. … After we have emphasized the aspect of the *ex-* in the phenomenon of ex-tension, by now we have to consider the tensional aspect of an ex-tension. What is the essence of an extension? Every extension is an expansion. But an expansion is also a tension in the sense of a tense intensity" (Nancy 2003, p. 123).

The Greek root of the word *tensio*, *tonos*, still emphasizes this tensional aspect of extensions. Bodies primordially *feel* the world-wide extensions of their appearance in the tones and tunes, produced in them by the world-wide relations they are corporally embedded in. (cf. Nancy 2003, p. 124) Emotionally tuned by the sound of their world-wide strings, inter-medially yoking a body with others, the realm of emotions produced in a body is never a "private" matter of an isolated thing. If anything, it is much more the result of world-wide relations, a body is involved in and engaged with as a mode of being-with-others.

To emphasize this *communitarian* sense of emotions, Nancy proposed to call them com-motions, because "[c]ommotion is a word that has the advantage to contain the prefix 'with' (cum). Commotion indicates the phenomenon of 'being-actually-moved-with'" (Nancy 2003, p. 125). The commotions of our souls, despite they are experienced *in* one, are effects, emotionally derived from external relations a body maintains in accordance with other bodies.

The etymology of the word "ex-perience" speaks a clear language. In Latin *experiri* means "going out," "moving away," "opening oneself for an adventure," a trip, without knowing whether one will return back home or get astray in the course of the journey (cf. NANCY 2003, p. 124).

In order to remember the fact that our souls are extended beings—souls are extended, but actually have displaced this truth—Nancy suggests that we have to recover foremost that *bodies substantially matter.* A doctrine that has to be developed up to the point where it becomes impossible for anybody to ignore the substantial weight of a body; either by spiritualizing the concept of a body in order to get rid of matter at all, or by reducing the essence of corporal substances to a massy "something," an isolated thing-in-itself, deprived and highjacked from its outside (cf. NANCY p. 126).

Conclusion

As far as the local place that takes place in a corporal manifestation constitutes the three dimensional *volume* of a *body* only from which the *world-wide* dimension of its earthly existence cannot be separate entirely or subtracted, it is the picture of the body as a *world-wide* entity that has to be recalled for the sake of an open model of bodies. Sensing the cosmic space that surrounds a body, the eyes, ears and mouth of a body suddenly opens. Astonished from the infinite vastness of its world-wide existence, it is on the way to expose and discover the brightness of its being.

> Now the word *aśva* must originally have implied strength or speed or both before it came to be applied to a horse. In its first or root significance it means to exist pervadingly and so to possess, have, obtain or enjoy. It is the Greek ἔχω (old Sanskrit *aśā*), the ordinary word in Greek for "I have." It means, also and even more commonly, to eat or enjoy. … Shall we not say, therefore, that *aśva* to the *ṛṣis* [sages] meant the unknown power made up of force, strength, solidity, speed and enjoyment that pervades and constitutes the material world? (AUROBINDO 1981, p. 337)

The *aśvas,* the vital powers of the horses are needed in order to let this open, out-standing *deha* actually take place in the dawn of its local birth, *uṣā*.

References

AUROBINDO (Sri) (1971): The Secret of the Veda. – 3rd ed. – Pondicherry.

AUROBINDO (Sri) (1981): The Upaniṣad: Texts, Translations and Commentaries. – 2nd ed. – Pondicherry. AUROBINDO (Sri)(1989): The Supramental Manifestation and Other Writings. – 2nd ed. – Pondicherry.

BÖHLER, A. (1996): Das Gedächtnis der Zukunft. – Wien.

DERRIDA, J. (1988): The Ear of the Other: Otobiography, Transference, Translation: Texts and Discussions with Jacques Derrida. – English edition by Christie MCDONALD. – Lincoln.

Desikachar, T. K. V. (1980): Religiousness in Yoga, Lectures on Theory and Practice. – New York/London.

Eliade, M. (1969): Yoga. Immortality and Freedom. – Transl. from the French by Willard R. Trask. – 2nd ed. – Princeton.

Nancy, J.-L. (2003): Corpus. – Berlin.

Nancy, J.-L. (2004): singular plural sein. – Berlin.

Nehamas, A. (2000): For whom the Sun Shines: A Reading of "Also sprach Zarathustra". In: Gerhardt, V. (Ed.): Friedrich Nietzsche, Also sprach Zarathustra. – Berlin, pp. 165–190.

Nietzsche, F. (1980): Sämtliche Werke: Kritische Studienausgabe. Vol. 3: Morgenröthe. – München.

Tholen, G. Ch. (2002): Die Zäsur der Medien. – Frankfurt a.M.

White, D. G. (2003): Kiss of the Yoginī. "Tantric Sex" in its South Asian contexts. – Chicago/ London.

White, D. G. (2004): Early Understandings of Yoga in the Light of Three Aphorisms form the Yoga-Sūtras of Patañjali. In: Cirutin, E. (Ed.): Du corps humain, au Carrefour de plusieurs savoirs en Inde. Mélanges offerts à Arion Rosu par ses collègues et ses amis à l'occasion de son 80e anniversaire. – Paris, pp. 611–627.

White, D. G. (2006): "Open" and "Closed" Models of the Human Body in Indian Medical and Yogic Traditions. In: Asian Medicine: Tradition and Modernity, Vol. 2, No. 1, pp. 1–13.

Yogasūtras of Patañjali = Prasāda, R. (Ed.) (1982): Patañjali's Yoga-Sūtras with the commentary of Vyāsa and the gloss of Vāchaspati Miśra. – Translated by Rāma Prasāda with an introduction from Rai Bahadur Śrīśa Chandra Vasu. – 3rd ed. – New Delhi.

The Body in Narratives and Ritual Performances

Rich Freeman

Untouchable Bodies of Knowledge in the Spirit Possession of Malabar

This paper concerns just part of a larger work I have been engaged in for some two decades which both theorizes spirit possession in the Teyyam worship of northern Kerala as a practice in relation to the "classical" image worship of Tantric Hinduism, and grounds this in the language, texts, and rituals of this practice (FREEMAN 1991; 1993; 1998; 1999; 2003). The present fragment of this work traces out the social stratigraphy of liturgical bodies of knowledge that bring on possession in this worship. Here I wish to explore a particular case of how such bodies of knowledge simultaneously disclose a knowledge of the body, a knowledge that is deployed by Teyyam performers of formerly Untouchable (*avarṇa*) castes to mount an explicit critique of the spiritual, and hence, moral illegitimacy of caste.[1]

That an Untouchable body should be the locus for revealing a higher spiritual ethic gives moral expression to the powerful cultural irony and performative rationale of Teyyam itself. For the entire complex of worship is indeed predicated on gods being invoked into and out of the bodies of ritually transformed and elaborately costumed dancers of the lowest castes. Once so possessed, these specialists dance, declaim, and ritually and verbally interact with their gathered devotees of all castes, as the living presence of the deity. Of course the ritual transformation of this body, and the performative ability to take on an alternate, divine personhood, inevitably raises questions about the cultural understanding of "the body" in such contexts. These issues are heightened once one realizes that possession practices form part of a larger cultural logic that similarly informs the worship of enshrined images. As I have long argued, spirit possession, on the one hand, and image worship, on the other, are so intimately related in south Indian religion as to confound notions of biological embodiment and consciousness that have become normative in the West. The flow of "conscious energy" (*caitanyam*), in both

[1] I use Untouchable here as a rough gloss on *a-varṇa*, literally "without-caste"; this latter, more literal, gloss is hardly suitable, since the *avarṇar* recognize many different castes among themselves. I do not use the currently widespread term Dalit, because aside from a small subset, mostly of Christian converts in my experience, these castes do not generally subscribe to wider Dalit identity politics. For the use of Untouchable, in the politically sensitive historical purchase that I can only aspire to, see R. S. KHARE 1984.

general and individuated forms, across the boundaries of animate beings, and between these and apparently inanimate objects and loci, is not just a regular feature of religious ritual, belief, and narrative in south Indian culture, but in many contexts, their very *raison d'être*. I have therefore been led to develop the theory that personhood in this culture is both more permeable and partible than our assumptions of a unitary "self" in Western learned and everyday contexts, and this, of course bears directly on how we understand and situate "the body"(FREEMAN 1999).

I have also argued, in terms of the cultural history of these practices, that it was the widespread Indic religious developments of Tantrism, with its emphasis on the immanent embodiment of divine powers projected into ritual worship, that provided indigenous south Indian possession cults their most salient articulation with Sanskritized patterns of worship (FREEMAN 1998; 2003). I want to distance myself, however, in theory, method, and much of the substance, from SMITH's (2006) evident adaptation of this model in his recent Indological survey. I do not believe "possession" can be usefully projected into a vaguely generic, pan-Indic model of personhood, abstracted from actual ethnological or cultural historical contexts, including textual ones. And aside from some specifiable engagements, as with certain Tantric formulations that are explicit, it seems evident that possession in any ethnologically meaningful sense was certainly not propagated at a pan-continental scale through the operations of a chimerical "Sanskrit culture," reaching back to the Veda.

The possession for which I developed these ideas is rather a set of actual ritual and discursive practices, culturally explicit and elaborated, historically based, and regionally and socially grounded. While I have extensively treated the ritual procedures and the medieval historical context of Teyyam elsewhere (FREEMAN 1991), my purpose here is to forefront our volume's thematic of "the body" in light of the genred discursive content and stratigraphy of just one deity's liturgical corpus. Aside from this basically narrative level which will be my focus here, there are other linguistic levels which further mediate between the liturgies, the genred features of performance, and the indexical engagement with ritual and verbal interactive frames in any given performance. These levels of framing of Teyyam have been analyzed elsewhere in some detail,[2] and I will here only briefly characterize them as background to the liturgies of a single deity, and return to them again, briefly, at the close of this paper.

[2] Aside from the published work and extensive thesis treatment referenced above, I have worked up several unpublished analyses of performance for lectures, a series of them in Paris, and one in Heidelberg (May 2007). I especially thank Francis Zimmermann for the former, and Bo Sax and Axel Michaels for the latter opportunities.

At a basic social level, the worship of Teyyams entails specialists of the lowest castes in northern Kerala, under specified lineage-entitlements, serving as mediums for the local Teyyam-deities in annual festivals of public worship. Arriving in advance of a performance to these Teyyam shrines, which are usually in the custody of castes higher than those of the dancers, these mediums undergo an elaborate make-up and costuming that transforms them into the living, iconic embodiment of the deity. Through this process they sing the liturgy of the deity, and engage in a concurrent series of ritual actions which symbolically conduct the conscious power of the deity into their bodies. This culminates through a series of highly formatted rituals into the onset of possession, when the performer takes up the weapons and insignia of the deity, dances as the deity through the shrine compound among the worshippers, and then speaks as the god in interaction with worshippers, receiving their offerings and distributing physical substances of grace and verbal blessings.

The bodies of knowledge in terms of the rituals, dance and drumming forms, costuming, make-up, and extensive corpora of sung liturgies, are the exclusive possession of these lowest castes. The liturgies themselves often tell the stories of the deities, who were prototypically local human beings who underwent death and apotheosis to return as Teyyam deities. While there are varieties of circumstances that eventuate in generating Teyyams, a major class of these deities are victims of varying sorts, who return from the dead to exact worship and bestow their blessings on the living.

At this social level of performance, then, the bodies of knowledge entailed in the enactment of Teyyam rites must be literally embodied through their practice by these specialists, as the manifestation of a ritual habitus acquired through years of training. Under the ideology of possession, however, this is not merely viewed as cultural knowledge, verbally and physically learned, but the spiritually transmitted conscious power of the deity itself, re-embodied in every performance, and across the generations. This transmission through the rituals, liturgies and performative experience of possession therefore encodes a knowledge that includes the body, but extends to a constituent field of far greater scope than we understand by mundane, corporeal inhabitance. The Tantric dispensation of god's consciousness being resident in and enlivening the human organism has here merged with the south Indian cult of spirit possession by the ancestral dead, and the merger has been mediated by multiply nested cultural forms of language, ritual, and religious ideology, as the liturgies themselves attest. The "body" under this ritual regime of possession comprises a range of dimensions from the gross form with its social identity and physical elements, to subtler metabolic and mental energies, up to a claimed identity with the luminous essence of divinity itself. These dimensions are further claimed to be accessible and transformable through the rituals, where the most comprehensively overt and concrete expression of this is the ancestral Teyyam animating the bodies of performers to walk and talk among the living.

The first phase of this transformation is wrought on the outer form of the Teyyam dancer's body, through make-up and costuming. Here the everyday body of the low-caste individual is refigured into the image of the god. Each deity has its own complexly individuated iconography of facial and bodily make-up, its own costuming, crowns, weapons, and insignia, that differentiate them, one from another, in their divine individuality. (Figure 1 shows a performer's graphically renderable knowledge of the body and facial make-up of one particular deity, and Figures 2 and 3 the rendering of this, with the accompanying crown and costuming, on an actual body in performance).

At the same time, of course, this transformation subsumes the individual human identities of different dancers into the particular Teyyam, across performances, and through the generations of different performers' lives. In the course of the rituals each performer is thereby aware of dedicating both his life-energies, and through the liturgies and rituals, his very consciousness, into this bio-artifactual assemblage, to transform it, and himself, into a living icon of the god.[3] There are further rituals of conduction through heat, light, smoke, fluids, substances, insignia and weapons, which symbolically ratify and intensify this cognitive and physical transformation. The corresponding

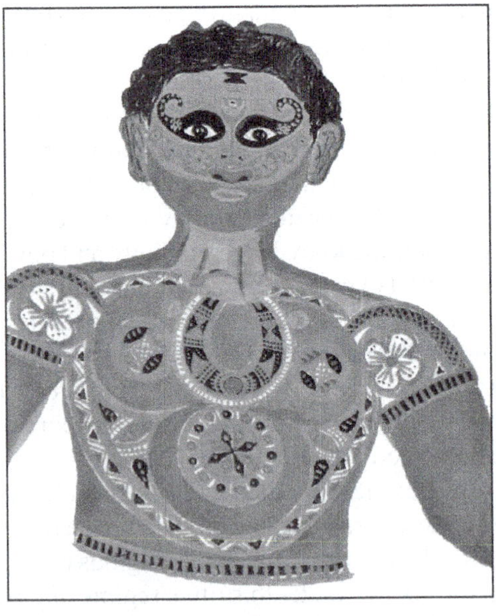

Figure 1: A performer's painting from a notebook illustrating his knowledge of the body and facial make-up for the deity Ūrpalacci (drawn by Kunhiraman Vaidyar, Pilikkode, Karsaragodu Dt, Kerala).

[3] For striking testimony to this process, related by performers themselves, see FREEMAN 1993, pp. 125ff.

Figure 2: The same deity, Ūrpaḷacci, as shown in the previous notebook, showing the facial make-up on the body of a dancer in performance.

Figure 3: The same deity as in Figures 1 and 2, showing the make-up, costuming and crown for the complete assemblage in performance.

rites between the worship of enshrined images of the gods, and those of the dancer undergoing possession not only mirror each other, but are indexically linked, making it clear that this is a relation not merely of formal analogy, but substantive flow. The vital difference, of course, is that the humanly embodied dancer takes on the actions of deity through dance and ritual, and the consciousness of the deity through its liturgy and subsequent speech. Let us turn, then, to a chosen liturgical corpus, to see what the discursive content of this consciousness is like, and how it reflects back on the Untouchable body and its truths.

***

The Teyyam deity whose performance and corpus I take up here is named Poṭṭan, the colloquial word for a "deaf-mute" or "idiot" (Figure 4). The most widely known version of this god's story comes from the performance corpus of the Malayan caste, a group whose traditional status, like that of all Teyyam performers, rendered them polluting under normal circumstances to all of the middle and upper castes. This telling of Poṭṭan's myth, one of several laminated into any single performance of his Teyyam, is in a fairly heavily Sanskritized Malayalam.[4] The story begins not with Poṭṭan, however, but with the birth and

Figure 4: Poṭṭan in his initial phase as Pulat-Mārutan.

[4] These liturgical materials include both transcriptions of tape-recordings made from the field in 1987 and two published versions (Bālakṛṣṇan Nāyar 1979, pp. 425–34; Viṣṇunampūtiri 1996). I will not belabor this exposition with specific differentiations of the slight variations by citing from the Malayalam in this paper.

education of the most famous Brahman sage of Kerala, and indeed, of India, Śaṅkarācārya. Śaṅkara, we are told, was born through a boon to a previously childless couple, through their vows to the god, Śiva. Through his prodigious intellect, Śaṅkara mastered all the scriptural learning available while still in his youth. To crown his accomplishments, he then set out to claim his right to occupy the "seat of omniscience" (*sarvajña-pīṭham*), an institutional center of higher-learning and universal acclamation. As Śaṅkara sets out on this journey, the liturgy abruptly shifts scenes to a cremation ground, describing how Śiva, in the form of a savage hunter, wreathed in snakes and accompanied by a bevy of ghouls, dances there while sporting with his chief consort, Pārvati. Announcing that they should put to the test the knowledge of this youth who sets out so arrogantly to declare his omniscience, Śiva, Pārvati, and their son, Nandikeśan, take on the guise of Untouchables in rags, and appear on the path before Śaṅkara, guzzling from a pot of liquor and singing obscene songs.

The norms of social pollution were such in medieval Kerala that not only were lower castes untouchable to the upper castes; they were unapproachable within fixed gradations of distance that varied with their respective degrees of lowness according to notions of atmospheric pollution (*tīṇḍal*). This meant that such castes could not use many public roads and had to withdraw from paths on the sight of upper-castes, especially Brahmans, who had criers accompany them to announce their approach.

In the present case, Śaṅkara was therefore astounded to find these lowest Untouchables cavorting on his path, using words "without fear," drinking, laughing, singing their obscene "hut-songs,"[5] and failing to withdraw with the requisite display of self-abasement. In anger and astonishment, Śaṅkara finally addressed his counterpart:

> You are an Untouchable who should leave the path
> and withdraw into the distance;
> When those whose minds are ignorant behold the coming of the wise—
> When the approach of the "Gods on Earth" (Brahmans) is beheld—
> There are none devoid of reverence,
> Not one among the four castes—as is well known.
> Ignorant of past, present, or future,
> You are of vile caste, wreckers of social norms.
> Your caste observes none of the rites of purification, ablution, and such.
> Your nature is crude and your regard for deity slight.

[5] These songs of the hut (*cāḷa*) (the significance of which is elaborated, below) are glossed by a modern editor of Poṭṭan's songs as the equivalent of *teṛippāṭṭu* (VIṢṆUNAMPŪTIRI 1996, p. 51, n. 20), songs of obscenity directed at deities when certain temples in Kerala are thrown open to deliberate pollution by lower-castes, prior to their purification for festivals. The sexual implications, accompanied by deliberate defiling with meat and liquor, suggests clear historical associations with Tantric celebrations.

Not only that—the stink of such as fish and flesh
Never leaves your bodies.
Your trickery which intends to wreck my journey—it is astounding!
Drop this cunning and clear the path,
You fool who lacks any discriminating knowledge.
Of vile race, you chief among rogues—begone!
If you dare to oppose me, you will be honored with a beating,
So clear the way! Stand aside, you magnificent idiot!

All of the caste arrogance is exhibited here which we would expect of those who styled themselves "Gods on Earth" (*bhūsuranmār*), and in the opening lines Śaṅkara directly asserts, through a grammatical parallelism, the equation of his social position, as Brahman, with the possession of wisdom. The Untouchable's failure to cede this position with a show of reverence is linked not just to his ignorance and insensibility to the rational order of caste, but to moral degradation indexed by his habits of worship and diet, his very nature as "crude" (*prākṛta*, which is also "natural"), and to the attribution of deliberate malice in his use and enjoyment of the pathway. That such linkages might not have been self-evident to Untouchables is made clear by Śaṅkara's final resort—the threat of violence. That upper castes might have caste-inferiors beaten and even killed for relatively trifling caste breaches, is amply attested in many folk-genres and colonial traveller's accounts. The necessity for such sanctions points to a counter-ideology, where, as we shall see, powerful alternatives are posed, reasoned arguments which question the basic orthodox Brahminical religious and philosophical stance. The ensuing exposition of the Untouchable renders ironic Śaṅkara's charge that he is devoid of any "discriminating knowledge:"

What is the path, and who is it that should stand aside?
What is pure and what is impure? What is eternal
and what transitory?
What is truth and what error? What is purity of mind?
What is feminine, what masculine, and neuter?
What things are gross and what subtle?
Who are 'those of the Veda' and what is a debased caste?
What is the path of rectitude? Point this out for us!
The basis for distinguishing between you and ourselves,
Please tell us, if indeed you are a knower of Brahman!

This leads Poṭṭan into a nearly exhaustive listing of all the ontological and psycho-physiological constituents of Sanskrit philosophical schools, including the gross and subtle elements, the sense faculties, humors of the body, etc. Such lists were used in Śaṅkara's Advaita Vedānta to analyze the person into its constituent parts, as an aid to self-realization. Questioning and rejecting each set of elements as not pertaining to the real self, the aspirant was to recognize his true nature as that indefinable entity which remained, the pure self-awareness that cannot be rejected.[6] That our Untouchable has this process in mind is evident from his next question, yet he redirects its application from analysis of self to analysis of other. For after breaking down body and mind into lists of their constituent elements, he asks, "What is it you apprehend here, that you have ordered me to withdraw into the distance?"

The implicit answer to this rhetorical question is that there is nothing of qualitative difference between Śaṅkara and the Untouchable which would render one pure and the other polluting. If we speak of the absolute self, it is admitted to be non-dual, pure awareness, shining the same in all beings. If we speak of individual selves as physically embodied, then such a view is itself constitutive of ignorance, and there can be no further basis for distinguishing between such erroneous perceptions of individuated selves as pure or impure, on the basis of these illusory bodies. Thus the Untouchable's follow-up question: "If the body (*vigraham*) is cut, can you tell any difference from the color of the blood between a Brahman and myself?"

Thus far, the argument has followed what could be viewed as the logical extension to social relationships of standard Vedāntic teachings. For after decomposing the body-mind complex into its constituents to discard it, it is of no further soteriological value to religious praxis. The word for "body" in the above quote, however, is *vigraham*, which also, and more ordinarily in Malayalam, refers to the consecrated image of a god. A case could be made that one of the hall-marks of Tantrism, as opposed to more orthodoxly Vedic, Brahminical religious practice, is a focal concern with the body as the locus and principal instrument of religious experience (Flood 2006). Thus, far from being denigrated or feared in its impurities, the body is cultivated as the vehicle for spiritual experiences. The "body" is indeed a living manifold of layered subjectivities, through which the aspirant ascends in more comprehensive fields of subsuming consciousness.[7] When we recall that the entire object of Teyyam is the invocation of a deity into the body of a dancer, in which he

[6] This rejection of the soteriological value of the "realities" (*tattva*s), in their various series, goes back to Śaṅkara's exemplar (or teacher's teacher, if one accepts the tradition), Gauḍapāda, in his commentarial *kārikā*s on the Māṇḍūkya-Upaniṣad, and Śaṅkara's comment on the same (Gauḍapāda 1936, II.26, pp. 130ff.); this is taken up as the spiritual method of negation (*pratiṣedha*) and rejectional meditation (*parisaṁkhyāna*) in Śaṅkara's own works, e.g. the Upadeśasāhasrī (Śaṅkarācārya 1979, II.3, pp. 251–54).

[7] See the penetrating analysis of this positively assimilative, yogic "conquest of the tattvas" (*tattva-jaya*) in Vasudeva's (2004) work on the Mālinīvijayottara Tantra, a root yogic text of Abhinavagupta's synthesis of the Trika school of Tantrism that becomes so prominent in later south India, as discussed below.

becomes its living icon, the affinities between Tantra and Teyyam become apparent. Under such a rationale, the fact that we are all similarly endowed with the human psycho-physical complex, shifts the interpretation from a Vedāntic declaration of bondage to a Tantric promise of realization. This is unmistakable in what immediately follows:

> That indestructible Lord who stands at the End-of-twelve (*dvādaśāntam*)
> As our teacher, who remains divorced from all desires, fetters, and defilements,
> Who, in you as in me, in the earth and the sky,
> Exists as One, bursting with radiance—
> Shooting from the Basal Center (*mūlādhāram*),
> It courses through the inner Channels (*nāḍi*),
> And passing up through the Six Centers (*-ādhāram*),
> Reaches that Cranial Lotus (*kapāla-padmam*) which stands above.
> Then crashing through that Rapturous Fissure (*suṣumna-randhram*),
> By that nectar which comes from the Disk of the Moon (*indu-maṇḍalam*),
> Comes drops (*bindu*) which reach the Basal Center—
> And when there is such a bliss,
> How can one have notions of duality?
> When you do not even know yourself, how can you have aversion to me?

The above description is that of the process of religious ecstasy as the Tantric schools map it out, tracing the course of the divine energy's movement through the human body's various channels (*nāḍi*s) and plexuses (*cakra*s) as it leaves the body to link up with the source of divine power, resulting in a kind of back-wash of "nectar" (*pīyūṣam*) through the body and mind, bathing them in bliss. Arcane as this sounds in translation, the terms and description are standard and immediately recognizable as Tantric mappings and soteriological practices concerning the subtle body. As such, these doctrines would also be rejected by most orthodox Vedāntins, as evidenced by the considerable polemical writings they expended against Tantrics. That each person's body provides direct access to the Lord (*īśan*) who is the unmediated teacher (*deśikan*), undermines the exclusive claims of Brahmans, both to deity, as embodied in their temples, (from which all lower, *avarṇa*, castes were excluded), and to salvational knowledge, as contained in their Vedas and Vedānta, from which non-Brahmans were similarly excluded.

In the lines which directly follow, our Untouchable asks how he can be reasonably expected to clear the way, for he bears a pot of liquor on his head, is carrying a child, and the way to either side is filled with thickets and thorns. From this plea for compassion, he immediately shifts topics to the metaphysical realm, calling attention to the Lord dwelling equally in all creation, then reverts again to asking why he should clear the way. Common conditions of human embodiment, social practices of discrimination based on material conditions, and spiritual insight are all explicitly linked in a direct inversion of Śaṅkara's earlier construal, and brought around to the ethical implications with a counter-imputation against the Brahmans. In specific application to the Kerala practice that precipitated this encounter he states, "It is merely from *pride in the body* (*dehābhimānam*), that you shout 'Ho! Ho!,' while we run, filled with terror."

He closes by pointing out to Śaṅkara the direct and necessary connection between one's spiritual development and his social perceptions, turning from Tantrism back to Vedānta's own claims to transcend bodily identification:

> For one who gives up the idea "I am the body,"
> There is no reason for harsh words towards me.
> For the Brahman who is freed of such delusion,
> There can be no cognizance of someone as "low-natured."

What follows after this is the denouement, precipitated in Śaṅkara's consciousness in response to hearing these truths, which redounds to his credit and proves his status as a sage "unequaled in the world." He recognizes that such words of wisdom could not come from one of the "debased" (*nīcan*); hence this must be the god Śiva. Śaṅkara falls at the Untouchable's feet and reels off lines of praise (*stuti)* to him in stock images of that god.

I believe the narrative framing of this caste-encounter through a Śaivite *deus ex machina*, is related to the context of Poṭṭan's unmistakable social message, in the changing context of his performance history. It should be borne in mind that this Teyyam is regularly performed in the households and shrines of the upper-castes and of Brahmans. Except in rare cases where Brahmans themselves were caught up in violent encounters or deaths, however, they do not seem to have been regularly implicated in generating Teyyams or their narratives. It does seem the case, though, that a number of upper-caste households had literati who composed some of the hymns of praise to the Teyyams that were incorporated into their liturgies. Given the overt assault on caste practices at the center of Poṭṭan's narrative, and in the context of an Untouchable performer voicing this as the embodiment of divinity before higher castes, I therefore believe the narrative frame of his being really Śiva, and merely posing as an Untouchable, was a later, Brahmanically inspired innovation. Indeed in the remainder of this paper, I will adduce textual evidence for this reworking, to be found in the linguistic and narrative stratigraphy of the rest of this deity's liturgical corpus.

***

I want to start, however, by briefly treating a still "higher" register of text, often performed within the Malayan corpus. This is a short text called the Manīṣāpañcakam ("The Five Credos") as a set of five verses in pure Sanskrit, with a couple framing lines, also in Sanskrit, that fits them into our story.

I have never heard of any Sanskrit poets among the Malayans, a caste traditionally unapproachable to Brahmans outside the Teyyam context, and their transcription of this Sanskrit text is often rather defective. So I believe we likely have here a little textlet of higher caste authorship incorporated into the performance. Indeed, the framing lines claim it to be the work of Śaṅkara himself, representing the verses of praise he composed for Śiva after this confrontation, when the latter relinquished his Untouchable disguise and revealed his true identity. Note the authorial effect this has: by comparison with the Teyyam, the wisdom-teachings are adroitly expropriated from the Caṇḍāla (as our Untouchable is called) and attributed to Śaṅkara instead. While I have researched these textual issues in some depth, I will here just summarize a complex skein of evidence I have been gathering.

As many Sanskritists will know, the rudiments of this narrative of Śaṅkara's confrontation with Śiva-in-disguise and his subsequent spiritual insights, are found in the longer narrative tradition of the variously dated Śaṅkara digvijaya, attributed to one Mādhava. This hagiography, "Śaṅkara's Conquest of the Quarters," as the title suggests, commemorates the sage's life and later travels through India and his vanquishing of philosophical and religious rivals *en route*, including prominent contests with low-caste Tantrics that end in their supernatural destruction. Later commentaries on both the Manīṣ āpañcakam (SUBRAHMANYA SASTRI, 1960) and on the hagiography (APTE 1891), try to relate these two texts integrally to each other, though there is nothing in the five verses themselves, other than the final line in the first two, which might suggest a thematic link. These lines laud the person of perfect non-dualist insight, claiming that "such a one … be he a Caṇḍāla or a Twice-born [Brahman], he is a Guru; this is my credo (*manīṣā*)". This is scant evidence that there was any original, organic link to our narrative frame or to Śaṅkara, and in fact a Sanskrit commentary points out that each of the first four verses are designed to exemplify one of the four "great utterances" (*mahāvākya*s) of Vedāntic teaching (BĀLAGOPĀLENDRAMUNI, 1960). So its naming as a discrete quintile (*-pañcakam*), the necessity of adding extra verses to link it thematically with this narrative, and its alternate rationale as exemplifying the *mahāvākya*s, all suggest the distinct likelihood of an independent existence from our narrative. Whether the episode in the hagiography was inspired by the stanzas, or the stanzas later prefixed with some lines of narrative to adapt them to the hagiography, is a matter I have not yet settled. What I am relatively certain of at this juncture is that the Śaṅkara hagiographic traditions of which this particular episode is a part were originally spawned around the creation of the Brahmanical monastic center (*maṭha*) of learning and worship at Sringeri, which dubiously claims it was founded by Śaṅkarācarya to perpetuate his lineage in south India (KULKE 1985). An evidently later rival tradition around a similar claim advanced for Kanchipuram in Tamil Nadu has generated its own raft of texts,[8] the rancor of competition between the two institutions breaking out in court cases from the mid-19th century down to recent times. This has made a partisan mess of the editing and scholarly assessment of the various hagiographies.[9] There is, however, no sober evidence that either of these corpora of traditions can claim any legitimate historical connection to Śaṅkarācārya, nor do the ties of any of this literature to either *maṭha* pre-date the 14th century; most of the texts are indeed much later productions.

As a matter of social history, I am more certain that the historical impetus for the celebration of Śaṅkara's "conquest" was the late medieval priestly colonization of a number of formerly rival sectarian sites, especially those of local non-Brahman and Tantric affiliation, by Smārta Brahmans under the dispensation of their putatively Śaṅkarite affiliation. It was this same movement that generated the proliferation of works of pseudo-Śaṅkara authorship, including numerous other tracts like the Manīṣāpañcakam, many *bhakti* hymns, and most improbably, many works of clearly late Tāntrika and Śākta affiliation. More specifically, this story of Śaṅkara's encounter with the Untouchable is found only in the hagiographic tradition of Mādhava,[10] a text almost certainly tied to Sringeri, which is only some seventy miles north of the performance area of Poṭṭan's Teyyam. For present purposes, this all builds towards the counter-argument I wish to entertain against the common assumption—given the apparent weight of the Śaṅkara legacy—that this Teyyam tradition is derivative of an originally Sanskritic one. The Sanskrit purchase on this narrative seems shaky and contrived even on its own

[8] Critical, to my thinking, in establishing the priority of Sringeri, is the fact that the oldest text establishing the claims of Kanchi, the Śrīśaṅkaravijaya of Anantānandagiri (Veezhinathan 1971), not only quotes a commentarial text of a Sringeri pontiff of the 14th century, at some length, but puts these words in the mouth of Śaṅkara himself (pp. 69, 160). This shows not only Anantānandagiri's later date, relative to this pontiff, but that he held this tradition in such esteem, and was so historically removed from it, that he conflated it with Śaṅkara's own works. I have confirmed these relations with the various works and colophons of this pontiff, Bhāratitīrtha, but the interested reader may see the brief note of Bader's (2000, p. 28, n. 21) and Sundaresan's treatment (2003, p. 118).

[9] For a rather complete survey of this literature and its political entanglements, but one that is itself overly generous to the partisan claims of Kanchi, see Bader 2000. For a similarly scholarly, critical overview, focused on the politics of this literature, and one that points to outright misrepresentation on the part of the Kanchi scholarship, see Sundaresan 2003. Clark (2004, Chapter 6) provides a rather thorough overview of Sringeri's and Kanchi's pontiffs related to the inscriptional and textual record, and confirms the lateness of claims to Śankarite affiliation.

[10] The episode is also treated in the Śaṅkarābhyudaya, a partial manuscript that Bader, following his Kanchi partisan, Antarkar, makes much of as a putative source of Mādhava's text, based on conjecture from negative evidence. I have examined the single, fragmentary manuscript in Telugu script in Mysore and suspect it may be a later copy of Mādhava from the Nāyaka period.

evidence, and is indeed rather troubling to its Brahmanical commentators, even in its euphemized form.[11] The further liturgies of Poṭṭan indeed testify against any originally Brahmanical connection, as I shall now argue.

***

Within the Malayan liturgical corpus is an alternative narrative of Poṭṭan, framed with a thematically very different set of hymns in a dialect that is Dravidian in vocabulary, rusticated in its local and low-caste idioms, and nearly devoid of Sanskrit influence. We should recall that though the Malayans are dominant in their performance claims to Poṭṭan, the protagonist himself is of the still lower Pulayan caste, a group whose status was so low that even their Teyyams were segregated from those of other castes. And indeed the Malayan performance begins with the Teyyam's charter, in which it is clearly stated that Poṭṭan's original shrines were all Pulayan, and that he only later passed to the higher castes through adoption by one Puḷiṅṅōttu Nāyar.

The hymns which set the scene for this version are all of paddy agriculture, in local idioms that code the fields, and bullocks, furrows, and crops, with mythical and mystical allusions to fertility and verdancy. An idealized version of the fields of Vāyanāṭu, an inland district of tribals and foresters, is projected as a kind of Pulayan Arcadia where crops magically flourish without pests or dangerous or irksome labors, and where the task-masters and overlords take no exactions of work, demand no deferential displays, and do not plunder the produce of Pulayan labor. This absence of encroaching social agents on this mythical landscape, however, anticipates their more realistic intrusion as upper-castemen in the following episode, in this text's parallel to the Śaṅkara encounter.

As Poṭṭan is introduced standing watch in the fields, a landlord or chieftain appears on the scene with his entourage of henchmen of various castes. When the Pulayan is abusively shouted at to clear the way, he responds with the plea that it is difficult for him, as he has a child on his hip, a pot on his head, and there is a thicket and thorns to either side. As an apparent buttressing of this plea for compassion, he then lists a series of parallel contrasts between the life-styles of his high-caste (probably Nāyar) antagonist and of Pulayans.

> While you, O Lord, go mounted on elephants,
> We go mounted on bullock's backs.
> While you daub on sandalwood paste,
> We daub ourselves with mud.
> You wear garlands strung of lotus blossoms,

---

[11] Since he ties the Manīṣapañcakam to the narrative of the hagiography, the Brahman commentator, Bālagopālendramuni, must defend against the possibility this seems to raise of an actual Untouchable functioning as a Guru (Subrahmanya Sastri 1960, p. 6).

We string ours with wildflowers and grass.
You wear the finest colored silks,
We wear cheap cloths with vegetable dyes.
You make offerings in your temples with bronze cauldrons,
We make them in our clearings with clay pots.
You go forth with sword and shield,
We go with our knife and paddy-stick.
Your domain is the chiefly realm,
Our domain is the irrigation ditch.

Items of dress, adornment, conveyance, occupational tools, and places and items of worship are all contrasted in similar lines. Many of these items were, in fact, specifically regulated in their use by the sumptuary rules of caste.

Rhetorically, these parallels function at two levels. First, and most overtly, they point out the disparities in goods and entitlements between the castes of the Nāyars and others and the Pulayans. We may read this, in connection with the lines preceding it, as an extended plea for sympathy and compassion. Simultaneously, however, they point out not just the substantive contrasts, but the functional equivalencies of each pair, as well, revealing the similarity of needs and aspirations, indeed the common humanity, which underlies these distinguishing markers of caste. Periodically, these pairs are therefore punctuated with the query,

Then how, O lord, can you revile our caste?
It's from pollution, isn't it, that you revile our caste?

This pollution referred to is that of "contact" (*tīṇṭal*) merely through atmospheric proximity, where the subtle stuff of bodies extended into invisible zones of penetration and vulnerability. This Brahmanical remoteness, though, is collapsed by Poṭṭan, making their contact intimate not just with reference to the shared needs and space of their respective bodies, but to their very insides and their common, human mortality:

If you are stabbed will there not be blood?
If we are stabbed, will there not be blood?
If you are cut will there not be blood?
If we are cut will there not be blood?
If you are set on fire, will you not feel the heat?
If we are set on fire will we not feel the heat?

With more than a little hint here of the potential for violence, the discourse shifts to actual material relations between them, and the role of the Pulayan's productive labor. Poṭṭan indeed targets the biological dependency of the Nāyars and others on this labor: "The very rice that you cook for your food, is the rice that we have threshed … Is it not the coconuts which we have broken, in which, Milord, you find the sweet water?" And consonant with the South

Asian linkages between feeding humans and feeding deities, the Pulayan can claim that from his humble labor, the very offerings which enable worship emanate:

> The bananas which we plant in manure,
> Is it not with these fruits that you make offerings to the gods?
> The tulasi (sacred basil) which we plant in manure,
> Is it not with this that you do pūja to the gods?

With this shift of context from the mundane towards the transcendent, the questioning refrain becomes not "Why do you revile our caste?", but, "What is the difference between us?" As the social register of caste is left behind, a personal dialogue is broached between one human being and another, on the ultimate truths of life, death, and salvation. The language becomes increasingly elliptical and pregnant with a sense of the mystical gravity of its portent.

> When thirty-three trees were planted,
> Three among them put forth shoots;
> A single flower blossomed from those,
> which I possess.

A local scholar's interpretation of this verse indeed seems convincing: the Vedic gods of Brahmanism, thirty-three in number, can be epitomized in the three principal manifestations of the Trimūrti (Brahma, Viṣṇu, and Śiva), whose essence is the non-dual consciousness which Poṭṭan, and indeed any human being may possess (Bālakṛṣṇan Nāyar 1979, p. 432, n. 13). Similarly humble, yet verbally effective analogies, depict life as a journey across a river. In an idiom familiar to English-speakers, we are all "in the same boat" of corporeal embodiment.

> That same boat in which you go,
> Is the same boat in which we go,
> So what difference is there between us, Milord?
> We paddle to push against the waters,
> You paddle to push against the waters,
> So what difference is there between us, Milord?

Ultimately, the journey of life, across its river, brings us to other shore, which stands, ambiguously, for either liberation in this life, or for death and what awaits us thereafter. In either case, this ultimate destination is envisioned as a temple; but unlike those under Brahmanical jurisdiction, which exclude and exploit Untouchables, this temple is under higher spiritual management, where Brahmans can claim no caste-advantage.

> When everyone goes to the temple of the Great One,
> You and I shall be made equal there,
> So why, Milord, do you revile my caste?

The final such text in this Malayan corpus I wish to examine occurs as a refrain during the performance, principally after there has been a change of costume to summon the incarnation of Poṭṭan's accompanying goddess, his wife, Pulacāmuṇḍi. It is an almost purely Dravidian vocabulary.

Long ago this precious hut,
By the carpenter was measured and hewn.
Four columns were arranged, one for each quarter,
With beams, too, on both sides.
And nine doors were set for this hut,
With different ones for coming and going.
The ridge-beam was laid and the rafters bound on,
And over the rafters, were tied ninety-six panels
of palm-fronds.
And over these fronds he bound on grass.
In the middle he crowned it with a suitable tile.
"With what shall I give this hut its sturdiness?"
He fixed fifty-one nails to make it firm.
"Whose is this hut to enter and sustain it?"
Twenty-one-thousand, six-hundred Cerumakkaḷ.
"When will this hut be demolished and fall?"
When it is, no one indeed can tell.

This remarkable piece, which goes on in this vein, in a literally homely metaphor, is a description of the body and its constituents, a reminder of the common mortality of all embodied beings. In pure country dialect it mirrors closely the sentiments of our first piece directed to Śaṅkara.

The hut is the body itself, fashioned by the carpenter who is deity. It is significant that the word used for this hut (*cāḷa*) specifies by its vocabulary that the body is an Untouchable's dwelling. The message is clearly that in the raw materials of our corporeality and consciousness, the noble is no different from the Pulayan. The columns and beams are the limbs, and the nine doors, the body's orifices, through which the "coming and going" of breathing and the other bodily functions operate. The ridge-beam is the spine and the rafters the ribs. This skeletal hut is thatched with the ninety-six panels, which are equivalent to the elements or principles of reality (the *tattvas*) of classical Indian philosophy.

The inclusion of these principles in the domain of Untouchable knowledge is quite remarkable, for they comprise lists of all the standard ontological elements of Sanskritic speculative thought. The lists include the gross and subtle elements, the constituents of the body, mind, the sense faculties and objective qualities of apprehension, the "vital airs" (*prāṇas*, which are manipulated in certain yogic-tantric techniques of realization), the psychic centers through which these are believed to operate, and a number of other such standardized sub-lists to which we will return.

After these psycho-physical constituents were put on the frame, it was covered with hair (grass) and atop the whole, at the peak, went the head (here, a potsherd or tile). There is a play on words here, (reflecting a more pervasive metaphorical model in Dravidian, as we will see), where the word *ōṭu* can mean skull as well as potsherds or clay roofing tiles.

The "fifty-one nails" which make the hut or body firm are the letters of the Sanskrit/Malayalam script. While this partly confirms the implications of the above reference to the *tattva*s regarding the transmission of Sanskritized knowledge, largely mediated through Malayalam, among at least a few of the lowest castes, we should not assume a unilineal language ideology of learning exemplified by written Sanskrit. Among the Pulayans, this particular knowledge seems to have been restricted to just a few of their gurus (*gurukkaḷ*), who indeed became divinized culture heroes, worshipped in the context of Teyyam. One is even celebrated as having operated a *kaḷari*, or gymnasium, on the model of the martial Nāyars, where the various branches of the martial and magical arts were taught. Such knowledge, among the higher of the Untouchable castes, was not so unusual, for they regularly possessed palm-leaf manuscripts, with at least a few members of each lineage who could read them and transmit the knowledge across the generations. But there were other channels of knowledge, indigenous and oral, in which the "letter," as the phonematic power of language and learning, was not restricted to Sanskrit and its written media. We will return to some evidence of this, later.

Finally, the number twenty-one-thousand and six-hundred refers to the number of breaths which a human being draws per day, which inhabit and sustain the body. In the tantric-yoga complex, physical respiration merges with its subtle counterparts, the various *prāṇa*s or "vital airs" (*uyir*). It is the techniques of manipulating this force within the psycho-physical complex which bestows yogic and magical powers, or, on a more elevated plane, spiritual insight. These very breaths which sustain and inhabit the body are said to be Ceṛumakkaḷ (literally, the "Little people"), a synonym for Pulayans. We have seen that the body itself is said to be a Pulayan's hut, and that it is the crops produced by Pulayans which feed it. That the very vitalizing breaths of metabolism are also toiling Pulayans completes this set of images to deliver the message that the high castes are not merely like the low, analogically, but that they are constitutionally and substantially the same. The final warning, that the hut may be demolished at any time, like the final summons to the Great One's temple, reminds the listener of his ultimate mortality, before which he is as helpless as the weakest member of society.

***

The original publishing of part of Poṭṭan's liturgical corpus made reference to songs of "Pulayans and other low communities" (Bālakṛṣṇan Nāyar 1979, p. 429), and segregated some of the verses on the basis of this attribution.

This selection was something of an editorial hodge-podge, however, clearly based primarily on the main public performing caste of the Malayan's version of the songs which wove pieces in a rustic folk-Malayalam together with the Sanskritized pieces that conveyed the Śaṅkara story. Indeed the character of the Malayan performance is very much one of pastiche, ranging as we have seen, from the Sanskrit of the Manīṣāpañcakam, through Sanskritized registers of Malayalam, into the most rusticated folk-idiom. With the more recent publication of the complete Pulayan version (VIṢṆUNAMPŪTIRI 1996, pp. 66–73), it now becomes possible to compare the two corpora, however, and both of these with a third, discretely related text, in order to treat more completely the processes by which these bodies of knowledge historically articulated.

Most strikingly, the Pulayan version indeed has no reference to Śaṅkara, or even clear reference to any Brahman.[12] Indeed, the antagonists in the Pulayan version of Poṭṭan appear in his fields as a group of dominant castemen, especially the martial and managerial castes, headed by the Nāyars, that the Pulayans would have had more direct contact with. Furthermore, the opening lines give the lineages of the Pulayan shrines and the origins of Poṭṭan in their community of worship, leaving no doubt that the Malayans have adopted Poṭ ṭan from this caste-community, and that it was likely through this adoption that the local liturgy was articulated into a Śaṅkara narrative, with an upgrading of the whole caste dynamic. It seems quite plausible that the Manīṣāpañcakam may have been provided with its narrative attribution to Śaṅkara in the context of this upgrade by some local, higher-caste Sanskrit scholar associated with Teyyam shrines, and eventually taken into the regional ambit of Brahmans associated with Sringeri, who incorporated this, along with many other such local legends into the Śaṅkara hagiography.[13]

In any case, the Pulayan liturgy is entirely the story of a paddy-laborer and watchman, beset upon by a pentad of upper-castemen, against whom he then delivered substantially the same declamation on the spiritual and moral perniciousness of caste as the lines that made their way into the Malayan liturgy. Furthermore, the entire analogy to the human body, built by God as a master

[12] It is often supposed, because of the assumption that the Śaṅkara narrative underlies Poṭṭan, that the addressive form, *Covvar*, means "Brahman" when these verses are borrowed into the higher-caste version of the Teyyam. In fact, I learned from performers that in their elaborated, archaic vocabulary of caste-keyed deference, the term *Covvar* is used of Nāyar and other dominant castes, and not of Brahmans.

[13] Candēra simply reports as a fact that one Kūrmāra Eluttacchan (the latter being a title for a learned Śūdra, or rarely, Untouchable teacher) was the composer of Poṭṭan's songs, but he presents no evidence for this. Being untutored, this Eluttacchan is said to have gained spontaneous learning through the blessing of a holy man (Candēra 1968, pp. 155f.).

carpenter is prominent, including the reference to the ninety-six elements, the fifty-one phonemes of the Sanskrit syllabary, and most dramatically at its close, the invocation of the 21,600 life-breaths, as the Pulayans who inhabit and innervate the very bodies of the high-caste protagonists. Significantly, the verb used for this inhabitation (*pularuka*) means both to illumine and to enliven.

The narrative of the encounter ends elliptically with the chief protagonist, a "noble" (*Covvar*), saying he did not know who Poṭṭan was, and then being instructed by the Pulayan to institute a Teyyam in that same series of costumes which he has worn. The plural use of "costumes" doubtless refers to the fact that Poṭṭan appears with his wife and child, and that the performance includes a change of costume by the same dancer, to successively render all three members of the Pulayan family, Pula-Poṭṭan, Pula-cāmuṇḍi, and Pula-mārutan, as separate incarnations. In the Pulayan liturgy, the Teyyam is further established, however, through the summoning of Poṭṭan's maternal uncle (*māman*), who is instructed whom to summon to institute the Teyyam, and various other social principals are also invoked and listed as a kind of charter for Poṭṭan's original worship.

I believe this information from the Pulayan liturgy allows me to hazard further interpretation of the cult's founding, based on similar patterns in other Teyyams. In a realistic rendering of any such encounter in medieval Kerala, it is difficult to imagine the Pulayan would not have been killed for his defiance in such circumstances, and I was indeed told in the village where the Malayan version of the Teyyam was founded, that this was the case. Typically, in other such cases where a Teyyam results from a murdered victim, his divinely empowered spirit returns, to force recognition of his divinity by visiting calamity on his oppressors and exacting tribute through worship. This indeed constitutes recognition of a new, post-mortem identity, as a god, and is often announced as such by the contrite worshipper. I think this may well be the portent behind the noble's plea that he did not know who Poṭṭan was, and his receiving subsequent directions for instituting his worship as a god. Furthermore, such worship is often also instituted through close family members of the deceased, (such as cousins and maternal uncles), who become initially possessed by the recent dead. The Teyyam then results from the subsequent institutionalization of this possession, through appointment of rites and dancers under the oracular instructions delivered through the possessed relatives. This is exactly what seems to happen here, and this is how I would interpret Poṭṭan summoning his own uncle to institute his worship. This makes no sense if, as in the Sanskritized Malayan version, Poṭṭan was originally conceived of as Śiva spontaneously appearing in Untouchable garb to establish his own worship; he would then clearly have no earthly Pulayan relatives. Finally, the suggestion of violence that is a usual part of this paradigm finds confirmation at the liturgy's close, with pleas that Pulayan children not be killed by nobles for various petty infractions and a plea to Poṭṭan himself to intercede in saving them in exchange for items of worship. In my reading, this is because Poṭṭan himself is the archetype of such victimization, now deified.

***

It turns out that the gnostic doctrines of the body that Poṭṭan teaches are rendered in a final body of knowledge that has an indirect, but significant, connection with this Teyyam. These Untouchable teachings, however, with the eponymous designation of their teacher, were circulated in other performative and possession arts in Kerala, as well, and the doctrines of the body and consciousness themselves go back to earlier Dravidian contributions to Tantric lore, as I shall show. The particular folk-text to which I refer has been published from an unattributed source, as an "ancient song" that is drawn upon in a number of folk-genres associated with non-Brahman festivals of worship in different parts of Kerala. The text is published as the Vaḷḷōkavi, the "poem of Vaḷḷōn"(VIṢṆUNAMPŪTIRI 1996, pp. 74–79). Though I know of no caste or community currently going by that name, the great lexicographer GUNDERT (1982) gives this full form, Vaḷḷuvan as "a priest of the Parayas, a low caste sage Vaḷḷuvaccāttan, Vaḷḷōn, who wrote the Vaḷḷuvacintu" (GUNDERT 1982, p. 924). Parayas (whence the English Pariah) were commensurate with Pulayas as the lowest of the agrestic slave castes, and Gundert's information leads to some other connections with this text, and with Poṭṭan. First, the Vaḷḷuvacintu is quite likely our very Vaḷḷōkavi, or a close congener. Secondly, the link with the old Dravidian personal name, Cāttan, recalls Poṭṭan's membership (in his Malayan version of the performance) in the pantheon of five *mantra-mūrti*s, or godlings of sorcery based originally at Kāḷakāṭṭu illam, the manor and shrine of the chief Brahman *tantri* (priestly authority) and *mantravādi* (sorcerer) of northern Kerala. The chief god of this pentad of deities is Kuṭṭiccāttan (*kuṭṭi* simply meaning child), and his liturgy relates his birth in a Paraya hut (the same word, *cāḷa*, as used of Pulayas) to Śiva and Pārvatī in their incarnations (*avatāram*) as a Vaḷḷōn and his Vaḷḷuvatti wife. The liturgy then tells of his adoption by this Kāḷakāṭṭu Brahman, and how though raised in the Brahman manor, he exhibits a pattern of disturbing and escalating sociopathic behaviors. Events come to an intolerable crisis, and his adoptive father is finally forced to kill him. This errant "child," however, returns as a cackling, murderous, vengeful spirit, and once its proves otherwise uncontrollable, is established in the manor as a Teyyam deity. It is quite clear that the quasi-demonic Kuṭ ṭiccāttan was a powerful Tantric sorcerer, and that many of his murders, his blood-lust, and sacremental consumption of meat and alcohol are driven by his Tantric rites. The struggles of the Kāḷakāṭṭu Brahman with him are thus reminiscent of those of Śaṅkara with similarly craven, low-caste Tantrics in his hagiographies. Here, however, the Tantric literally has the last laugh, when the cackling spirit of Kuṭṭiccāttan undergoes a post-mortem elevation into a Teyyam, following his would-be destruction at Brahman hands. If there were any doubt about the Tantric ideology of this complex, Kuṭṭiccāttan's companion among the five *mantra-mūrti* Teyyams is Bhairavan, the chief god of the leftist Śaiva Tantrics throughout India. While I have written at length of these gods elsewhere, and their local assimilation and relations in the Teyyam pantheon (Freeman, 2008), the point I wish to underscore here is that the company Poṭṭan keeps in his upward elevation from a Pulayan to Malayan performance, in the context of a fraught and sanguine "Brahmanization," is unambiguously Tantric in its religious validation. Further, and despite the trend of most Sanskrit scholarship on Tantra to depict it as primarily driven by a Brahmanical dynamic, I believe this points up the important role that further regional language scholarship, particularly in the Dravidian south, will bring to light on the varied social strata caught up in these histories.[14]

In terms of the Vaḷḷōkavi itself, the song seems deliberately coded for obscurity, but in this case the meanings are not so occluded that we cannot grasp the overall claim for a hidden, liberating gnosis, inherent in the person and life-world of the Untouchable. In terms of our earlier texts, one can immediately see that many lines and locutions, as well as distinctive themes and specific treatment of the body, gnosis, the life-world of Pulayan labor, and caste relations, are taken up into the Pulayan, and Malayan liturgies of Poṭṭan from this source. The idioms are both heavily agricultural, but also come in cryptic, enumerating sequences. Both of these are reflective of older Dravidian and non-Brahman gnostic codings such as we find in the literature of the Tamil *Cittar* (< Siddhas), an eclectic body of yogic works that goes back to its foundational work in Tamil, the Tirumantiram. From there similar idioms are traceable even further back, into the Tamil *bhakti* canon of the Śaiva Nāyanmārs. Finally, we may note that one of the earliest formulary gnostic texts in Tamil, the Tirukkuraḷ, is traditionally assigned to the sage Tiruvaḷḷuvar, "the sacred Vaḷḷuvan."

Our Vaḷḷōkavi, in any case, begins with exactly the image of the body as Untouchable hut (*cāḷa*) that features in the Teyyam liturgies, similarly fashioned by the divine, master carpenter. He further states that it is a sacred temple (*kōvil*), which, in the context of Kerala temples being archetypically

[14] I would note, for instance, how even Alexis Sanderson, who has brought us enormous gains in knowledge of the predominantly Brahmanical Sanskrit corpus of Śaiva Tantrism, has recently made exciting connections and discoveries on the early history of a complex of strange, gestural gnosis (*chummā*s) in the Krama school, from works in Old Kashmiri (Sanderson 2007, pp. 333f.). He has further been led to some intriguing connections with Dravidian etyma (Sanderson 2007, pp. 283f., n. 172) on these, which converge with some of my own recent findings on the Tamil/Malayalam side.

the epicenters of Brahmanical norms of purity, was surely provocative. And as before, this body-hut has its 21,600 agrestic slaves (*Ceṟumakkaḷ*) to enter, exit, and maintain it, (in a clear parallel to the three functions of the great gods of Hinduism, to create, maintain, and destroy the material universe). As the life's energy (*uyir*), however, this enumerated supply of daily breaths is inexhaustible, pointing beyond mere bodily metabolism to the infinite life of consciousness: "If you draw it in to fill it, it will never be full; if you take it and expel it, it will never empty." That the nature of this breath merges into supramundane consciousness is clear from the immediate role of Vaḷḷōn as the imparter of gnostic knowledge of this body in the next lines, for he is the master (*nāthan*) of the mystic, mantric syllable *oṁ*, and summons the soul to a higher knowledge imparted in secret illumination.

In a furrow ploughed by Ōṁkāra-nāthan,
In secret-light sown, the seed has sprouted;
At a time unknown, there to the temple of bliss
For a difficult work he calls me,
Ōṁkāra-Vaḷḷōn, to study the letter.

The word for seed in the image also means semen and lineage, implying both the convergence of sexual, metabolic, and mental energy in Tantrism, as well as the propagation of knowledge from Guru to student on the model of biological reproduction, passed in secret-light through the formation of Tantric lineages.[15] The temple of bliss is the mind-body complex, and the letter is both the discursive content of the teaching, as well as its sonic embodiment in mantras, which also picks up on a homonymous meaning of "seed" as "knowledge." A parallel meaning, clearly implicated from similar lines elsewhere that play off similar images, also suggests an alternate scenario of liberation through death. This is our final summons, a difficult work that delivers us to God's temple of bliss, and is the reading of our fate, in the idiom of writing.

In any case, the immediately following lines make it clear that this knowledge is bodily rooted for,

The tendrils are three, for the base-root,
There are tendrils spread all through the base,
For the tuber of knowledge, the tendrils are four,
There are tendrils spread all through the knowledge.

---

[15] The word *oḷivu* in Malayalam is a homonym for both "secret" and "light." I was tempted to chose one over the other, but I believe the ambiguity is deliberate on the model of verses from the Tirumantiram, e.g. vs. 2765 (Tirumūlar 1991, p. 426) which deliberately and unambiguously exploit both meanings; hence I have rendered the single word, *oḷivil*, as a somewhat oxymoronic compound.

The reference here is to the basal *cakra* (*mūlādhāra*),[16] in the perineal area of the subtle-body in Tantric teaching, which has three main channels or arteries leading from it, the central of which conducts the body's *śakti* to the deity in or above the head where liberating bliss occurs. There are indeed later verses which describe Vaḷḷōn's female counterpart, his *śakti*, Ōṁkāra-Vaḷḷōtti seeking him out along this "basal highway" (*aṭi-peruvaḻi*) to join him. The body's main metabolic energies radiate through other channels spreading from this center. The allusion to the archetype of knowledge, the four Vedas, follows, but it too is literally rooted in this bodily form, and the bodily tendrils of its Tantric revelation seem to enmesh the former's claims to supremacy. Indeed the lines immediately following repeat those on the Vedic pantheon cited by Poṭṭan, above, wherein the thirty-three Vedic gods are reduced to the single flower of non-dual consciousness, which the true adept possesses (but here Vaḷḷōn further teaches one should adorn one's head with this blossom and go forth with it into the world). There are many similar allusions, such as to the subtle body, the senses, the subtle elements, etc., mapped into agriculture, herding, and other images, only some of which I've decoded, and some of which are polyvalently obscure. But the portent of all these individually and collectively is clear,—that there is an esoteric knowledge, clearly more-than-the-body, whose access point is the mundane body and mind we all possess, and which has been transmitted as a specifically Untouchable gnosis. Near the end of the piece we again revert to the image of the body as a hut, covered in the ninety-six elements of its thatch.

I wish to close the discussion of this body of knowledge with a cursory exploration of the cultural-historical roots of these enumerations and images of bodily esoteric knowledge, going back to earlier textual sources. This knowledge, as I noted earlier, draws on two cultural complexes, one reaching into the regional, Dravidian past, and one into the Sanskrit strata of Tantrism. The regional complex both drew on Tantric sources, but no doubt also contributed to them. The Malayan performers have listings of the ninety-six elements which Poṭṭan invokes, that they have preserved in memory and reduced to writing at present in their notebooks. This includes the listings of gross and subtle physical elements, sense faculties, bodily humors and physical substances, as well as cognitive faculties, states of consciousness, circuits of divine beings, and overlords in the body. This list is itself broken down into sub-sets, and this is one of the commonest structuring devices for presenting esoteric, doctrinal teachings one encounters in Dravidian religious literatures, both classical and folk.

[16] This is ingeniously glossed into Malayalam, using the Dravidian word for root or tuber, *kilaṅṅu*, as equivalent to one meaning of the Sanskrit *mūlam*, compounded with the latter word in the meaning of "base" giving the notion of a kind of root or bulb at the base of the body, which is how the *mūlādhāra* is envisioned.

The old Tamil text which, I am convinced, bears the closest connection to the tantric-yoga milieu of our Poṭṭan and the Vaḷḷōkavi, the aforementioned Tirumantiram, begins (vs. 1)[17]:

> The one, he himself, the two, his sweet grace,
> In the three he stood, the four he conceived,
> The five he conquered, the six he pervaded,
> The seven realms he entered,
> And remaining himself, conceived the eight.

The multiple possible meanings for these enumerations (on which modern commentators have expended much ingenuity) need not detain us here. My point in the present context is that such enumerations abound in this text, and especially in application to a bodily gnosis. Parts of the text's teachings may date from as early as the 8th century, but many elements are clearly no earlier than the 11th or 12th centuries.[18] The text is a doctrinal amalgam of the southern Śaiva-siddhānta Tantrism with elements of the headier, leftist Śaiva and Śākta Tantrism, harnessed to the practice of a hybrid yoga, but all of this rendered into the idioms of a rusticated, elliptical Tamil. All of the images we have encountered of the body and the spiritual path in Kerala abound in the Tirumantiram, including that of the body as simultaneously humble thatched hut, and divine temple. Many models of the enumerated elements of metabolic energies as channeled towards liberation are found as well, and many of the rustic images of growing crops and herding cattle as analogies to controlling the breaths, mental energies and senses, which occur in Poṭṭan and Vaḷḷōkavi, are also found in the Tirumantiram, often even in the same linguistic idioms.

Finally, the reference to what, in Sanskrit, are the *tattvas*, the "elements" of the body, or levels of constituent "realities" or "essences," find various enumerations, according to different schools of reckoning, but culminating in exactly the highest, stock number of ninety-six, which our Kerala texts and modern performers take as authoritative. The other standard numbers of the Sāṁkhya school's twenty-four *tattvas*, and the Śaivas' thirty-six are also

---

[17] For quotes from this text, I cite the most commonly available translation and follow the Tamil text and its numbering there, but supply my own translations (TIRUMŪLAR, 1991, p.3). Coincidentally, I now find GOODALL (1998, p. 174, n. 41) has cited the same verse of this text as an instance of "ornamental numbering" for comparison with a Sanskrit text, but perhaps without full cognizance of this as a pervasive feature of Dravidian literatures across many genres.

[18] I follow Goodall (1998, pp. xxxiv–xxxix) in his identification of many later Śaiva doctrines for the later strata of this text, but I think some strata may be earlier, given their conformity to the earlier Nāyanmar idioms and locutions, and the heterogenous nature of the composition.

common in the Tirumantiram, but ninety-six seems to have been the number settled on as incorporating these earlier strata compounded with other lists of elements such as the *dhātus* (gross physical fluids and constituents of the body). The centrality of the Śaivas' segregated thirty-six "realities" (and relatively diminished unimportance of the others) is suggested by a stock enumeration, "thirty and thirty and thirty-six." This is a phrasing which indeed goes back to Appar, one of the foundational Śaiva *bhakti* poets of Tamil Nadu (probably of the 7th or 8th century), but which he also uses uncompounded, simply as ninety-six.[19] Furthermore, the word he commonly uses for body (*kurampai*) is actually the word for a hut, where the *tattvas* are also clearly a kind of "thatch" exactly as with Poṭṭan. Other related words for this stratum of Tamil (such as *kūrai*), derive from the same root-metaphor of the body-as-thatched hut, filled with wind (*vaḷi*) or life's breath (*uyir*). In other images the ninety-six are viewed, along with "the five" (senses) as inhabiting the hut and demanding sustenance.[20] Liberation is the way the Lord shows for exiting the hut, and while we have here, as with some verses from Poṭṭan, the notion of salvation in death, we must also recognize a prominent notion of *liberation in the body*, that we find with the more Tantrically inclined Tirumantiram (vs. 2550):

> The one who's mixed into the body,
> The ruler of the body's domain,
> The Lord who pervades the body, within;
> Those who search about for him in the land,
> Don't comprehend that he's based in the body.

The specifics of the other enumeration, the 21,600 breaths, which, we recall, is represented in our Kerala texts by the same number of Untouchables who innervate the body, has a clearer lineage in the opposite textual direction, in the Tantric Śaivism that Abhinavagupta made a subcontinental phenomenon from his base in Kashmir. I have found references teaching this enumeration of breaths in the Tantrasadbhāva (Dyczkowski, 2006, vs. 24.48–50) and Vijñānabhairava (Singh 1979, vs. 155–56, pp. 143ff.), works of the Trika school of leftist tantrism to which Abhinavagupta belonged. The Vijñānabhairava verses were cited and commented on by Abhinava's chief disciple and expositor, Kṣemarāja (11th century) in his own commentary on the Śivasūtras (Vasugupta 1978, III.27, pp. 189ff.), a synthetic exposition of the school's

[19] The apparent antiquity of this enumeration in Tamil is intriguing, and I have found this in Sanskrit only in the so-called Yoga Upanishads (Srinivasa Ayyangar 1952) (e.g. Varāhopanishad, p. 399), which seem to be late medieval productions, and exclusively south Indian.

[20] These observations are taken from the indices and text of the Tēvāram in Chevillard/Sarma (2007).

various yogas. Most interestingly, this latter commentary was given a summary exposition by one Varadarāja, a south Indian who indeed treats the teaching of these precisely enumerated breaths in his text (Varadarāja 1925, p. 34). Varadarāja was a disciple of Madhurāja, an ascetic based at Madurai in Tamil Nadu whose works specialize in praising Abhinavagupta's lineage. The major works of Abhinava's school, and the celebration of the lineage's southern extension by this Madhurāja, are in fact found in Kerala in Malayalam script, strongly suggesting the presence and activities of this lineage there.

The content of the teaching of the 21,600 breaths bears further relation to our Kerala folk-texts, since this is not merely reported as some oddity of folk-biology, but intended as a meditative technique.[21] The number is that of the times we respire each day, with the out-breath making the sound, "sa" and the in-breath the sound "ha," forming the mantra "haṁsa" associated both with non-dualist awareness of the self as God (the inversion of "so'ahaṁ", "I am He"), and with a Tantric doctrine of these as male and female syllables mating as Śiva and Śakti, in the body. The mantra is incessant and metabolically automated, making of our bodies a continual machine of prayer (*japa*), which, when one is aware of it, bestows the highest non-dual consciousness as the very life-system of the body. These teachings thus have an evident Kashmir-to-Madurai textual propagation, with clear attestation of the school's extension into Kerala. What is remarkable is that we now have proof that some of the traditionally lowest castes of Kerala, through their gnostic gurus, had assimilated these teachings into folk Malayalam, and continue to embody them today in performance.

The performative evidence of this stratum of Untouchable yogis actually comes mid-way through Poṭṭan's performance. The dancer removes his mask, sits before it, his paddy-knife and paddy-tool, and an array of lit offerings, and he then performs an abbreviated but very solemn Tantric *pūjā* in a meditative pose (Figure 5). Called the *mukha-pūja*, "worship of the face," he ministers to the image of the god that he himself has become, before donning the mask again, to actively resume the god's persona.

***

With this return to the performative frame, I wish to remind the reader that these textual strata eventuate in the liturgies of the present, which are literally embodied not simply through rote memorization of content, but through the

[21] While this enumeration of the breaths itself occurs in probably earlier Śaivasiddhānta texts, (such as the Sārdhatriśikakālottara and Kiraṇāgama), it seems not to have been the basis for the same śākta elaboration into the meditative technique which it finds in Abhinavagupta's legacy, and it is this latter which seems to trace here more readily into the Kerala tradition.

Figure 5: Poṭṭan performing the Tantric yogic rite known as mukha-pūja, "worship of the face."

lived ideology of possession—of today's Malayans and Pulayans actually becoming Poṭṭan. They speak in his voice, as their ancestors did, and they will continue to do so, I suspect, long after we are all dead and gone. This brings us finally, by way of conclusion, to the voice in the body, and the link from there to consciousness, for the two are inseparably bound up with each other (Hanks 1996; Lee 1997).

As I have worked out in a series of lectures and analyses, most as yet unpublished, the liturgies of Teyyam are framed by invocatory genres that involve a complex set of indexical mappings in ritual speech between the body of the performer, physical objects in the shrine, and the bodies of textual knowledge. While these mappings are too complex to elaborate here, we can summarily note that their semiotic modes entail the following: relatively presupposing reliance of speech on objects, bodies, or bodily constituents actually present; relatively creative projections of speech onto these, so as to change or resignify their constitution; some entirely creative projections onto empirically non-present objects, spaces, or bodily constituents; and finally, cross-mappings that combine these in various ways.[22] When we add to this the

[22] The analytic of indexicality having two relational modes to context, one relatively presupposing and the other relatively creative, has been developed in many of Silverstein's writings, e.g. (Silverstein 1993, pp. 36ff.)

insight that all of these are issued in speech, from out of the bodily matrix as a performative, kinetic and gestural center, we can begin to appreciate just how complexly constitutive the indexical properties of speech are, in the context of possession (cf. HANKS 1990).

This "context," however, is not something over and against the "text," for the very textuality of the textual corpora is the achievement of cohesion through similarly indexical, but "co-textual," or intra-textual ties (HALLIDAY/HASAN 1976; SILVERSTEIN 1993). In structural terms, these invocatory genres thus project both outwardly, into the extra-textual world of performance, and inwardly, into the contents of the narratives. But both of these reflexes are actually embodied in the voice of the performer as he retrieves them from his consciousness, and utters them in the speech of the ritual context. He therefore enacts a kind of inner dialogue with himself, his surroundings, and his narrative, embodying the contents of a semiotically mediated consciousness that leads him, by stages, into that of the divine protagonist he becomes. This textualized consciousness, of course, is not his own invention. It is the consciousness of ancestral gods, learned from his family gurus, and backed by the authority of the legacy that has become his by birth, and through years of practice.

There comes a phase in the performance, however, when he leaves the text, and speaks as the god himself, in interaction with his worshipers. This is the ratification that the divine consciousness, which his ancestors have passed on to him, lives demonstrably within his body, and in the present. In such a state, I have seen and heard "Poṭṭan" argue, as the god, with his higher caste patron, that he is the source and basis of his patron's wealth and power. On this occasion, the patron had to back down and cede the dancer a greater share of the shrine offerings than he thought was the performer's due. A bit of reflection on such cases and their negotiation makes it evident how complex the mediation is between this essentially medieval body of knowledge that constitutes the textually conditioned consciousness of the god, and its projection out through the present circumstances of a contemporary performer in a present-day shrine. What this, and the whole verbal reproduction of this knowledge points to, going forward as it were, is that there must also be a corresponding temporal depth and historical dimension that conditions and informs these textual corpora going back in time.

It is this historical dimension, necessarily caught up in the present case with the social dimensions of caste and its religious valorization, that I have tried to document here, in the narrative of just one Teyyam deity, out of hundreds. I have also tried to show its linkages into a more general religious ideology of locally wrought Tantrism, a body of knowledge that was at once a knowledge of the body, as the only fleeting hold that the chronically disempowered could claim over their spiritual lives. This knowledge of the body, however, revealed the body to ultimately consist of consciousness itself, the consciousness of god. This knowledge asserted that when corporeality could express the very embodiment of conscious illumination, the bodies of Untouchables, as themselves bodies of knowledge, were positively *untouchable* to the physical and social degradation of caste. This knowledge has been promulgated through the voice of the god they call, with a deliberate sense of irony, Poṭṭan, the "Deaf-mute".

References

Apte, M. C. (Ed.) (1891): Śrīmacchaṅkaradigvijaya by Vidyāraṇya: With the Diṇḍimā of Dhanapatisūri and the Advaitarājyalaks̩mī. – Pune. (Ānandās'rama Sanskrit Series Vol. 22)

Bader, J. (2000): Conquest of the Four Quarters: Traditional Accounts of the Life of Śaṅkara. – New Delhi.

Bālagopālendramuni (Ed.) (1960): Madhumañjarī (ṭīkā on Manīṣāpañcakam). – Kumbakonam.

Bālakṛṣṇan Nāyar, C. T. (Ed.) (1979): Kēraḷabhāṣāgānaṅṅaḷ: Nāṭanpāṭṭukaḷ. – Trichur.

Candēra, C. M. S. (1968): Kaḷiyāṭṭam: Paṭhanavum Pāṭṭukaḷum. – Kottayam.

Clark, M. (2006): The Daśanāmī-Saṃnyāsīs: The Integration of Ascetic Lineages into an Order. – Leiden.

Chevillard, J-L./Sarma, S. A. S. (Eds.) (2007): Digital Tēvāram. – Pondicherry.

Dyczkowski, M. S. G. (Ed.). (2006): Tantrasadbhāva. – Muktabodha Indological Research Inst. Digital Library, Cat. No. M10011 from NGMCP: A 188/22; A 44/1; and A 44/2: URL: http://muktalib5.org/digital_library.htm – Download from 22.4.2009.

Flood, G. D. (2006): The Tantric Body: The Secret Tradition of Hindu Religion. – London/ New York.

Freeman, J. R. (1991): Purity and Violence: Sacred Power in the Teyyam Worship of Malabar. – Philadelphia. (Unpublished PhD Thesis, University of Pennsylvania)

Freeman, J. R. (1993): Performing Possession: Ritual and Consciousness in the Teyyam Complex of Malabar. In: Brückner, H./ Lutze, L./Malik, A. (Eds.): Flags of Fame: Studies in South Asian Folk Culture. – New Delhi, pp. 109–138.

Freeman, J. R. (1998): Formalized Possession among the Tantris and Teyyams of Malabar. In: South Asia Research, Vol. 18, No. 1, pp. 73–98.

Freeman, J. R. (1999): Dynamics of the Person in the Worship and Sorcery of Malabar. In: Assayag, J./Tarabout, G. (Eds.): Possession in South Asia: Speech, Body, Territory. – Paris, pp. 149–181. (Special Issue of Purushartha 21)

Freeman, J. R. (2003): The Teyyam Tradition of Kerala. In: Flood, G. (Ed.): A Companion to Hinduism. – Oxford, pp. 306–326.

Freeman, J. R. (2008): Shifting Forms of the Wandering Yogi: The Teyyam of Bhairavan. In: Shulman, D./Thiagarajan, D. (Eds.): Masked Ritual and Performance in South India. – Ann Arbor, pp. 147–184.

Gauḍapāda. (1936): Māṇḍūkyopahishad with Gaudapāda's Kārikā and Śankara's Commentary. – Transl. by Swami Nikhilananda. – Mysore.

Goodall, D. (Ed./Trans.) (1998): Bhaṭṭa Rāmakaṇṭha's Commentary on the Kiraṇatantra. Vol. I: Chapters 1–6. – Pondicherry. (Publications of Indology Department Vol. 86.1).

Gundert, H. (1982): A Malyalam and English Dictionary. – 1st edition 1872 – New Delhi.

Halliday, M. A. K./ Hasan, R. (1976): Cohesion in English. – London.

HANKS, W. F. (1990): Referential Practice: Language and Lived Space among the Maya. – Chicago.

HANKS, W. F. (1996): Language and Communicative Practices. – Boulder.

KHARE, R. S. (1984): The Untouchable as Himself: Ideology, Identity, and Pragmatism among the Lucknow Chamars. – Cambridge, Cambridgeshire/New York.

KULKE, H. (1985): Māhārājas, Mahants, and Historians: Reflections on the Early Historiography of Vijayanagara and Sringeri. In: DALLAPPICOLA, A. (Ed.), Vajayanagara – City and Empire. – Stuttgart, pp. 120–143.

LEE, B. (1997): Talking Heads: Language, Metalanguage, and the Semiotics of Subjectivity. – Durham, N. C.

SANDERSON, A. (2007): The Śaiva Exegesis of Kashmir. In: GOODALL, D./PADOUX, A. (Eds.): Tantric Studies in Memory of Helene Brunner. – Pondicherry/Paris, pp. 231–582.

ŚAṄKARĀCĀRYA. (1979): A Thousand Teachings: The Upadeśasāhasrī of Śaṅkara. – Transl. by S. MAYEDA. – Tokyo.

SILVERSTEIN, M. (1993): Metapragmatic Discourse and Metapragmatic Function. In: LUCY, J. A. (Ed.): Reflexive Language: Reported Speech and Metapragmatics. – Cambridge, England/New York, pp. 33–58.

SINGH, J. (Trans.) (1979): Vijñānabhairava: Or, Divine Consciousness. – Delhi.

SMITH, F. M. (2006): The Self Possessed: Deity and Spirit Possession in South Asian Literature and Civilization. – New York.

SRINIVASA AYYANGAR, T. R. (Trans.) (1952): Yoga Upanishads. – Madras.

SUBRAHMANYA SASTRI, S. (Ed.) (1960): Madhumañjarī (ṭīkā on Manīṣāpañcakam) of Bālagopālendramuni. – Kumbakonam.

SUNDARESAN, V. (2003): Conflicting Hagiographies and History: The Place of Śaṅkaravijaya Texts in Advaita Tradition. In: International Journal of Hindu Studies, Vol. 4, No. 2, pp. 109–184.

TIRUMŪLAR (1991): Tirumantiram. – Transl. by B. NATARAJAN. – Madras.

VARADARĀJA (1925): Śivasūtra-Vārtikam. – Srinagar. (Kashmir Series of Texts and Studies Vol. 43)

VASUDEVA, S. (2004): The Yoga of the Mālinīvijayottaratantra: Chapters 1–4, 7, 11–17. – Pondicherry. (Collection Indologie Vol. 97)

VASUGUPTA. (1978): Śiva Sūtras. – Transl. by J. SINGH. – Delhi.

VEEZHINATHAN, N. (Ed.) (1971): Śrī Śaṅkaravijaya of Ānandagiri. – Madras.

VIṢṆUNAMPŪTIRI, M. V. (Ed.) (1996): Poṭṭanāṭṭan. – Kottayam, Kerala.

William S. Sax

Performing God's Body

How can one describe the body of god? In some non-literate religions, god's body is identified with the earth. For Christians, god's embodiment is the central event in history, offering the possibility of human salvation. For mainstream Judaism and Islam, the idea of god's body is nonsensical, unthinkable, even blasphemous. But in the numerous religions that make up what we call "Hinduism," god is frequently embodied, or, to put it more precisely, the numerous gods, goddesses, and demons of the Hindu pantheon have a startling variety of embodied forms, ranging from the zoomorphic (Vishnu's fish-, turtle-, and boar-incarnations; the "monkey-god" Hanuman), to the anthropo-zoomorphic (Narasimha the "man-lion:" Ganesha with his human body and elephant's head) to the human (Rama, Sita, Krishna), and the hyper-human (Durga with her eight arms, Brahma with his three heads, Ravana with his ten heads). In many Hindu temples, iconic representations of god are treated like human beings: fed, clothed, bathed, serenaded, and put to sleep (WAGHORNE/CUTLER 1985). Indeed, the sheer exuberance and fantastic variety of Hindu representations of divine embodiment contributed to the rejection of the very notion of embodiment by the various *nirguna bhakti* movements of the medieval period, who elevated the recitation of god's ineffable name over the worship of his embodied form (HAWLEY/JUERGENSMEYER 1988). The boundaries between divine, human, and demonic realms are quite porous in popular Hinduism, with humans often achieving divine embodiment, in myths as well as in popular practice (i.e. the striving to achieve an immortal, divine body through yoga, or alchemy, or meditation; the embodied performance of god's body that is the focus of this article), while the gods take on human bodies either to save human beings, as in the incarnations of Vishnu, or to enjoy more earthly pleasures, as for example in the *Mahabharata* where Kunti summons various gods to impregnate her, resulting in the births of Karna, and four of the five Pandava brothers.

In this article, I discuss the body of the Hindu god Bhairav,[1] as it appears in popular myth and ritual in Chamoli District of Garhwal, a former Hindu kingdom that is now part of the north Indian state of Uttarakhand in the Central Himalayas. Bhairav is the central deity in a cult of ritual healing that is the

[1] In Sanskrit he is called Bhairava, but in the languages of North India, including the dialect of Hindi spoken in Garhwal where I conducted my fieldwork, the final "a" is omitted.

subject of my recent research.[2] One of the forms taken by Bhairav in this cult is particularly associated with the lowest castes of the region, locally known as Harijans.[3] These forms are described in myths, songs and rituals, and they are performed by low-caste persons when the god enters their bodies; that is, when they are possessed. It is that body, and these performances, that are the focus of this article.

In many parts of India, the oppression of the lowest castes is extreme. One reads regularly in the newspapers of atrocities of various kinds committed against them: villages burned down because low-caste persons dared to use the wells of higher castes, inter-caste lovers captured and executed by village councils, or even by their own parents, the sexual exploitation of low-caste women, the brutal persecution of those who stand up for their legal rights. The lowest castes in India are truly a "community of suffering."

In addition, the lowest castes are often landless, with nothing to sell but their own labor, and caste prejudice is exacerbated by such extreme dependence. In Garhwal however, as elsewhere in the Central Himalayas, most Harijans have at least a small piece of land, and there are few if any reports of caste atrocities. In general, their situation is not nearly so bad as in other parts of the subcontinent. Still, the suffering of the Harijans in the region is very real. They endure constant humiliation and discrimination; they are not allowed to enter the homes of the highest castes; they are often addressed as "boy" or "girl," using the familiar pronoun ("tu") that is otherwise reserved for children and animals; they must wash their own cups at the village tea-stall; they are expected to defer to higher castes when they go shopping or ride the bus; and they must endure numerous other insults every day. They usually have much less land than the higher castes, and are therefore often compelled to work for them as dependent day-laborers, with all of the humiliation such labor entails.

How do such forms of oppression affect the minds and bodies of low-caste people? Generalizations are difficult here, because the level of oppression varies greatly, even between neighboring villages. As Polit (2005) has pointed out, when Harijans constitute the minority in a village and are surrounded by higher-caste people, they experience a high level of oppression. But the

---

[2] Sax 2009. The material is this article is drawn primarily from the second chapter.

[3] The decision about which term to use for the lowest castes in Garhwal has political as well as epistemological dimensions. "Untouchable" is offensive to those so designated, and "untouchability" is in any case illegal in India. "Scheduled Caste" is a cumbersome and rather vague term, though it is popular among many people of this group. "Dalit" (literally "oppressed person") is preferred by those who are politically active and aware, but the term is hardly used in the region where I conducted my fieldwork. In this article I use the term "Harijan," a term coined by Gandhi that means literally "child of god," because it is the most widely-used and ideologically neutral term in the region.

level of felt oppression in an exclusively Harijan village is much lower, since daily interactions are more likely to be characterized by relations of near-equality. Moreover, the youngest generation of Harijans has been thoroughly exposed to modern discourses of equality in school and in the media, and more recently in the activities of low-caste activists, especially those from the BSP or "Majority Socialist Party" (*bahujan samajwad parti*), a political party claiming to represent India's lowest castes. The Government of India has tried to eliminate or moderate caste discrimination by giving loans to low-caste businessmen, providing places for low-caste people in institutions of higher education and in government service (as teachers, judges, village headmen, regional council members), and taking many other measures. As a result, there is now a younger generation of low caste people—sorted by the government into such categories as "Scheduled Castes" (SCs) and "Other Backward Castes" (OBCs)—that has taken advantage of these programs and is more confident and assertive, more educated and articulate, than their parents ever were.[4]

But for that older generation, forms of insult and stigmatization are so much a part of life that they have been internalized by the Harijans themselves, whose very way of inhabiting their bodies—what Bourdieu would call their *hexis*—reflects their constant oppression and stigmatization. A friend of mine, a brilliant Harijan musician from Garhwal, inevitably bows and joins his hands in respectful greeting when he meets a higher-caste person. He habitually addresses such persons as "mom and dad" (*ma-bap*), and finds it intolerable to sit while they are standing. Other Harijans of his generation often display the bowed shoulders, the immediate folding of the hands in greeting, the ready smile, the obsequious language, and the avoidance of eye contact that are the hallmarks of Harijan *hexis*.

In what follows, I will discuss the cult of Bhairav, and especially a particular form of Bhairav that is closely associated with the Harijans of Chamoli District. I shall argue that this embodied form is intimately related to the bodies of local Harijans, that it both reflects and ameliorates the oppression and suffering that is part of their lives. Bhairav's body has a history, which I attempt to capture by means of local memory and oral history, as well as oral texts; and it has an iconography, which is revealed in his descriptions in songs and rituals. Ultimately, I shall argue that Bhairav's appearance in the body of a "possessed" devotee is his most important mode of embodiment, and that it tells us a great deal about what it means to be a Harijan.

---

[4] This is one of the reasons why some scholars argue that anthropologists have paid far too much attention to caste (Daniel 1987, pp. 1ff.; Quigley 1993, pp. 12–20), and that it is time to move on to other topics.

Bhairav's First Embodiment

In the Sanskrit tradition one of the earliest, prototypical forms of Bhairava (lit. "the terrible one") is the god Virabhadra, who led Shiva's followers when they took revenge on Daksha Prajapati. The story is one of the most popular Hindu myths: Shiva was married to Sati, the daughter of the sage Daksha, also called Prajapati, the "lord of creatures." Daksha held a fire sacrifice and invited all the gods and sages except his son-in-law Shiva, whom he deliberately insulted by excluding him. Shiva was inclined to ignore the insult, but not his wife Sati. She attended her father's sacrifice and leaped into his sacrificial fire, thereby not only killing herself but also lending her name to the subsequent practice of self-immolation by widows. When Shiva heard what had happened, he was filled with grief and rage, and sent his followers, led by Virabhadra, to take revenge. They decapitated Sati's father, Daksha, and killed many of the sages who had taken part in the sacrifice.[5] In tantric Vajrayana Buddhism as well, Bhairava is strongly associated with the themes of anger, revenge, and violence.[6] In Garhwal, Bhairav takes a number of forms, but the one most closely associated with the Harijans is Kachiya, often called "Kachiya-Bhairav."[7] His most important cult center is the temple of Kaleshwar (colloquially known as "Kaldu"), a few miles east of Karanprayag on the Badrinath road. Here is how Shanti Lal, a particularly knowledgeable priest of Kachiya, described the god's origin.

> The local story is that one of our ancestors came from Kumaon.[8] He reached a place near Bhatoli village where two families lived: one of Smiths and one of Musicians.[9] He had brought a very fierce god with him, and when he gave the command, this god would attack[10] people. This kept happening, and the people in Bhatoli became angry. They said, "Either we get rid of this guy, or we murder him." Someone told him that he should leave, because his life was in danger. So he took the god and his special things—the fire tongs and the Timaru staff near the temple—and left. He went to Karanprayag—for people in those days, it was as far as Delhi is for you these days—and then he came up this way. He slung his basket on his back, came here, and sat down. When he arrived he saw that the land was very good: broad fields, very nice land. He put down his basket, and when he tried

[5] For more on the story of Daksha's sacrifice, see O'Flaherty 1973, pp. 214, 236; Goswami 1982, pp. 4.II.13–15, 4.III.3–4, 4.IV.6–8.21, 5.11–16; Mertens 1998.

[6] For more on Bhairava, see Stietencron 1969; Slusser 1982; Erndl 1989; Sontheimer 1989; Chalier-Visuvalingam 2003.

[7] I have been told that "Kachiya" means "the brilliant/shining one."

[8] Kumaon is a former Hindu kingdom, roughly the same size as Garhwal and lying to the east. Together, Garhwal and Kumaon constitute perhaps 90% of the area of Uttarakhand.

[9] *Lohar* (smiths) and *Das* (musicians) are both Harijan castes.

[10] Underlining indicates that the words were spoken in English.

to pick it up again, he found that he was unable to do so. He kept trying, but he couldn't lift it! Now he had a problem; he had to stay the night here. And during the night, the god spoke to him through a little bird, saying, "I like this place. I want to stay here." And because he was a very spiritual man, he stayed here.

They say that this old grandfather of ours was very powerful. He would tell the god to bring him tobacco, and the god would bring him tobacco! This was four or five generations ago. Later on the place became very famous, and everyone started giving much respect to the god. They believe that he has a lot of power, and that his decisions are just (*sahi-sahi nirnay*). But our ancestors thought it inappropriate to build him a temple, and so they didn't. This is because he was staying on the bank of the river, where the cremation ground is. They kept him just as he was. The *tantrik* method is that the god should be kept in the earth itself. And because there is a cremation ground there, with burning corpses and all … it's all under his control. Even today. He is the in-charge (of that place)… He adjudicates problems, helps people obtain powerful positions, gets them promotions, saves them from destructive quarrels … He does all this work for people from the entire area (*kshetra*). People have faith in him. And the greatest thing is that he is the only power in the hands of the weaker sections of society, the Harijans …

There is one more very important thing that I want to tell you, something that is of great importance, not only for our nation but for the whole world, and this is that my ancestors joined two deities together: a Muslim deity and a Hindu deity. Bhairav is a god of the Hindus, Nar Singh is a god of the Hindus, and with them is a Muslim deity whom we call Maminda [a corruption of "Muhammad"] …

If one wants to worship the god, then we will be the priests. The god is pacified (*shant*) only when one of us is there. It's not even necessary that the priest is an adult—he can be a child as well. He can be anyone from the lineage. For example, if I'm in another village, but my son is here, and if by the way the god is angry or something, this can be resolved through our children. If some woman gets sick in that village over there, if the god is showing his anger, if he's punishing her, and if one of our children has gone there for some other reason, then someone may say, "He's a priest of Kaleshwar." And they may ask the child to apply some of the god's sacred ash (*vibhuti*), and if it's truly Kaleshwar's affliction, then she'll be cured by that ash.

W. S.: Earlier you told me the history of your ancestor. Was his name Kaldu? Is that why they call this place "Kaldu Beach"?

Shanti Lal: This god is Kal Bhairav.[11] They used to call him "Kachiya of Kaldu." He was black, so we call him *kala* (black). And that's why this place is known as Kaldu Beach.

---

[11] "The Bhairav of time/death," one of the best-known forms of Bhairav. His most famous temple is in Varanasi (Benares), and he is often said to be the "policeman" (*kotwal*) of that city.

W. S.: An oracle near Nauti told me that the god originated in Dol village, and from there he spread here, and to Kankhul, and to other places.

Shanti Lal: The Kachiya of Dol is this one's class-fellow. What happened in Dol was this: someone buried a child—alive! Some enemy must have done it. The child screamed there under the ground, and died, and his *atma* took the form of a supernatural power, and he became the god of that whole area. And because he was very powerful, he went along with all his *disa-dhyanis*.[12] And that is why he was made the in-charge of the cremation ground here.

W. S.: Kachiya is that child?

Shanti Lal: That very child. Even now when he comes in a dream, he takes the form of a child. There are a lot of stories connected to this god—how can I tell them all?

Later in the interview, Shanti Lal told my friend Mr. Nautiyal that his work as a lawyer was rather similar to Kachiya's work: "He alone is our judge, and he is our surgeon. He is our everything. He is our deputy. He is our District Magistrate. I think that our ancestors who settled here, who were of a weaker section (of society) brought him as a helper. Even today, he is a powerful ally."

In this interview, Shanti Lal mentioned several things that are fundamental for understanding local forms of Bhairav, especially in his form as Kachiya. These include the fact that he is thought of as a god of justice,[13] that his cult spreads when he accompanies his out-marrying "village daughters" to their new homes, and that he is strongly associated with the Harijans, who are his priests at this particular temple. (Shanti Lal himself belonged to the caste of *tamata* or Coppersmiths who, along with carpenters, are one of the highest-ranked Harijan castes.) Subsequent interviews with other priests confirmed the centrality of all these themes in stories of Bhairav's origin.

The Appearance of Bhairav as a Savior

Low-caste people in Chamoli often tell stories of how Bhairav appears as a savior who intervenes to rescue weak people when they are exploited and abused by the powerful. Such stories are rarely, if ever, told by high-caste

---

[12] *Disa-dhyani* is the term for "outmarried village girl." In other words, Kachiya's area of influence spread because he went along with village girls when they got married and moved to their husbands' homes.

[13] Ideas of local gods as providers of justice are not uncommon in the region. One of the best examples is the Kumaoni god Golu (known in Garhwal as Goril; see Agrawal 1999). The god Pokkhu in the upper Tons valley is referred to by his followers as a "god of justice and injustice" (*nyay-anyay ka devata*). During the royal period, he was officially authorized by the king to settle local disputes. Even nowadays, people who consider themselves victims of exploitation go to him for justice.

persons: they are in a sense the intellectual property of local Harijans, recited when high-caste people are out of earshot and thus examples of what SCOTT (1990) calls "hidden transcripts." One such story is that of Lalu Das, which I reproduce here exactly as it was told to me by one of the god's priests. It should be noted that in Chamoli District, the Das caste of Musicians is the lowest caste, while Bhartwal is one of the highest-ranking Rajput castes.

> Lalu Das lived with his six brothers in Nagpur. He was a very small person. Jasu Bhartwal also lived in Nagpur. He was a very big person. He kept the handcuffs to bind criminals, and he kept the key to the leg irons as well. Lalu Das's family used to plough Jasu Bhartwal's fields and care for his livestock, take them grazing and so on, and they lived on whatever they could scrounge from their labors. What happened? One day, one of their children had gone with Jasu Bhartwal's cows and buffaloes to graze, when Bhairav manifested himself. His *linga* appeared there, and the buffalo gave all its milk to that *linga*.[14] Naturally Jasu Bhartwal was angry, because he wasn't getting any milk from the buffalo. He thought that the shepherd boy was sitting in the jungle and drinking the buffalo's milk, the bastard! So he took that little boy and cut off his hands and his feet! And when he did this, Lalu's wives cried, "He has amputated our child's hands and his feet!" And the men were very angry and upset, too.
>
> After that, what happened? Bhairav took the form of a yogi and went to a stream of water. It was a cremation ground, with corpses lying around. There was a cave there, and he took up residence and lit his *sadhu*'s fire there.[15] He just sat there, and didn't worry about his food and drink. He didn't beg for anything, he just sat. Lalu's senior wife went there to fetch water. She saw the *sadhu* and asked him what he ate. (She thought she should ask him, since he had been there for so many weeks and months.) She told him that she hadn't even seen him stand up in a long while. He answered, "Mother, I'm just sitting here and worshiping God on an empty stomach." She asked, "Will you eat something?" and he replied, "I will be the support (*vastuk*) of whoever feeds me something." So Lalu's wife went back to her house and took a bit of whatever was cooking there. They were poor, so they ate whatever came to them: sometimes lentils, sometimes boiled rice, sometimes simply roots and flowers. Now, the *sadhu* had an earthen pot (*handi*). He said "Mother, you keep putting food in my pot, and I will cook it and eat it." And the woman brought him food, morning and evening.
>
> After that what happened? It was time to plough. And the *sadhu* spread cholera in the home of Lalu Das. The whole family got sick. Everyone's oxen were in the fields

---

[14] The *linga* is the phallic sign of Shiva, the god with whom Bhairav is associated. The motif of a linga spontaneously appearing and a cow offering its milk to it is extremely common in India.

[15] A *sadhu* is a Hindu ascetic, or holy man. A *sadhu*'s fire is called a *dhuni* and is of particular importance for the cult and rituals of Bhairav, as well as for the Gorakhnath tradition of *kanphata yogi*s with which it is associated (see below).

ploughing, but Jasu Bhartwal's oxen remained tied to their posts, because there was no one to plough his fields—all the Harijans were sick. Jasu Bhartwal took his golden staff in his hands, and climbed to the top of a big cliff, and shouted out, "Lalu Das! Lalu Das! Have your sons all died? Everyone is ploughing their fields, but my oxen are still tied to their stakes!" But the Harijans couldn't answer—they were dying! The *sadhu* disappeared. He hid himself. The woman brought food for him, but he wasn't there. She felt very sad, because the *sadhu* had become like a member of her family. But he was gone, so she picked up his pot and took it home and put it on her hearth. She cooked all her food in that pot. And that's how they ate. Then Jasu Bhartwal reached there with his golden staff, and saw that the whole family was lying on the ground, sick, and he put the handcuffs and the leg irons on Lalu Das, and led him away. He put him in his "silver courtyard" (*candni cauk*). It was mid-Winter, the month of Paush, and very cold. Snow was falling.

Now, Jasu Bhartwal had seven queens. They were so modest that they didn't bathe during the daytime—they didn't want the sun to see them. And they didn't bathe in the evening either, after the moon had come out. They were chaste wives (*pativrata nari*), so they only bathed at dusk, when there was neither sunlight nor moonlight. When they came out in the evening, they saw that Lalu Das's handcuffs and leg irons were open, and that he had escaped and gone home. They went inside and told Jasu Bhartwal. He was furious, and said, "Where is the bastard who thinks he's bigger than me? I have the key! I'm his master! Who has let him loose and taken him away?" They said, "His wife took him away—Lalu Das's wife saved him!" So Jasu Bhartwal went and found Lalu Das's wife, and seized her. He shouted, "You whore! You helped him escape!" And he put her in his jail. But at night, Bhairav returned. He loosened the bonds of Lalu Das's wife, and helped her escape.

After that, the sickness in Lalu Das's home went away, and everyone improved, but then the cholera spread in Jasu Bhartwal's home. Now, Jasu Bhartwal had seven sons and fourteen grandsons. He had twelve twenties[16] of buffaloes, twelve twenties of cows, twelve twenties of goats, twelve twenties of oxen. Gold, silver, riches, grain—he had everything! But still, they got cholera, so he went to an oracle. He reached a pass with a crossroads. Bhairav was sitting there; he had taken the form of a *sadhu*. Jasu Bhartwal said, "Greetings, *sadhu*!" and the *sadhu* replied, "Greetings, my disciple. Oh man (*narain*), where are you coming from and where are you going?" Jasu Bhartwal said, "*Sadhu-ji*, do you know how to read palms?" and the *sadhu* answered, "I've grown old reading palms." So Jasu Bhartwal said, "Read my palm, and tell me what my problem is." The *sadhu* read it and said, "Look brother, do the seven Lalu brothers take care of your livestock, and plough your fields?" Jasu Bhartwal said, "Yes." "Was there a boy in that family who used to graze your animals?" Jasu Bhartwal said, "Yes." "Did you amputate his hands and feet?" Jasu Bhartwal said, "Yes." The *sadhu* said, "He didn't drink your milk! There was a Bhairav shrine there—it was Bhairav who drank the milk! You did a great injustice when you cut off his hands and feet! And when there was cholera at

[16] Counting in units of twenty is a traditional way of reckoning land and livestock throughout the Central Himalayas.

his home, did you bind him and bring him to your square?" Jasu Bhartwal admitted that he had. The *sadhu* said, "It was Bhairav who let him go." Jasu Bhartwal said, "What must I do now?"

Now, Jasu Bhartwal used to do his evening worship while sitting above his big front gate. And the *sadhu* said, "You will have to build a shrine for Bhairav there, and divide all of your grain, wealth, gold, silver, cows, buffaloes, and land: seven portions for your sons, and seven portions for Lalu Das's sons. Are you willing to do it? For seven days, Lalu's seven brothers will dance at your home. And if they dance along with Bhairav for seven days at your home, and if you make the guru's ritual seat (*dulaici*) there, then you will retain your wealth—otherwise you will be ruined!" Jasu Bhartwal said, "I'll do it, Maharaj! I'll do just that!" And he divided all his grain, wealth, *maya*, *lakshmi*, and land into fourteen parts, and Lalu and his brothers danced at Jasu Bhartwal's house for seven days. And then Jasu Bhartwal's seven queens also began to dance! Bhairav rocked them, and they danced naked! He possessed those seven chaste wives. "You were so chaste, but now I have destroyed your honor!"

Here Bhairav appears as a renouncer from the Nath order of Yogis (see below), and as a savior who provides justice for the poor, low-caste people oppressed by the cruel Jasu Bhartwal. One striking feature of the story is how Bhairav afflicts not only the oppressive Jasu with cholera, but also Lalu Das and his family, evidently as a mark of his favor. This conforms to a common pattern in Hinduism, where certain diseases—especially those associated with pustules and fever, such as smallpox and chicken pox—are regarded as a sign of "possession" or divine selection (Egnor 1984; Nicholas 1981).

The story of Jasu Bhartwal was recited to me in prose, but many similar narratives take the form of songs. There are many such songs, but by far the most important is that of Umeda and Sumeda, which in many ways is the "mythical charter" for the cult, since it not only explains how Bhairav first came to Garhwal, but also contains features that appear in cult rituals. Here I reproduce the story in narrative form, as it was told to me by the god's priest Darpal:

Once upon a time, the high-caste Myur Rajputs of Panthi Bagwan were building a temple. Big rocks had to be cut for this temple, and the Myurs said to the low-caste Coppersmiths, "Fetch the rocks, you bastards!" The Coppersmiths lifted the lighter rocks and brought them, but they left the large rocks behind—they weren't able to lift them. So the Myurs seized them and beat them, and kidnapped their beautiful daughters Umeda and Sumeda, and sold them in slavery to the Gurkhas.

So the girls' fathers Udotu and Sudotu went to Tibet to visit their spiritual teacher, a Tibetan lama. They said to him, "Hey mother's brother, the Myurs have done us a great injustice; they have sold our daughters into slavery, and flayed the skin from our backs. We have no one!" Their story brought tears to the Lama's eyes, and he made a pot, a round red pot. He filled its belly with forty-two heroes (*vir*), fifty-two

> ghouls (*bahiyal*), eighty-four fierce goddesses (*kali*), sixty-four witches (*jogini*), and ninety man-lions (*narasimha*). He put all of them in the pot's belly, and told them to "play their game." Then he covered the pot and closed its mouth by tying it with a cloth, and said "Lift it, sister's son: lift this pot!" Udotu tried to lift it, but it was very heavy. He couldn't lift it, and he said, "Guru, I won't be able to place this pot on my head." So the guru himself lifted it and put it on the coppersmith's head! And he said "Go, sister's son, and take this red pot to the land of Uttarakhand! Take it to the land of your enemies!"
>
> So the coppersmiths went to Tilkhani Bar. They lay down to sleep, but Sudotu heard a buzzing sound inside the pot. He was curious about what was inside, so he lifted the cover a little bit, and out came Bhairav. Now at this time they were performing a Pandav Lila[17] in Dobari Village, and Bhairav took the form of a yogi and reached the village where they were dancing. He said to the villagers, "Give me a nice spot that I can call my own." They said, "Where have you come from, you lazy son of a bitch?" and they beat him and drove him away. He joined his hands in supplication and said, "Give me a bit of land where I can raise buffaloes, goats, a few cows and some oxen." They said, "Go! Get out! Where the hell have you come from?" So he took the form of a leopard, and destroyed all their cows, oxen, sheep, goats and buffaloes. He cursed them (*dosh lagaya*), and since that day, the Pandavas have never again danced in Dobari. From there, Bhairav went to Kob Bar where the Myurs lived, and exterminated them. He took the form of cholera and killed them all. Two corpses were carried to the cremation ground every day, until the Myurs were totally destroyed.

Once again, Bhairav appears as a renouncer, a Nath Yogi, who defends the weak and brings a swift and terrible justice to their powerful oppressors. It is interesting that according to the story, Bhairav came to Uttarakhand from Tibet, and not from the Indian plains. Bhairav is, in fact, an important deity in Tibetan Buddhism, and most if not all of the priests I met said that the tradition in general, and its rituals in particular, came from the other side of the great Himalayan range. They were said to have been brought to Uttarakhand by the so-called "Bhotiyas," a high-altitude community that formerly conducted the trade between India and Tibet. And some of the language of the cult of Bhairav suggests a connection with the tradition of the "eighty-four siddhas," which is closely associated with Tibet as well as with the Kanphata yogi tradition, as I explain in the following section.

The Iconography of Bhairav

Many of Bhairav's songs evoke a monk from the Gorakhnath tradition, one of the Kanphata ("split-ear") Yogis, so called because fully initiated members of the order split their ears and wear large earrings. This order was very

---

[17] A ritual drama focusing on India's great epic *Mahabharata* (see Sax 2002).

influential in north India during the medieval period. It was allegedly founded by the medieval Hindu ascetic Gorakhnath, who is also associated with the Siddha tradition.[18] In Garhwal, some of Bhairav's mantras explicitly mention Gorakhnath, other mantras and stories make explicit reference to his guru Matsyendranath, and still others mention the names of unknown Nath yogis who presumably were involved in the founding of the cult. When oracles are possessed by Bhairav, or when they call upon him in trance, they often call out "*alak*" and "*adesh*," terms that are associated with the Kanphata tradition. The adjective *alak* (from Sanskrit *alakshana*, "without characteristics") is used by Nath yogis and theologians to designate the formless absolute, while the noun *adesh* ("permission") is conventionally used by them when requesting permission to join or leave a group of fellow Naths. The oracle's frequent use of these terms, along with other aspects of the cult, suggests that the Nath order was active at some time in the past in the Central Himalayas (cf. Chatak 1990, p. 311), as indeed it was throughout North India. Other items mentioned as part of the iconography of Bhairav and Kachiya Bhairav, and usually also found in their shrines, are associated with renunciation, the worship of Shiva in general, and the Nath order of Yogis in particular. These include:

1. a staff of Timaru wood (*tejmal ka sotha*)
2. the fire-tongs from "Dhuni Pass" (*dhunidhar ka cimta*—the noun *dhuni* refers to a renouncer's fire; see footnote 16)
3. a saffron-colored cloth bag (*gerua ki jholi*)
4. a trident surmounting an iron pole (*danda trishul*)
5. a strip of saffron-colored cloth (*path ka mekhala*)
6. a loincloth of iron (*loha araband*)
7. a *langoti* (the cloth that renouncers use to bind their genitals) of stone (*shila ki langoti*), and
8. a *phavari* of stone (*patthar to phavari*). The *phavari* is used in ritual contexts, and is made of iron or tin, in the shape of palm with bent fingers (see Figure 1). It is heated until it is red-hot and then licked, in order to demonstrate the authenticity of the trance.

The priests I knew best nearly always began major rituals with a praise-song to Bhairav in which the image of a Nath renouncer with these accoutrements found its most complete expression. The following translation is taken from one such song, recorded live in performance.

---

[18] For more on the Nath tradition, see Briggs 1973 [1938]; Vaudeville 1976; Lapoint 1978; Chalier-Visuvalingam 2003; Banerjea n.d. For the "eighty-four siddhas," see Dowman 1985; Robinson 1996; Davidson 2005, p. 14. For the relationship between Nath and Siddha traditions, see White 1996, chap. 4, esp. pp. 80–85 and 107ff..

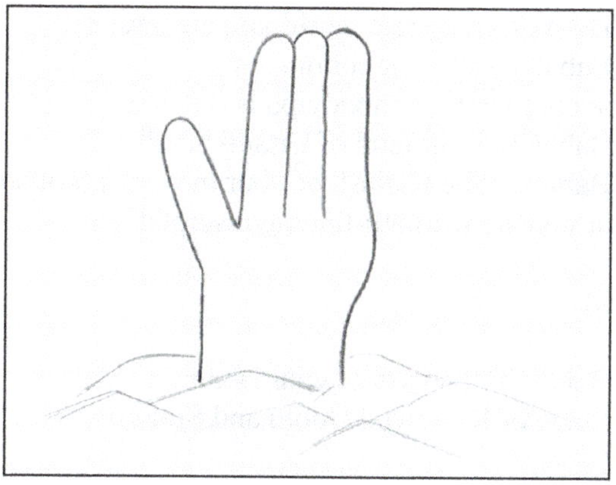

Figure 1: A *phavari* (drawing by Ariane Petney).

1. Victory to the guru, victory to the guru, victory to the deathless swami
2. What game did the deathless swami play in this world?
3. Other gurus play other music, swami, (but) yours is the music of the Huraki-drum[19]
4. Which guru split your ears, which guru shaved your head?
5. Which guru showed you the path?
6. Who will go with you, who will speak with you, my deathless Siddha?
7. The [Timaru] staff will go with you, the fire-tongs will speak.
8. My Siddha Swami, you wear a *mekhala* cloth
9. A *mekhala* cloth, (and you carry) the fire tongs from Dhuni Pass
10. My deathless swami, the *phavari* of stone
11. Swami, you (wear) a *langoti* of stone.

(tune change)

12. Guru-ji plays the cruel-hearted music that makes you weep![20]
13. The sound of my drum and the words of my mouth reach your ears

[19] The *huraki* is a small hourglass-shaped drum with two goatskin heads, the tightening straps of which are attached to a harness which he wears around his back, so that when he plays the drum he can, by pulling on the straps, cause it to make an unusual sound, which is especially effective in invoking the spirits. Priests of Bhairav normally play this drum, and are accompanied by the *thakalyor*, who plays an inverted metal platter with two wooden drumsticks, and usually by a third man, the *bhamvar* or "bumblebee," who echoes the final lines of each verse of the song.

[20] *kuro dilo nad*,; also called *krodhi nad* or "furious music."

14. Adesh, Baba! To the great world you created!
15. Adesh, Baba! To all your continents!
16. Of all the continents, Jambudvipa is the first
17. Adesh, Baba! To your land of Uttarakhand!
18. Adesh, Baba! To the Kailash of your mother's brother (Shiva)!
19. Of whom you are the path-finding disciple!

(tune changes)

20. Adesh, Baba! To the Kob of your Bhairav!
21. In the village of Kob lived Udotu and Sudotu

(tune changes)

22. The coppersmiths Udotu and Sudotu lived in the village of Kob
23. Oh God! Their daughter was called "Cheta"
24. And her beautiful daughters were named Umeda and Sumeda …

Having summoned Bhairav and praised him, the guru begins to sing the song of Umeda and Sumeda. In effect, the song has changed from an invocatory prayer to a narrative. But for now, let us return to Kachiya, the form of Bhairav that is most closely associated with the Harijans. If Bhairav is represented as a Kanphata Yogi, then Kachiya is represented as an Aghori *sadhu*, which is a type of "left-handed" tantric renouncer. Members of the so-called Aghori (literally "without fear") sect live in cremation grounds, their meditative practices focus on death, they use the coals of cremation fires to cook their food, and occasionally practice necrophagy (Barrett 2005; Svoboda 1994; White 1996). The point of their *sadhana* or spiritual practice is to train themselves to cease distinguishing between pure and impure, beautiful and ugly, food and filth; to become like infants, as they put it. The songs of Kachiya do not however concentrate on such theological details, but simply emphasize his impure, disgusting actions. This can be seen in the following song (rather freely translated)[21] that is sung during Kachiya's rituals, particularly when someone is possessed by him:

1 Awaken! Father Kachiya, in your leather blanket
2 In your house of filth on the burning ground
3 With your demoness lovers, in the warm springtime
4 Where skeleton waists dance ever around
5 Awaken, O Kachiya! in this mortal world

[21] Recorded April 1999 by Darpal Lal Mistari.

Where the red-hot skillets dance ever around
Awaken, O Kachiya! at the meeting of rivers
In your leather blanket, in your house of filth
Ghosts wail in pain, but you hear sweet music
Awaken, O Kachiya! half the night here, and half the night there
At the burning ground, you light a torch
At the burning ground, the axe is resounding
The corpses are being chopped into pieces!
So awaken! O Kachiya, at the burning ground
Where a burning corpse is your fire altar
For many long days, no corpses have come!

(The priest continued in Hindi:)

Three-hundred and sixty corpses come from Jaunsar, they seize their shrounds and bind them on their heads. Kachiya wears a *bhagoya* (an archaic style of dress where the cloth crossed over the chest like an "X" and tied behind the back), he twirls the corpses by their feet; he fries the corpses' flesh and eats it; he cooks rice pudding in their skulls, and mixed rice and lentils on their funeral pyres.

Even Kachiya's perceptions are inverted and rather perverse. According to one verse, "Ghosts wail in pain but you hear sweet music." When I recorded this song, the priest spoke the line (probably by mistake) in Hindi rather than in dialect, and subsequently explained, "All the ghosts on the burning ground weep, but Kachiya hears an auspicious wedding song (*mangal git*)." Later, he said that when Kachiya chops up corpses, he uses the blunt edge of the axe instead of the sharp edge!

Kachiya has other embodiments as well. Many people claim to have seen him at night, or in their dreams, where he appears as a black, hairy, dwarf-like figure. In some of his mantras, he is described as being extremely violent and threatening. When the priest summons Kachiya to appear at the séance, he sings out a series of commands, telling him to "tear up Mt. Meru and come," to "drink the well dry," to come "chewing iron pellets … breaking iron bars … roaring like a lion … roaring like a leopard." He is told to take away the seats of other gods and replace them with his own. These are fierce forms, frightening forms, and so is the most basic form taken by Kachiya, when he possesses one of his devotees. It is this form—a person possessed by Kachiya—that Garhwalis most often see, and it is probably the one they think of when they picture the god. A person possessed by Kachiya falls to his knees, or crouches on the floor, twists his or her hands painfully—the effect reminds me of a bird claw (Figures 2 and 3)—and often scratches him- or herself uncontrollably. I was once told that Kachiya does this because, when Shiva sent Virabhadra and his minions to destroy Daksha Prajapati's sacrifice (see above), Kachiya

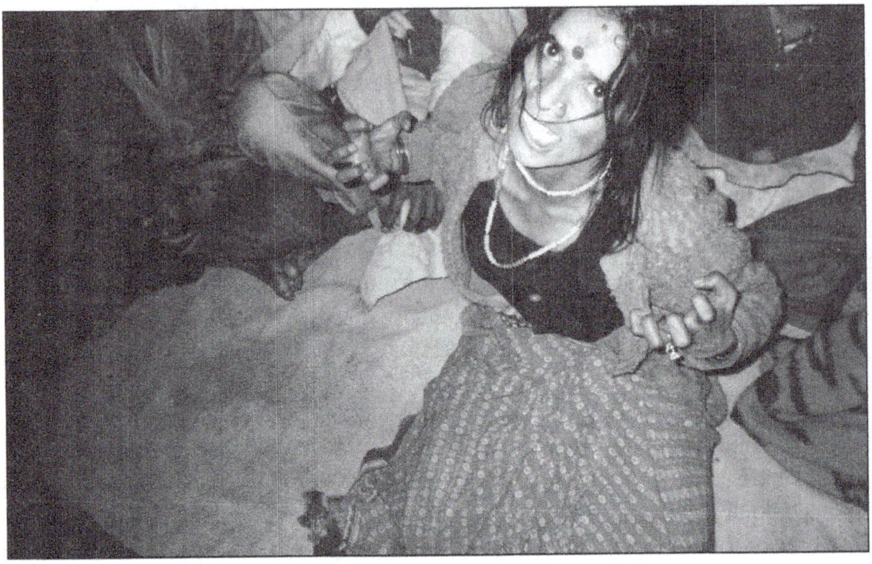

Figure 2: A woman possessed by Kachiya (photo by William Sax).

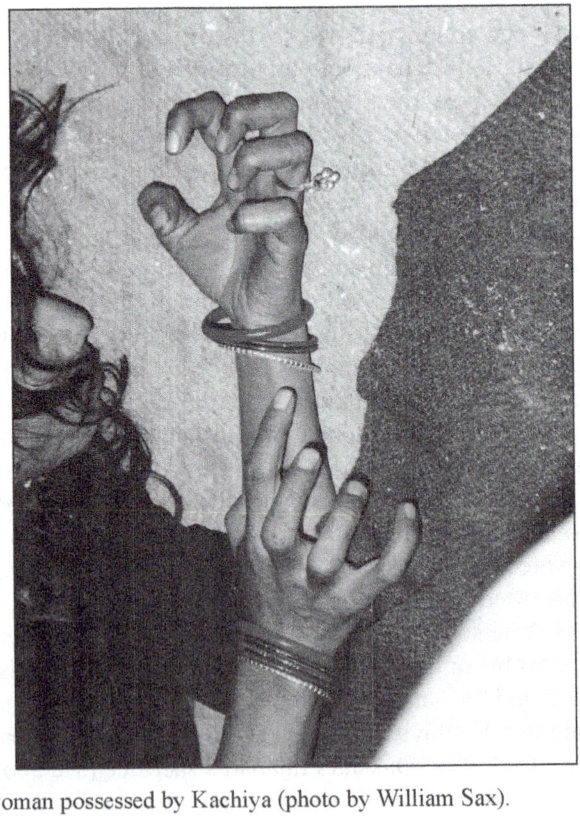

Figure 3: A woman possessed by Kachiya (photo by William Sax).

was the last one to return. When he admitted to Shiva that he had not managed to accomplish much, Shiva cursed him to "eat his own flesh," and he has done so ever since. Such images create an effect of supernatural horror and disgust, involving extreme impurity and the reversal of conventional norms of behavior, which is of course consistent with Kachiya's songs. I was told that until a decade or so ago, when local Harijans were possessed by Kachiya, they would sometimes go behind the house, to the place were dishwater and rotten food are tossed and where people urinate, and drink the water there, to demonstrate the authenticity of their possession. Once I was present during a brief pause in a major ritual, when the priest asked rhetorically, "What sort of people worship Kachiya?" And he answered his own question: "Those of low birth (*nic yoni*)." After one particularly impressive ritual in Kaleshwar lasting several days, a local Harijan leader gave a speech in which he said that his low-caste brothers and sisters should reject the cult of Kachiya, that they should give it up, because it was contributing to the negative stereotypes that high-caste people had of them; it was one of the reasons for their low status. Nevertheless he participated in the final ritual feast, and when it was over he told a fascinating story of how once, years before, a particularly effective priest had come to his hamlet and caused practically everyone in it to get possessed. They had all danced to the cremation ground, where they found a half-burned corpse on the riverbank, which some of them began to eat! The next morning, he said, they were in a state of shock. They could hardly believe what had happened, and swore that they would not participate in the cult any longer. But because Kachiya had such a strong hold on them as Harijans, they were unable to give it up.

Such ideas are not limited to the Harijans. When I asked upper-caste people about why Kachiya was so strongly associated with the lower castes, or why they seemed to be so much more deeply involved with these matters than the higher castes, they usually said that the lower castes were "weaker," more vulnerable, and therefore more susceptible to Kachiya. A local Brahman priest put it like this:

> Bhairav is a divine being, an incarnation of Shiva. And Kachiya is his angry form—he is filled with rage. For example, you are peaceful. But if a certain kind of experience happens to you, you will become very angry. That itself is the angry form of Kachiya … He is the god of the lower classes. He does the dirty work, that's why his shrine is below the ground … Kachiya is nothing but *tamas*.[22] Only the angry form … He goes everywhere. When a great injustice is done and there is no redress, he says, "Let's go," and goes to save them … (Such gods) only have

[22] According to the Samkhya philosophy, everything consists of a mixture of three *gunas*, or "strands." The *guna* of *tamas* is associated with darkness, decay, and sloth or inertia.

> power over a weak man. But they don't have power over someone who knows the scriptures, someone who has knowledge. They belong to weak men. I know this, because I worship all these gods: Bhairav, Kachiya, Narsingh, etc. I worship them all. I am their priest. And in my view, based on my experience, these are the gods of weak people, people who have little spiritual power (*atmabal*). It's like a light-bulb. Light-bulbs are of different strengths. Some are high-power and some are low-power. If too much power comes into a low-power bulb, it will explode.

A Brahman priest of the god told me it would be very unlikely that I would ever be afflicted by Bhairav. "You are strong," he said. "You have a healthy body and lots of money, and you are intelligent. You are a big person. But these Harijans are small people. They are poor and weak, and that is why they are vulnerable to all kinds of affliction from the gods and so on. They have no one."

Performing God's Body

The stories I have related above do not correspond to the classical Sanskrit myths about Bhairava, but are instead the "property" of the Harijans, their "hidden transcripts." In these stories, as well as in his iconography (which does in fact resemble the more classical image of Bhairva), he appears as a Nath Yogi who helps the poor and the oppressed, while Kachiya Bhairav appears as a tantric Aghori renouncer who is closely associated with the Harijans. I have reproduced these myths and iconographies as words on a page, but this medium is far removed from how Bhairav and Kachiya Bhairav are actually experienced in the lives of the people of Chamoli. Such stories are never read in a book; rather, they are *performed* as songs, and indeed the singing of these songs is one of the most powerful techniques for summoning the god and making him present. The songs are never sung in private, but always rather during rituals. Even when I asked the gurus to sing them into my tape recorder, we first had to purify the atmosphere, to pray and light some incense, before I switched the tape recorder on. And a full-scale ritual involves very much more than that. Many people, friends and relatives, gather at night, expecting to be visited by fierce and unpredictable deities. There is an atmosphere of excitement, a crush of warm bodies packed tightly together on the earthen floor. The music is strange and exciting: the high-pitched clanging of the inverted metal platter rapidly beaten with two wooden sticks, the voice of the guru reaching out above the weird sounds of his two-headed Huraki drum with its unmistakable "*vhoo-vhoo*!" sound, the hypnotic echo of the third musician, a singer who echoes the final words of every line sung by the guru. When the performance is effective, the atmosphere is charged, and many persons dance and/or become possessed. This is called *siddhi*, "supernatural power," and it has an electrifying impact. The crucial line is "I have no one." When this line is sung, it is a cue for possession to occur. Many listeners fall into trance; women loosen their hair so that it hangs loosely, then whip it back and forth in the air as they "dance" wildly, on their knees, to the beat of the drum; people roll about on the floor, grimacing and writhing in pain, their hands twisted into the shape of a bird-like claw, the characteristic sign of possession by Kachiya. This is the most persuasive and powerful appearance of the god, more compelling than any iconographic description and more immediate than any story. Kachiya possesses a person sitting next to you, and he is visibly transformed: the bared teeth, the bent waist, the dancing on his knees on the floor, the cramped and claw-like hands. This is a physical embodiment of Bhairav, and devotees see it often enough to persuade them that he is quite real. Indeed, when I asked my friends if they "really believed" in Kachiya, their most common response was, "Of course I do. How could I not believe in him? He comes and dances, and you can see him right there in front of you!"

This is the pivotal moment of the rituals, when myth and iconography, context and social memory, power and morality, all come together. It is the moment when, as GEERTZ (1973, p. 112) puts it, ritual fuses together "the world as lived and the world as imagined." From the local point of view, such ritual possession confirms the power and presence of Bhairav. If possession does not occur, then the ritual has failed. Possession defines the moment of maximum ritual efficacy, and this is always a performative moment. But what, exactly, does it mean to say that possession by Kachiya is "performative"?

In the first place, it is performative because at the core of the ritual is a musical performance in which the guru summons the god by singing the stories of Puriya, Umeda and Sumeda, and the others. BAUMAN (1978, p. 11) has defined performance as "a mode of spoken verbal communication [that] consists in the assumption of responsibility to an audience for a display of communicative competence." For Baumann, such competence is demonstrated by the ability to speak in socially appropriate ways, and it is evaluated by an audience, which judges the relative skill and effectiveness of the performer's display of it. Such a definition can also be applied to the ritual performances of gurus, who assume responsibility to an audience (their clients) for a display of ritual competence (a successful ritual). Such competence is not simply taken for granted, and a guru's success in summoning and controlling a deity like Bhairav is never guaranteed. The relationship between the guru and the god is often agonistic, so that the guru has to strive mightily to make Bhairav appear at all. This "striving" is primarily musical and performative—the guru uses his drum, his songs, and also his mantras to compel the god to appear and dance. And the markers of success, the signs of competence, are also dramatic and performative: in particular the *siddhi* or power that is generated by the guru's music. It is by such markers—especially an exciting atmosphere, and the appearance of the god—that the audience judges the efficacy of a performance, and the authenticity of the god's appearance.

There is another important sense in which possession by the god might be said to be "performative." In recent discussions of ritual, Austin's theory of performativity in speech has received a great deal of attention. Austin (1962) argued that many forms of speech, including ritual speech, are not merely descriptive statements about the external world that can or should be evaluated according to their propositional content. Rather, to make an utterance is usually also to perform an act, and should be evaluated as such. When I make a promise, take a vow, or greet someone, it makes no sense to evaluate my utterance in terms of its propositional content. In other words, when I say "Hello" to you, it makes no sense to ask of this utterance, "Is it true?" Rather, my utterance should be evaluated in terms of whether or not it has been successful ("felicitious" in Austin's terms). The appropriate question to ask of my utterance "Hello" is rather, "Have I successfully greeted you?" An important implication of Austin's model—but one that is not noticed as often as it should be—is that successful performative utterances (or "felicitious perlocutionary acts" as Austin puts it) index antecedent social conditions. This is obvious enough in the case of ritual and ceremonial speech. When the priest says "I now pronounce you man and wife," or the judge says "I sentence you to five years in jail," the speech act will be efficacious only if particular antecedent social conditions have been fulfilled: the priest must be properly ordained and legally entitled to conduct weddings, the bride and groom must be willing to enter into the marriage contract; the judge must be legally empowered to pronounce the sentence, etc. Austin's accomplishment was to turn the attention of linguists and philosophers of language away from purely formal, linguistic analysis, and toward the social conditions and contexts of actual language use.

Can we say that the ritual appearance of Kachiya-Bhairav in the body of a possessed person is "performative" in this Austinian sense? Perhaps, but only to a limited extent. Of course the rituals contain many examples of performative speech, and the summoning of the god is an illocutionary act (i.e. it is a "summoning") with hoped-for perlocutionary effects (the appearance of the god) that index antecedent social conditions (the guru must be a "real" guru who has knowledge of effective mantras, etc.). When the god is reluctant to come—and this often happens—the "summoning" becomes a command by the guru, or even a threat. Members of the audience on the other hand may plead, beg, and entreat the deity to have mercy on them, to come and hear their prayers (cf. Schömbucher 2006). All of these are illocutionary acts, and thus by definition "performative" in the Austinian sense.

But our question is, "How do songs like that of Umeda and Sumeda work to bring about Bhairav's embodiment?" In other words, how do they cause possession, sometimes so powerfully that *siddhi* seems to roll in waves across the audience? Why does the recitation of these songs have such an intense emotional impact? It seems to me that Austinian performativity does not take us far in answering this question. The appearance of the god is not the perlocutionary effect of an illocutionary act. In fact, it is not a linguistic phenomenon at all. Rather, it is a bodily phenomenon. The god "dances" (*nacna*) or is "made to dance" (*nacana*) by the guru; he "comes/sits on the head" of (*sir pe ana/ baithna*) or "comes over" (*upar ana*) the possessed person, referred to as the god's "beast" (*pasva*) or "little horsie" (*dungariya*). Kachiya Bhairav appears *in the body* of a possessed person: his appearance is a matter of embodiment, not of language. It calls for a hermeneutics of the body and not a hermeneutics of the text.

And yet a hermeneutics of the body is much more difficult to conceive than a hermeneutics of the text, for all the reasons that CONNERTON (1989, pp. 100f.) suggests in his brilliant study of social memory. "Inscribing practices," he writes "have always formed the privileged story, incorporating practices the neglected story, in the history of hermeneutics". Hermeneutics has always taken inscription as its privileged object, not only because it arose from philology and inevitably returns to it, but also because hermeneutic activity itself became a textualized object of reflection. And all of this—the interpretation of texts and the textual interpretation of the interpretation of texts—was facilitated by the fact that texts are fixed, that they have an independence and a solidity that body practices like possession lack. They are permanent and objectified, and thus lend themselves much more easily to the interpretations of a hermeneutic community. Similarly in the natural sciences, argues CONNERTON, the body was "materialised," regarded as one material object amongst others, so that bodily practices were "lost from view."

> A newly-constituted object-domain, the communication of meaning according to rules, could in principle include the body in its domain but in practice it did so only peripherally. The object-domain of hermeneutics was defined in terms of what was taken to be the distinctive feature of the human species, first consciousness and later language ... When the defining feature of the human species was seen as language, the body was 'readable' as a text or code, but the body is regarded as the arbitrary bearer of meanings; bodily practices are acknowledged, but in an etherealised form (1989, p. 101).

To put it simply, texts are easier to interpret than bodily practices, and this is why so much interpretive social science privileges the text; why, as JACKSON (1983, p. 328) put it in a brilliant article on the topic, "the 'anthropology of the body' has been vitiated by a tendency to interpret embodied experience in terms of cognitive and linguistic models of meaning"; why language rather than the body is taken as a privileged metaphor—or even as a model of—society; why "performativity" is for Bauman primarily linguistic and not bodily; why even this chapter threatened to become a discussion of texts and songs rather than of the embodied performances which are in fact the central mode of Bhairav's appearance. I chose to begin with songs and texts because I address a community of readers whose hermeneutics is primarily textual, but even now, when I turn to bodily practice, I immediately transform it into text by *writing* about it. For an academic, the textual inscription of practice is (practically speaking) impossible to avoid.

Nevertheless I want to attempt a hermeneutics of the body, the contorted body, the body in pain, which marks the appearance of Kachiya Bhairav. This body is so utterly transformed, so disturbing and even frightening, and at the same time it is so central to the cult of Kachiya, that it calls out for interpretation. And the interpretation that suggests itself is the one that was made by many of my informants, and that is repeated over and over the songs and stories: that the suffering of Kachiya is the suffering of the Harijan. This, I believe, is what Guru Darpal meant when he said that only those of "low birth" worship Kachiya; it is the reason why the Harijan political leader urged his followers to give up worshiping Kachiya; it is the reason why, according to the Brahman priests, Kachiya attaches himself to "weak" and low-caste people; it even explains why Kachiya loves such people so much, and why he always comes to their rescue.

In order to understand this whole complex we can invoke yet another notion of performativity, that of Judith BUTLER (1990, 1993; see also SALIH 2002). It is important to emphasize at the outset that Butlerian "performativity" is neither dramatic performance nor Austinian performativity. For Butler, performativity is unconscious, unwilled mimesis. It is the way one learns to be a female or a male—primarily by imitating others, by conforming to the (heterosexual) "law" and *performing* masculinity or femininity until one becomes that which one has performed. One *learns to* be a man or a woman at the same time that one is *defined as* such, primarily through discursive practices such as speech acts. One of the more controversial of Butler's assertions is that such discursive speech acts, along with the mimetic activity of the subject who performatively embodies the ideology ("the law") lying behind them, actually *create* the gendered body. Accordingly, she has been criticized for defending the absurd proposition that physiological differences are socially caused. But in the end, Butler does not argue for pure social constructionism. Although discursive performativity appears, like an Austinian speech act, to produce what it names (that is, although gender appears to be performatively produced), its power to do so actually derives from a structuring law. For Butler, this is the law of patriarchy. Can we not also speak in this sense of the law of caste?[23] Caste is also performatively produced, and that is why I began this chapter by describing the bodily *hexis* of Harijans, thereby illustrating how "being a Harijan" (or being a Brahman for that matter) is something that one learns to do, not by studying a set of rules, but rather in everyday interactions such as greeting, purchasing a cup of tea, riding a bus, etc.[24]

---

[23] See LIECHTY 2003, p. 23 for a similar notion applied to class.

[24] For a brilliant discussion of such caste-based *hexis* in a ritual context, see OSELLA/OSELLA 2000.

For Butler, the strength and enduring nature of gender lies in its being continuously, daily performed, in a thousand little dramas of reiteration, interpellation, etc. But what about the extraordinary, non-mundane actions that we call "rituals"? As I have argued elsewhere (SAX 1991, 1995, 2000, 2002), public rituals are the sites *par excellence* where identities and relationships are created, re-affirmed, reiterated, and sometimes reconfigured. As self-defining actions, rituals are powerful precisely because they do not work simply at the level of language, but at the more fundamental level of the body. This is what CONNERTON means when he argues that collective, social memory consists of "images of the past and recollected knowledge of the past ... [that] are conveyed and sustained by (more or less ritual) performances" (1989, pp. 3f.).[25] And that is, after all, how the story of Umeda and Sumeda is understood, as a founding event in the collective and religious history of local Harijans which, when recited in the context of a ritual, causes a profound change in the consciousness of the (largely or exclusively) Harijan audience, resulting in Bhairav's embodiment in a possessed person. But the possessed body is contorted and in pain, because what is being collectively affirmed here is not simply an historical event, but rather the whole experience of suffering and affliction that is the mutual bond of the Harijans. This is why the song is almost never performed in front of the higher castes.

In short, I am arguing that the songs of Puriya, Umeda and Sumeda, and more generally the appearance of Kachiya in the painfully contorted bodies of his subjects, constitute a collective creation of identity through ritual performance. But is the memory only a memory of suffering? Is the Harijan body only a body in pain? Is there no way out of this circle of embodied suffering and injustice? Here again we can draw on Butler, who insists that because the gendered subject is itself a product of disursive performativity, it cannot transcend the law that fashions it. One does not choose one's caste or gender role like an actor in a play; rather one is more-or-less constrained to play a particular role. If there is agency, says Butler, if there is to be subversion and change, then it must express itself in those practices themselves.

References

AGRAWAL, C. M. (1999): Kumaom Himalaya ke Nyay Devata Golu [Golu, God of Justice of the Kumaon Himalaya]. – Almora.

AUSTIN, J. L. (1962): How to do Things with Words: The William James Lectures Delivered at Harvard University in 1955. – Cambridge, Mass.

BANERJEE, A. K. (n.d.): Philosophy of Gorakhnath. – Gorakhpur.

[25] For a discussion of possession as historical consciousness in Africa, see STOLLER 1989; for the "alternative" consciousness of subalterns, see CHATTERJEE 1989, pp. 169–209; HAYNES/PRAKASH 1992; OMVEDT 1995.

BARRETT, R.(2005): Aghor Medicine: Pollution, Death, and Healing in Northern India. – Berkeley.
BAUMAN, R. (1978): Verbal Art as Performance. – Rowley, Mass.
BRIGGS, G. W. (1973): Gorakhnāth and the K Yogīs. – Reprint. – Delhi.
BUTLER, J. (1990): Gender Trouble. Feminism and the Subversion of Identity. – New York.
BUTLER, J. (1993): Bodies that Matter. On the Discursive Limits of "Sex." – New York.
CHALIER-VISUVALINGAM, E. (2003): Bhairava: terreur et protection. – Brussels.
CHATAK, G. (1990): Bhāratiya lōka samskriti kā saṇdarbha: madhya himālaya. – New Delhi.
CHATTERJEE, P. (1989): Caste and Subaltern Consciousness. In: GUHA, R. (Ed.): Subaltern Studies No. 6. – Delhi, pp. 169–209.
CONNERTON, P. (1989): How Societies Remember. – Cambridge.
DANIEL, V. E. (1987): Fluid Signs: Being a Person the Tamil Way. – Berkeley.
DAVIDSON, R. M. (2005): The Rebirth of Tibetan Culture. – New York.
DOWMAN, K. (1985): Masters of Mahamudra: Songs and Histories of the Eighty-four Buddhist Siddhas. – Albany.
EGNOR, M. T. (1984): The Changed Mother or what the Smallpox Goddess Did when there was no more Smallpox. In: Contributions to Asian Studies, Vol. 18, pp. 24–45.
ERNDL, K. M. (1989): Rapist or Bodyguard, Demon or Devotee? Images of Bhairo in the Mythology and Cult of Vaisno Devi. In: HILTEBEITEL, A. (Ed.): Criminal gods and Demon Devotees: Essays on the Guardians of Popular Hinduism. – Albany, pp. 239–250.
GEERTZ, C. (1973): The Interpretation of Cultures. – New York.
GOSWAMI, C. (Ed.) (1982): Srimad Bhagavata Mahapurana: With Sanskrit text and English Translation. – Gorkhapur.
HAWLEY, J. S./JUERGENSMEYER, M. (1988): Songs of the Saints of India. – New York.
HAYNES, D./PRAKASH, G. (Eds.) (1992): Contesting Power: Resistance and Everyday Social Relations in South Asia. – Berkeley.
JACKSON, M. (1983): Knowledge of the Body. In: Man New Series, Vol. 18, No. 2, pp. 327–345.
LAPOINT, E. C. (1978): The Epic of Guga: A North Indian Oral Tradition. In: VATUK, S. (Ed.): American Studies in the Anthropology of India. – New Delhi.
LIECHTY, M. (2003): Suitably Modern: Making Middle-class Culture in a New Consumer Society. – Princeton.
MERTENS, A. (1998): Der Daksamythus in der episch-puranischen Literatur: Beobachtungen zur religionsgeschichtlichen Entwicklung des Gottes Rudra-Siva im Hinduismus. – Wiesbaden.
NICHOLAS, R. W. (1981): The Goddess Sitala and Epidemic Smallpox in Bengal. In: Journal of Asian Studies, Vol. XLI, No. 1, pp. 21–44.
O'FLAHERTY, W. D. (1973): Asceticism and Eroticism in the Mythology of Shiva. – Delhi.
OMVEDT, G. (1995): Dalit Visions: The Anti-caste Movement and the Construction of an Indian identity. – New Delhi.
OSELLA, C./OSELLA, F. (2000): Movements of Power through Social, Spiritual and Bodily Boundaries: Aspects of Controlled and Uncontrolled Spirit Possession in Rural Kerala. In: Purusartha, Vol. 21, pp. 183–210.
POLIT, K. M. (2005): The Effects of Inequality and Relative Marginality on the Well-being of Low Caste People in Central Uttaranchal. In: Anthropology & Medicine, Vol. 12, No. 3, pp. 225–237.
QUIGLEY, D. (1993): The Interpretation of Caste. – Oxford.
ROBINSON, J. B. (1996): The Lives of Indian Buddhist Saints: Biography, Hagiography and Myth. In: CABEZÓN, J. I./JACKSON, R. (Eds.): Tibetan Literature: Studies in Genre. – Ithaca, pp. 57–69.

Salih, S. (2002): Judith Butler. – London.
Sax, W. S. (1991): Mountain Goddess: Gender and Politics in a Central Himalayan Pilgrimage. – New York.
Sax, W. S. (1995): Who's Who in Pandav Lila? In: Sax, W. S. (Ed.): The Gods at Play: Lila in South Asia. – New York, pp. 131–55.
Sax, W. S. (2000): In Karna's Realm: An Ontology of Action. In: Journal of Indian Philosophy, Vol. 28, No. 3, pp. 295–324.
Sax, W. S. (2002): Dancing the Self: Personhood and Performance in the Pandav Lila of Garhwal. – New York.
Sax, W. S. (2009): God of Justice: Ritual Healing in the Central Himalaya. – New York.
Schömbucher, E. (2006): Wo Götter durch Menschen sprechen: Besessenheit in Indien. – Berlin.
Scott, J. C. (1990): Domination and the Arts of Resistance: Hidden transcripts. – New Haven.
Slusser, M. S. (1982): Nepal Mandala: A Cultural Study of the Kathmandu Valley. – Princeton.
Sontheimer, G. D. (1989): Pastoral Deities in Western India. – New York.
Stietencron, H. V. (1969): Bhairava. In: Zeitschrift der Deutschen Morgenländischen Gesellschaft, Supplementa I, Teil 3, pp. 863–871.
Stoller, P. (1989): Fusion of the Worlds: An Ethnography of Possession among the Songhay of Niger. – Chicago.
Svoboda, R. E. (1994): Aghora, at the left hand of God. – Calcutta.
Vaudeville, C. (1976): Braj, Lost and Found. In: Indo-Iranian Journal, Vol. 18, No. 3–4, pp. 195–213.
Waghorne, J. P./Cutler, N. (Eds.) (1985): Gods of Flesh, Gods of Stone. – Chambersburg, PA.
White, D. G. (1996): The Alchemical Body: Siddha Traditions in Medieval India. – Chicago.

Cornelia Schnepel

Bodies Filled with Divine Energy: The Indian Dance Odissi

1. Introduction

This article is based on fieldwork which I conducted in Bhubaneswar, the capital of Orissa, in the autumn and winter of 2001. The immediate topic of my research was a dance known as Odissi, which, despite its strong regional flavour, achieved the status of a "classical" all-Indian dance around the middle of the twentieth century. In order to conduct "participant observation" in the social anthropological sense of the term, I enrolled for two months as a pupil in the Odissi Research Centre, a dance school on the outskirts of Bhubaneswar which at that time was headed by a renowned dancer called Kum Kum Mohanty. There, every day I joined about twenty other female students of the dance, who were between 14 and 25 years of age, in order to become acquainted with the dance on its own terms, which, of course, I did in the time span available to me, only with limited success. In a wider orientation of my project, I sought to link my research on Odissi to more general questions concerning present-day constructions and negotiations with regard to establishing an all-Orissan regional tradition and identity in a steadily globalizing world. For this reason I visited archives and libraries and conducted a number of interviews with both practitioners and connoisseurs of the dance.[1] In this article, I wish to re-focus the data and the findings of my research activities, this time with regard to the theme of the "body in India."

The Odissi dance is a curious mixture of centuries-old traditions, and relatively new "inventions."[2] It is based on ideas and practices that stem as much from old Sanskrit writings and late-medieval temple practices as they do from the contemporary (and in Orissa much intertwined) realms of popular Hinduism and tribal religion and art. From the actors' points of view, the dance basically represents a form of devotion to the Orissan "state deity" known as Jagannath, who is considered by many to be a manifestation of Krishna and is worshipped in his main temple of Puri.[3] Consequently, Odissi is understood

[1] Some of the results of this research can be found in C. Schnepel 2005.

[2] The 1970s in particular seem to have been a "hey-decade" of the inventions of traditions in Orissa.

[3] On the political theology of Jagannath, see Kulke 1979, as well as the articles in Eschmann/Kulke/Tripathi 1978; and Kulke/Schnepel 2002.

by the actors as a "spiritual dance" through which a relationship, if not a dialogue, between the god and his adherents is established or performed; for some, practising Odissi even means that the god is embodied in the dance(rs).[4] Generally, then, the attitude exhibited by dancers and audience alike is one of spirituality, and this spirituality is usually characterized by the well-known concept of *bhakti*, devotion or loving surrender to a deity,[5] which is meant to be experienced not only mentally, but also physically. Through the dance, it is sought to turn the presence of the deity into a somatic experience in which the senses are involved, not only as far as the dancers are concerned, but also for those who watch the dance in a spiritual mood. The spirituality of the Odissi dance is often seen by its Orissan practitioners and interpreters as being rooted in a more general Indian state of mind. "Spirituality," we learn from, for example, a leading Orissan expert on Odissi, "is the core of Indian art. Evolved out of spiritual passions, art in India has gone hand in hand with religion since time immemorial—spirituality is a divine experience of communion with the divine" (Patnaik 1990, p. 7). While these and many similar statements which could be cited in this context are hardly to be disputed in their generality, the specific kind of spirituality connected with Odissi only reveals itself to us when we examine more closely the dance's historical and aesthetic-performative aspects.

2. The Odissi Dance in Historical Perspective

The name "Odissi" is relatively recent, being traced back to the Orissan poet and scholar Kalicharan Pattnayak, who coined the term in 1955. But the dance that is known as Odissi today is already mentioned as the "Odra Nruyta" or "Orissa Dance" in a Sanskrit scripture known as *Abhinaya Chandrika*, probably produced some time in the fifteenth century (cf. Patnaik 1990). Apart from this regional text, which links the dance with the cult of Jagannath, like other Indian classical dances Odissi has been raised to the national, pan-Indian level by being traced back to quasi-divine knowledge as revealed in two Sanskrit texts of classical quality, namely the *Natyasastra* dating back to the fifth century A.D., and the *Abhinayadarpana* written some time in the twelfth century A.D. For Odissi we also have late Sanskrit writings such as the *Nartananirnaya* and the *Abhinaya Chandrika* just mentioned, in which we find quite detailed descriptions of the postures called *chauka*, *tribhanga* and *abhanga*, which are typical of this dance (see Bose 2001).

---

[4] I have discussed the issue of "love and surrender," or of the "dialectical relationship between 'agency' and 'patiency'," exhibited in and through the dance in an article (Schnepel forthcoming) in a volume edited by K.-P. Koepping, B. Schnepel and C. Wulf.

[5] For discussions of *bhakti*, see especially Michaels 1998, pp. 277–285 and Fuller 1992, pp. 155–181.

The origin of Odissi is traced back by many to the beginnings of the cult of Jagannath in Puri. During the early twelfth century, Jagannath, who probably started his "career" as a local deity of tribal origin (see ESCHMANN 1978a; 1978b), was raised to the status of "state deity" by the Ganga kings, who also built the magnificent temple in Puri for him. This temple, which also has a big festival hall, was the venue of dance rituals which a group of women known as *devadasis* or "servants of the god" performed daily in front of the wooden effigy of Jagannath in order to please him as part of the general *puja* activities in this temple.[6] In about the same period we can locate the making of an important literary work, namely the *Gitagovinda* of the poet Jayadeva, which had a great impact on the arts of Orissa. The poems and divine praises which can be found there were performed in the songs and dances of the *devadasi*s.[7] Contemporary practitioners of the Odissi therefore regard their dance as being rooted in the *devadasi*s' dance tradition, with the *Gitagovinda* being the basis for many Odissi choreographies, especially when they deal with the *lila* of Radha and Krishna.

During the sixteenth century, the dance was practically moved out of the temple of Jagannath and the palace of the Gajapatis, and was then performed in other more common venues, being enacted by the so-called *gotipua*s, young boys dressed up as girls. The rise of the *gotipua* tradition is linked to the decline of the *devadasi* tradition which lost its moral respect first under Muslim and then under British rule. The development of the *gotipua* tradition is also associated with the Vaishnava prophet Caitanya (1486–1533), whose teachings were characterized by a strong impetus towards *bhakti*, advocating the devotional surrender of the believer to Krishna as his loving (female) servant. It is likely that the adherents of *Caitanya* and other followers of a *bhakti*-dominated form of religiosity used the *gotipua* tradition to spread their ideas and messages (see PATNAIK 1990, pp. 73–77; KOTHARI 2001, p. 94).[8] The history of the Odissi, then, has three strands of influence which have converged more and more as time has passed: 1) *Shastric* Sanskrit texts through which the dance is linked to the so-called "Great Tradition" and qualifies to be called "classical;"[9] 2) the tradition of the female temple dancers known as *devadasi*s;

[6] The temple rituals are well described by RÖSEL (1980). The *devadasis* are the object of an elaborate study by MARGLIN (1985). See also PATNAIK 1990, pp. 62–73 and C. SCHNEPEL 2005, pp. 21–36.

[7] Jayadeva, a fervent adherent of Krishna, was probably married to a *devadasi*. On his art, life and the evening rituals in Puri, see DAS 1995.

[8] On Caitanya's influence in Orissa, see MUKHERJEE 1978, pp. 309–319.

[9] In India, classical dances belonging to the so-called "Great Tradition" are called *marga*, while local and rural dances of the "Little Tradition" are characterized as *desi*. See BOSE 2001, p. 3; MICHAELS/BALDISSERA 1988, p. 42 and VATSYAYAN 1980, p. 5f.

and 3) the Vaishnava *gotipua* tradition performed by young male dancers in female attire. But there is a fourth strand, not to be forgotten here: the Federal State of Orissa contains a relatively high percentage of tribal populations as compared with other regions of India, and these have mixed with popular forms of Hinduism to form a quite characteristic mixture.[10] There are indicators that this strong influence of tribal and popular religion and culture on Orissan history and culture has also affected the Odissi dance. To the three strands of influence or traditions that have formed the Odissi, one must therefore add considerable influences from popular Hinduism, as well as from tribal art and culture. These have entered the dance both through the cult of Jagannath, which in itself contains some important tribal elements, and independently through other avenues. It is significant that, despite the importance given to the Odissi as part of India's classical "Great Tradition," many of the gurus of the Odissi whom I interviewed emphasized this tribal aspect to the dance, thus following a new "cultural logic" in Orissa (and probably also India as a whole) which has started to re-evaluate tribal culture and art positively.

3. The Dance's Aesthetic Qualities

Experts on Indian dances often describe the Odissi as being one of the most lyrical and feminine of all Indian dances. The Odissi fascinates experts and ordinary spectators alike through its graceful, gentle, soft, round movements (see C. Schnepel 2005, pp. 49f.). The Odissi consists of two forms, first an aesthetic or "pure" dance, and secondly an "expressive" dance, also known as *abhinaya*.[11] Both these forms of the dance are part of stage performances, no matter whether they are carried out by individual dancers or by dance ensembles. These performances usually consist of five parts, starting with an invocation and greeting to Jagannath, which is followed by one "pure dance" sequence. In this sequence the basic rhythmical movements and postures of the dance are shown, most of them being quite "sculptural" in character, reminding one of those well-known sculptures on the outsides of temple walls. During those phases that belong to the "expressive" kind of dance, the dancers enact the poems, legends and stories of divine beings, Krishna first among them. The dancer incorporates a god or goddess and makes it visible to the audience both mimically and through bodily gestures. Yet another

[10] See, for example, the "Dance of Punishment" (*dando nato*), recently described by B. Schnepel (2008).

[11] The expressive form of the dance or *abhinaya* is also described as a dance pantomime. The movements of the hand and the fingers, known as *mudra* and *hasta* respectively, represent words, phrases, ideas or even heroes and divine beings. More detailed information on this can be found in Michaels/Baldissera 1988, pp. 50–76; Patnaik 1990, pp. 88–100 and Puri 1998, pp. 241–260.

"pure-dance" sequence, known as *moksha* or "release," will round off the performance. As the title suggests, this sequel is soteriological in character, promising salvation and unity with the divine.

As has been mentioned before, practising the dance is understood as a form of worship. This religious dimension to the dance also emerges through how it is taught. As in so many other ways of transmitting sacred knowledge in India, acquiring an expertise in Odissi can only be achieved fully, so it is understood, by submitting oneself as a dedicated pupil to a guru (and his own particular ways and contents of teaching). Generally, for this a prolonged period of time is considered necessary, if not a life time. When I started out with my own endeavours in learning this dance, I was soon told by Kum Kum Mohanty that it takes a minimum of ten years to be able to perform it properly, at least in order to learn or rather to internalize the complex and standardized repertoire of bodily movements, gestures and mimicry. It is also considered imperative for any pupil to acquaint him- or herself intimately with the "texts" that are enacted on the stage.

The dance is understood as an embodiment of divine aesthetics, which comes to the fore especially in the "pure dance;" and it is also seen as a divine instrument with which to convey messages, which is achieved through the "expressive" form of the dance. The "somatic vocabulary" of this part of the Odissi is not only used to illustrate the myths, legends and stories of divine beings, but also to express and bring forth emotions. This aim is based on an "aesthetics" of moods and emotional states which are described and standardized in the various Sanskrit manuals of dance as well. The intention is to generate a specific emotional state (*bhava*) which produces a corresponding emotion, known as *rasa*, within the spectator. In order to achieve this aim, the dancer needs to have empathy with these emotional states and to identify with them, if not to internalize and *embody* them. Members of the audience will then be able to sense and feel this emotion in themselves too. Through the Odissi dance, then, aesthetic performance is transmitted into a sensuous and even somatic religious experience.[12]

4. The Gurus' Points of View

The "love and surrender" attitude encapsulated in the term *bhakti* is prominent in statements made by gurus when characterizing the dance. In interviews, they stressed to me repeatedly that they have devoted their lives not only to the

[12] On the construction of emotion, see the articles in Lynch 1990. According to Marglin (1990), the dance rituals of the *devadasis* stimulate and incite an "erotic emotion" (*srngara rasa*) in the believing spectators, who by watching so intensely somehow become actors themselves; this emotion Marglin calls "body-emotion-thought."

god, but also to the dance. Dedicating one's life to the dance means dedicating one's life to the true and beautiful, and ultimately, therefore, to the divine. The dance itself is *bhakti*, I was told by Guru Gajendra Panda—*bhakti* and Lord Jagannath/Krishna. To dance Odissi for Panda is a religious activity dedicated to praising Jagannath. And through Jagannath, Panda also argued, the Odissi dance attains its regional and tribal flavour, because Jagannath is originally a tribal god, and Odissi is therefore in essence a tribal dance (see C. SCHNEPEL 2005, pp. 62–65).

For another guru, Gangadhar Pradhan, to dance the Odissi is likewise an expression of one's love of Jagannath. Pradhan, however, connects the Odissi less with a tribal tradition than with the "great" cultural heritage and tradition of Orissa. Consequently, in 1978 he founded his dance centre, containing a school and a performance hall, in the famous temple city of Konarak, not far from the acclaimed Sun Temple built in the twelfth century. In one of his choreographies called "Konarak Jagan: Sun temple come into light, the awakening of the statues of Konarak temple", he expresses the desire of the heyday of the temple coming to life again. Proudly he led me through his premises, calling himself repeatedly a "tradition lover." He was ambitious to make his *ashram*, as he called it, sooner or later into an internationally famous spiritual centre for teaching, performing and spreading Odissi and Oriya culture. His centre also contains a school for *gotipua*s, where he boards young village boys, giving them a common school education, but also training them in Odissi and *gotipua*. "Odissi is a refinement of *gotipua*, *devadasi*s and folk dance," he explained.

Bidut Kumari Choudhury, another Odissi performer of some standing, is "Lady Principal" of the government-run *Utkal Sangeet Mahavidyala* in Bhubaneswar. For her, the dance is a gift from the gods. In the training sessions, she places a great deal of attention on the *mudra*s of the expressive dance or *abhinaya*, because it is this form of the Odissi which to her mind best establishes a relationship with the audience. In an Odissi manual written by her for students, we read:

> The body gestures in the dance give pleasure to the eyes of the audience ... While watching the dance being performed, our mind and heart is also influenced ... But dance is not only vision, it flows in two streams for the purpose of audience as spectacle and audible. (CHOUDHURY 1999, pp. 1ff.)

And:

> It is a flow of dance or drama to the audience. The rhythm of any animal, bird or man and its thougs the Gods and Goddesses is enacted in the form of Abhinaya ... Forgetting one's self, enacting someone else other than yourself with such engrossment is known as Abhinaya. (CHOUDHURY 1999, p. 67)

According to Choudhury's explanations, then, a dancer is qualified most of all by mastering the *abhinaya*. The interpretation of a poem, song or divine story by means of a dance, if performed well and with an "authentic" expression of emotions, will trigger sentiments and emotions among the audience as well.

Another practitioner and teacher of the Odissi dance is the Italian Ileana Citaristi. For more than thirty years now, this fervent adherent of Odissi has been living in Bhubaneswar, where she runs a well-reputed private dancing school. According to her own account, following a personal spiritual quest she was led to Orissa, where she finally found her destiny in Odissi as taught by Kelucharan Mohapatra. We can read on her homepage: "Here, completely dedicated to the sacred art of Indian dance at the feet of my guru Kelucharan Mohapatra, I am able to give shape to the inner striving of the soul and overcome the anxiety of human existence" (Citaristi n. d.). With her book *The Making of a Guru*, she wrote a personal homage to her guru Kelucharan Mohapatra, who is considered by many to be the most important dancer and guru of the Odissi dance. Among his pupils there are not only many Orissans, but also, like Ileana Citaristi, quite a number of people from abroad. Not a few of his pupils today lead dance schools and dance ensembles of their own, thus continuing to teach and propagate their guru's style. It is said that *bhakti* and the worship of the God Jagannath have determined Mohapatra's life, and many Odissi dancers elevate Mohapatra himself to a divine status. Citaristi writes in her book:

> He dances on stage as if possessed by a divine spirit which acts through him; never repeating himself, always recreating with total involvement. For his disciples he is like god ... Kelucharan receives all these demonstrations of love with grace and offers everything to his beloved Lord Jagannath; on stage, as in his life, devotion fills his gestures and radiates from him. (Citaristi 2001, pp. 180f.)

The American Odissi dancer Sharon Lowen describes him as "the embodiment of the transformative power of Indian Classical performing arts. His performances moved audiences to tears of wonder and joy in villages, temples and capital cities around the globe" (Lowen 2004). Mohapatra's daughter-in-law called him a "creator," and, when anyone masters his style, she spoke of him/her as an "embodiment of Mohapatra." The most important thing for Kelucharan Mohapatra was "to forget oneself:"

> Observe and feel, don't mimic or look in a mirror ... Before coming to the stage, I put on my makeup and begin to focus on the role or character, salute my guru, and only think of what that character, whether Nayika or Hanuman or Kevat will do. I am already transformed before I enter the stage. You have to forget yourself, your own identity totally. (Lowen 2004)

For Rekha Tandon, as well, the dance is a spiritual matter; spirituality to her is inherent in and essential to Odissi. She also advocates a close connection with yoga, especially *hatha yoga*, which she practices herself and in which she sees a physical activity through which one is enabled to re-unite (in her words) "body awareness" and "psychic awareness." As she explained to me: "The combined body and mental awareness is to activate the seven chakras" (see Schnepel 2005, p. 74). And in another context she says of the spirituality of the dance:

> To remain true to its spirit, Odissi needs to be a "sacred channel" drawing in "divine energy through the material form of the body and providing an access to inner space." Due to its inherent structures, the language it articulates best is that of devotion to God. (Tandon n. d.)

For Tandon, then, the dance is a spiritual medium to activate divine energy, not only in the dancer, but in the audience as well. One day, while performing in Brazil, she felt an extraordinary energy enter her body, lifting her into another sphere. She described this experience to me as follows: "All of a sudden I saw myself floating on the ceiling and my body moving in a vortex. I felt like being used." In her own interpretation of the matter, this energy was transmitted to her through the audience at a certain stage of her performance. At this moment her body was taken over by a supernatural power, an energy that made her feel liberated from space, time and body.

After this experience in Brazil, Tandon left her guru and ensemble. Together with her husband Michael, an English musician and film-maker, she founded a dance centre of her own called Dance Routes. This is meant to be both a "school" to learn the established Odissi art and a "laboratory," i.e. a place which is open to experiments and new ideas. Thus she is breaking with a too strict adherence to traditionalism and "guruism," and also wants to transcend regional and even national cultural boundaries. The audience which she wishes to address and to make receptive to the emotions conveyed through the dance is not only an Orissan and Indian audience, but also an international one. In this way, Tandon also intends to react to the fact that, in India itself, young boys and girls are increasingly losing their interest in the dance, which to them is too complex and takes too long a time to learn, while Bollywood dances gain in attraction. Tandon thus wants to make a classical traditional dance enjoyable and attractive to contemporary spectators and dancers, including non-Indian ones.

Consequently, her own dance projects often focus on the tension and interplay between tradition and modernity, a theme which she also addressed in her dissertation entitled "Classicism on the Threshold of Modernity: Expanding the Physical Parameters of Odissi Dance for Contemporary Audiences" (Tandon 2005), which she submitted at the Laban Centre/City University in

London. In her own choreographies, she combines classical performances of Odissi with pieces of music, literature and film from various other cultures, whenever a dialogue with the divine is part of the artistic imagination of these genres. In one of her performances, for example, she dances Odissi to a poem by Rabindranath Tagore which is recited in English; in another she lets the spirit of an old and empty London manor house come to life through dancing in Odissi style.[13] In yet another choreography, she dances Odissi more traditionally to a poem called "Hymns to the Goddess" in a temple near Bhubaneswar, expressing through her movements and gestures the greatness and beauty of the divine mother Saraswati. All in all, then, for Tandon, as for her colleagues, Odissi is a religious affair. However, she also lets "Western" and/or "modern" elements and influences flow into her interpretation of the dance. While her *bhakti* is addressed to Jagannath and other Hindu deities as well, in the end the "divine" with whom she seeks to communicate and convey through the dance is more universal. For her the dance is about developing, expressing and liberating the self in a more Western or universal understanding. For this purpose she experiments by combining elements from various artistic backgrounds, whether yoga, popular or classical dances.

4. The Body Outside-In

The human body is an instrument for the dance. Through it the dancer expresses stories and emotions and conveys messages. But in the context of the Odissi and many other non-Western art genres, the body is not only *ex*pressive, it is also *im*pressive, i.e. it is a medium into which something enters. As we have seen, especially in Tandon's case, the body of the Odissi dancer is a receptacle for deities and divine energy. In Odissi, the body is, then, more than just an instrument to express something, it is also medium and vessel through which the divine communicates and into which it can come.[14] Through years and years of practice, pupils learn and exercise the complicated techniques and the intricate "body language" of the dance again and again. The aim, at the highest level, is to dissolve one's self in order to be able to let the divine enter into one's body. On top of this, pupils have to acquaint themselves with the

---

[13] In the film depicting this performance, Tandon moves through the empty rooms of the house, her body sometimes disappearing and then suddenly re-appearing. There are shadows moving, and one can see, among other things, a calm pond, a cat licking her paw and other images conveying calmness, but also vital life energy. The choreography is supported by music from a piano, an oboe and a syntheziser. By showing Odissi in the medium of "film" (and not on stage or in a temple) and having it accompanied by musical instruments that are foreign to this dance, Tandon wants to show the continuity of the traditional dance, albeit in another time and place.

[14] For a similar argument, see B. Schnepel 2000 and 2008.

philosophy, mythology and religion of Orissa, thus turning the body-mind into a container which stores the region's (religious) history and culture. One could say that the body, as a container, becomes a *lieu de mémoire*, remembering Jagannath and Krishna and the all-embracing love and spirituality which they stand for and bring to life in their adherents.

As far as the postures and movements of the "pure dance" are concerned, one can compare these to the stone sculptures of temples, of which the sun temple in Konarak, with its splendid erotic figurines, is one of the leading examples not only in Orissa, but in India as a whole. The pure dance is an embodiment of a divine aesthetic, and the dance which makes this embodiment possible is regarded as a gift of the gods. Mohanty sees Odissi as an expression of beauty and aesthetics. Her own focus in teaching and performing the dance is thus on "pure beauty," her intention being to capture the parameters of this beauty in a "script" which she has been preparing for some time. Beauty was also linked by Mohapatra to harmony, or rather to a sense of harmony. This sense has to be felt rather than known in the conventional sense: "The limits are not dictated by the style but by your aesthetic sense; there is an inner harmony which is common to the movement composed, the underlying music and the context of the meaning to be expressed. If this harmony is not achieved you will instinctively know that something is wrong and you will continue the search for it until that harmony is achieved and when it is realized you will instinctively know" (cited in Citaristi 2001, p. 157).

The gestures and mimics, which are so special to Odissi and other Indian dances in general, form a language with which stories (usually of gods) are told. Through the dance deities speak to the human beings, especially if the dancer has given up his or her self. "Forget yourself totally," as Mohapatra emphasized.[15] As far as the expressive dance or *abhinaya* is concerned, this is also considered by many actors as a kind of (body) language intended to establish a dialogue and interaction with the audience. As we have seen, Tandon understood her experience in Brazil as a communicative act between herself and her audience. According to her own interpretation, the spiritual energy she experienced was created in the space or interaction between dancer and audience. She dances not *for* the audience, Tandon explained, but *with* the audience, and more precisely with the energy of the audience. She plays and dances with this energy and with anything that she can absorb, including the venue of the performance, which she visits, without an audience being present, before each performance in order to communicate with it and, in her words, to "sanctify the space."

---

[15] It is said that not a single female Odissi dancer manages to perform the "sensuous walk" of Radha as convincingly as he did.

This leads me to the observation that Odissi is always danced in front of two audiences, one human, the other divine. This is expressed by the fact that, at the start of a performance, the dancer always bows to both the audience in the front and to her or his god, usually Jagannath, who is represented by an anthropomorphic idol or *murti* located at a seat of honour at one corner of the stage. During the dance the audience is brought closer to the deities and/or the divine energy. But when they enter the dialogue or better trialogue with the deities and the dancers, the members of the audience are no longer just spectators. If the performance is successful (and this means effective but also affective in an emotional sense), the spectators become actors themselves. This phenomenon of religious moods, sentiments and emotions arising from the interaction and communication between dancers, audience and gods could be characterized as an "emerging" and "emergent" reality.[16] It can also be understood with reference to Lienhardt's concept of *passio* (cf. LIENHARDT 1961), with which we can best understand a basically non-western view in which extra-human powers are seen to have agency, while the human beings whom they enter in trance, dreams, possession, shamanistic séances or other techniques (like dance) are just passive and hence the "patients" of these active powers. Only after, and through, making themselves open to *passiones* can the dancers and spectators experience and develop spiritual energy and hence agency.[17]

5. Conclusions

The Odissi dance has moved out of the temples and, from being a religious tradition to honour the gods, has acquired more secular venues of performance. Nevertheless it has maintained its spirituality and is still seen as a medium through which to contact and enter into a dialogue with the divine. In doing so, the body assumes an important role because a deeper knowledge of the dance's somatically expressed techniques and of the "sacred lore" associated with the dance is still seen by all performers and gurus as essential for connectivity with the divine. It is regarded as imperative that all the detailed postures and movements of body, hands and fingers, as well as the eye movements and various facial expressions described in the *Natyasastra* and the *Abhinayadharpana*, are not only mastered, but somehow internalized. The natural body, which is compartmentalized in the process of learning the dance, is put together anew the more this learning is completed and perfected. Mastering the *abhinaya* also means first to forget oneself, then to remember

[16] Here, of course, I am referring to an important concept of "performance theory" as put forward especially by SCHIEFFELIN (1976; 1998).

[17] On the dialectics of "agency" and "patiency," see B. SCHNEPEL forthcoming.

the movements and stories connected with the dance, and finally to dance in a way which is understood or rather emotionally and physically felt by the audience as being an authentic representation of the gods and of divine energy.

References

Bose, M. (2001): Speaking of Dance. – New Delhi.

Choudhury, B. K. (1999): Odissi Dance. – Bhubaneswar.

Citaristi, I. (2001): The Making of a Guru: Kelucharan Mohapatra, His Life and Times. – New Delhi.

Citaristi, I. (n. d.): Ileana Citaristi. – kalinga.net/ileana: URL: http://www.kalinga.net/ileana/ – Download from 23.4.2009.

Das, D. (1995): Dance. In: Pathy, D./Panda, B./Rath, B. K. (Eds.): Jayadeva and Gītagovinda in the Traditions of Orissa. – New Delhi, pp. 87–91.

Eschmann, A./Kulke, H./Tripathi, G. C. (Eds.) 1978: The Cult of Jagannath and the Regional Tradition of Orissa. – New Delhi.

Eschmann, A. (1978a): Hinduization of Tribal Deities in Orissa: The Shakta and Saiva Typology. In: Kulke, H./Tripathi, G. C. (Eds.): The Cult of Jagannath and the Regional Tradition of Orissa. – New Delhi, pp. 79–97.

Eschmann, A. (1978b): The Vaishnava Typology of Hinduization and the Origin of Jagannatha. In: Kulke, H./Tripathi, G. C. (Eds.): The Cult of Jagannath and the Regional Tradition of Orissa. – New Delhi, pp. 99–117.

Fuller, C. J. (1992): The Camphor Flame: Popular Hinduism and Society in India. – Princeton.

Kothari, S. (2001): Odissi: From Devasabha to Janasabha. In: Pal, P. (Ed.): Orissa Revisited. – Mumbai, pp. 93–104.

Kulke, H. (1979): Jagannath-Kult und Gajapati-Königtum. – Wiesbaden.

Kulke, H./Schnepel, B. (Eds.) (2001): Jagannath Revisited. – New Delhi.

Lienhardt, G. (1961): Divinity and Experience: The Religion of the Dinka. – Oxford.

Lowen, S. (2004): Kelucharan Mohapatra: the Undisputed Master. – narthaki.com: URL: http://www.narthaki.com/info/profiles/profil40.html – Download from 22.4.2009.

Lynch, O. (Ed.) (1990): Divine Passions: The Social Construction of Emotion in India. – Berkeley/Oxford.

Marglin, F. A. (1985): Wives of the God King: The Rituals of the Devadasis of Puri. – New Delhi.

Marglin, F. A. (1990): Refining the Body: Transformative Emotion in Ritual Dance. In: Lynch, O. (Ed.): Divine Passions: The Social Construction of Emotion in India. – Berkeley/Oxford, pp. 212–236.

Michaels, A. (1998): Der Hinduismus: Geschichte und Gegenwart. – München.

Michaels, A./Baldissera, F. (1988): Der Indische Tanz: Körpersprache in Vollendung. – Cologne.

Mukherjee, P. (1978): Caitanya in Orissa. In: Eschmann, A./Kulke, H./Tripathi, G. C. (Eds.): The Cult of Jagannath and the Regional Tradition of Orissa. – New Delhi, pp. 309–319.

Patnaik, D. N. (1990): Odissi Dance. – 1st edition 1971 – Bhubaneswar.

Puri, R. (1998): The Interpretation of Abhinaya in Indian Dance: The Communication of Meaning in the Medium of Movement. In: Waterhouse, D. (Ed.): Dance of India. – Mumbai, pp. 241–260.

RÖSEL, J. (1980): Der Palast des Herrn der Welt. – München.
SCHIEFFELIN, E. (1976): The Sorrow of the Lonely and the Burning Dancers. In: WILLIAMS, D. (Ed.): Anthropology and Human Movement: The Study of Dances. – Lanham, Md./ London, pp. 166–197.
SCHIEFFELIN, E. (1998): Problematizing Performance. In: HUGHES-FREELAND, F. (Ed.): Ritual, Performance, Media. – London.
SCHNEPEL, B. (2000): Der Körper im "Tanz der Strafe" in Orissa. In: KÖPPING, K.-P./ RAO, U. (Ed.): Im Rausch des Rituals. – Hamburg, pp. 156–171.
SCHNEPEL, B. (2008): "Tanzen für Kali:" Ethnographie eines ostindischen Ritualtheaters. – Berlin.
SCHNEPEL, B. (forthcoming): Die Dialektik von "Agency" und "Patiency." In: SCHNEPEL, B./ WULF, C./KÖPPING, K.-P. (Eds.): Paragrana: Internationale Zeitschrift für Historische Anthropologie.
SCHNEPEL, C. (2005): Odissi: eine ostindische Tanzform im Kontext der Debatten um regionale Traditionen und kulturelle Identität. – Halle (Saale). (Südasienwissenschaftli che Arbeitsblätter Band 6)
SCHNEPEL, C. (forthcoming): An der Decke schweben. In: SCHNEPEL, B./WULF, C./KÖPPING, K.-P. (Eds.): Paragrana: Internationale Zeitschrift für Historische Anthropologie.
TANDON, R. (2005): Classicism on the Threshold of Modernity: Expanding the Physical Parameters of Odissi Dance for Contemporary Audiences. – London.
TANDON, R. (n. d.): Research. – danceroutes.com: URL: http://www.danceroutes.com/ ac.htm – Download from 22.4.2009.
VATSYAYAN, K. (1980): Traditional and Indian Theatre: Multiple Streams. – New Delhi.

Ute Hüsken

Ritual Competence as Embodied Knowledge

This essay points at the importance of considering questions concerning the body and embodiment in a ritual tradition which is usually seen as text-dominated, and strictly rule-governed. I argue that this perspective provides us with an additional analytical tool, which takes into account not only the textual layers, but also the praxis-related aspects of traditions that comprise of both, ritual texts and performance.

Here, the case study is the initiation into priesthood in South Indian Hindu traditions that consider the god Viṣṇu as the main god (these are called Vaiṣṇava traditions in what follows). The basis of this essay is both, field research among the present day practitioners and the analysis of the relevant Sanskrit texts, because in contemporary South India these Vaiṣṇava traditions are very lively and active ritual traditions and their main representatives usually emphasise that their rituals are even today faithfully performed according to certain ancient ritual texts in Sanskrit (the so-called Āgamas or Saṃhitās).[1]

The site of my field research is the Vaiṣṇava Varadarāja Perumāḷ temple in the South Indian temple town Kāñcipuram, situated ca. 70 km west of Chennai (Madras), the capital of India's southernmost state Tamil Nadu. Within this huge Viṣṇu temple, my research concentrates on the hereditary temple priests (*arcaka*), who are mediators between the god and the humans who come to the temple to interact in one way or the other with the god.

These priests have special rights and obligations with regard to the god Viṣṇu who is worshipped in this temple in his form as Varadarāja, the "Gift-bestowing King" (see Figure 1). As the only group allowed to touch the images of the god, the priests invoke the god and thus make him present in his iconic representations installed in the temple. They thereby facilitate his worship in the temple in general. Moreover, they serve the god like a human being (the god is frequently compared to a child or a king): they give him bath, they dress and feed him, they decorate him and present the devotees' offerings to him. The priests perform the ritual ablutions on him with water, milk, honey, and oil, and they accompany him as his servants during the processions.

[1] While the traditions claim that these Sanskrit ritual texts have been revealed to their mythical founders by the god Viṣṇu himself, they were compiled in or after the 8th to 10th centuries CE according to Western researchers.

Figure 1: The decorated image of the god Varadarāja, used for the festivals (*utsavamūrti*).

All these ritual actions are, the priests claim, performed "according to the Āgamas"—at least they should be, because critique on the performance of others usually is expressed by phrases such as "this is not done according to the Āgamas" or "this is against the Āgama regulations." The Āgamas invoked here are the above mentioned medieval ritual texts in Sanskrit.[2] In the Varadarāja temple these are the texts of the so-called Pāñcarātra tradition,[3] and the major text referred to here is a metrical Sanskrit text called *Pādmasaṃhitā*.[4]

These texts are also invariably invoked when questions are raised about the priests' right, obligation, and competence to perform rituals in this

[2] On the historical background of this claim see Hüsken 2009a and 2009b.

[3] For an overview over Pāñcarātra literature see Schrader 1916, Smith/Venkatachari 1975 and 1980, and Rastelli 1999a, 1999b, 2006.

[4] On the *Pādmasaṃhitā* see Smith/Venkatachari 1975, pp. 197ff.

temple. In such conversations, members of the concerned Vaiṣṇava groups invariably refer to their eligibility (*adhikāra*) to act as priests, as determined by "tradition." This tradition nowadays is mainly understood as being fixed in and by the mentioned medieval Sanskrit texts.

Nevertheless, more recently also ritual handbooks are printed, which are in one way or the other based on these mediaeval Sanskrit texts, but which in addition include commentaries and explanations in vernacular languages such as Tamil, Kannada or Telugu. These explanations make the content comprehensible to those priests who have no or only little knowledge of Sanskrit. And in spite of the constant reference to the Sanskrit Āgamas, it is rather these ritual handbooks than the Āgama texts that are used even during ritual performances (see Figure 2).

However, this physical use of printed texts in actual practice is assessed ambivalently: while on the one hand the use of texts during performances is appreciated as a proof of "following the authentic tradition," on the other it is also evaluated as a deficiency, since it reveals the lack of knowledge of the acting priest who has to resort to guidelines in the form of a text.[5] Thus, in

Figure 2: Two priests, using a ritual handbook during a public festival.

[5] Thus, the scene depicted in Figure 2 was strongly criticized by some participants. And in fact, the persuasiveness of the performances, even for me as an outsider, exists in an inversely proportional relationship to the degree of reference to the text.

spite of the authority attributed to the texts, in practice they are not necessarily conceived as models that should be followed word-for-word (see WELBON 1984, p. 97; FULLER 2003, pp. 81, 87).

A word-for-word execution of these ritual instructions is anyway impossible without a considerable amount of pre-knowledge, as a close look at the Sanskrit ritual texts reveals:[6] the rituals prescribed therein have to be constantly adapted to the concrete place and circumstances of their performance.[7]

In addition to an understanding of these texts performative knowledge, gained mainly through experience, is required to translate text into practice. Knowledge of texts *and* knowledge of how to apply them, including knowledge of how to react creatively and convincingly on contingencies is an essential part of priestly competence. Text and performance are therefore never 100% congruent—yet the priests' claim that their rituals are performed "according to the Āgamas" is perfectly valid, too, because the understanding and the application of the ritual prescriptions is subject to interpretation.

As I have shown elsewhere, even in cases when identical texts are used during diverse enactments of one and the same ritual, the actual performances differ greatly (see HÜSKEN 2009a and HÜSKEN 2009b). This holds true, for example, for the initiations required for a future temple priest in the Varadarāja temple. Their enactments differ partly from their prescriptions in the authoritative text *Pādmasaṃhitā*: the performance nowadays is usually abbreviated and depends on the candidate's family background, his affiliation to one of the two dominant Vaiṣṇava sects (Teṉkalai and Vaṭakalai), and many other aspects.[8]

The concrete circumstances external to the ritual proper most likely always have been highly relevant for which rituals are performed and how. Thus, the familial and professional background of the participants, the economic situation under which the rituals are performed, the spatial situation, and many more factors contribute enormously to a ritual's enactment.

Ritual knowledge is moreover, above all, embodied knowledge. As pointed out by FULLER: "How well a priest uses his body is interpreted as an index of how correctly he can perform ritual" (2003, p. 108). It seems that knowledge

[6] If ritualised actions are in fact to be understood as units or elements always already constituted by rules, as HUMPHREY/ LAIDLAW argue (1994 p. 88f.), then for the rituals discussed here these rules are evidently not (only) the written instructions of the ritual texts.

[7] Most of the Pāñcarātra texts were compiled without reference to specific places or circumstances.

[8] Thus, instead of the *samaya, putraka, sādhaka*, and *ācārya dīkṣā* which are prescribed by the texts, today the familial background —since in this temple priesthood has become hereditary some when in the 19th century— and the temple politics as executed by the temple officials (representatives of the government) are extremely important to be allowed to serve as a temple priest in this temple (see HÜSKEN 2009b).

of rituals leads to knowing the meaning of the texts, not the other way around.[9] At least in present day practice the written instructions ideally serve rather as guidelines than as rulebooks, and ritualised reading (recitation) is a ritual presentation of texts rather than a means of getting information.

Clearly the fact that especially those rites *not* elaborately described in the texts are performed in a very similar manner in different performances and by different actors points to the importance of ritual practice and experience rather than knowledge and understanding of texts. To give an example: the basic rites (building-blocks of many rituals) used in the course of many domestic rituals are embodied in every ritual specialist. These are for example the recitations, the body postures, and the hand gestures during the "formal declarations" (*saṃkalpa*) that mark the beginning of every Brahmanic ritual (see MICHAELS 2005), and the offerings into the sacrificial fire (*homa*). These rites are performed very similarly in different contexts, even though these rituals are rarely described in detail in these texts. The consultation of written ritual instructions is not necessary. On the other hand, rituals that are rarely performed are often highly individual and during their enactment frequently ritual texts are resorted to (see HÜSKEN 2009a).

The existence of a common pattern and at the same time the individuation of the rituals by the performers, dependent on the performance context and the experience of the ritual specialist, suggests that the performer and the process of how he acquires his ritual competence are extremely important factors in a rite's concrete enactment. A crucial question is therefore how the priests acquire their ritual competence and how this is reflected in the rituals' performances.

The above-mentioned Sanskrit ritual texts deal with ritual competence, too. They usually contain a statement about who may act as a priest. However, these statements frequently emphasise the priests' *right* to act as mediators between god and the devotees, irrespective of their individual capacity to do so. Thus, a ritual text of the Vaikhānasa tradition explicitly says:[10]

> The one and only one who may worship Viṣṇu, *whether he is well equipped or badly equipped*, must come from a Vaikhānasa family and is marked by a Cakra already before birth.

This statement can be interpreted as a license to ignorance, but it can also be read as a reference to the embeddedness of the neophytes into a setting

---

[9] This is evidenced also by the fact that the use of ritual handbooks during the performances is seen as deficiency rather than a safety measure to ensure the quality of a ritual (see above).

[10] Free translation of *Ānandasaṃhitā* 8.2: *ayogyo vā suyogyo vā garbhacakreṇa lāñchitaḥ/vaikhānasodbhavo Viṣṇum arcayed itare na tu//.*

(a family of hereditary performers) that enables them to know how to enact the rituals and how to do it right. As it turns out, this ascribed competence also enables the performers to deviate from the rules, and opens up a possibility for ritual creativity, which clearly hints at the priests' superior ritual competence and in no way devalues their ritual performances.

As I have argued elsewhere (HÜSKEN 2007), we can gain important insights into the processes by which the concrete form of the ritual emerges by considering deviations from ritual norms which are evaluated negatively (flaws, mistakes, errors, slips etc.). Thus, in one performance of a prenatal life-cycle ritual I witnessed, due to a slip in reading the ritual text, the priest allowed one ritual element to be performed twice. Moreover, occasionally the prescribed mantras were not recited, or recited at a point different from that mentioned in the texts, rites were left out or were fused with one another. Yet these deviations from the written norms did not lead to the ritual or parts of the ritual being judged as "wrongly performed." Rather, it became clear that one can only speak of "mistakes" when the leading priest explicitly or performatively declares certain acts or recitations to be mistaken. Here, as indicated by the textual statement quoted above, the ritual competence ascribed to a certain person (the priest) interacts with his performative competence.

Both forms of competence are, of course, no infallible mechanisms, but together they are extremely powerful and make the main actor into a competent ritual agent who has the power to react creatively to contingencies and also to deviate from the norm. Although the ritual texts are always referred to as authoritative and ultimate "source of tradition" by the performers themselves, the priests can deviate from the ritual rules given therein, at least to a certain extent. Their ritual competence is therefore not only established through knowledge of and adherence to rules given in the ritual text, but also through the ascribed competence, and through the priests' interactive and improvisational skills (see SCHIEFFELIN 1998, p. 198).

Nevertheless, the text quoted earlier also clearly states that ritual competence follows from the fact that the respective person belongs to a certain group:

> The one and only one who may worship Viṣṇu, whether he is well equipped or badly equipped, *must come from a Vaikhānasa family and is marked by a Cakra*[11] *already before birth.*

The definition of such a group or of boundaries that create an "inside" and an "outside" is an important aspect of human interaction in general (see SELIGMAN et al. 2008), although the modes of creating these boundaries might be different from tradition to tradition and change over time. Thus, a major

[11] The "marking by the Cakra" refers to a prenatal initiation here (see HÜSKEN 2009a).

conflict between the two rival groups of temple priests in South Indian Viṣṇu temples is about whether the right to act as temple priest is acquired by birth or by initiation. Other conflicts are about the concrete enactments of the relevant life-cycle rituals and initiations. These rituals clearly change over time, responding to the changing demands of their setting, but retain their importance as long as the competence acquired through them is valued (see HÜSKEN 2009a).

Such rituals that create a group's boundaries, whether these are (prenatal) life-cycle rituals or rituals of initiation, can be labelled "hard qualifications."

Apart from that there are other qualifications which have to be fulfilled, if young men want to become temple priests in the Varadarāja temple. These shall be termed "soft qualifications" here, because these are in many cases a matter of negotiation and interpretation—although reference to them is made in present day discourse among the ritual performers as well as in the mediaeval ritual texts in Sanskrit.

One of these "soft qualifications" is for example that the young men have to show from early age on some interest in the proceedings going on in and around the temple (see Figures 3 and 4). They must feel and show some

Figure 3: The acting priest's sons watch him performing a *homa*.

Figure 4: The grandson of the acting priest watching what is going on in the ritual arena.

attraction to the temple priest's profession, as I am frequently told. Rituals are a major field of socialization, and this holds doubly true in traditions such as those of the Vaiṣṇava priests dealt with here; especially as in this tradition the priests are considered the impersonation of the god and the priest's body is considered the residence of the god.

In addition to individually shown interest, some education in the recitation of Vedic texts and the Tamil Divyaprabandhams, and, most importantly, some knowledge of the above-mentioned medieval Sanskrit ritual texts is required.

Moreover, those who aspire to become temple priests also need a thorough practical training, enabling them to translate the words of the texts into action, or to link textual passages with specific ritual acts.

Apart from this specific knowledge and practice, their constant exposure to public surveillance requires future temple priests to "behave properly." This concerns their style of living, including efforts to maintain their ritual purity through restrictions concerning food, drink, clothing, hair style, action, and contact. Moreover, they are required to fully dedicate themselves to the service to the god: the priests at this temple may not take upon themselves for example a regular part time job elsewhere.

While the above-mentioned "hard qualifications" (membership to a group, through rituals of initiation and life-cycle rituals) refer rather to a person's *eligibility*, the "soft qualifications" rather concern their *ability*. While the "hard" factors remain important, it is only in combination with a priest's ability that full ritual competence is acquired.

Nowadays, many temple priests' families in Kāñcipuram, who enjoy hereditary rights to perform worship in the Varadarāja Perumāḷ temple, encourage their youngsters to subscribe to courses in governmental approved so-called Āgama schools and earn a certificate of sorts there, because a service rule issued in 1964 by the Hindu Religious and Charitable Endowment Department demands that every newly appointed priest needs such a certificate issued by an Āgamic school.

However, in contrast to the traditional way of learning by participating in the life of the teacher, in many of these rather recently established Āgama schools, learning of texts and theoretical knowledge is emphasised. The lack of emphasis on practical training is evidently one of their major disadvantages. This, however, is already built into the very concept underlying these institutions, namely that knowing the Āgama texts inevitably implies that one is capable of performing the rituals, and that standardised texts alone are perceived and represented as the source of authoritative knowledge (see Fuller 2003, p. 86).

In contrast, interviews among the young priests of the Varadarāja temple who attended courses in these Āgama schools, but also among the experienced elder priests clearly show that the ability to perform the rituals is *not* acquired in these schools. They achieve this thorough knowledge in the rituals' practical performance in the first instance from learning with their fathers, or with other male relatives. To quote two of the main ritual actors in the Varadarāja temple, with whom I was talking about how they learnt what they are doing:

> Naturally, my father was doing it. I was sitting with him and doing this. For many years it was like that. Finally, when he got very old, he got his eyes operated at one stage. At that time I was sitting personally and he would be sitting by my side to supervise me. Now also my son comes and joins me in doing this.

Another main performer says:

> As I have been working in the temple since the age of fifteen, I know what the custom is in the temple. So in a way I am grown up with it and experienced through the long years of service. Moreover, I went with the Prabandha Ghoṣṭhi [the group reciting the Tivyapirapanta hymns] and I also have experience from a very young age of all the practices at the temple. I grew up here. My Periyappa [the elder brother of his father] was the one who taught me the Prabandhas. I also went with the now eldest of the temple priests, Sīmā Bhaṭṭar. With him I learnt a lot. Every Kumbhābhiṣekam [temple inauguration] I have watched before I got my position.

> So it became very natural for me to take on the job. I have also travelled a lot with elder members of the community and visited other temples. So a lot of my authority is derived from the fact that I have learnt also from the elders. The younger people who come to the temple know that I have been with the elders and have learnt from them.

In face of this evidence, it seems legitimate to perceive initiation as a process, rather than an isolated ritual event: "initiating and initiation goes on all the time" (Grimes 2002, p. 89). Although certain points within this process are ritually stressed and marked by "initiation rituals," it is important to emphasise that by the initiation ritual a person is made into somebody he or she yet has to become (see Figure 5). While "initiation" often is seen as a rite of passage that effects an irreversible status change, here "initiation" is understood not just as a specific ritual, but rather as a process. The ritual of initiation is a marker taking place at a certain point of time in this process. Initiations are embedded in a "long and complex multidirectional process of increasingly somatic practice" during which the body gradually becomes a "body-in-practice," as Bado-Fralick (2009) terms it. She convincingly argues that in

Figure 5: Mr. Varadan Kattiyam and his sister's son Jishnu.

this long process the body is increasingly involved not only as an acting agent, but also as "knower" of the skills necessary for ritual work. The physical body thus emerges as "equally important to belief or intellectual knowledge." In the context at hand, ritual has clearly more to do with embodied practice than with disembodied belief.

Since practice, participation, experience in and exposure to ritual are major factors in this process, it is worth while looking at the physical and bodily aspects of a ritual in addition to its textual representation.

Repeated practice creates memory, which is, according to Thomas J. Csordas, always also bodily memory.[12] Even perception is in principle a bodily process (see Figure 6) since our bodies are integral part of the perceiving subject

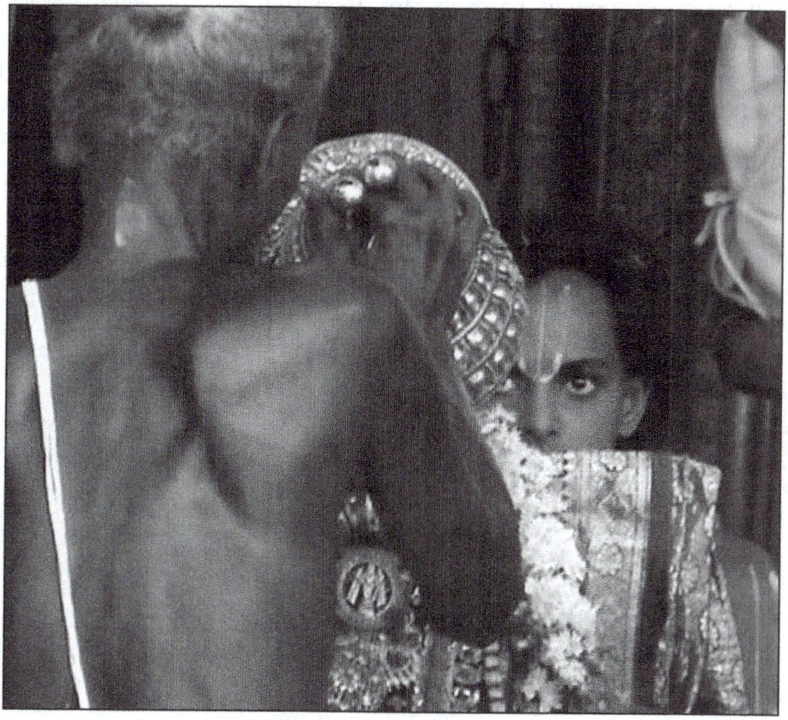

Figure 6: A child watches closely what the acting priest is doing.

[12] This reminds us that, when trying to explore rituals and their transformations, we have to pay attention to the fact that rituals are constituted by text, performance, *and memory* (see GRIMES 2006). Csordas takes Bourdieu's notion of "the socially informed body" as the "principle generating and unifying all practices" (*habitus*) and argues in his seminal article on embodiment that "a theory of practice ca be best grounded in the socially informed body" (CSORDAS 1990, p. 8).

(Csordas 1990, p. 5). On the level of perception it is therefore not legitimate to distinguish between mind and body, although our bodies may *become* objectified through the process of reflection (Csordas 1990, p. 36).

Following him in taking "embodied experience as the starting point for analyzing human participation in a cultural world," a new perspective on the acquisition of ritual competence in South Indian Vaiṣṇava temples opens up.

Even in those parts of the practical education of future temple priests in which ritual texts are used, the major role of the body is evident (Figure 7). The ritual prescriptions are learnt together with the respective action: while the relevant sections of the texts are recited the corresponding actions are performed. In such a way the relation between text and performance is established and, in the long run, embodied—the body remembers it. Even the memorisation of textual passages for recitation can be characterised as important kind of bodily technique, albeit combined with literate learning (Figure 8). The correct vocalisation of texts (including stress, pitch, rythm) are important features of priestly education (Fuller 2003, pp. 86, 102f.). Therefore, while the existence of texts in printed form helps in memorizing

Figure 7: Mr. Krishnasvami Bhattar reads the "Invitation to the gods" during a festival.

Figure 8: Boys and young men taking class in recitation.

the texts and thus in fact improves the young priests' capacity to recite them by heart, priestly education still is mainly based on practical training.

Therefore, even in those largely "textual" traditions the importance of the body as learning agent, acting on the mind as much as the mind acts on the body, must be emphasised. Ritual, as action, visibly enacted or enacted in imagination, must be seen as action of the body. While the meaning and function of the ritual may differ for the diverse performers, its enactment is its unifying element. This does not only apply to the ritual performance in the narrower sense, but to the learning process as well: attendance, repetition and practice precede and create understanding.

Mimesis as means of transmitting priestly knowledge is a crucial issue in priestly education. The heart of mimesis is attention (see Figures 9–11). While "attention" is thought of as "watching" in the first place, it is usually conceptualized as a process of the mind rather than a bodily process. Csordas, however, argues for a strong emphasis on the body: "… one is paying attention with one's body. Attending with one's eyes is really part of this same phenomenon, but we less often conceptualize visual attention as a 'turning toward' then as a disembodied, beam-like 'gaze.' We tend to think of it as cognitive function, but should rather see it as a form of bodily engagement" (Csordas 1993, p. 138).

Figure 9: Hidden behind a pillar a boy watches attentively the priests' performance.

Figure 10: The acting priest's sons watch him performing.

Figure 11: A boy watches the priests through a fence.

But Csordas' notion of somatic mode of attention signifies not only attention to and with one's own body, but includes "attention to the bodies of others with one's own body ..." (Csordas 1993, p. 139; see Figures 12–14).[13]

Mimesis, however, is not only attention, but attention paired with imitation. A great deal of priestly competence is achieved through watching, "being with elders," but also by playing priest, and imitating their ritual actions (Figures 15–17). Children, especially boys, are always around. They are entrusted with small tasks, such as fanning, bringing ritual utensils, and accompanying the elder performers. Through time spent in the ritual arena they become accustomed to the ritual performances, it becomes "natural" for them. They are encouraged to have and maintain their own small idols, do decorate and feed them, and so on (Figure 18). The priests' male children learn what they will do when grown up through watching the grown ups, being with them, and playfully imitating them (Figure 19).

[13] At the same time Csordas cautions that the ways we are attend to and with our bodies, and even the possibility of attending, are neither arbitrary nor biologically determined, but culturally constituted. Diverse forms of somatic modes of attention, as forms of embodied intersubjectivity, are culturally determined and differ. This becomes especially evident if we consider the differences between the "somatic modes of attention" presented by William Sax in this volume, and the forms of attention referred to here.

Figure 12: Children watch a procession passing by.

Figure 13: A child sits close to the altar.

Figure 14: A boy waits for the procession to arrive.

Figure 15: The priests' sons on the vehicle carrying the god.

Figure 16: A boy holding the fan for the god.

Figure 17: Children carrying the fan for the god.

Figure 18: Arun decorates his idols.

Figure 19: A priest's child plays with a drum that is used during processions.

One of the main factors contributing to ritual competence is thus "the magic of imitation" which is "a fundamental human faculty:" "making *oneself* similar to an other" involves becoming something other that what one is, says STEPHENSON (2007). Attention, participation, imitation and repetition gradually transform the neophytes. Mimesis is not only a way of acting but also a way of knowing, although mimetic knowledge is not necessarily conscious knowledge. Although associated with the acquisition of body techniques, this "somatic mode of attention" (CSORDAS 1990) recedes into the background once the technique is mastered (see also BADO-FRALICK 2009).

It turns out that—alongside with theoretical and textual knowledge and the formal qualifications such as initiation—performative learning, acquired through "being with elders," bodily presence during ritual performances, gradual involvement and mimesis are the most important means of internalisation of ritual competence, taking place by means of and in the body. In the end, this competence does not only include the correct execution of ritual rules, but also the ability as main actors to convince the audience and to maintain this conviction through contextual knowledge, technique (cf. GRIMES 1988), and interactive and improvisational abilities (cf. SCHIEFFELIN 1998 p. 198; 1996, p. 62f. and 80).

Taking into account diverse aspects of ritual competence, its definition in a given context, its transmission and its confirmation thus illustrates how a ritual tradition is maintained and changed at the same time (cf. WELBON 1984, p. 97). The bearers of this ritual competence have the authority not only to perform the ritual, but also to adapt it to contextual needs. They inherit, individuate, and transmit tradition through their embodied knowledge.

References

Primary Literature

Ānandasaṃhitā by Marīci = Bhaṭṭācārya R. P. (Ed.) (1998): Śri vaīkhānasa bhagavacchāstrē bhagavan-Marīci maharṣiprōktā Ānandasaṃhitā, 4 Vols. – Reprint. – Tirupati. (TTD Religious Publications Series, 509)

Pādmasamhitā = PADMANABHAN, S./SAMPATH, R. N./VARADACHARI, V. (Eds.) (1974/1982): Padma Samhita, 2 Vols. – Madras. (Pancaratra Parisodhana Parisad Series 3–4)

Secondary Literature

BADO-FRALICK, N. (2009): The Body-in-Practice as the Ground of Ritualized Negotiation. In: HÜSKEN, U./NEUBERT, F. (Eds.): Negotiating Rites. – Oxford/New York.

CSORDAS, T. J. (1990): Embodiment as Paradigm for Anthropology. In: Ethos, Vol. 18, No. 1, pp. 5–47.

CSORDAS, T. J. (1993): Somatic Modes of Attention. In: Cultural Anthropology, Vol. 8, No. 2, pp. 135–156.

FULLER, C. J. (2003): The Renewal of the Priesthood: Modernity and Traditionalism in a South Indian Temple. – Princeton.

GRIMES, R. L. (1988). Infelicitous Performances and Ritual Criticism. In: Semeia 43, pp. 103–122.

GRIMES, R. L. (2002): Deeply into the Bone: Re-inventing Rites of Passage. – Berkeley/Los Angeles/London.

GRIMES, R. L. (2006): Rite out of place: Ritual, media, and the arts. – Oxford/New York.

HÜSKEN, U. (Ed.) (2007):. When Rituals Go Wrong: Mistakes, Failure, and the Dynamics of Ritual. – Leiden. (Numen Book Series 115)

HÜSKEN, U. (2009a): Viṣṇu's Children: Prenatal life-cycle rituals in South India. – Transl. into English by Will SWEETMAN. – Wiesbaden. (Ethno-Indology: Heidelberg Studies in South Asian Rituals 9)

HÜSKEN, U. (2009b): Challenges to a Vaiṣṇava Initiation? In: ZOTTER, A./ZOTTER, C. (Eds.): Hindu and Buddhist Initiations in India and Nepal. – Wiesbaden. (Ethno-Indology: Heidelberg Studies in South Asian Rituals).

HUMPHREY, C./LAIDLAW, J. (1994): The Archetypal Actions of Ritual: A Theory of Ritual Illustrated by the Jain Rite of Worship. – Oxford.

MICHAELS, A. (2005): Saṃkalpa: The Beginnings of a Ritual. In: GENGNAGEL, J./HÜSKEN, U./RAMAN, S. (Eds.): Words and Deeds. Hindu and Buddhist Rituals in South Asia. – Wiesbaden, pp. 45–64. (Ethno-Indology. Heidelberg Studies in South Asian Rituals 1)

RASTELLI, M. (1999a): Zum Verständnis des Pāñcarātra von der Herkunft seiner Saṃhitās. In: Wiener Zeitschrift für die Kunde Südasiens 43, pp. 51–93.

RASTELLI, M. (1999b): Philosophisch-theologische Grundanschauungen der Jayākhyasaṃhitā: Mit einer Darstellung des täglichen Rituals – Wien.

RASTELLI, M. (2006): Die Tradition des Pāñcarātra im Spiegel der Pārameśvarasaṃhitā. – Wien.

SCHIEFFELIN, E. L. (1996): On Failure and Performance. Throwing the Medium out of the Séance. In: LADERMAN, C./ROSEMAN, M. (Eds.): The Performance of Healing. – New York/London, pp. 59–89.

SCHIEFFELIN, E. L. (1998) Problematizing Performance. In: HUGHES-FREELAND, F. (Ed.): Ritual, Performance, Media. – London/New York, pp. 194–207.

SELIGMAN et al = SELIGMAN, A. B./WELLER, R. P./PUETT, M. J./SIMON, B. (2008): Ritual and its consequences: An Essay on the limits of sincerity. – New York.

SCHRADER, F. O. (1916): Introduction to the Pāñcarātra and the Ahirbudhnya Saṃhitā. – Madras. (Adyar Library Series Vol. 5)

SMITH, H. D./VENKATACHARI, K. K. A. (1975): A descriptive bibliography of the printed texts of the Pāñcarātrāgama, Vol. 1. – Baroda. (Gaeckward's Oriental Series Vol. 158)

SMITH, H. D./VENKATACHARI, K. K. A. (1980): A Descriptive Bibliography of the Printed Texts of the Pāñcarātrāgama. Vol. 2: An annotated Index to selected topics. – Baroda. (Gaeckward's Oriental Series Vol. 168).

STEPHENSON, B. (2007): Ritual, Ritual Studies and the Mimetic Faculty. – Lecture held at Heidelberg University.

WELBON, G. R. (1984): Mahāsaṃprokṣaṇa 1981: Āgama and actuality in a contemporary temple renovation. In: VENKATACHARI, K. K. A. (Ed.): Agama and Silpa. – Bombay, pp. 69–102.

S. Simon John

Human Body, Folk Narratives and Rituals

Introduction

The social construction of the body differs from the medical construction in so far as it positions the body in the center of human interaction. That is, the body is seen as the existential basis of human interaction within given social, political, economic, cultural, and environmental conditions (cf. HALL 1977). Robert CRAWFORD (1984) described the human body as a cultural object. As our most immediate natural symbol it provides us with a powerful medium through which we interpret and give expression to our individual and social experience. "Human nature," the category of the inevitable (and often the desirable), finds its truth in the body. We live within a nature/culture opposition and the "natural body" confirms our place within a more "authentic" order. It is a vital foundation upon which behavior and values are predicated. Conversely, as a symbol of nature the body must be contained and transformed by culture. We invest the body with culture, thereby distinguishing ourselves from the rest of nature. Moreover, our biological being, always mediated by culture, delimits many of our most important social roles. It defines us in relation to others in kinship, sex, age groups, and larger social units such as race or caste. Bodily states are key markers in which the social definitions of the self are invested—not only regarding role, but normality and abnormality. The body also supplies a universally experienced model of a living and dynamic unit, an organic whole, a prototype from which we can draw in our attempts to explain and give meaning to larger social units and experiences. It is our richest source for metonymy and metaphor (cf. CRAWFORD 1984).

The human body is subject to social power structures and relations because it is shaped, almost configured, according to them (cf. Shil l ing 1993). The body is the bearer of the human being and at the same time the expression of his/her existential, i.e., economic, political, social, cultural and environmental condition. Individual and social biographies are represented in the body as are the social and cultural circumstances in which it has been developed. Body awareness, bodily experiences and bodily expressions are not only subject to individual choices of one lifestyle over another; they are primarily structured by social communication and interaction, both of which are dependent upon the symbolic structure of the social system, i.e., the value system, normative expectations and symbolic categories such as health, wealth, happiness, satisfaction, power, etc. (cf. Wenzel 1983). The human body is constantly being altered by natural and cultural processes. These alterations leave visible traces, which, in many societies, are associated with religious ideas, beliefs and forces. Biological growth itself leaves marks on the body. Adolescence brings changes in physical structure to members of both sexes. Ageing alters the coloring and density of body hair. Firm flesh wrinkles; teeth drop out further more, accidents at work and play mar, scar, mutilate, and deform the body. Such biological and accidental changes in many cultures are evidence of the operation of invisible beings or powers, such as deities, ancestors, or witchcraft. Or compensatory supernormal powers may be attributed to the lame, to the malformed, to the blind, and to albinos. Just as certain kinds of divines may read hidden meanings in such natural phenomena as the flight of birds or the spoor of foxes in sand, so, too, may the will of invisible entities be read in to the natural marks left on the body by growth, illness and violent mishap (cf. El iade 1987).

Rituals are centers on the body, and if we understand ritual we shall have to take the body seriously as a vehicle for religious experience. It is evident that without a body we would have no awareness of a world at all. Much ritual symbolism draws on the simplest and most intense sensory experiences, such as eating, sexuality, and pain. Such experiences have been repeated so often or so intimately by the body that they have become primary forms of bodily awareness. In ritual, they are transformed into symbolic experiences of the divine, and even into the form of the cosmic drama itself. Ritual is more than merely symbolic action. It is hieratic. Almost all human activity is symbolic, even the most "rationally" pragmatic. However, ritual underlines and makes emphatic its symbolic intention. Ritual behavior is repetitive and consciously follows a model. Repetition, after all, is a natural way for the body to proclaim, enact, and experience the choice of true as opposed to false things and ways, and to dwell self-consciously in determinative model realities in the "holy."

In ritual, people voluntarily submit to their bodily existence and assume very specific roles with highly patterned rules—rules and roles that conform the self to all others who have embodied these typical roles in the past. To contact reality, in short, the conscious self must sacrifice its individual autonomy, its freedom in fantasy to "be" anything. Edmund Leach (1968) suggested that the term ritual should be applied to all "culturally defined sets of behavior," that is, to the symbolical dimension of human behavior as such, regardless of its explicit religious, social, or other content. For Leach, such behavior should be regarded as a form of social communication or code of information and analyzed in terms of its "grammar." Ritual is treated as a cognitive category.

We shall understand as "ritual" those conscious and voluntary, repetitious and stylized symbolic bodily actions that are centered on cosmic structures and/or sacred presences. Verbal behavior such as chant, song and prayer are of course included in the category of bodily actions. Even more fundamentally, ritual is intentionally bodily engagement in the paradigmatic forms and relationships of reality. As such, ritual brings not only the body but also that body's social and cultural identity to the encounter with the transcendental realm. By conforming to models or paradigms that refer to the primordial past and that can be shared by many people, ritual also enables each person to transcend the individual self, and thus it can link many people together into enduring and true forms of community. Rituals draw into itself every aspects of human life, and almost every discipline of the social sciences and humanities has something to say about it. The body is evidently more important in religious experience than is often thought (cf. Eliade 1987).

Rituals are one mode of cultural praxis through which bodies, knowledge, powers, agency and selves have been repositioned through practice. Practices are those modes of embodied doing through which everyday as well as extra daily experiences, realities and meanings are shaped and negotiated. As discussed by Mauss (1973), De Certeau (1984) and Bourdieu (1977) everyday practices include such habitualized and routine activities as walking, driving, hygienic practices, etc. Extra daily practices are those practices such as rituals, dances, theatre performances, the recitation of oral narratives, religious practices, martial arts, etc., which require the practitioner to undergo specialized body training in order to become accomplished in attaining a certain specialized state of consciousness, body, agency, power and so on. Extraordinary energy, time and resources are often invested by a society to create cultural specialists whose embodied practices are the means by which personal, social, ritual and cosmological realities are created and enacted.

With this brief understanding of the socio-cultural construction of the human body and rituals, this paper described three important folk religious ritual celebrations of Tamil Nadu, South India. They are rituals of Periandavar worship, rituals performed by Kaniyan community and the Hook swinging ritual celebration. This research is an attempt to understand the association of human body in rituals. How the human body is culturally professed, purified, transformed and healed through rituals is the important subject matter of this paper. It is an effort to understand the socio-cultural construction of human body in a particular cultural context. Empirical data have been documented through fieldwork in the natural cultural context of ritual performance and the triangulation research methodology i.e. observation, interaction and visual documentation have been followed.

"Submission of Body"—Rituals of Periandavar worship

A festival of Periandavar—a male folk deity is celebrated for fifteen days once in two years at Kulianoor village in Darmapuri district of Tamil Nadu, south India. The very first ritual of the festival is *kall naatuthal*, i.e. posting a stem.

For this, the village people worship the deity and dig a small pit on the right side of the temple. Then they take a lengthy branch of Neem tree and apply turmeric powder, vermilion, and sandal paste and wear garland on that branch. Then the important persons in that village and the temple administrators join together and post the branch on that pit. This ritual is called *kaal naatuthal*. This signifies that the festival has been inaugurated.

From the day of *Kaal naatuthal* people in that village, especially those who are actively engaged in various ritual activities in the festival, give special attention to their body in order to purify them. They abstain from meat, have a bath twice a day, and have conjugal continence. They do not wear footwear inside the village. All the core rituals of the celebration are performed during the last two days of the celebration. Rituals are performed at two places. One at the temple situated in the center of the village and the other in the paddy fields two miles east of the village. Both temples are temporarily erected during the celebration. At the beginning of the ritual, two deities made of clay are kept in the center of the village. A small shelter thatched with Neem leaves is erected above the deities. The name of the deity is Periandavar. They apply sandal paste and vermilion on the deity. In front of the deity, they spread banana leaf and upon it, coconut, bananas, betel leaves, vermilion, turmeric powder and sacred ash are placed. By that time, people start gathering around that temporary shrine. Then two people come near the deity performing music called Pambai (percussion musical instrument). When they start performing Pambai, people join in clapping their hands joyfully. After the music one of them begins to sing a devotional song and the others repeats it. At that time, the men folk put their two fingers in their mouth and make a whistling voice in order to invoke the deity.

Then the shaman brings two feet long swords and place them in front of the deity. He lights the camphor and waves the flame around the deity. During this the male mediums among the crowd are possessed by the deity and dance vigorously. Each person picks up a sword kept in front of the deity and begins to beat it vigorously across their chest, first looking at the deity and later turning to the people. On completion of this, each male medium prostrates before the deity and receives the sacred ash from the priest and applies on their forehead and chest and become normal. When the last male medium begins to dance with the sword the noise of the crowd is very loud. He dances for a while and then run for a distance of nearly three Kilometers. There in the midst of the field, he placed the sword into the ground immediately a rope fence of two meters radius is put up in that place. Fifteen young men begin to dig a well on the spot marked by the male medium. The persons who dig the well have go through the ritual prescriptions. They are forbidden from wearing footwear and eating meat. They must adhere to the practice of conjugal continence. They have not cut their hair. The tools like spades, iron rods, buckets used for digging have been kept away from contact.

The young men who digs the well are tied their mouths with a cloth to avoid polluting the place by their saliva. The digging began at 10.30 pm. At about 4.30 am the water begins to ooze from the well. When people saw the water springing forth they shouted in joy. The diggers came out of well, bowed in reverence to it and covered the well with coconut leaves. If water is found soon it signifies more agricultural production for the ensuing years. If it is late, people believe there would be less agricultural production.

The ritual of purification or driving away the evil spirit from body is held in the outskirt of the village on the 14th day of the festival. Music is performed vehemently and the shaman runs at a high speed to the place where devotees possessed by evil spirits are waiting. The shaman wears flower garlands around his neck and carried a terracotta horse on his shoulder. Two men on either side hold the horse from falling. At a specific place about two hundred women and few men laid down to the ground faced towards the earth in order to submit and surrender their body and self (Figure 1). The shaman walks faster upon the men and women who lay there. This is repeatedly done. When he walked like that some evil possessed women begins to dance. At that time the shaman stamped harder upon the possessed women (Figure 2). Once the shaman took off his feet, the possessed women are pulled by few men folk (Figure 3) to a tamarind tree nearby. There they took a small bunch of their hair, and nailed it to the tree. They made three knots and clip off their hair. They believe that the evil spirits are go with the hair.

On completion of the ritual "driving away evil spirit" the ritual of "whipping" is commenced (Figure 4). Three young men whipped the devotees who come forward with hands rising above their head. The young men beat them

Figure 1: Devotees submit their body for healing ritual in Periandaver worship.

Figure 2: A shaman stamped upon evil possessed women in Periandavar worship.

Figure 3: An evil possessed woman pulled to a tamarind tree in Periandavar worship.

Figure 4: Whipping ritual in Periandavar worship.

rapidly on their hands. Some women are seen massaging their hands being unable to bear the pain. They believed that the evil or sin in them would be removed in that way. Womenfolk are dominant in the purification rituals. Traditionally these purification rituals are also related with the "fertility" of the female body. It is believed by the womenfolk that by participating in these rituals would bless with good health and fertility. Another important factor associated with women body is "menstruation." Menstruation is traditionally considered as profane in Tamil societies. It is a traditional rule that women should not take part in any rituals during menstruation. They would be severely punished by the deity if they violate it.

"Human body and sacred narratives:" Rituals of Kaniyan

Most of the traditional communities in the world have narratives or myths explaining their own origin. The origin myth of communities plays a traditional role in the functioning of the community. The traditional rituals, occupations, performances etc are determined by the origin myths of the particular community. Here I have analyzed the role of origin myth of Kaniyan community and its impact on the body of the menfolk of the community.

Kaniyan is a tribal community, occupies a low status in the social hierarchy, and lives in Tirunelveli region of Tamil Nadu, South India. Generally they are uneducated and live in poverty. They are considered untouchable and uncultured by the upper caste people. The literal meaning of "Kaniyan" in the Tamil language is "to calculate." Formerly, the Kaniyan were experts in astrology. The men of the Kaniyan community are traditionally experts in *koothu*. In the Tamil language *koothu* refers to a play or a performance, which consists of dance, music, narration and singing. The type of *koothu* performed by the Kaniyan community is known as *Kaniyan koothu*. There are typically several *koothu* teams in a Kaniyan community. Their traditional occupation is to perform *koothu* during the annual celebration to worship Sudalai (a male folk deity) which is sponsored by the non-tribal communities. Apart from the *koothu* teams there are Kaniyan men who function as shamans in the annual celebration, where they lead all the core rituals of the worship of Sudalai. Generally, these shamans are older people who have retired from performing *koothu*.

The role of the Kaniyan community in the worship of Sudalai is highly significant. Although the non-tribal communities worship Sudalai, the core rituals of the annual celebration of Sudalai are to be performed by the men of the tribal Kaniyan community. This means that though the Kaniyan community is socially backward, it occupies a dominant role in the ritual performances of the annual celebration. The Kaniyan proudly claim themselves to be *Deiva Kaniyan*, that is "Divine Kaniyan." The following origin myth supports this claim:

> One day Shiva, Parvathi, and other Hindu Gods were dancing in the heavenly place called Kailasam. While dancing, Parvathi fell down and two bells from her anklet came off. The God Tirumal took these bells and created two children, and he named them as Kaniyan and Kambar. After some days Parvathi found it difficult to identify Lord Shiva and God Brahma because both of them had five heads. So she complained to Shiva about her problem. On hearing this, Shiva cut off the middle head of Lord Brahma and made him four-headed. But the head which was cut off stayed in the hands of Shiva, causing him to suffer from *Brahmahathi tosham* (a kind of divinely inflicted illness as punishment for trangression). To cure this *tosham*, Tirumal asked Kaniyan to cut his hand and sacrifice his blood. Kaniyan did so, and this cured the Shiva's condition of *Brahmahathi tosham*. Then Tirumal took the crown from the severed head of Brahma, and from it he made a *makudam* (drum) and a *mani* (bell). Then he gave the drum to Kaniyan and the bell to Kambar, and asked them to do *pooja* (priestly service) in the temple of Sudalai. They did as they were asked, with Kambar acting as priest while Kaniyan performed the rituals of Sudalai. (John 2008, pp. 125)

Rituals associated with the body of Kaniyan in Sudalai worship

In Tamil literature, there are two meanings for the word Sudalai. One refers to the ground for the burning of corpses—a graveyard. The other refers to a deity, also known as Sudalai Madan or Sudalai Madasamy, whose sanctuary is usually situated near a graveyard. This deity is widely worshipped by the scheduled caste and backward communities of the region, as the hundreds of Sudalai temples found in this area demonstrate. The deity Sudalai is considered a chief and head of all the evil spirits and demons. A Sudalai temple is also known as *pai kovil* (temple of demons). There are separate Sudalai temples for each village or caste. These temples are generally situated on a road side, the banks of a river, the outskirts of a village, or in a graveyard. Normally Sudalai is represented by altars or stone statues. The size of the altars varies from place to place, ranging from three to thirty feet. These altars are situated in the open air—there are neither roofs nor bounding walls. All Sudalai temples are oriented toward the east. Generally there is no regular or daily worship in Sudalai temples. In some of the popular Sudalai temples, though, worship takes place on Tuesdays and Fridays, in others on the last Tuesday and Friday of every Tamil month. Worship varies from place to place and from temple to temple. However, devotees celebrate an annual festival for Sudalai, which is locally known as *kodai*. This annual festival is celebrated in all Sudalai temples but in different seasons. *Kodai* is generally celebrated for three days, with a Friday or Tuesday as the central day. It can occur once a year, once every two years, or once every several years, depending upon the financial situation of the devotees.

Based on the origin myth, the body of Kaniyan is culturally constructed as "sacred" and it functions as a medium between the "human" and the "divine" in the rituals of Sudalai worship. The body of menfolk of Kaniyan community plays a significant role in Sudalai worship. Here the body also includes the verbal chants, narration and the bodily actions or performances. A number of rituals are performed by Kaniyan during the annual worshipping celebration of Sudalai. However, here I have described and analyzed only few ritual performances that are directly associated with the body of Kaniyan. They are *Kaniyan Koothu* (play or performance), *kaappu kathuthal* (wearing a sacred cord), and *Kaniyan Kaivettu* (blood sacrificing by the shaman). A team of Kaniyan men performs the *Koothu* in order to invoke the spirit of Sudalai, and a shaman who also belongs to the Kaniyan community performs the ritual of *kaappu kathuthal* and *Kaniyan kaivettu*.

Kaniyan koothu

Kaniyan koothu performance (Figure 5) is performed in the annual worshipping of Sudali in order to invoke the spirit of the deity. In this performance the performers sings and narrate the origin myth of the deity accompanied with dance and music. During this performance the *komarathadigal* (the male mediums) are possessed by the spirit of Sudalai and dance vehemently. The main function of a *Kaniyan koothu* performance is to invoke the spirit of Sudalai upon the *komarathadigal*.

Kaniyan koothu is performed by a team normally consisting of six Kaniyan men. The team includes a lead singer, an assistant singer, two drummers, and two dancers dressed in female costume. In *Kaniyan koothu* the performers narrate the myth of Sudalai accompanied by music and dance. The name of the musical instrument, a drum, is *makudam*; therefore the *Kaniyan koothu* is also known as *makudatam* (*makudam* dance). The lead singer, or *annavi*,

Figure 5: Kaniyan Koothu ritual performance.

is the leader of the entire *Kaniyan koothu* performance. It is his role to sing and narrate the myth of Sudalai. He stands in front of the deity and cups his left hand behind his left ear, while at the same time extending his right hand towards the deity as he sings the myth. While the leader sings the myth in a high pitched voice, the *komarathadigal* becomes possessed by the divine spirit and dances vehemently. Another man, the assistant singer, repeats part of each sentence performed by the lead singer. He frequently expresses doubts and asks the *annavi* questions about the myth. He is also responsible for ensuring that the performance continues if anything should happen to interrupt the lead singer.

In *Kaniyan koothu*, two men perform on the musical drum *makudam*. This drum is a small circular one-headed drum hung from the left shoulder and tapped with the fingers of both hands. The drum is made of poovarasu (*Thespesia populnea*, or "Portia tree") or neem (*Azadirachta indica*) wood. Boards of this wood are bent into circular shape and the skin of a young buffalo is attached to one side of the frame using glue prepared from Tamarind seeds. Based on the sound of the drum, or more specifically its pitch, two types of *makudam* are distinguished: the *vucha makudam* (high pitch drum) and the *mantha makudam* (low pitch drum). Both drums are used in the *Kaniyan koothu*. The two drummers perform standing adjacent to the lead singer.

Finally, to complete a *Kaniyan koothu* team, two male dancers are costumed as women. Generally these performers grow their hair down to their shoulders and tie and curl it using hairclips. They put flowers around their hair and wear ear studs and bangles. They apply lipstick and perfumed powder on their faces.

They dress themselves in blouses and saris. To form breasts they put paper or cloth inside their blouses. They don anklets in the final stage. The anklets are considered sacred because they give rhythm to the dancers' steps, and before donning the anklets the dancers worship the deity. When they have finished putting on their costumes they look so much like females that it is difficult to recognize them as males. These performers dance to the accompaniment of song and music.

Only the Kaniyan community performs this *koothu*, and it is the traditional play of that community. There are no formal classes or coaching to learn this performance. Kaniyan men who are interested in learning it accompany the performers whenever and wherever they perform. They assist the artists whenever necessary. This familiarizes them with the myth, the techniques, and the formulas of the performance. Whenever the opportunity arises they take up the *makudam* and practice the music. Those who are interested in singing stand near the lead singer and sing with him, while those who are interested in dancing dance together with the performers during an actual performance. Whenever the juniors commit a mistake the senior artists correct and guide them. Similarly whenever the juniors have uncertainties they clarify them by asking the seniors. In this manner they learn the performance by participating in its natural context.

Apart from the *koothu* performers there is a shaman (Figure 6) from the Kaniyan community whose role is to perform rituals such as *kaappu kathuthal* (wearing a sacred cord), *Kaniyan kaivettu* (blood sacrificing by the shaman),

Figure 6: A Kaniyan Shaman.

usually this is an elderly person who has retired from the *Kaniyan koothu* performance. He works as a shaman and leads the entire ritual component of the annual worshipping ceremony. The rituals described below are those performed by the shaman.

Kaappu katuthal: Wearing a sacred cord

On the central day of the annual celebration, that is, on a Friday or Tuesday, the shaman ties a *kaappu* around the wrists of the *komarathadigal* (spirit-possessed persons). In Tamil, *kaappu* means "to protect" or "to prevent." Here, *kaappu* refers to a yellow cord with several items attached to it. A small iron ring is fastened to its center, while a piece of turmeric is tied to one end of the cord and some betel leaves to the other. The whole is called *kaappu*. The *kaappu* is placed into a tray together with a coconut, incense sticks, saffron, vermillion, betel leaves, and areca nuts, and all of this is given to the shaman. The priest or the temple administrators put twenty-one rupees on the tray as an offering to the shaman. The shaman receives this tray and ties the *kaappu* around the wrists of the *komarathadigal*. This ritual is known as *kaappukatuthal*, or "tying the sacred cord." *Komarathadigal* believe that the *kaappu* will protect the body from evil spirits, because the iron piece they use in making the *kaappu* serves as a protective device. The *kaappu* will be removed by the shaman at the end of the *kodai*.

Kaniyan kaivettu: Blood sacrificing by the shaman

The most important ritual in the annual worshipping ceremony of Sudalai is the sacrificing of blood by the shaman. This ritual is known as *Kaniyan kaivettu*, which means that the shaman cuts his own hand. It too is performed on the central day of ceremony following the *kaappu katuthal*. The shaman puts bananas, betel leaves, a coconut, incense sticks, and a mask made of clay or fiber representing the evil spirit into a tray and offers it all to the deity. He walks three times around a stone mortar used to make flour, finally stepping up onto and standing upon the stone for a time while wearing the mask on his face. He rubs his left hand, the one he is going to cut, with the coconut and circles it three times with the coconut. Then he ties his left arm tightly with a cord and cuts the upper part of his wrist with a small sharp knife until blood begins to flow. He clenches his hand tightly and pours the blood on some plantain leaves, which are spread out in front of the *komarathadigal*. The shaman often sprinkles water on the wound to keep the blood from clotting. The blood sacrificed by the shaman is mixed with bananas and eaten by the *komarathadigal*. Devotees believe that only those whom the spirit of the deity has entered can eat the blood. After sacrificing his blood, the shaman removes the cord from his arm and covers the wound with it. By doing this, the shaman told me, the wound will quickly heal without the use of other medicine. In a similar kind of ritual known as *Kaniyan naakuvettu*, blood is again sacrificed, but this time by cutting the Kaniyan shaman's tongue. The shaman bites his tongue tightly, then looks into a small mirror held in his left hand while cutting his tongue with a sharp knife until blood begins to flow. Then he pours his blood on plantain leaves and has it eaten by the *komarathadigal*.

"Second Birth"—The Ritual of Hook Swinging

A ritual of Hook swinging is performed every year at the Venkanji Mudipura temple situated at Kollemkode village in Kanyakumari district, Tamil Nadu, South India. This festival is locally known as *Thooka Thiruvizha or Pillai thookam*. In Tamil language *Pillai* refers to the new born babies and *thookam* refers "to lift." Therefore *pillai thookam* means, "lifting the babies." The festival starts on the day of *Bharani* star in the month of *Meenam* according to the vernacular calendar. The ritual of hook swinging is primarily performed as a fulfillment of the vow by the parents to the deities. Those womenfolk made a vow to the deity in that temple that she would perform the hook swinging ritual for her child if she is blessed with fertility. Therefore after the child birth the parents perform the ritual of hook swinging for their child as a thanks giving and fulfillment of vow. Thousands of parents with their newborn children are participating in the ritual of hook swinging celebration. Those parents, who wish their child to be swung in the festival employ a separate person to hold their child and swing in the sacred cart. These people are known as *thookkakkar* i.e. swinger (Figure 7) Sometimes the father or maternal uncle

Figure7: The 'swingers' in the ritual of hook swinging.

of the children may act as swinger. Thousands of swingers are reserved in advance in order to lift the children and swing in the sacred cart.

These swingers are considered as sacred by the parents and devotees and there are traditional rites to purify their body. In order to purify their body, these swingers have to abstain themselves from their family contacts and have to stay in the temple premises for about ten days from the day of flag hoisting of the hook swinging celebration. On the first day, an identity number is given by the temple administration to each swinger and thereafter they are identified with their respective number only. During their stay at the temple premises, they have to eat vegetarian food made of rice and vegetables that is provided by the temple administration; have to stay away from the consumption of alcohol and tobacco; should not wear foot wears; have to take a bath twice in a day both morning and evening and had conjugal continence; prostrate and worship the deity in the prescribed time and have to apply sacred ash on the forehead and body. All these things have to be strictly followed by the swingers in order to purify them.

Anka piratacinam i.e. "circumambulation by the limbs"—rolling their body in the auspicious clockwise direction around the temple with their arms outstretched over their head is an important ritual in order to purify the body. *Namaskaram* i.e. prostration is another core ritual performed by swingers on the ninth day of the festival. In this ritual, all the swingers take a bath in the sea, prostrating and perform a number of physical exercise in a much disciplined manner. It is believed that all these rituals purify and prepare their body in order to perform the swinging ritual on the tenth day of the festival.

On the tenth day of the festival thousands of devotees are gathered to witness the festival. A team of people prepare the swingers in order to swing in the cart. On this occasion all the swingers wear half trousers with bare body. A thick rope is tied across the swinger's chest and waist and the iron hook is fixed on the rope at the back body of the swingers. They tightly tie the iron hooks on the back body of the swingers.

It is a custom that before performing the ritual of hook swinging, the swingers must sacrifice their blood to the deity. A priest thumps the fleshy part of the swingers back body and takes few drops of blood and mixes it in the water that is kept in front of the deity. While sacrificing the blood, the devotee should not show any sign of pain because he is already purified and prepared for this ritual. If he shows any sign of pain during this ritual it is believed that he has violated the codes prescribed by the temple.

After blood sacrificing by the swingers, the temple administration announces the identity number of the swingers. Accordingly that particular swinger and the parents who employ the swinger with their child are fastened to the beam or pole of the cart. There is a huge traditional sacred cart made of thick timber meant for hook swinging in the temple. Two wooden beams which are approximately 100 feet length and one feet diameter are placed through the hole at the top of the cart and balance in the middle like a huge seesaw. It takes at least an hour to setup the sacred cart. The whole arrangement of the car is such that, lowering one end of the long beam to the ground, and fasten a man to it, and then pull down the other end by the ropes could raise the man the air a height of hundred feet more (Figure 8). The cart, poles and the ropes are considers as sacred objects.

Figure 8: The sacred cart.

A team of menfolk is engaged to fix the swingers in the front portion of the cart and another team of menfolk are sitting on the back portion of the cart in order to operate the beams. Soon after the swingers reach the cart they are tied in the front beams of the cart. At a time four swingers are attached to the beam. The swingers are connected to the beam by two steel hooks, which joined to the clothes and tied around his chest and waist. After fixation of the swingers in the beam of the cart, parents handover their child to the swinger's arm. The swinger holds the child carefully and then the beams are lifted up and up. The swingers swing with children in the air for about hundred feet high from the ground (Figure 9). Hundreds of devotees enthusiastically drag the cart and the cart slowly moves around the temple. Parents and devotees are whole-heartedly pleading to the Goddesses to be blessed with good health and wealth for the children as well as family members. It takes at least five minutes for the cart to complete a round around the temple. Similarly more

Figure 9: Swingers swing with children in the cart.

than one thousand children swing on this festival of hook swinging. After the car reaches the starting point the beam is pulled down and the children and swingers are removed from the clutches. Parents are pleased and cheerfully offer new clothes, gold rings and money to the swingers after the successful completion of the hook swinging. It is believed by the parents and devotees that the child who performed the hook swinging ritual is "reborn."

Conclusion

All the above described ritual ceremonies are traditionally celebrated in particular regions of Tamil Nadu. The nature of these ritual ceremonies is purely socio-religious and the participation of people is voluntary. The important function of these ritual ceremonies is to satisfy the Gods and Goddesses in order to get good health and prosperity. The human body plays a vital role in most of the rituals and it is shaped by the social communication and interaction through rituals.

The rituals of Periandavar worship clearly indicates that the human "body" and "self" is submitted to the divine spirit and get purified by the shaman. The body of the shaman is considered as sacred. During his sprit possession, his body is the medium for the divine spirit. In order to submit his body to the divine spirit the shaman performs certain rites to purify his body. Being abstained from meat and spicy food, alcohol and tobacco; having bath twice a day; regular worship and applying sacred ash on the fore head and chest;

staying away from the funeral rites and conjugal continence are the habits that are performed by the shaman in order to purify his body. In the ritual of driving away the evil spirit, hundreds of womenfolk submit their "body" and "self" and the shaman walk upon their bodies in order to identify the evil spirited women. After having identified the evil spirited women, the shaman beats and slabs the woman's body with his legs and hands and a bunch of her hair is pulled and nailed in a tree and then cut off. It is believed by the people that the evil spirit is driven away through the hair. Similarly In the ritual of whipping the devotee submits their body to get whipped by the shaman. The purification rituals are also related with the fertility of women body. It is a traditional belief that their "body" and their "conscious self" must be surrendered in order to purify their soul. Another important observation is the belief about human "saliva" and "menstruation." While digging the well, the people who dig the well are covered their mouth in order to protect the well from spit. The womenfolk should not take part in any rituals during menstruation. The saliva and menstruation are traditionally considered as profane.

The rituals of Kaniyan reflect that the body of Kaniyan plays a dominant role in the Sudalai worship. The rituals performed by the Kaniyan in the worship of Sudalai have a mythological background. The origin myth of the Kaniyan community says that the Kaniyan were created by Lord Thirumal from the bells of Parvathi's anklet. The boy Kaniyan was asked by Lord Thirumal to sacrifice his blood in order to heal the *Brahmahathi tosham* of Shiva. Then Lord Thirumal created a musical drum and asked Kaniyan to perform ritual services at Sudalai's temple. This sacred narrative gives "divine" status to the Kaniyan's body. Based on myth, the cultural construction of the body of Kaniyan is considered as a sacred and powerful medium between "human" and the "divine." His performance and bodily actions in *Koothu* invoke the spirit of the deity upon the male medium; his blood is considered as the blood of the divine and has to be eaten by the male medium; the sacred cord tied by him to the devotees' wrists protects their body from the evil spirit. All these are strong proofs that folk narratives or myths play an important role in the socio-cultural construction of the human body.

The body of the *thookkakkar*, i.e. the swingers plays an important role in the ritual of hook swinging. A number of rituals are performed during their ten days stay at the temple in order to purify their body. Vegetarian food; conjugal continence; bath twice a day; rituals of circumambulation by the limbs, prostration; regular worship and applying sacred ash on the forehead and chest are all the rituals to purify the body of the swingers. These purification rituals prepare the body of the swingers to be possessed with the spirit of the deity during the ritual of hook swinging. The swingers act a medium between the "child" and the "divine." The child on the hands of the swinger in the cart is believed as if the child were in the hands of the deity and the parents and devotees believe that nothing dire will happen during hook swinging. The significant aspect of this hook swinging ritual is that the body of the new born child is submitted to the divine power in order to be blessed with good health and prosperity. It is believed by the parents and devotees that the child is "reborn" by performing the ritual of hook swinging. The fertility of the body of the womenfolk is also associated with the ritual of hook swinging. The womenfolk made a promise or vow to the deity that she would perform the ritual of hook swinging for her child if she is blessed with fertility. It is believed by the people that this vow would definitely bless her with fertility.

The above ethnographic notes of rituals clearly shows that the human body serves as a religious vehicle and it also refers to the cultural transformation of the human body. The ritual performers undergone a specialized body training and rituals in order to become accomplished in attaining a certain specialized state of consciousness, body, agency, power and so on. The "sacred persons" or the shamans of the above mentioned ritual ceremonies perform certain rituals in order to purify their body in which are possessed by the spirit of the deity during the ritual performances. Staying at the temple premises; eating vegetarian food made of rice and vegetables; staying away from the consumption of alcohol and tobacco; avoiding foot wears; bathing twice in a day; conjugal continence; prostration and circumambulation by the limbs and worshipping; applying sacred ash on the forehead and body are all the common purification rituals for the above mentioned ritual ceremonies. These rituals transform the body of the shamans from the state of the profane to the sacred and the conscious "self" of the shaman is sacrificed during the ritual performance. The body of the shaman acts as an agency between human and divine and performs several rituals in order to purify or heal the devotees.

The traditional awareness of human body is closely associated with the religious ritual practices. People in these regions relate certain bodily illnesses like barrenness, mental disorder, chickenpox etc with supernatural powers. It is believed by the people that these kinds of bodily illness happen when the Gods and Goddesses are angry with them. Therefore to cure these illnesses they submit and surrender their body and self through certain rituals like driving away the evil spirit, whipping, hook swinging etc in order to satisfy the supernatural power. These rituals are the traditional cultural process through which the human body is altered.

References

Bourdieu, P. (1977): Outline of a Theory of Practice. – Cambridge.

Crawford, R. (1984): A Cultural Account of "Health:" Control, Release, and the Social Body. In: McKinlay, J. B. (Ed.): Issues in the Political Economy of Health Care. – New York.

De Certeau, M. (1984): The Practice of Everyday Life. – Berkely.

Eliade, M. (1987): The Encyclopedia of Religion. Vol. 2. – New York.

Hall, E. T. (1977): Beyond Culture. – New York.

John, S. S. (2008): Kaniyan: Ritual Performers of Tamil Nadu, South India. In: Journal of Asian Ethnology, Vol. 67, No. 1, pp. 123–135.

Leach, E. R. (1968): Ritual. In: Sills, D. L. (Ed.): International Encyclopedia of the Social Sciences. Vol. 13. – New York.

Mauss, M. (1973): Techniques of the Body. In: Economy and Society, Vol. 2, No. 1, pp. 70–88.

Shilling, C. (1993): The Body and Social Theory. – London.

Wenzel, E. (1983): Lifestyles and Living Conditions and Their Impact on Health: A Report of the Meeting. In: Scottish Health Education Group (Ed.): European Monographs in Health Education Research. Vol. 5. – Edinburgh, pp. 1–18.

Zarrilli, B. P. (1998): When the Body Becomes All Eyes. – Delhi.

The Body in Visualisations and Images

Monica Juneja

Translating the Body into Image: The Body Politic and Visual Practice at the Mughal Court during the Sixteenth and Seventeenth Centuries*

> … the body is a tool and an instrument for the soul, like the tools and instruments used by artisans and craftsmen. It is not, as some people conceive, the souls's receptacle or locus …
>
> (Nasir-al Din Tusi, *Akhlaq-i Nasiri*)

> He [i.e. the King] is continually attentive to the health of the body politic, and applies remedies to the several diseases thereof. And in the same manner that the equilibrium of the animal constitution depends upon an equal mixture of elements, so also does the political constitution become well-tempered by a proper division of ranks … a multitude of people become fused into one body.
>
> (Abu'l Fazl Allami, *Ain-i Akbari*)

Ethico-political writings of pre-colonial South Asia define moral and political authority in bodily terms, postulating an indissociable relationship between the physical body of an individual and the body politic. In this constellation of ideas, which remained in sway for nearly three hundred years, the king, the body and the land were described as composed of mixtures of different humours which gave them their distinct attributes. A balance of these elements was held to be the secret of good governance, social harmony and ecological plenitude. Such a notion of the body politic was intended to secure a sense of community: good governance came to be an "embodied" science rather than an abstract one, one which through references to bodily experiences worked towards cementing subjects to the kingdom (cf. Bayly 1998, pp. 12f.). This article addresses the ways in which the body was configured within visual practice at the Mughal court as a medium to transmit ethical conceptions of the polity. Harnessing the body as medium also meant making the body a subject of visual representation. Translating ethical texts into images was a complex process that involved negotiating multiple regimes of visuality which made up the pluralistic cultures of north Indian courts during the sixteenth and seventeenth enturies, and arriving at pictorial choices that did not necessarily create a direct equivalence with the written word. My arguments draw upon

---

* For Neeladri Bhattacharya and Kumkum Roy, companion historians and friends of many years. I wish to acknowledge my debt to Muzaffar Alam whose authoritative writings on the languages of political Islam in South Asia have been a rich source of knowledge.

important recent studies of north Indian political culture, especially those of Muzaffar Alam, Chris Bayly and Rosalind O'Hanlon. At the same time this essay engages with the research of these historians to argue for the vital agency of the visual in constituting political culture. Visual representations were on the one hand integral to Mughal manuscript production that juxtaposed images to texts. Yet the communicative modes of the visual medium followed a dynamic that was not a rehearsal of the path taken by texts. Composers of painted images inevitably drew upon an available reservoir of political ideas, narrative themes and normative precepts expounded in politico-ethical writings and which circulated through multiple channels and interpenetrated popular wisdom. Reconfiguring these as image was a more slippery process, as we move to a domain in which different sensory routines and ritual habits that impinge on the specific corporeal experience of vision come into play directly and with urgency. This also meant that as images cut across distinctions formulated elsewhere and drew up new boundaries, they worked to refine and pluralise the understandings of political culture beyond the normative. Pictorial experiments were often open ended, created a new field and range of sensibilities, especially the corporeal, that could then be reworked into a language to define new ideals of the political body, which historians have closely examined and eloquently written about.[1]

The *Akhlaq-i Nasiri* by Nasir-al din Tusi (1207–1274) was among the several popular ethical treatises, referred to as *akhlaqi* literature, which circulated in the courts of north India in a variety of recensions from the fifteenth century onwards. Tusi's text, since its arrival in Gujarat in the late fifteenth century (cf. ALAM 2004, p. 50), drew up a model of virtue that was premised on the notion of bodily purity and perfection. The model referred to three domains regarded as homologous: the kingdom, the household and the body (cf. O'HANLON 2007). Thus the first discourse in Tusi's work deals with *tahzib-i akhlaq*, that is the regulation of different aspects of an individual's bodily and moral dispositions, the second deals with the regulation of households and the third with the wider domain of the state. Virtue consisted of a proper balance between natural (i.e. bodily) desires and emotions, the ruler's duty in turn was to balance different elements and types of people within the polity, making justice or equity (*adl*) the highest political virtue. Tusi's text was widely read and enjoyed considerable authority among Mughal political elites. In the 1580's it was copied, illustrated, sumptuously bound and kept in the imperial *kitabkhana*, where precious manuscripts were both produced as well as preserved. A large number of recensions and copies proliferated

[1] See especially ALAM 2004; O'HANLON 1999; O'HANLON 2007; RICHARDS 1998a; BAYLY 1998.

through the seventeenth and eighteenth centuries and were also referred to by rulers of the regional courts following the shrinking of Mughal sovereignty, more so as these ideas found an echo in texts from non-Muslim traditions such as in Vijayanagara, Rajasthan or Maharashtra (cf. ALAM 2004, pp. 61–80; BAYLY 1998, pp. 13ff.).

In the 1580's Akbar's court historian and close friend Abu'l Fazl drew substantially on the tenets of Nasirean ethics while formulating his political ideals of enlightened monarchy in the monumental illuminated history *Akbarnama* and its compendium the *Ain-i Akbari*. In this ideological format of a divinely sanctioned kingdom, Akbar emerges as "the perfect man" (*insaan-i kamil*) whose virtues of self-control, renunciation of worldly desires and ability to enforce justice were the groundwork of an empire where universal harmony (*sulh-i kul*) prevailed. This and other contemporary histories are replete with information about norms of bodily comportment, marriage regulations, sexual practices among imperial servants, especially in relation to homosexual love (O'HANLON 2007, p. 892). In Abu'l Fazl's history Akbar emerges as the embodiment of moral and physical perfection, a paternal figure for the kingdom and above all a man in full control of his exceptional bodily powers. Indeed the emperor's perfect body came to function as a metonym for the health of the body politic. Such a notion found expression in court rituals such as the *khilat*, or granting of a robe of honour, an artefact associated with the king's person, to a loyal subject (cf. GORDON 2001): acceptance meant incorporation into the kingdom through the medium of the royal body.

Between *tahzib* and *darshan*

The ideas enumerated above came to be enmeshed with the cultural fabric of the north Indian courts not least through their visual articulations. Painting signalised one important kind of public moment in which the body functioned as instrument of the soul. The centrality of the visual medium to communicative habits and practices of the north Indian regions meant that most court histories and manuscripts from the sixteenth century onwards were composed as a combination of text and images, with images intended to illustrate the text and fix its meanings. In practice however the relationship between the two tended to be more ambivalent and slippery. The image, because of its imprecision, open-ended qualities and possibility of multiple readings, lent itself less easily than the written word to functioning as a sign of absolute truth. Less abstract than the calligraphic word, the image opened up more to the eye through sensual perception and comprehension. Indeed the act of viewing involved a bodily experience of placing oneself in relation to a painted image, which in its turn possessed the powers of evoking more directly and effectively experiences and memories of bodily routines.

For these reasons, that made it difficult to fully control the workings of images, the choice of visualisation as a communicative mode was caught up in a series of tensions between courtly patrons and members of the Muslim orthodoxy. The arts of figural representation in the Islamic regions proliferated in spite of continuing conflicts with theological authority. Muslim rulers on the Indian subcontinent in addition encountered belief systems in which images were created and maintained in a constant ritual context of devotion, service and attendance.[2] Practices of visual representation at the Mughal and other regional courts had therefore to negotiate multiple traditions, not only to repudiate bondage to orthodox opinion, but to realise a visual ideal of *tahzib-i akhlaq*, of perfect regulation of bodily and moral dispositions. In a well-known passage of the *Ain-i Akbari*, Abu'l Fazl draws a parallel betweeen the way the mystic uses his body to reach God and the practice of the artist, who through the medium of paint and brushes transforms earthly substances into an ethereal notion of beauty (cf. *Ain-i Akbari*, Vol. 1, pp. 113f.). The viewing of a work of art too—at close, intimate range, solitary and with intense concentration—imbued the act of seeing with a devotional quality that was also in a special sense a physical one. Unlike a larger canvas painting where the viewer moves back and forth physically to locate himself in relation to the painting, a viewer of a miniature had to find an imaginary path to complete bodily and emotional immersion in a work as a condition of access to it.

Visibility, vision and visuality—all formed channels through which ritual practice, bodily experience and images interposed on and codified each other. The Sanskrit term *darshan* meaning both "sight" or "vision" and also the "act of beholding," was central to Mughal court ceremonial, marked by regular appearances of the emperor, often several times within the space of a day. The religious concept of *darshan* had been under the Hindu monarchies of the early medieval period transferred to the institution of kingship (Inden 1998, pp. 74f.). Its adaptation and codification into a ceremonial practice by the Mughals served as a sign of distinction that set them apart from their Safavid and Ottoman counterparts. In the ceremony of *jharokha-i darshan* instititued by the Mughal rulers, the emperor together with the rising sun appeared before his subjects at the *jharokha*, a special window of his palace which framed his appearance and overlooked a gathering of devoted subjects assembled below. Many of these subjects would fast before they viewed the emperor's face. This spelt the assurance of his continued existence without which they feared the collapse of their universe. Painted images, in turn, were animated by the ritual of viewing the royal person. By "re-presenting" a body that was once present, but no longer is, royal portraits in Mughal painting sought to

[2] Discussed at length in Davis 1997.

bridge an absence in time by effecting an omnipresence of the royal body. The image drew from the ritual its sacral force, its accumulation of emblematic plenitude, in turn it assured to the ritual its fixity.

And yet the ritual of *jharokha-i darshan* was caught up, both in practice and its visualisation, in tensions engendered by the opposing pulls of the *tahzib-i akhlaq* and the anthropomorphism that inhered in Hindu devotional practice. In Hindu ritual the act of seeing is contingent on reciprocity, on the belief that the deity is endowed with powers that are mobilised through the ocular relationship between the devotee and the deity which flows from the act of *darshan*. The corporeal and emotional experience of *darshan* could only be engendered by the presence of a deity that "gazes directly back" at the beholder (cf. PINNEY 2003, pp. 115f.).[3] The Mughal ritual, on the other hand, was framed architecturally and spatially in a way that the two gazes, that of the subject and the emperor, never met.[4] The normative demands of the *akhlaq-i tahzib*, which expounded in great detail the attributes of a virtuous ruler in full control of passions (cf. *Akhlaq-i Nasiri*, First Discourse, esp. pp. 122ff.) translated into a language of disjuncture that came to be built in the ritual as also in the pictorial idioms that were animated by it. Royal portraits framed the appearance of the emperor by encasing it within multiple painted borders, or *hashiyas*, which the eye had to traverse, one after the other, in order to gain access to the imperial person.[5] The unvarying painterly choice of the profile presented a face that could be gazed at, but never looked back, never presented a personality that revealed signs of unfolding, of imperfect control. Painted faces came to possess a visual quality that was ostensibly similar to deities—distant, flat, iconic, and inscrutable—rendered through thick overpainting and burnishing, and yet ocular asymmetries prevented the gaze from functioning as a mode of sensual enchantment.[6] Instead the artists rebounded on the rest of the imperial body as the locus of ideals—physical hardiness, valour, intrepidity—and as the expressive medium par excellence within visual practice.

---

[3] There is a growing literature on *darshan*: ECK 1981; BABB, 1981; GELL 1998. In her exemplary study of popular media in recent times, Christiane BROSIUS (2003) has elaborated the notion of "intervisuality" to flesh out the ways in which new media harness older practices of seeing.

[4] A description of the ritual in ROE 1967.

[5] See for instance the portrait of the emperor Shah Jahan on the peacock throne, attributed to Govardhan (c.1635, the *hashiya* was completed in 1645), Harvard University Art Museums, Private Collection (651.1983), colour reproduction in the exhibition catalogue, BRAND 1996, no. 71, p. 104.

[6] Commenting on this quality, François BERNIER (1992, p. 255) had described the Mughal painters as being "chiefly deficient ... in the expression of the face."

Journeys through the painted page

Transforming the body into an image, to render it tangible as an "instrument of the soul," confronted the court painter with a set of challenges. Visualisation demanded that the power of the king's body be represented as outwardly directed and expressive, suggesting at the same time a concentration of inner energies. While the artist had to find an expressive medium to constitute physical prowess and bravery as embodied qualities, these qualities needed to purged of any hint of excess, or of unrestrained emotional fervour, so as to add up to an image of a complex, yet resolved individual in full control of his powers and passions. The text of the *Akbarnama* is full of descriptions of Akbar's heroic feats—of dramatic elephant fights, of rebellions successfully crushed, hunting expeditions and victories on the battlefield—descriptions which leave little doubt as to his extraordinary bodily strength and courage matched by moral perfection. Rendering these textual images in paint was however not a tension free process, also in view of the iconographic choices artists at the north Indian courts had to constantly negotiate. Well into the third quarter of the sixteenth century, *paramparas* (pictorial traditions) from different regions of north India provided the Mughal atelier with a substantial core of artists who, together with a handful of Iranian *ustads* (master artists), conceptualised and gave shape to the emergent Mughal *qalam*. Early products of the atelier are marked by a visual practice that resorted to a minimization of means, a synoptic mode of rendering objects and gestures, often brought to light by rapidly modulated suggestions of movement, calligraphic and otherwise.[7] Such a practice was premised on a fairly sophisticated code of communication, which each of these traditions had internally evolved and whose specific meanings and communicative strategies would have been accessible to those familiar with its complex manipulative range. A painting visualised through shared conventions, additively plotted, generally possessed an open-endedness[8] that enabled the viewer to add elements so as to conjure it fully. In other words, the body of a painted image remained partially empty until the eye of an informed viewer inhabited it by inserting fresh perceptions. Such a possibility of investing personal visions brought with it the perils of ambiguity which threatened to destabilise the certitudes of ideology.

As opposed to indigenous *paramparas*, new forms of naturalism transported by European works of art, that had made their way into the Mughal *kitabkhana* from the 1570's onwards, seemed at first glance better equipped to translate into paint the powerful ideals contained within the notion of *akhlaq-i tahzib*. At the same time the naturalistic idiom brought with it different

[7] See for instance the illustrated manuscript of the *Tuti-Nama* (Tales of a Parrot), completed in the 1580's. While one version is located in the Chester Beatty Library, Dublin, there is another in the Cleveland Museum of Art. On the latter, Chandra 1976.

[8] This quality has been referred to as the "*gestalt* of an incomplete work of art," see Sheikh 1997, p. 15.

conceptions of perspectival norms—the Italian Albertian and the Flemish North European[9]—that animated European works of art of the sixteenth and seventeenth centuries. Both these systems of representation transformed that which was depicted into "image-as-memory," by placing the viewer in a privileged position of control that at the same time led him to forget his presence and agency. In other words, by fixing the gaze within the frame of an image, perspective created the fiction of a gaze disengaged from the body (cf. Belting 2008, pp. 24f.). Negotiating these different visual regimes, Mughal court artists constantly strove to balance an idiom of creating tactile bodily forms with an image that involves the viewer as active participant in an unfolding narrative. The Albertian organisation of space wherein the human body, placed at the centre of the perspectival grid, functions as the measure of all things, came to be bypassed in north Indian painting of the sixteenth and seventeenth centuries in favour of bodies picturised according to symbolic size, and above all to privilege a mode of viewing wherein the viewer "travels" through the composition, unit by unit, to piece it together. Such a choice meant seeking recourse once more to more corporeal forms of traditional viewing experience akin to those built into Hindu rituals.

The ways in which such a process of balancing and selection was effected can be observed in the double page miniature of the *Akbarnama*, painted by the artists Miskin and Mansur, which portrays the emperor Akbar engaged in a hunt near Lahore (figs. 1–2). The artists strove to incorporate and compress into a single two-dimensional picture space different stages of the narrative of an event that spread over a number of days and nights. The textual account of this was plotted in chronological sequence over several pages of the manuscript (cf. Akbarnama, Vol. 2, pp. 416ff.). The image of the hunt starts off on the left page, where the emperor is shown galloping vigorously across the middle ground of the double page pictorial area, first having shot an arrow which pierces into the rear of an antelope, and then continuing onto the next page in pursuit of further prey. At the same time hundreds of beaters bearing burning torches herd—and have already herded—the game into the hunting area encircled by a makeshift wooden fence. In the middle ground, to the right hand, the captured game is being skinned. The royal tent too has been brought from its customary location at a secure distance from the site of the hunt to be placed in the middle of the densely packed hunting circle. The intense drama and vibrant energy of the hunting expedition, which signified a struggle with and suppression of the potentially threatening and evil forces of the universe, is communicated through a partially naturalistic mode that breaks from earlier synoptic codes to show a sea swirling with lithe animal bodies, counterposed by the intense vitality of the emperor's body, fixed in perfect control over his

[9] For a discussion of these distinct modes, Alpers 1983, p. 133–142.

rapidly galloping steed. The pictorial choice of the artists is not for a narrative centred around a single point; rather movement is denoted through redrawing space and locating objects and persons in it at multiple points. At the same time the mobile plasticity of the hundreds of bodies—of deer, antelopes, cheetahs and of humans—that populate this image, prevent it from disintegrating into fragments. This is achieved through a composition which moves in a spiral, taking off from the tent in the centre and continuing in concentric circles out to the fence perimeter. The spiral also creates a space for Akbar at the centre, without detracting from the suggestion of lightning pace with which he gallops cross the picture space. While painted faces are held within the firm grip of the graphic line, flattened so as to suppress expressive tremors, modelling is applied selectively to the animal and human bodies, even as they retain their predominantly linear aesthetic. It is significant that the division of labour among Mughal artists was organised according to principles which distinguished between the three separate functions described above: devising the composition (*tarah*), rendering the faces (*chihra nami*) and colouring (*rang amezi*), which included the modelling of bodies.

The paintings of the *Akbarnama* are replete with images like the one described above—that is, crowded with figures, each one characterised by individual bodily movement and energetic gestures, the whole composed around complex geometrical patterns that direct the viewer's gaze through the stages of the narrative. We see Akbar leaping onto a wild elephant, trying to tame it as it tramples over a bridge of boats, while terrified retainers and nobles flee or appeal to providence,[10] elsewhere supervising building operations at the site of the new capital Fatehpur Sikri.[11] In other scenes, where the emperor is not physically present in the picture frame, closely knit groups of people held together by variety of posture and gesture—in short through a special new language of bodily codes—are crucial to narrative strategies of these images.[12]

[10] Double page miniature by Basawan and Chitra depicting Akbar's adventures with the elephant Hawai, Victoria and Albert Museum London, repr. in SEN 1984, plates 21–23, pp. 70–73.

[11] Miniature painted by Tulsi (composition), Bandi (modelling) and Madhu Khurd (faces), Victoria and Albert Museum London, repr. in SEN 1984, plate 61, p. 138.

[12] In a painting illustrating the seige of the Rajput fortress of Ranthambhor, reputed for its impregnability, the artists, Miskin and Paras have succeeded in creating a pictorial expression of compressed bodily energy and effort. It is an image of some hundred men and bullock carts forcing their way uphill through a narrow and steep gorge in the valley of the Ran, so as to transport heavy cannons to the top of the hill from where the troops could fire at the fort of the Rajput rule of Ranthanbhor. The deliberate massing of bodies, each caught in a distinct movement and collectively pushing and heaving includes the viewer who, too, journeys across the steep diagonal of the composition, participating in the physical momentum of the whole. The miniature belongs to Akbarnama manuscript housed at the Victoria and Albert Museum London, repr. in SEN 1984,plates 52–53, pp. 120ff.

Frequent instances draw our attention to the ways in which artists worked their way through dif-ferent cultural codes and struggled with the problem of resolving these pictorially. To take one example: the expression of physical courage and bodily strength needed to be distinguished from unrestrained anger or martial rage that would disrupt the complex balance that made up the *tahzib-i akhlaq*. Tusi's ethical model drew upon Aristotlean philosophy of sufficiency and moderation to argue for bodily health as a path to ensure the health of the soul (cf. *Akhlaq-i Nasiri*, p. 118). It presented man's inner being as composed of three faculties: the rational, the irascible and the concupiscible. The first was located in the brain, the "seat of reflection and reason," the second in the heart, the source of anger, bravery, drive, in short "the mine of innate heat," and the third in the liver, the body's "organ of nutrition and of distribution" (*Akhlaq-i Nasiri,* p. 43). The first discourse of the *Akhlaq-i Nasiri* juxtaposes a description of anger with a prescription of how to remedy it through restraint and self control. The physical manifestations of anger, a motion of the soul, are rendered as: "… the blood begins to seethe, and the brain and arteries are filled with a dark vapour, so that the intelligence is cut off by a veil … the human frame becomes as a mountain cave, filled with a blaze of fire and choking with flame and smoke, from which are recognized only noise and sound …" (*Akhlaq-i Nasiri,* p. 128). After outlining the ten causes of anger and the seven categories under which its consequences could be classified, Tusi prescribes "the management of the intelligence" as the treatment of this "disease." The discourse alternates between description, prescription and resolution which is summed up as: "… the course of intelligence and respect the condition for Justice, which necessarily produces equilibrium." (*Akhlaq-i Nasiri*, pp. 129–135). The political culture of the Mughal court, constituted through a continuous engagement with a plurality of regional traditions and practices, meant reaching out to and incorporating concepts that did not always focus on a resolution of the kind advocated as *tahzib-i akhlaq*: for example, notions of honour such as the Rajput idea of direct personal sacrifice, articulated through explicit emotionality, through practices and a habitus in which the bodily and the emotional fused. Mughal politics was marked by efforts to bring about a transfer of this particular sense of personal honour from the lineage onto a more impersonal register of imperial pride and belonging (cf. Richards 1998b, p. 288).

An effort to grapple with these positions and challenges in the domain of the visual can be followed through in a painting, again from the *Akbarnama*, composed by the artist Miskin, who also painted the faces, and by Shankar who executed the colouring and modelling of figures.[13] The narrative, recounted through several pages of the text, centres on an incident where Akbar, seized

[13] *Akbarnama*, Victoria and Albert Museum London, repr. in Sen 1984, plate 25, p. 76.

by fury, punishes his foster brother Adham Khan for conspiring to assassinate the imperial *wazir*, by flinging Adham Khan down from the terrace of the upper *zenana* apartments. The towering rage prompting this action is rendered pictorially through a series of contrasts: between the rigid, expressionless figure of the emperor, framed by the doorway of the terrace apartment and the panic-stricken figures below, fleeing in different directions, moving and gesticulating rapidly; between the austere white wall and stairway and the frenzy of colour patterns and contrasts that resonate through the agitated bodies, and above all in the dramatic plummeting form of Adham Khan which, marked by the archetypal contrast of red, green and black, creates a chromatic focal point. The same contrast is mirrored in the reverse in the dress of the fugure of the messenger, Farhat Khan, standing above. The contrast of red and green, often used to draw attention to imperial figures in portraits, and signifying an embodied resolution of oppositions, is significantly transposed here on to the object of imperial action, while the main actor, the emperor, is dressed in subdued colours that draw our attention only through the contrasting dark frame of the doorway. The action itself is one inspired by the larger motive of justice but executed through an act of uncontrollable rage. Again, the figure of the emperor, face in inscrutable profile, remains iconic and distant—only the rigid stance of his flexed limbs and above all the hand tightly gripping the scimitar suggest the tension inherent in anger and the need to govern it.

Beyond likeness

The agency of bodily codes in the public construction of elite status and above all of imperial authority meant that portraits came to acquire a new importance as a painted genre. By representing a body no longer charged with kinetic energy and in constant movement, portraits of members of the imperial elite, by their quality of being more contained images, registered a different and perhaps shifting understanding of humoural aspects of the body in relationship to material environment and inner equilibrium. While portraits were designated as "likeness" (*taswir, citra*), they did not necessarily strive to achieve perfect individuation as a means of recognition, in the sense contemporary European portraits sought to do. Abu'l Fazl's oft cited statement in the *Ain-i Akbari* observes: "His Majesty himself sat for his likeness, and also ordered to have the likenesses taken of all the grandees of the realm. An immense album was thus formed: those that have passed away have received a new life, and those who are still alive have immortality promised to them." (cf. *Ain-i Akbari,* Vol. 1, p. 115) "Drawing the likeness" (cf. *Ain-i Akbari,* Vol. 1, p. 113) however meant drawing upon a reservoir of normative materials that laid down the physical attributes of persons according to rank and gender, so that a portrait would enable recognition on the basis of those qualities that were held to mark individuals as kings or noblemen.

Literary discussions of portraiture on the Indian subcontinent before the advent of the Turkish and Mughal rulers focus primarily on gods and kings, leaving the painter more or less free to render other social groups according to his own imaginative preferences. An important iconographic text of the sixth century AD, the *Citralakshana* of Nagnajit deals extensively with the *lakshanas* or bodily attributes of men of rank, especially the *Cakravartin* (lit. wheel-turning master, universal ruler). His arms, for instance, are precisely described: "The upper arm of the Master of Men is symmetrical as the tail of a bull; when he stands erect, both the hands touch the knees." Further *lakshanas* according to Nagnajit: "…the nails should resemble the half moon, should be of red colour and lustrous, illumined like the pupils of the eye…," the teeth "even shaped, thickly set, shining pure, sharp and white, white as the pearls, as cow's milk, as the stem of the lotus, as a heap of snow… The Great Man turning the Wheel should be represented … with the gait of the King of Elephants … he has the sharpness of mond of the leader of Bulls, the strength of a King of Lions, the majesty of a King of Wild Geese; such is the outward apearance of the Master of Men." (citation by Goswamy 1986, p. 195). Long descriptions based on similies drawn from flora and fauna inspired the stylisation of the human body to add up to an image of extraordinary majesty.

While literary texts that created a blueprint for portraits circulated in courtly milieus over many centuries, painted portraits themseves made an appearance from the sixteenth century onwards, primarily under the patronage of the Mughal elite. Other north Indian courts as well as those in the Deccan responded to the Mughal example, so that from the mid-sixteenth century onwards a veritable efflorescence of the genre can be observed. Following from Ananda.K. Coomaraswamy's sharply drawn distinction between Rajput and Mughal painting, most art historical writing well into the present operates on the assumption that as opposed to Rajput and other north Indian regional styles, Mughal portraits were inspired overwhelmingly by naturalistic concerns, and their execution followed from an observation of physical details and inner states. The term "psychological realism" has been used in connection a discussion of European "influence" on Mughal art. Yet Mughal portraits too drew upon panegyric descriptions by court historians, on mythical traditions, symbols of royalty and importantly on cultural ideals of etiquette such as *adab*, and other textual constructions of ideal masculinity for their inspiration. High sounding names which Mughal emperors assumed upon accession—Jahangir (he who seizes the world) or Shah Jahan (king of the world), Alamgir (lion of the world)—all resonate with the panegyric flavour of *Cakravartin*. Portraits systematically assimilated into their pictorial programme symbolic objects such as the globe, the lion and the lamb, the nimbus, the weighing scales, to translate such rhetoric. The symbolism of light—rendered through the halo, or often emanating from within the figures, painted in luminous colours against plain, dark backgrounds, had its origins in an imperial myth: the story handed down by generations of chroniclers wherein the semi-mythical ancestress of the Mughal clan, the Mongol princess Alanqwa, was impregnated by a miraculous ray of divine light that then was transferred from one emperor to the next. The distant view of the emperor's profile which became the norm for elite portraits was, as seen earlier, hardly an effective idiom within which to render an unfolding personality. Bodily defintions in Mughal portraits followed their own set of conventions rather than a concern for physiognomical exactitude. In his memoirs the emperor Jahangir describes his father Akbar as follows:

> In stature he was of medium height. He had a wheaten complexion and black eyes and eyebrows. His countenance was radiant, and he had the build of a lion, broad of chest with long hands and arms. On his left nostril he had a very beautiful fleshy mole, about the size of a chickpea. Among those who have some expertise in the science of physiognomy such a mole is considered a sign of great good fortune. His august voice was very loud, and he had a particularly nice way of speaking. In his conduct and manners there was no comparison between him and the people of the world—a divine aura was apparent around him. Both greatness in personal worth and regality in lineage, you would say Solomon had placed his ring on his finger. (Jahangirnama, p. 36)

Physical details in this account are framed by panegyric, convention, symbolism of light, while the long arms resemble in all likelihood a favourite *laskhana* of kings formulated by Nagnajit.

The *Mau'izah-i Jahangiri* (Admonitions of Jahangir), a collection of ideas and maxims assembled from Persian, Arabic and Indian sources by an imperial governor, Muhammad Baqir Najm-i Sani, an Iranian migrant to Mughal India, sets out to describe the qualities required by the ideal of *adab* that an individual should cultivate (cf. ALAM 2004, pp. 61, 75).[14] Though the work itself was never accompanied by illustrations, there appears to be an association or reciprocity between the language of portraits and Baqir's themes and discussions on the inner and outer perfectibility of a cultivated person, on the conventions of dress and the markers of the ideal male body. For instance one of the bodily criteria of ideal manliness named by Baqir was a man whose physique was *kamar band*, that is "waist bound up," meaning at all times prepared for battle and heroic action (cf. O'HANLON 1999, p. 64). This meaning was articulated in portraits, even before Baqir set out to compile his text,[15] which invariably depict the standing male body as firm waisted, a corporeal attribute set into focus by the broad ornamental sash in exiquiste

[14] Discussed at some length in O'HANLON 1999, pp. 56ff.

[15] See for instance the portrait of Jahangir with bow and arrow, painted c. 1604, Arthur M. Sackler Gallery, Smithsonian Institution Washington DC (S 1986.408), excellent colour repr. in *The Jahangirnama*, p. 47.

silk or brocade, the *patka*, that was worn by every imperial servant appearing in public. Further devices—the sword or dagger, a jewel—functioned to focus attention to the waist as a critical marker. It has indeed been argued that the strong male waist, significant in a military culture that attached exceptional importance to cavalry skills and wielding heavy weapons on horseback, made this feature constitutive of ideal masculinity, which was then counterposed to being "feeble waisted," meant to denote debility or base actions, often associated with women (O'Hanlon 1999, p. 64). It is significant however that portraits of aristocratic men and women do not deploy the language of gender difference in the way it has been ascribed to Baqir's text. The portrayal of both men and women by court artists is surprisingly similar, often even interchangeable. Both are marked by almost identical bodily contours, delineated through diaphanous draperies, same delicate facial features, both dress in silks, satin, sumptuous brocades and fine muslins and appear to enjoy shared pleasures in pearls and gems. The quintessential Mughal nobleman is usually shown holding a flower, a jewel or a mirror in a gesture that draws attention to the hands as a marker of refinement (Figure 3).[16] Difference in bodily attributes here cuts across gender lines, instead it is drawn with clarity along the boundaries of social class. The aristocratic body, male and female, transporting ideals of *nazaqat* and *tahzib* (delicacy of demeanour and courtesy) can be effectively counterposed to the working bodies of labourers—male and female—rendered with poignant care in miniatures such as those showing building operations at the Agra fort (figs. 4, 5). Even while contained within the graphic line, the postures, gait and stances of men and women carrying weights, transporting blocks of sandstone along a ramp, driving nails to split a large stone block, seated on their haunches while laying bricks or mixing lime—all appear to be articulated through recall of memories of the body in work routines. Observations are however reworked into pictographic formulae, rapid codes such as short, stocky torsos, excessive girth, straining arms that speak their language more effectively than facial expression, which however shows traces of greater differentiation in terms of complexion and features as compared to the aristocratic visage.

The prolific production of portraits at the Mughal court inspired regional principalities to follow this example in an effort to partake of the cultural and political prestige associated with such visual practice. Larger regional kingdoms chose to follow the Mughal format in that portraits were painted with figures

---

[16] Of the large number of Mughal portraits in this genre only two examples will be cited: Prince Salim as a young man (holding a jewelled mirror), painted by Bichitr, c. 1635, Minto Album, Victoria and Albert Museum London, repr. in Okada 1992, no. 201, p. 168; Shah Jahan standing on a globe, holding a turban jewel, by Hashim, Dublin, Chester Beatty Library, repr. in Jones 1987, no. 35, p. 53.

clearly detached from coloured backgrounds, rendered in flat colours, though their tones were stronger than those used by Mughal artists—pure yellow, carmine red, sage green. Also rendered in profile, the subjects portrayed were endowed with greater bodily fullness and monumentality, with the forms occupying the picture space till the edges and often threatening to break out of its frame.[17] Interestingly smaller principalities, such as the kingdom of Mandi in the Punjab hills, experimented with their own idiosyncratic modes of portraiture, especially at the beginning of the eighteenth century, a time when the authority of Mughal imperial power was confronted by serious challenges from regional groups such as the Marathas, the Deccani nobles and Pathans. In seeking to assert a distinct regional identity, painters of Mandi drew upon the reservoir of prescriptions for bodily forms, the *lakshanas*, found in traditional texts and interpreted these in unusual ways to created images of extraordinary dramatic force. A particularly striking example is to be found in a series of portraits of the ruler of Mandi, Raja Sidh Sen, from around 1700. To take one example that attempts to give pictorial form to attributes couched in panegyric descriptions found in earlier texts[18]: it shows the Raja bare chested, wearing a Mughal style turban, a long, flowing robe, open down the front to reveal a pair of striped shorts and long, powerfully built thighs and legs that would appear to echo the description of the king Harsha composed by court poet Bana in the *Harshacharita* (7th century): "… his broad chest shone like [Mount] Kailasa with a cliff of crystal … his two thighs were ruby pillars, set to bear the weight of the earth which rested in his heart." (citation by Goswamy 1985, p. xxii). Equally striking are the height of the striding figure and the length of his arms, which the painter has extended to make long enough to reach his knees, one of the most characteristic *lakshanas* of a great man. While the Raja wields a sword, wears a turban ornament, rings, pearl and ruby earrings in the manner of Mughal princes and nobles, he also wears the wooden clogs of a *saiva* ascetic, a necklace with an amulet and a white and red auspicious mark on his forehead, all of which refer to his attributes as a religious devotee of Siva. It would seem that one path to the articulation of regional identities in relation to the powerful imperial centre was through the reinvention of earlier, distinct cultural models, wherein the image of the body could function as an important marker to create new forms of allegiance.

---

[17] See for example portraits of Raja Gaj Singh of Marwar by a painter of Jodhpur, mid 17th century, National Museum Delhi (63.1789); Raja Karan Singh of Bikaner, mid-17th century, Private Collection, Portrait of Mian Mahipat Dev of Mankot, Mankot c. 1660, Government Museum and Art Gallery Chandigarh, all three repr. in Desai 1985, plates 27, 28, 30, pp. 31, 34.

[18] Raja Sidh Sen of Mandi Walking, c. 1700, Government Museum and Art Gallery Chandigarh (2725), repr. in *Desai 1985*, plate 32, p. 37.

Embodying the exotic

The political culture of the Mughal court during the sixteenth and seventeenth centuries was informed by exchanges of many kinds—material goods, political concepts, visual motifs—with world regions—Europe, Ottoman Turkey, Central Asia—as well as with regions of the Indian subcontinent. Exchanges formed part of a field in which boundaries between the material and the cultural were often fluid, as objects participated in cultural transactions such as practices of gifting, ritual incorporation or missionary efforts. An object had both material value and form, at the same time, as a gift or ritual object, it incorporated the charisma of the giver or particular cosmological notions. Since most material objects entered the Mughal repertoire through alien cultures, they transported different kinds of and often contradictory messages. On the one hand they worked to enhance the prestige of those elites who possessed them, by generating new values such as cosmopolitanism, connoisseurship, access to luxury and the habitus of conspicuous consumption, values which then came to be codified in the genre of *Mirza Namah* texts as attributes of *mirzai*, of cultivated urban gentility.[19] At the same time alien objects, which made up a truly mixed bag—ranging from horses and slave girls to jewels and textiles, clocks of different kinds, porcelain objects, globes, mirrors in gilded frames, crucifixes, maps, paintings and prints—were often a source of diplomatic irritations, especially when drawn into the cultural economy of gifting, for they did not always conform to Mughal codes of value and prestige and produced uncertainties about their display and location.[20] One way of dealing with the alterity of an object seemed to be pictorial incorporation. The body as image now came to function as a stage on which to display luxury goods: naturalistic techniques of representation were selectively and sensitively deployed to render radiant and richly patterned silks, the transparency of muslin, the sheen of pearls or the glitter of rubies on a sword handle. Colour could generate the synaesthetic experience of heat, airiness, the sounds of rippling water or the heady smells of flowers and perfumes. Such visions furnished the existing conceptions of humoural mixtures and the inner equilibrium of the body with sensibilities that enabled their articulation in a new guise. The sensual qualities of an individual's physical environment—its colours, fragrances, textures and sounds—all came to be increasingly regarded as important to creating the right measure of resolution and equilibrium between the body and inner life (cf. O'Hanlon 1999, p. 69).

---

[19] The emergence of the ideal of *mirzai* has been discussed at length and persuasively by O'Hanlon (1999, pp. 68ff.), who however does not address the ways in which the pictorial translation of objects into an image as early as the late 16th century could have been constitutive of these later ideals.

[20] For examples, Mukhia 2004, pp. 104f.

Bodily incorporation of alterity in the pictorial realm, a response to the mimetic pull exercised by otherness, also became a way of cognition and a mode of repositioning the self within a relationship of power. An exotic object translated into an image frequently came to be associated directly with the king's persona, a body that was a metonym for empire. One object which lent itself in remarkable ways to embodiment, transporting in the process a clear ideological message, was the globe. Sumathi Ramaswamy has charted the trajectories of this object which, in its original European setting stood for rationality, intellectual advances and terrritorial expansion, now relocated could be made to serve a different ideological purpose. The globe was an effective way of pictorialising panegyric titles of the Mughal emperors such as Jahangir and Shah Jahan and their claims to being world rulers; it also functioned to build a bridge between Islamic and Hindu cosmological conceptions of creation (cf. Ramaswamy 2007, pp. 751–782). The meanings of the relocated globe resonated in particular ways primarily through the unmistakeable association that paintings forged between the king's body—the most intimate part of the self—and an alien object. Portraits of Mughal emperors show the king either standing on the globe, holding it, handing it over as part of conferring sovereignty to a successor or sitting with it firmly under the feet.[21] In other words, an object originally belonging to the realm of the intellect came to be visualised as an extension of the emperor's body so as to reconfigure the relationship of power the object was intended to spell out.

Modes of pictorial incorporation, like in the case of the globe, furnished a fresh and tangible undergirding to the mutually constitutive relationships between the body, politics and ethics that characterised north Indian court cultures. Yet drawing a close association between an alien object and the king's body also had the potential of generating subversive arguments—stimulated by an excess of signification produced through a multi-layered presence of different visual regimes and the unpredictable entanglement of their original and potential symbolic meanings within the space of a single image. The destabilising arguments in this case centre on the transience of the human body, they are equally about the nature of power and about visual representation itself. This becomes apparent in a particular work—an unusual and at the same time extremely well-known portrait of the emperor Jahangir painted by the artist Bichitr and which is housed in the collection of the Sackler Gallery at the Smithsonian Institute, Washington DC[22]. It is an image,

[21] Several examples can be cited, a number have been reproduced in Ramaswamy 2007.

[22] A miniature from the *Jahangirnama* showing the emperor seated on an hour glass, offering a book to a Sufi. A detail is reproduced on the splendid dust jacket of Thackston, *The Jahangirnama*, a full page reproduction on p. 257. For an extensive discussion of this image, Juneja 2002.

I wish to argue, which derives its disruptive power through the interaction between the imperial body and a series of alien objects, an interaction that works to produce disjunctures and drive a wedge into a carefully moulded edifice of an imperial portrait. This oft reproduced painting shows the emperor Jahangir seated on an hourglass transformed into a throne. In a familiar topos, the emperor presents a book to the Sufi saint Hasan Chishti while ignoring the other, more "worldly," figures placed in a descending row along the left edge of the picture space. These are the Ottoman sultan of Turkey, the English monarch, James I and, interestingly, the painter of this miniature, Bichitr—who positions his self portrait at the end of this line of kings, referring to his symbolic role as "king of the arts." The overt intention was therefore to articulate a mythical claim of the Mughal emperor to universal rulership, and the artist Bichitr was instructed to create a variation on a theme executed by another court artist, Abu'l Hasan, where Jahangir displays the same arrogant stance while receiving the poet Sa'di and ignoring the presence of Turkish diplomatic representatives.[23] The object associated with the king's body in Bichitr's painting is not the globe but an hour glass, a Christian symbol of death and transience. The seated figure of Jahangir is framed by an enormous refulgent aureole that embodies both sun and crescent moon, a symbol which spells a notion of infinite time. In this image it exists in a state of tension with a competing notion of temporality symbolised by the hour glass, whose original associations with death continue to shimmer through the dense accoutrements of a Pax Moghulica. For the artist has deployed the language of naturalistic representation to draw our attention to the sands of time which have run out. In a gesture as if to exorcise the inexorable flow of time, two cupids inscribe directly upon the hour glass the words: "O Shah, may the span of your life be a thousand years." A comparison of this representation with a more or less contemporaneous portrait of Jahangir embracing his political opponent Shah Abbas[24], renders the inbuilt tension more evident. While the latter image shows an emperor still in possession of a powerful physique, robust and well-built, Bichitr's rendering presents us a considerably more aged and haggard-looking Jahangir, as if consciously registering the ravages of time on his body, made tactile through skilfully painted transparent draperies. Death—the disappearance of the body—becomes the all-encompasssing horizon that organizes the experience of time and generates all efforts to overcome its

[23] The left folio of this double page miniature (c. 1615) is located at the Walters Art Gallery Baltimore (W. 688, folio 37) and the right one in the Freer Gallery of Art, Smithsonian Institution Washington DC (F46.28). Both are reproduced in Thackston, *The Jahangirnama*, pp. 170f., the right page which shows Jahangir seated with the globe under his feet also in Ramaswamy 2007, Figure 5.

[24] Jahangir embracing Shah Abbas by Abu'l Hasan, Freer Gallery of Art, Smithsonian Institution Washington DC (45.9), repr. in Thackston, *The Jahangirnama*, Frontispiece.

workings. The creation of images, generated by the supra-temporal theme of death, was meant to hold a place for the body of the dead person among the living, as Abu'l Fazl had described the objective of the Mughal album of portraits (cf. *Ain-i Akbari,* Vol. 1, p. 115).[25] In this respect too, the artist has pushed disruption to a final point of irony.[26] This portrait, uniformly labelled as an imperial portrait, is at the same time a self-portrait, for the artist, Bichitr, places his persona in the same image, at its lowest edge. Here we have the unusual instance of a painter in the strictly regulated system in which this miniature was created, seeking to share the pictorial space of his patron. The framed picture he holds up may be read as a reference to his art[27], both as creation and at the same time as a salaried activity: an elephant stood for a reward and the salary of painters like that of all other employees in the service of the Mughal court was calculated in terms of foot soldiers (*sawar*). Vision then comes to rest on a mundane transaction between artist and patron for painted mythologies. A central prerequisite of viewing as a sacral vision, as *darshan*, was the invisibility of the artist, the effacing of all traces of his painterly activity. By making his presence visible, the artist transforms vision into an act of representation. He introduces a note of ontological uncertainty, playing ironically as he does on issues of artifice and representation, ideal and reality, the transient body and eternal fame.

Ordering nature

The subject of death in a sense brings us back to the primordial earth, the third element in the body-kingdom-land triad. Here again, various strains of thinking were present within a culturally diverse court. Like the body, the land too, in various ethical, agronomic and political doctrines, was governed by different humours, which kingdoms and communities had to keep in equilibrium: the soil could be toned up by planting trees and crops, and by digging wells. Equally, the settlement of learned men and great saints could implant virtue in the land (cf. Bayly 1998, p. 16). Many martial traditions of the subcontinent venerated the land as that for which the sons of the soil sacrificed their lives. For instance mortally wounded Rajputs mixed their blood with the land to form a ball of clay, or food made from the produce of the land, which they offered to ancestors who had conquered and husbanded the land before they did.[28] An ecological harmony between the body and nature—the plant and

[25] For an extensive discussion of the death image as the true vanishing point of every picture, Belting 2001, chapters 5 and 6.

[26] For a more extensive discussion of other disjunctures that operate within this image, Juneja 2002.

[27] On the recurrence of this topos in Mughal self portraits, Juneja 2008, p. 201.

[28] Norman Ziegler, cited in Bayly 1998, pp. 11f..

animal world—was therefore as necessary to a healthy body politic, as was balancing different types and groups of people in a polity. While nature was perceived as a source of life and beauty, it was at the same time feared to be potentially inimical and destructive if left uncontrolled. "Civilising" nature through laying down formal gardens, orchards, through building activity, were all canonised in texts and practice of the sixteenth and seventeenth centuries as acts of piety. Akbar's historians describe the transformation of the countryside around the village of Sikri during the course of construction activities to create a new township in the following terms:

> The lands which were desolate like the hearts of lovers ... attained freshness, purity, splendour and value like the cheeks of the beautiful ... in the environs which had formerly bee the habitat of rabbits and jackals ... mosques, bazaars, baths, caravanserais and other fine buildings were constructed... (*Tarikh-i Akbari*, p. 35)

In artistic representations an important aesthetic value was accorded to the principles of formal linear harmony and symmetry through which human agency would impose its own order and stylisation on nature, so as to draw out its beauty and to intensify the experience and enjoyment of it by those privileged to do so.

The Mughal emperors spent considerable portions of their lives, during their frequent journeys, military and hunting expeditions, in direct contact with nature. This provided the occasion for pictorial narratives to work their way through different idioms that would communicate the idea of a fine ecological balance between the imperial body and the land. The intrinsic presence of violence and mutually hostile forces within nature, a continuing struggle for power and survival, was a continual theme privileged by artists—a favourite topos was the portrayal of powerful animals devouring the weaker ones. The motif of a lion killing a gazelle, or a rabbit, or a bird or a bull or at times even a human bieng was a recurring one. Intervention in this struggle involved domestication of threatening forces and an imposition of order, balance and harmony through curbing nature's unruliness. Once domesticated, animals come to acquire humanised expressive qualities, serve as a metaphor for perfect justice *adl*.[29]

---

[29] For instance the miniature from the Polier Album (Staatsbibliothek, Preußischer Kulturbesitz Berlin), showing Jahangir and a lion with his Vizier, repr. in Rogers 1993, plate 79, p. 113; or observe the rendering of the lion and the ox in the miniature from the Windsor *Padshahnama*, wherein Jahangir presents Prince Khurram with a turban ornament, painted by Payag, c. 1640, repr. in Milo/Koch/Thackston 1997, Plate 39 and Figure 31 (detail). A number of similar examples exist.

The subject of the hunt, a favourite of Mughal artists, centred on some of these issues, though pictorial practice did register shifts here while trying to accommodate different understandings of the hunt.[30] Many different meanings and functions have been ascribed to the hunt in north Indian political culture; alone in Mughal texts the list valorising the hunt beyond being simply a favourite royal pastime is a long one, and visual representations moved over time between privileging one or the other. In many parts of early modern Asia hunting was endowed with special significance as an attribute of rulership. François Bernier, the French traveller to Mughal India in the seventeenth century, described a successful hunt as being a "favourable omen," as the escape of an animal was a portent of "infinite evil to the state" (cf. Bernier 1992, p. 379). Among the Hindu kings of early medieval India, the ritual of enthronement (*rajyabhiseka*), the placement of the imperial body at the sacral centre of the kingdom, was enacted with the throne set over five skins of hunted animals, those of a wolf, a civet, a leopard, a lion and a tiger (cf. Inden 1998, p. 74). In the double page miniature portraying a hunting scene from the *Akbarnama* discussed earlier in this essay, the artists Miskin and Mansur focus primarily on the bodily relationships between the hunting emperor, the hundreds of beaters, torch bearers and other helpers, and an equally large number of animals, all contained within a composition which locks man and nature within swirling movements. Yet the image also contains a clear ideological reference to the virtue of *adl*, justice: its upper right hand edge makes space within the hunting enclosure for an incident that had taken place previously and was described in the *Akbarnama* (Vol. 2, pp. 417f.). A certain Hamid Bakari had committed an offence against a court official. The punishment meted to him is part of this image, symbolically the site of justice: the culprit is shown, head shaved off, mounted on an ass and being taken around the hunting area as an act of public humiliation. Hunting in this sense has been described as a form of bodily action that brought the emperor regularly to far flung regions of his empire, enabled him to keep an eye on his subjects, and gain knowledge about their condition (cf. Akbarnama, Vol. 2, pp. 417f.; Koch 1998, p. 12). The relationship between bodily action and spiritual purpose is articulated through images in which Akbar is portrayed as experiencing a moment of mystical communion and enlightenment in the midst of a hunt.[31]

[30] On the theme of the hunt in Mughal painting: Skelton 1969, pp. 33–48; Smart 1979, pp. 396–400; Okada 1992, pp. 319–327; Koch 1998.

[31] Miniature from the Victoria and Albert Museum *Akbarnama*, by Mahesh (composition and modelling) and Kesu (faces) which portrays Akbar experiencing a spiritual seizure in the midst of a hunting expedition in the desert, reproduced in Sen 1984, plate 60, p. 136.

This was followed by a resolution, Abu'l Fazl informs us, not only to restrain his hunting activities, but also to impose bodily restrictions on himself through consuming a vegetarian diet once a week (cf. *Akbarnama,* vol. 2, pp. 522f.). Images of the hunt from the mid-seventeenth century shift to a more contained, or resolved, idiom which resorts to increased naturalism to locate the physical imperial presence within the heart of nature, in greater harmony with the land and its flora and fauna, as in a painting from the Windsor *Badshahnama.*[32] Embedded in the receeding image, is a scene of a peasant working on the land, while another draws water from a well. Their distant bodies merge with nature and the colours of the earth, conveying an unmistakeable message of harmony and resolution, effected by an imperial power in perfect control over a realm that encompasses the land, its plant and animal life and the bodies of the subjects that work it.

The variety of pictorial experiments to create images that worked as both *of* the body and those which stand *for* the body, had the power to function across regional identities in more than one way: they shaped a language that could generate cohesion among multi-ethnic and pluri-religious imperial elites in north India during the sixteenth and seventeenth centuries and could equally be reappropriated by these to define anew the boundaries between the empire and the regions. This dynamic accelerated with the transition to the eighteenth century, a time marked by imperial disintegration and the emergence of new political formations, courtly and market cultures, processes which have all been competently analysed by historians over the past decades. These years were also a time of cultural shifts, when court artists sought employment with new patrons espousing different forms of political and bodily cultures—the Marathas, Sikhs, the Deccani elites, now joined by the trading officials of the East India Company. Examining the ways in which visual culture participated and constituted the historical fortunes of these decades promises to be an exciting and rewarding undertaking.

[32] Shah Jahan hunting (c. 1645), repr. in Beach/Koch/Thackston 1997, plate 33, p. 85 and figure 62 (detail), p. 155.

List of illustrations

Figures 1–2: Akbar engaged in a hunt near Lahore, double page miniature from the *Akbarnama*, painted by Miskin and Mansur, Victoria and Albert Museum, London.

Figure 3: Mughal Prince offering wine to his mistress (c. 1740), San Diego Museum of Art.

Figures 4–5: Construction workers at the Agra Fort, double page miniature from the *Akbarnama*, painted by Miskin, Sarwan and Tulsi Khurd, Victoria and Albert Museum, London.

References

Ain-i Akbari of Abu'l Fazl Allami = The Ain-i Akbari, Vol. 1 (2001). – Transl. by H. BLOCHMANN. – Reprint. – Delhi.

Akbarnama of Abu'l Fazl Allami = The Akbarnama of Abu'l Fazl Allami, 3 Vols. – Transl. by H. BEVERIDGE. – Reprint. – New Delhi.

Aklaq-i Nasiri of Nasir-al din Tusi = The Nasirean Ethics by Nasir ad-Din Tusi (1964). – Transl. by G. M. WICKENS. – London.

ALAM, M. (2004): The Languages of Political Islam in India 1200–1800. – Delhi.

ALPERS, S. (1983): The Art of Describing. – Chicago.

BABB, L. A. (1981): Glancing: Visual Interaction in Hinduism. In: Journal of Anthropological Research, Vol. 37, pp. 387–401.

BAYLY, C. A. (1998): Origins of Nationality in South Asia: Patriotism and Ethical Government in the Making of Modern India. – Delhi.

BEACH, M. C./KOCH, E./THACKSTON, W. (Eds.) (1997): King of the World – The Padshahnama: An Imperial Mughal Manuscript from the Royal Library. – Washington DC.

BELTING, H. (2008): Florenz und Bagdad: Eine westöstliche Geschichte des Blicks. – Munich.

BELTING, H. (2001): Bild-Anthropologie: Entwürfe für eine neue Bildwissenschaft. – Munich.

BERNIER, F. (1992): Travels in the Mughal Empire AD 1656–1668. – Transl. and ed. by A. CONSTABLE and V. SMITH. – Reprint. – New Delhi.

BRAND, M. (Ed.) (1996): The Vision of Kings: Art and Experience in India. – London.

BROSIUS, C. (2003): Hindutva Intervisuality: Videos and Politics of Representation. In: RAMASWAMY, S. (Ed.): Beyond Appearences? Visual Practices and Ideologies in Modern India. – New Delhi.

CHANDRA, P. (1976): The Tuti-Nama of the Cleveland Museum of Art. – Graz.

Citralakshana of Nagnajit = GOSWAMY, B. N./DALLAPICCOLA, A. L. (Ed.) (1976): An Early Document of Indian Art: The Citralakshana of Nagnajit. – Delhi.

DAVIS, R. H. (1997): Lives of Indian Images. – Princeton.

DESAI, V. N. (Ed.) (1985): Life at Court: Art for India's Rulers 16th–19th centuries. – Boston.

ECK, D. (1981): Darsan: Seing the Divine Image in India. – Chambersburg.

GORDON, S. (Ed.) (2001): Robes and Honor: The Medieval World of Investiture. – New York.

GOSWAMY, B. N. (1985): Of Devotees and Elephant Fights: Some Notes on Subject Matter in Rajput and Mughal Painting. In: DESAI, V. N. (Ed.): Life at Court: Art for India's Rulers 16th–19th centuries. – Boston.

GOSWAMY, B. N. (1986): Essence and Appearance: Some Roots on Indian Portraiture. In: Skelton, R. (Ed.): Facets of Indian Art. – London.

INDEN, R. (1998): Ritual Authority and Cyclic Time in Hindu Kingship. In: RICHARDS J. F. (Ed.): Kingship and Authority in South Asia. – Delhi.

Jahangirnama = The Jahangirnama: Memoirs of Jahangir, Emperor of India (1999). – Transl. and ed. by W. M. THACKSTON. – Oxford/New York.

JONES, D. (1987): Patrons of the Art – The Mughals and the Medici. In: Marg, Vol. 39, No. 1.

JUNEJA, M. (2002): Jahangir auf der Sanduhr: Überlegungen zur Lektüre einer Visualität im Spannungsfeld zwischen Eigenem und Fremdem. In: SCHNEIDER, G. (Ed.): Die visuellen Dimensionen des Historischen: Hans-Jürgen Pandel zum 60. Geburtstag. – Schwalbach/Ts., pp. 142–157.

JUNEJA, M. (2008): Braided Histories? Visuelle Praktiken des indischen Moghulreichs zwischen Mimesis und Alterität. In: Historische Anthropologie, Vol. 16, No. 2.

KOCH, E. (1998): Dara Shikoh Shooting Nilgais: Hunt and Landscape in Mughal Painting. In: Occasional Papers of the Freer Gallery of Art (Smithsonian Institute), New Series 1. – Washington DC.

MUKHIA, H. (2004): The Mughals of India. – Oxford.

O'HANLON, R. (1999): Manliness and Imperial Service in Mughal North India. In: Journal of the Economic and Social History of the Orient, Vol. 42, No. 1, pp. 47–93.

O'HANLON, R. (2007): Kingdom, Household and Body: History, Gender and Imperial Service under Akbar. In: Modern Asian Studies, Vol. 41, No. 5, pp. 889–923.

OKADA, A. (1992a): Indian Miniatures of the Mughal Court. – New York.

OKADA, A. (1992b): Le Prince Salim à la chasse: Une miniature inédite peinte à Allahabad. In: Artibus Asiae, Vol. 52 (3–4), pp. 319–327.

PINNEY, C. (2003): "A Secret of Their Own Country:" Or, How Indian Nationalism Made Itself Irrefutable. In: RAMASWAMY, S. (Ed.): Beyond Appearences? Visual Practices and Ideologies in Modern India. – New Delhi.

RAMASWAMY, S. (2007): Conceit of the Globe in Mughal Visual Practice. In: Comparative Studies in Society and History, Vol. 49, No. 4, pp. 751–782.

RICHARDS, J. F. (Ed.) (1998a): Kingship and Authority in South Asia. – Delhi.

RICHARDS, J. F. (1998b): The Formulation of Imperial Authority in Akbar and Jahangir. In: RICHARDS, J. F. (Ed.): Kingship and Authority in South Asia. – Delhi.

ROE, T. (1967): The Embassy of Sir Thomas Roe to the Court of the Great Moghul 1615–1619. – Ed. by W. FOSTER. – Reprint. – Liechtenstein.

ROGERS, J. M. (1993): Mughal Miniatures. – London.

SEN, G. (1984): Paintings of the Akbar Nama: A Visual Chronicle of Mughal India. – Calcutta.

SHEIKH, G. (1997): The Making of a Visual Language: Thoughts on Mughal Painting. In: Journal of Arts and Ideas, 30–31.

SKELTON, R. (1969): Two Mughal Lion Hunts. In: Victoria and Albert Museum Yearbook 1969, pp. 33–48.

SMART, E. S. (1979): A Recently Discovered Mughal Hunting Picture by Payag. In: Art History, Vol. 2, No. 4, pp. 396–400.

Tarikh-i Akbari of Muhammad Arif Qandhari. In: BRAND, M/LOWRY, G. D. (Eds.) (1895): Fatehpur Sikiri: A Sourcebook. – Transl. by M. BRAND and G. D. LOWRY. – Cambridge (MA).

Christiane Brosius

The Multiple Bodies of the Bride: Ritualising 'World Class' at Elite Weddings in Urban India

> For a bride, her wedding day is like walking the red carpet. It's her big moment, when countless eyes are watching her every move. And every bride wants to look her absolute best. But reaching that stage requires preparation and dedication. Because you don't want your audience, much less the bridegroom, to notice flabby arms, dark circles under the eyes or love handles. (Srinivasa 2007)

This quote from *Savy*, a lifestyle magazine, bridges the gap between the wedding and the beauty or fitness industries, underlining how closely they are connected by means of 'marketing the body' and how much pressure is put on aspiring candidates in terms of their performance. The beautiful and the fit body of women as well as men have moved centre-stage in the feel-good ideology promoted in neoliberal urban India. Its celebration is a relatively recent phenomenon: The first time I met with the passion and disgust aligned to the physical body of worldly India was in 1996, when the first Miss World contest was hosted in India and became a contested issue in various media (cf. Butcher 2003; Runkle 2004). Then, a highly moralistic debate was led about the commodification of the female body, the question as to whether the display of "so much skin" was not insulting to the eye of the traditional beholder, and whether the idealised female Indian body should be exposed that way in the light of a booming consumption industry based on pleasure (instead of motherhood, at least so it seems). Another aspect underlining this recent development, and so far rather marginalised, is that despite all the talks about the commodification of the woman, there might be genuine pleasure in the ways in which women participate in these events. I would argue that there are regimes of disciplining and empowerment at work, and the body and its manifold sensories, is the key stakeholder of this arena of negotiations.

In this paper, I am not so much focussing on the changing role of women in the mass media[1], indigenous conceptions of interrelatedness or specific constructions of familial personhood. Instead, I examine "big fat Indian" weddings as a stage for the display of "world-class" lifestyle and pleasure.

---

[1] On the subject of gender, liberalisation and media, see Fernandes 2006, Munshi 2001, Oza 2006, Reddy 2006.

These weddings set a new trend in India since the 2000s. As marathon celebrations of exuberant volume, usually lasting about ten days, and even though budget-wise they must be a matter of the social elites, they have come to stir discussions about the "vulgarity" of the "new rich" in India. Yet, these "Big Fat Indian Weddings" set the tone of lifestyle magazines and impact on wedding choreographies of less wealthy families.

Possibly more than any other social performance, these lifecycle rituals help us understand the effects of economic liberalisation on urban social life. In this context, the body becomes the central stage of communicating these new concepts (as if they were essential, given) in a highly ambivalent space. The wedding industry is vast and specialises in the creation of pleasure and desire, distinction and status, the marketing of travel destinations and culinary and other sensual experiences, status, style and etiquette. Through the romanticized, "ethnic" and "cultured" body of the bride, a moral universe of neoliberalism (conspicuous waste), of tourism (destination weddings and honeymoon) and of commercial film (romantic, free love) is constituted. That way, the wedding ceremony becomes a soundboard for the moral economy of the middle classes, rendering the bridal body at once docile and energetically seductive, helping to shape vernacular cosmopolitan middle-classness.

This paper evolves around the concept of the body-at-marriage as it is developed and staged by new lifestyle-experts, magazines and performative environments in contemporary urban India. The bridal body does not dwell at one site but is nourished by an intervisual mobility: it moves from popular magazines, to commercial films, to photostudios and "Page Three"-events such as the weddings of film-stars or millionaires. These people, media and events, have come to specialise in the provision of various kinds of well-being and pleasure to affluent middle class consumers in the course of economic liberalisation since the 1990s. They have taken over the bridal family's agency of usually hosting and designing a wedding, and the priest as ritual specialist and key authority. Centre-stage of this agglomeration of rites, rituals and ritualisations is the concept of conspicuous consumption and an event, the celebration of wealth which can at times even be referred to as "conspicuous waste." It has become a crucial part of the economy and performance of material wealth and excess on the one hand and a means of drawing borders based on distinction in order to negotiate the concept of an Indian-specific "world class" as cultural capital on the other hand. The body, in particular, the female body, surfaces in many visual and performative empires of weddings, beauty, tourism and wellness as much as these industries feature centrally in lifestyle media and discourses and must be understood as elements of new identifications and subjectivities, notions of intimacy and romance as well as affluence and aspiration. I argue that the aspiring middle classes' dream of self-transformation and a "good life" is made accessible by the wedding industry into which the ritual has to some extent been transformed. The body of the bride is tamed and used as an index of how much value is within can be accumulated and displayed in a ritual of conspicuous waste. The argument thus evolves around what I call different types of bridal bodies through which different regimes of values and ideas of womanhood are played out against each other. The paper examines some of the physical categories with respect to pleasure and taste: the "themed" bridal body as "ethnic" and "cultured" moving between icon and idol, ritual gift and fetish.

Pleasure, taste and distinction

The bridal body patrols and transgresses borders between tradition and modernity, taste and vulgarity, global and local flows. The performative concepts of ritual, heritage, leisure and exhibition are important to understand the complexity of lifestyle politics in neoliberal India. Notions of love and romance that entered into current wedding rhetoric, for instance, were shaped in the colonial context, both in appropriation of a model of loving partnership as well as against strictly moral and patronising tones of colonial rulers towards "Indian society" (see Sreenivas 2003). The notion of liberalised sexuality among members of the aspiring middle classes enables women to think of their own sensuality and sexual desires vis-à-vis those of the groom, on the one hand. Yet it is simultaneously restricted by a bourgeois ideology that aims at disciplining female sexuality by means of rendering her docile to (male) codes of honour and appealing to the value of chastity, on the other hand (see Kakar 1989). Canons of taste are written into and defined by codes of distinction in rituals and festivities, dress and fashion, and at sites and performances of consumption. In weddings now, as in all public consumption, but heightened because of it being a *rite of passage*, the crucial question from the perspective of anthropological reckoning is not how much is spent, though size does certainly matter, but in what way it is spent. Thus, taste is an elementary aspect of value-constitution. Much has changed with economic liberalisation: The wedding ceremony is no longer the sole expression of two families' consensus about their contractual fusion and wealth by means of an arranged marriage. It has also become the sign of a couple's choice ("arranged romantic love"), their attempt to acquire friends' and relatives' recognition of their sexual relations as well as their effort to be accepted as members of the social category of the new middle class, or even social elite (see Adrian 2003).

In his study on advertisement and globalisation in urban India, William Mazzarella (2003) takes up the topic of sexuality and consumption. He elaborates how the dogma of family planning (including forced sterilisation; see Tarlo 2003) and planned development in the first three decades after India's independence considered and rejected the desire of citizens for consumption as a sign of a bourgeois lifestyle and deficient civil, collective responsibility. The Indian citizen was rendered dutifully committed towards public welfare.

This logic was drastically reversed in the 2000s. The citizen's duty was to ensure national growth through consumption. Pleasure as a means to reach satisfaction and happiness became the driving motor of this new citizenry, the new middle classes.[2] The body is no longer a site of re/production but a source and site of different pleasures assigned to different agents. Consumption, so Mazzarella, moves from vice to virtue. The anthropologist defines this shift as "progress through pleasure" (2003, p. 101). The desiring self challenges the demanding state by means of shifting loyalties and priorities. Moreover, despite the paradigmatic shifts of national identity, and the alleged weakening of the state, the concept of the (joint) family receives remarkable attention as the prototypical element of a changing nation. The joint family now becomes the custodian of heritage and modernity, of new lifestyles and national identity, as many commercial films made in Bollywood have come to underline in the last fifteen years or so (cf. Dwyer 2000, Uberoi 2006). Their narratives evolve around concepts of romantic love versus familial duty, and are increasingly concerned with national identity, particularly since they are set firmly in transnational contexts.

To study wedding rituals in the context of consumption and pleasure is a fascinating task because seemingly dichotomous entities seem to clash and be resolved in and through them. Even more so, the bridal body as a field of discourse conveys these conflictuous relationships. It is my interest to look into the cultivation of the bridal body as a tradable item of "world class" and national taste.

The themed body

> Here in India, weddings are meant to be grand, meant to be big. Weddings, in fact, are the biggest celebration of a person's life. The size and scale of your wedding determines your pecking order in society… But suppose, you can't quite manage an Antwerp or Bali wedding and a French chateau is totally out of the reckoning: you can always create a Venice in Goa, a Rajasthani fort in Mumbai or a tropical forest in Delhi. As disposable incomes grow healthier, more couples than ever are opting for professional planners to see them through their weddings rather than depending on the sage advice of uncles and aunts who would otherwise have pitched to help with wedding preparations. … Today, you too can have your own version of the big fat Indian wedding! (Menon 2007, p. 37)

In order to convince, new taste, new pleasure, and new sensuality localise the body in a themed environment, that is, a choreographed narrative that

[2] The new middle classes are made up of several segments: aspiring, affluent and arrived (cf. Brosius 2009; Varma 1998). There are approximately 200 million people that can be counted into this growing class.

managed to generate a trend. It is here where the themed wedding and the destination wedding began their career. Many "theme weddings" are a monumentalised extension of photostudios, where people could dress up in trendy costumes, and pose in front of colourful backdrops (see PINNEY 1997). There would be replicas of the Kremlin in Moscow, of the Moulin Rouge in Paris or the White House in Washington. The most glamorous weddings took place in 2004, for instance, when the owner of the Sahara Business Group got his two sons married on Valentine's Day. Moreover, Laxmi Mittal, Steel industry baron from London rented parts of a grand castle near Paris for his daughter's wedding in 2004 for 30 million pound sterling. All 600 rooms at the Hotel le Grand Intercontinental in Paris were booked for wedding guests. Dancers, *mehendiwallis* (Henna painters to decorate the womens' hands and feet) for the wedding were flown in from Delhi and Mumbai. Another example are the week-long wedding festivities of New York hotel and restaurant owner Chatwal's son Vikram and Priya Sachdev from Delhi (a model and investment-banker) in 2006 included a masked "fantasy party" at the palace-city Udaipur in Rajasthan, as well as a "Queenie and Raja (king, CB) party" in Bombay. The wedding planner from New Delhi ensured that the painted elephant, 50 thousand kilos of flowers from Bangkok and Amsterdam, three chartered jets and 70 private cars arrived at the right time to transport and surprise the over one thousand guests. For one of the events, the Rajasthani theme, to be as "authentic" as possible, the wedding venue of a five star hotel was transformed into a Rajasthani village. Folk artists performed traditional dances and guests had been instructed to dress in Rajasthani outfits. Why Rajasthan has become the most popular region to stage "India" is part of an auto-orientalist self-perception: the colours and fashion of the desert state, the density of exotic palaces and maharajas, have always served as fairy-tail backdrops for all kinds of "romantic" colonial and neo-colonial narratives.

Theme weddings do not just represent a fashion that goes by. Instead, they stand for a concept that cultural geographers or sociologists refer to as "themed" environment, that is, the design of a public or private space or site according to a particular theme and event that invokes pleasure and aspirations in the beholders. Themed environments seem to become the fingerprint of neoliberalisation, not only in India, but also in Dubai, or Shanghai. The most obvious term for this is Alan BRYMAN's "Disneyisation of society" (2004). However, I am not referring to this specific term because in my view, this would lead to impression that India undergoes Americanisation. But "Big Fat Indian Weddings" are not just a big showdown of conspicuous waste in the age of late capitalism. The performances surrounding the wedding rite are staged to create cosmopolitan bodies that come eye to eye with "the West" and be both: global and local, pretend to speak in the world's tongue—but also display national and even neo-colonial chauvinism. Cosmopolitan mimicry here is an act of seeking to position modernity in an Indian context—place value of family, of tradition, of nationality, even affluence as a value. It is also a test of dressing up and fusing successfully the rustic, ethnic and rural versus a global and urban body. The importance given to a "special" wedding by celebrating it abroad or by recreating the world *en miniature* in the backyard is part of one's display of cultural capital. In some ways, weddings and the bodies related to them are structured and organised like theme parks and their props, appealing o the desire of self-transformation through consumption.

Cosmopolitan Indianness then is the capacity to cite, and to move in and around the world: For this, new ritual spaces and displays are required for new desires and needs and bodies/performances. But instead of locating them isolated, they are tied up to other, "traditional" rituals. For this, various bodies of the bride are required. In the next steps, I shall examine two kinds of intertwined bodies: the "ethnic body" and the "cultured body."

"Ethnic body" and "cultured body"

The bridal industry, states Patricia UBEROI (2008) is all about the making of class, ethnic identity, gender, and family relations. Even though these notions are fluid, the role of the bride has probably changed least, and is still confined by concepts of chastity and devotion to the husband. What is considered to be suitable or appropriate is highlighted in the next example. Ashok S., senior manager at one of India's leading marketing and consultancy agencies with its head office in Gurgaon tells me that while weddings in the 1980s and 1990s would even sport western suites for the groom and guests, therefore documenting their cosmopolitan attitude, this was hardly fashionable any more today. Today, "trend-conscious" urbanised persons wear "ethnic" dress of royal and historical background, mostly Punjabi or Rajasthani style with long and beautifully embroidered coats for special occasions. "Ethnic chic" is associated with knowing one's culture, being proud of and willing to show it. The new middle classes display such an increasing fascination with ethnic stereotypes, something rather unpopular fifteen years ago, for one's own fashioning of the body as a status symbol. Until the 1990s, ethnic elements were usually attributed to define the "Other," such as the peasant or the tribal (*adivasi*). To constitute oneself as urban, educated *and* ethnically conscious is a development of growing globalisation and economic liberalisation. Anthropologist Emma TARLO (1996) coins "ethnic chic" as an urban and upper middle class phenomenon of a new "ethnic chic," where the past is romanticised and appropriated into a sanitised, ordered and hygienic present. In terms of the bridal body, we find a rustic, seductive, and yet chaste woman as key symbol of urban nostalgia and exotic fantasies of "tradition" and "indigeneity." The village girl is considered innocent and pure (naive and uneducated), her body appears civilised but with traces of the untamed. Often, such an allegedly naïve and uneducated woman is considered ideal for the male professional living overseas whose family wants him to revitalise his Indianness through the genuinely traditional bride and her voluntary self-sacrifice for the preservation of "traditional values."[3]

Cultural diversity is one aspect of the bridal body's celebration as ethnic and authentic. Another is cultural heritage and "cultural consciousness." Historical costumes from nineteenth century colonial north India have a strong impact, especially since blockbusters like *Devdas* (2002, dir. Sanjay Leela Bhansali). Rajasthani "folk style," too, has been "gentrified," for example, with films like *Lagaan* (Tax, 2001, dir. Ashutosh Gowariker) or *Paheli* (2005, dir. Amol Palekar). Moreover, elements appropriated from religious practices are no longer perceived as auspicious Hindu items in the first degree but become part and parcel of a material culture and circulation systems that define a social value instead. In this context, Hindu rituals become scripts for new narratives of an ethnic underlining. Most of all, while the marriage rite of the couple by a *pandit* (priest) would have absorbed most of the time in a "traditional" wedding, today the fact that choreographies last over several days, involving elements that have become independent "items," such as the engagement, the *sangeet*[4], or the reception, clearly show a reduction of the key rite in favour of other modes of entertainment. Previously only the weddings of the upper class, senior politicians and royals would count more than hundreds of guests from all kinds of regional, religious and caste background, while traditional weddings kept to themselves, that is, within a regional compound of face-to-face contacts. Today, a middle class wedding event might add up to 500 guests and involve a host of diverse participants. The latest "fashion" for so-called A-grade weddings is to clad the wedding *mandap* (pavilion) in orchids from Thailand and Swarovsky jewellery, to fly in Bollywood film stars, or prominent personae from the west, for instance, Bill Clinton. What remained more or less the same, however, is that at conservative urbanised high-caste, upper class weddings, no alcohol is served on the day of the ritual ceremony itself, that for the wedding rite, groom and bride wear traditional dresses, and that a *pandit* (priest) is called to perform the wedding rite according to an auspicious date and time.[5] "Ethnic" brides (and tribes) are a trope through which the Indian state but also the wider popular imaginary of Indianness has been visually manifested and circulated; on postal stamps, bazaar prints, at state parades, beauty pageants, or calendars.

[3] See Uberoi's (2006) excellent analysis of diaspora films such as *Pardes* (Foreign Land, 1997, dir. S. Ghai).

[4] *Sangeet* means a pre-marital gathering of family, accompanied by singing and story telling.

[5] The caste and class specific requirements here demand more research in terms of urban contexts. Moreover, there are many weddings, e.g. in the Himalayan region, that request alcohol even at the ritual occasion, thus it is not always a taboo.

In themeing Indian cultural heritage, young and upwardly mobile Indians take a fresh look at "traditional" India, turning its culture into the property and repository of a heritage exhibition and performance, making it an extension of new consumer culture. In this context, a central and ever growing category of wedding event clients and trendsetters are the NRIs. They have started to claim custodianship over heritage. The *Delhi Times of India*, a section of the newspaper *Times of India* that predominantly reports about "society" events such as exhibition and restaurant openings, business fairs, and weddings, takes the New York hotelier Chatwal's son Vikram with "Delhi party girl" Priya Sachdev on Valentine's Day in 2006 as a marker of affirmation of at once knowledge of western habits (Valentine Day as the celebration of romantic love) and India's self-esteem (celebration of India's ethnic diversity). The event is said to have spread the "India everywhere-mood," a feel good-factor metaphor related to the rhetoric of the economically booming subcontinent. The newspaper cited Vikram saying: "Oh wow, this is such fun. I just love the magic around Indian weddings". And the bride's father saw no reason in feeling embarrassed about the following description of his son's "initiation" to India: "I strongly feel that it's very important to understand one's roots. Becoming an Indian (by marrying a model and ex-banker from India, CB), Vikram needs to see and feel the country, its culture, tradition and its diversity. In Rajasthan, he saw how kings lived, in Delhi he gets to discern the cosmopolitan flavour of an international city, just like New York is." The bodies of the groom and the bride thus become markers of the rite of passage, the transition to something Vikram will probably only remember as magnified "Queenie and Raja" party, "just like New York."

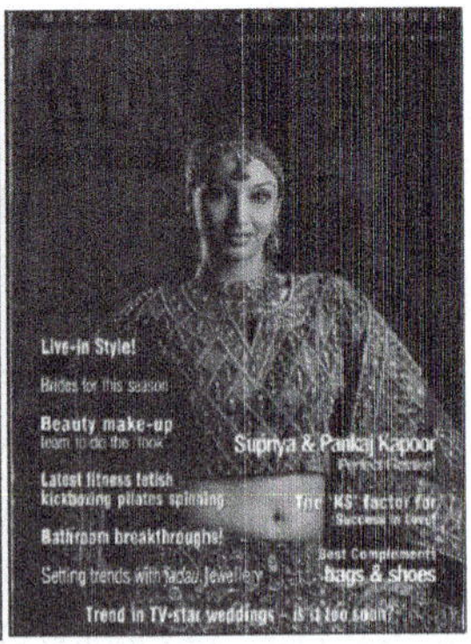

Figure 1: (left): Stamp from India, entitled "Bride-Bengal" (1980). Figure 2 (centre): "Indian Bride," popular bazar print, Delhi (2006). Figure 3 (right): Frontpage of bridal magazine *Wedding Affair* 7(4), 2006.

With respect to the bridal's body as "ethnic body," we can argue that dress and posture have become important markers. There is an interesting dynamic in that ethnic fashion had been outdated as element of self-constitution (not as element of constructing the other) among the urban middle classes and elites until the mid-1990s. It was conceived as "backward" and unmodern. After "the west" started to consume and promote it as "exotic" and fashionable, along with yoga or Ayurveda, Indian "folk" was reimported and became appreciated by the aspiring Indian middle classes. Those who felt that it was part of a cosmopolitan rhetoric could appropriate the "ethnic." In the shaping of the upper middle classes and social elites as an aesthetic community of cosmopolitans, the "cultured" body came to play an important role. To know one's culture, and to be able to place it among other signifiers of themed weddings, such as *Carneval of Venice* or *Moulin Rouge*, citing the world without being dominated by it (rather the opposite), is part of status disctinction.

Traditional wedding: the bridal body as ritual gift

In order to better judge changes occurring in wedding ritual and embodiment, let's recapitulate for a moment to see what is new, or what seems new. While weddings are important in that they are a key life-cycle ritual, the idea that they are the biggest celebration *of* an individual person's life is rather recent. Today, this is part of a shared imaginary of a largely urbanised and educated audience considering individual choice (romantic love) above, or at least equal to collective norms and values (e.g. arranged marriage). To be sure, a "traditional" wedding does not acknowledge the individual. It underlines the contract between two families by means of marrying two of their members to each other, a rather asymmetrical alliance between families in which the bride is "given" to the groom (*kanyadan*, that is, the gift of the virgin, the purest of all gifts; cf. Raheja 1988; see also PURI 1999*)*. During the ceremony, highly complicated family networks but also social and business relationships are enacted and negotiated, almost as if explosive substances are mixed together carefully. Who interacts with whom, who gives and who receives a gift, who eats what kinds of food and when is crucial for the efficacy of the ritual itself (cf. Kolenda 1984). But the meaning of status and lifestyle declaration has become very important, as has that of romance and intimacy. It is here where the bridal body comes centre-stage. Traditionally, marriage alliance is moderated by the concern with monitoring the "purity" of women. And it still is. The bride to be given to the new family had to be a virgin. The imperative of the Hindu religious ideal of *kanyadan* that ensures that wife-takers rank higher than wife-givers (hypergamy) is not that relevant any longer (while endogamy still is). In the ritual of *kanyadan,* the bride delivers herself, and is delivered by her father, to the prospective future family of her groom. In commercial films as well as home videos, the moment of farewell, obviously following the marriage ceremony, is marked by the public display of sadness, close-up of faces of the bridal family and herself crying. The camera also pays attention to her touching the feet of the elders of the family as a sign of obeisance and respect. This scene is still a part of the choreography, even though one can observe that behind the veil, the face of the bride is a smiling one.

Moreover, traditional weddings have long been key stages of conspicuous consumption and thereby the production of a cycle of symbolic capital. What is new in the case of the weddings explored here is their scale and the public, media-savvy, glocal aesthetics, taste and means of distinction imbued in them. Today, a wedding is highlighted as a celebration in certain contexts such as in lifestyle magazines or a commercial Hindi film. It has become an act of declaring romantic love, where two companions deliberately decide to devote their life to each other (and not the whole family). While the bridal body in weddings prior to the "Big Fat Indian wedding" trend used to be covered, rather static and passive objects of a ritual economy, the new bridal body must be agentive, seductive and pro-active. While "before," the bridal body was predominantly veiled and moved like a statue with little agency of her own, it is now publicly displayed, rendering itself performatively available to the public. Then, the couple did not know and had not even seen each other before the ritual ceremony itself. Now, the couple has to stage its fascination of being in love with each other, and wanting to be intimate. Many of the bridal magazines I examined over the past few years deal with the question of how to be intimate, how to find the right words, the right gestures, the right tricks. And how to be all at once, including love, trust, honesty, respect, fidelity and patience. Only bridals of the 2000s consider the paradox situation of wanting, and even having to explore sex-life, make it erotic and romantic and yet be able to share a joint family household.

The wedding ritual, as a rite of familial separation and incorporation for the bride and a display of social relations and cultural desires, has been studied in anthropological terms as to how the rite consolidates traditions and trends of marriage and family in the transition from traditional society to modern consumer and "Erlebnis"-media society. We deal with the transformation of intimacy in modern times, with weddings as visual expressions of social status and cultural capital, as markers and display of visual competence (taste). Visual spectacle is a crucial means of display and analysis of bodies and rituals. In our case it relates to cultural imagination, fuelled by the media, and propelled by the desire for life betterment, individual choice and solitude.

Bodies of Lineage

There is a host of associations aligning women to marriage, and I will only briefly mention a few: usually, it must be underlined that marriage alliance is moderated by the concern with monitoring the "purity" of women, and to ensure that her entering into a new family is not threatening that family's stability and purity. This is why belonging to the same caste and having the right horoscope matters vitally to conservative contexts. A couple of gendered concepts are cited from time and again, even in modern weddings, and often indirectly: goddess Sita and Mother India as representatives of the sacrificial, nourishing and devout wife and mother, then the figure of the courtesan from Mughal courts of North India, and more recently the beauty contestant Miss India or Miss World.

The incarnation of the dutiful, chaste and obedient woman reappears in the modern bride: Sita is still often referred to in lifestyle magazines, etc. Prototypical models for the ideal Indian bride/wife are pan-Indian "classics" such as the Ramayana or the Mahabharata, depicting romantic celebration of conjugal love and self-sacrificing wifely devotion—themes which had an enormous "Orientalist" appeal for Europeans as well, in particular the scene where Sita undergoes the divine ordeal by fire to prove her purity and devotion to husband Rama. The role of the mother, and obviously, motherhood, are key concepts of the married woman, and pressure on young women is still high to produce a child, preferably a son. However, with urbanisation and modernisation of middle class environs, this concept of being a mother only is increasingly challenged, or, at least paired with the ambitious workingwoman who is both mother and businesswoman. The idea of the duty to reproduce is also nourished by the independent nation-state, however, under the banner of population control and family planning (resulting in mass sterilisation campaigns in the 1970s). With economic liberalisation, as Mazzarella maintains, pleasure as progress shifts the attention from restriction to celebration. The female body becomes the centre of attention for a revitalised desire for sensual events and selves. These new sensualities also mirror in the bridal body as it goes on a honeymoon of intimacy, as it is fetishised, and as modern selves evolve increasingly around caring for and experiencing oneself corpothetically, for instance, by means of travel and tourism, or Asian spas. Several surveys have found that despite womens' growing articulation and awareness of their own sexual desires, urban educated Indians are still a far cry from what is considered as equality and emancipation in the West (being aware that these concepts are often as unreal for "westerners").[6]

Fetishised Feet: The Groom's Pleasure

A large part of the bridal media universe is occupied by film/video. From this, we can understand some of the regimes that monitor the contemporary bridal body. Commercial cinema of the 1960s and 70s marked the wedding choreography of the years to follow. Films like "An Evening in Paris" (1967, dir. S. Samatha) depict love and romance of honeymooning couples in Europe,

[6] Several surveys have been published in mainstream journals such as *The Week* or *India Today* between 2005–06.

away from home, then the ultimate and possibly only site of modern romance and love, where the couple could dwell in solitude and intimacy. But besides opening up an imaginary space for romantic love, the bridal body has its own choreography and iconography in film. Filmic language and actual wedding performance reinforce each other. Every wedding must be documented by a photowallah and a videowallah (at least), that is, professional camerapeople. Their craft is imbued by visual, ritual and normative traditions elaborated in popular film and studio photography since the beginning of the technologies. In wedding videos, eyes, hands and feet of the bride (the groom hardly features) play a vital role in the fetishisation of the female body. The camera flirts with the eyes of the bride, loading the scene with seductive meaning (see SENGUPTA 1999). This play with the eyes is a clear reference to the dance numbers in Hindi cinema where the courtesan's gaze towards the camera carried a great deal of erotic charge for the largely male audience. In this process, her body is marked as territory of the gaze, rendered available for the groom and the male public. The (unmarried) courtesan is the only element through which open seduction of the bride can be alerted to. The underlining narrative of such elements is that the courtesan longs to marry but must not out of status reasons. Famous Hindi films have narrated dramas evolving around courtesans in the 1970s and it is interesting that these films have recently enjoyed immense popularity again, pinpointing a nostalgia for Mughal and colonial history, and dramatic romantic narratives. This revival has also impacted on the bridal fashion.[7]

Wedding videos both celebrate and examine the bridal body in lengthy sequences. First comes her dress, the jewellery and other ornaments. Then body parts are studied in close-ups, eyes (often veiled), hands and feet, in order to show the elaborate henna patterns that decorate them and mark her as bride. These close-ups, as SENGUPTA argues, are "bearers of highly charged erotic meaning. ... This convention derives from a literary, and largely poetic code of expressing erotic sentiment by referring to the ornaments that mark a woman as a bride—a legitimate object of sexual interest, if not an active sexual agent" (1999, p. 292). According to Uberoi, the visual celebration of the courtesan's (and now the bridal's) feet generates mystery and (male) desire. For Uberoi, the feet are corporeal signifiers, and coins this as "podo-semiology" and "podo-erotics." This then is a culture-specific form of fetish-creation that renders her between the role of courtesan and bride, virgin and divine mother.

Interestingly, bridal magazines pick up on this idea of fetishised feet, translating it into spirituality and moral value of a (Hindu) Golden Age, underlining what I referred to above as intervisuality, or possibly intermediality of

[7] The most famous film of this genre is *Pakeezah* (1972, dir. Kamal Amrohi).

a particular signifier moving through various media domains, generating its own life. What western feminists would call suppression of the woman is now interpreted as respect and recognition of traditional essential givens. In an article entitled *Traits of an Ideal woman*, Yogi ASHWINJI (2007, p. 156f.) from the spiritualistic Dhyan foundation in North India tells us how to choose a perfect girl to marry by looking for significant attributes in her:

> Contrary to the belief which is prevalent in today's world that women were suppressed and ordered around, in the Vedic times, the fact was that they were most respected and considered to be *Devis* in whose hands the whole future generations were dependent. A wrong selection of a wife was considered as a reason for the destruction of the family *(kul)*. ... The most important traits of a woman lie not in her face but in her feet. ... Feet which are not too big and not very small with neatly developed toes, where the big toe is the longest toe and the other toes are descending in order, the toes are well-shaped and ... there are no gap in the digits—such women bring intense happiness into the family which they go to and also they age very slowly. ... a woman whose second digit is longer than the toe thumb was considered to be dominating and authoritative. The soles of the feet should be slightly rosy in colour. ... Such women were said to bring financial gains wherever they go. ... a woman with strong well-formed nails was considered to have the capacity for bearing healthy children. ... If the thighs are very thin and along with it if the complexion is slightly brownish i.e. towards the darker and not fair, the girl was considered to be very talkative and husbands of such women should be extra cautious about their heath.

This way, what has been analysed as the production of male fetishes by Sengupta and Uberoi is further heightened as stigmatising stereotype by means of putting such a fetish into a structure of religious ideology, constituting the woman as product of external forces by claming to empower her. A slim empowerment, however.

Bridal Pleasures?

Independent women are still considered threatening, both for the groom and his family. And often, this perception has been internalised by the women too. Weddings, as they are presented in bridal magazines, are a ritual where exactly these floating parameters are given attention but still marginalised (for the lifestyle magazines are inherently conservative in their moral values). There is an interesting emphasis on bride's sensuality and her sexual desires that mark the coming of the wedding in various articles in bridal magazines, most of all, with respect to the wedding night's promise of erotic pleasure (a rather western concept, shifting attention from reproduction to pleasure). Moreover, there are many articles too about possible hang-ups and crises after the wedding, where the wife's body is still locus of failure or success. An anonymous author suggests the following in the bridal magazine *Wedding Affair*:

> Be subtle... be seductive... be wild too... It's important to make the chemistry ... And what is most important is to keep the pleasure going. Say cheers, expose, explore...and experiment... because this is what the trend is! (Get Rocking 2006, p. 168)

This quote alerts us to a range of topics that will be discussed in this paper. There is the emphasis on the bride's responsibility to be subtle, seductive, wild in order to ensure the relationship holds. And there is the notion of doing something because it is mainstream, "trend." Responsibility does not lie in reproduction any longer, or pleasing the inlaws—it seems. Instead, the relationship's "chemistry" and sustainability is what worries and matters.

Bridal magazines are not just about shopping, preparations and the celebration of the wedding day. They also introduce the urban bride and groom to tabooised themes such as lovemaking, impotency or jealousy. Some even advice the bride to get pre-marital sex counselling, others suggest "outdoor sex" and "sex in the shower," if the first attraction has paled (cf. Steam up your sex life (2008), pp. 158f.). In the chaos of wedding preparations and family negotiations, the individual desires and fears of the married couple are usually marginalised. And they have in fact not really mattered much until recently, unless with respect to childbirth. Intimacy, romance, pleasure and trust, are largely talked about since economic liberalisation. The issues are coined by conservative bridal and lifestyle magazines, sometimes with a surprising openness. Themes such as sexual desire, unwanted pregnancy, impotency are addressed in lifestyle magazines such as *Women's Era*. Post-marital conflicts, too, are mentioned: arguments, nagging, familial tensions. Time and again the issue of "making love" instead of "having sex" is underlined as both a challenge and a huge pressure on the newly wed. And many unmarried people now seek their first sexual experiences through magazines or online forums instead of depending on their parents' choice. Online Dating is a popular way of getting in touch and having pre-marital experiences and exchanges with others. Lifestyle culture takes over from dry official state discourses, encouraging citizens to dream the dream of self-transformation. But rather than being liberating, new pressures are enforced on the couple's bodies. Thus, we can read the following statement by a skin expert in the popular bridal magazine *Celebrating Vivaha:* "Brides and grooms should ideally start their beauty and skincare regime about 45 to 60 days prior to the wedding, since there has to be a gap of seven to 10 days between sessions. We also give couples last-minute skincare tips and home remedies for any blemishes that may appear" (6(3) 2007, p. 27). Groom and bride must care for the fetishised parts of their body: "Hands and feet need attention. Moisture them at night and protect with gloves and socks" (ibid., p. 28). Moreover, arms, as the entry quote to this paper underlines, must not be flabby, and so forth. A regime of beauty and fitness is enforced upon bride and groom's bodies in order to appear as "lively" and "pleasurable." Self-surveillance and self-discipline become key tasks in this context.

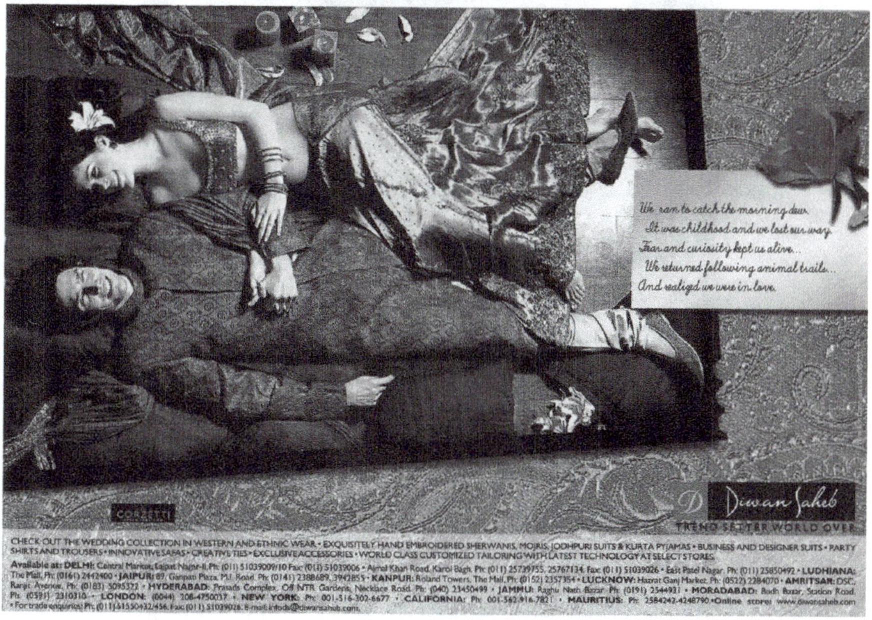

Figure 4: Staged intimacy: Diwan Saheb advertisment preparing the wedding night as relaxed, friendly event (2005).

Pleasure is possibly a new means of liberation for some. In the context of the weddings, it means new forms of disciplining and enforcing social and moral universes upon the body. The bridal body, as we encounter it in bridal magazines that feature "Big Fat Indian Weddings," is made up of different layers, historically and symbolically. In the wedding ritual, the bride does not only become a wife, but somehow the soundboard for different values and concepts that have shaped with economic liberalisation. Judith Butler has maintained that, "to be a woman is to have *become* a woman, to compel the body to conform to an historical idea of ‚woman,' to induce the body to become a cultural sign, to materialize oneself in obedience to an historically delimited possibility, and to do this as a sustained and repeated corporeal project" (2003, p. 394). Thus, when we look at the following advertisement (Figure 4), we can see the seeming lightness of intimacy as a new phenomenon of modern sexuality, we can see the ethnic body, the enjoying and beautiful body spread out in front of our eyes.

Figure 5: Erotic underwear, preparing for the wedding night. Source: *Indiawali Brides* Oct-Nov 2006, p. 97.

Conclusion

This paper examined different regimes of values and ideas of womanhood as they are played out against each other via the bridal body. The body is rendered vulnerable, dangerous and dynamic in the wedding as an act of transferring the bride as ritual gift, transcending borders of various kinds. In this course, different physical categories and concepts evolved with respect to pleasure and taste: the "themed" bridal body as "ethnic" and "cultured," moving between icon and idol, ritual gift and fetish. The key domains in which the bridal body is traded in those magazines are pleasure, taste and distinction, predominantly with respect to "world class." In transgressing and drawing borders between tradition and modernity, taste and vulgarity, global and local flows, the bridal body is an ideal means of analysis of rituals in the context of lifestyle politics in neoliberal India. Yet, what has also become evident is that beyond the liberating lifestyle spectacle of a wedding, surveillance and disciplining operate.

References

Adrian, B. (2003): *Framing the Bride: Globalizing Beauty and Romance in Taiwan's Bridal Industry.* – Berkeley/Los Angeles/London.

Ashwiniji (Yogi) (2007): Traits of an Ideal woman. In: *Celebrating Vivaha*, Vol. 6, No. 3, pp. 156–7.

Brosius, C. (2009): *India Shining: Cosmopolitan Pleasures of India's New Middle Classes.* – New Delhi/London/New York.

Bryman, A. (2004): *Disneyization of Society.* – London.

Butcher, M. (2003): Transnational Television, Cultural Identity and Change: When STAR Came to India. – New Delhi.

Butler, J. (2003): Performative Acts and Gender Constitution: An Essay in Phenomenology and Feminist Theory. In: Jones, A. (Ed.): The Feminism and Visual Culture Reader. – London/New York, pp. 392–401.

Dwyer, R. (2000): *All you Want is Money, All you Need is Love: Sex and Romance in Modern India.* – London.

Fernandes, L. (2006): *India's New Middle Class: Democratic Politics in an Era of Economic Reform.* – Minneapolis/London.

Get Rocking (2006). In: *Wedding Affair,* 7(4), p. 168.

Kakar, S. (1989): *Intimate Relations: Exploring Indian Sexuality.* – New Delhi.

Kolenda, P. (1984): Woman as Tribute, Woman as Flower: Images of "Woman" in Weddings in North and South India. In: *American Ethnologist*, Vol. 11, No. 1, pp. 98–117.

Mazzarella, W. (2003): *Shoveling Smoke: Advertising and Globalization in Contemporary India.* – Durham.

Menon, J. (2007): Wedding Vows. In: *Femina Bridal Yearbook,* pp. 24–40.

Munshi, S. (2001): Marvellous Me: The Beauty Industry and the Construction of the "Modern" Indian Woman. In: Munshi, S. (Ed.): *Images of the "Modern Woman" in Asia: Global Media, Local Meanings.* – Richmond, pp. 78–93.

Oza, R. (2006): *The Making of Neoliberal India: Nationalism, Gender and the Paradoxes of Globalization.* – New Delhi.

Pinney, C. (1997): *Camera Indica: The Social Life of Indian Photographs.* – London.

Puri, J. (1999): Woman, Body, Desire in Post-Colonial India: Narratives of Gender and Sexuality. – New York.

Raheja, G. G. (1988): The Poison in the Gift: Ritual, Prestation, and the Dominant Caste in a North Indian Village. Chicago.

Reddy, V. (2006): The Nationalization of the Global Indian Woman: Geographies of Beauty in Femina. In: *South Asian Popular Culture*, Vol. 4, No. 1, pp. 61–85.

Runkle, S. (2004): Making "Miss India:" Constructing Gender, Power and the Nation. In: *South Asian Popular Culture, Vol.* 2, No. 2, pp. 145–59.

Sengupta, S. (1999): Vision Mixing: Marriage-Video-Film and the Video-Walla's Images of Life. In: Brosius, C./Butcher, M. (Eds.): *Image Journeys: Audio-Visual Media and Cultural Change in India.* – New Delhi, pp. 279–307.

Sreenivas, M. (2003): Emotion, Identity, and the Female Subject: Tamil Women's Magazines in Colonial India, 1890–1940. In: *Journal of Women's History*, Vol. 14, No. 4, pp. 59–82.

Srinivasa, K. (2007): Body Beautiful. In: *Savy*, October Issue, p. 64.

Steam up your sex life (2008). In: *Wedding Affair*, 9(6), pp. 158–59.

Tarlo, E. (1996): *Clothing Matters: Dress and Identity in India.* – Chicago.

Tarlo, E. (2003): *Unsettling Memories: Narratives of the Emergency in Delhi.* – New Delhi.

Uberoi, P. (2006): *Freedom and Destiny: Gender, Family, and Popular Culture in India.* – New Delhi.

Uberoi, P. (2008): Aspirational Weddings: The Bridal Magazine and the Canons of "Decent Marriage." In: Jaffrelot, C./Van der Veer, P. (Eds.): *Patterns of Middle Class Consumption.* – Delhi, pp. 230–262.

Varma, P. (1998): *The Great Indian Middle Class.* – Delhi.

Iris Clemens

Lost in Transition? Managing Paradoxical Situations by Inventing Identities

Call Centre Agents in India: "John and Jane" in trouble

The documentary "John and Jane" by Ashim AHLUWALIA (2005) describes the living conditions, life styles and ambitions of six call centre employees in Mumbai at a time when call centres were not yet questioned in respect of their working conditions or social implications—the reason why the director had almost completely free access to this today carefully guarded, enclosed world. As the director said in an interview, his aim was not only to show the work and life of the call centre agents he was accompanying for about three years, but also to document the transition of Asian countries at that point of time, shortly before "Amway and discount coupons" started to become commonplace there too (cf. AHLUWALIA 2006a). The call center agents almost perfectly embody this time of transition in India: Average Indians during day time who have never been abroad but become well trained Americans in the night, a setting that is only possible due to globalization and the inventions of the new media. This divided life spent in two completely different spaces has a great influence on those who live in this transitional state. The ways they observe their environment, their expectation regarding their lives and biographies, their images about a good life in general; in short their whole way of thinking and their identity is affected by oscillating between two worlds. I want to use the case of the call centre agents as an example to analyse some of the implications life in this transitional state has. With reference to the differentiation of person, body and consciousness described by Niklas Luhmann, I will discuss especially implications for identity constructions in such transitions, focusing mainly on the case of the call-centre agent "Naomi" and her strategies of identity management. The role the body plays in these transformation processes becomes obvious in this example. The documentary is chosen, as it seems to reflect the situation of the call-centre agents quite realistically, as an expert discussion in the Museum for Communication, Frankfurt/Main in September 2006 with the director Ashim AHLUWALIA (2006b) and Vinod SHETTY (2006), an advocate for human rights in Mumbai and member of the Young Professional Collective, also suggests. The IT industry has immense significance in India, and call-centres are seen as part of it. While the Indian middle class in general is seen as the motor of modernization by various authors (e.g. VARMA 1999), recently DESHPANDE (2003) or FERNANDES (2000) have pointed out that Indian

IT workers—both those who are working in India and in the diaspora—have gained the upper hand over the definition of "Indianess" itself. Therefore the question of call-centres and their social implications are widely discussed in India today.

John and Jane: Working in an Indian Call-Centre

In his documentary, Ahluwalia shows us impressions of a call-centre as a workplace, a world of its own, somehow disconnected from the world "outside" India. We get a feeling of what it means for the call-centre agents to work in night shifts in Mumbai in an almost clinically clean office, surrounded by the symbols of American culture such as the flag and talking to Americans the whole night. "Glen," "Sydney," "Osmond," "Nikki," "Nicholas" and "Naomi" are answering service calls from American consumers or try to sell products by phone for American companies, the body is in India, but the mind is overseas. In the beginning one anonymous call centre agent describes this situation when he says: "It's great to speak to the Americans by phone. I have the feeling that I am *in* America, talking to Americans. They are so nice." In the following we will see that this feeling of actually being in America while calling is one important facet of the experience of the call centre agents.

The transformational dynamic the work in the call-centre develops, affects all three dimensions of meaning construction: the time dimension (1), the spatial dimension (2) and the social dimension (3).

(1) The most obvious changes or even challenges the agents are facing are related to the time dimension. Their shifts end when night is falling in America and the day is starting in India. When they go home and try to sleep, the "Maximum City" Bombay (Mehta 2004) is awake, making sleeping very difficult. As a result they are always tired and their rhythm of life is disconnected from that of their family and friends. That means that they live in a different time zone from that of their every day surroundings. This of course implies an alienation from their every day world, too. The commonly shared experiences with their social surroundings become fewer and fewer; their reality seldom overlaps with that of the others at all.

(2) The same division can be observed with regard to the two spaces the agents are living in. Sydney puts it this way: After a whole night shift you are *back* in India. And Nicholas later tells us that he wishes he could stay in the centre and not have to go out into this "hassle dazzle" at all. Similarly, Osmond expresses his admiration for the perfect organisation of the call center as one of the things he most likes. In fact, he adopted the precise organisational structure of the call centre for his whole life, planning 24 hours of his day. It follows that one can assume that the call centre is conceptualised by the agents as exactly the opposite of what they consider to be Indian or Indianness. To explain to the Indian agents the customs and habits of buying and selling in America, one of the coaches who is teaching in the call center

all about America makes the students compare Indian vegetable markets with shopping facilities in America. In comparison to the image of crowded and chaotic Indian markets she shows them photos of American supermarkets, endless rows with a huge variety of products, neatly piled up, everything shining clinically. This comparison of the places seems vividly to sum up the images behind the statements of Sydney, Osmond and Nicholas. On the one side the image of a systematic, well organised, rich, modern, clean and beautiful place called America, reproduced in the call centre reality, and on the other side the "hassle dazzle" of India.

The interesting fact however, is that the call centre can then be seen as an "in-between" space: Although not located in America itself, it seems to be a perfect copy of the country, at least for the centre agents, as none of the six persons have ever been abroad, let alone been in America. In any case it is a place completely different from the daily life of the agents and their experiences and living conditions. Sydney's statement of being back in India after a shift has to be seen in this context. In consequence, the call centre as an in-between space is like a "virtual space shuttle" which the agents enter every evening; placing them in another world altogether (compared to the daily life of India outside) most of the time of their time awake and even while sleeping. We are told that they also dream of the call centre, answering calls in their dreams, even moving their fingers to type while sleeping. And Sydney tells us that while lying in bed, he always thinks about the last call: Was it a good call? Did he mess up something? That means as a consequence, that the agents spend most of their time actually in a space that is disconnected from everything that might have been around them before joining the call centre: their Indian daily life. And of course the *comparison* is always in their mind.

It is therefore surely not by chance that transitional stages and times like waking and sleeping are shown in the documentary, situations of transition of the consciousness where the agents have to find themselves back in one reality that has not much in common with that one they spend most of their time in. After waking up they are back in their noisy, hot and small flat, the old fashioned furnishings and equipment, the restrictions of a family, the lack of understanding of their situation, the demands that might let them flee their homes once again like Glen. With regard to the spatial dimension, a clarification of the description given above is necessary. While the minds or the consciousnesses of the agents may be in America while calling and speaking to Americans the whole night, their bodies are *not* in India (in the sense of the chaotic "hassle dazzle" that seems to represent India in the images of the agents, especially in comparison to America), but in the in-between space of the call centre. I will come back to this later while analysing the case of Naomi.

(3) The most far-reaching consequences of becoming a call centre agent and working and living under these specific conditions can be assumed with

regard to the social dimension. In the call centre, the agents were trained in all aspects of their job. Speaking English is a must for the agents of course, but the real challenge is to speak like Americans. To achieve this goal, teachers from the US were brought to India. Sydney speaks so fast that even one American customer is not able to understand what he is offering him, and Nicolas admires the way Americans speak English and feels sorry that he will never be able to speak like that. When we meet Naomi, the Gujarati girl, she is speaking with a Midwest accent, and even Glen, the only introduced agent, who hates his job and the call centre, has adopted American slang (including saying "fuck" as often as possible). All of them also speak English outside the call centre now. The language is a sign and symbol of the transformation of the consciousness of the agents. Nicholas tells us that earlier, he used to talk in Hindi mostly, but after entering the call centre, he changed to English: "English started coming into me, an American feeling that I started to have. That culture has gone into me."

To make sure that is exactly what happens, the agents were trained in many aspects of the American way of life apart from the language. When they enter the centre, they pass a map of America, decorated with the flag and famous slogans such as "Don't mess with Texas!". They study advertising brochures, catalogues and photos of shopping malls, repeat nursery rhymes and learn the values of the average American man and woman, John and Jane, which are individualism, achievement and success, patriotism, privacy, progress and striving for happiness according to the coach. The goal of this training is obvious: to be able to sell to Americans, the call centre agents should not only talk like them, but also think like them. The goal is a transformation of the individuals, eliminating certain Indian habits and ways of thinking and taking over a schematic and simple version of Americanism that is offered by the call centre company and which cannot be questioned by the agents because they have never been to the US. Therefore the process of giving these employees new, American names is an excellent symbol for the transformation of the Indian agents. They should become just like "John and Jane," the average American man and woman, those people to whom they sell the products by phone, and should suggest to the customers that they are talking to compatriots. Therefore, when the documentary starts and we hear one woman introducing herself with "my name is John Doe," it sounds like a hint for the extent to which the agents should transform their personalities. As explained later, in America an unidentified dead body is called John Doe—another fact of the American everyday world the Indian agents are learning.

Inventing Identities in Transition

But the agents fill their "average American" identities with life and personality apart from the sterile image the call centre is offering. And as shown in the course of the movie, they also start using these names outside the call centre, taking certain parts of this world with them: the culture that has gone into them. They transform the virtual personality developed only for economic purposes into a lively part of their identity. In consequence my suggestion is that the emerging identity of the agents is neither an American one nor do they stay "Indians," but that they develop an identity that is as much transitional as the in-between space of the call centre itself and directly connected to its specific working conditions and lifestyle.[1] In the following one could say that they are not getting Americanised but "Indian call-centreised."

The meaning of the term "transition" or "transitional" has to be defined here. When talking about transition, it is not suggested that there are somehow stable states—like being an Indian or being an American—and that through a certain process an individual crosses from one form to another. Instead transition has become a permanent fact and condition of identity constructions in modernizing societies. Just as gender has become a matter of negotiation and sub-differentiations (Reddy 2007) and the range of sexualities goes far behind a "Third Gender" (Chakravorty 2007), identity is dynamic and unstable. As a result, the individuals have to oscillate between different frames of their everyday world permanently while observing themselves and re-constructing their identities. The same is true for the division into a virtual and a real world. In a commercial for Indian call centres shown in the documentary, the slogan is: "Call centres have made the virtual world into reality." It was created with regard to the fact that Indians now sell insurance to people in America. But developments and changes provoked through the possibilities of the new media as shown in the documentary go far beyond this, up to the point where the division of the virtual and the real itself becomes questionable. If employees in India doing "virtual" jobs, supported by the internet, people in Europe or America might lose their job in "reality." If a scientist joins a subgroup for a specific research question via internet, he might get "real" information, publications or invitations for congresses. Managers join weekly internet conferences and may never meet in reality but their decisions can change the reality of many people completely etc. And no one can decide on the basis of some objective criteria whether the friends a teenager has found in his internet community are less "real" friends than those he meets at the bus stop.

Especially when it comes to identity constructions, the influence of the images delivered through the media cannot be overestimated, and the division between the real and the virtual world erodes. As a consequence, identity construction is in permanent transition for those living under the conditions of a modern media society. Living in transitional states itself is a characteristic of

[1] One should not forget that the conditions in Indian call centres are very specific and much worse than in other countries.

this society. This becomes extremely problematic if the different living worlds get into competition with each other and one is seen as inferior in comparison to the others. This leads to the schizophrenic situation where the individuals would prefer one of the options but have to live in the transition, have to divide their lives and live at least partly in worlds they despise. The call centre agents are however an extraordinary and explicit example for constructing identities under the conditions of transitions, and a creative way of dealing with the demands of the very different worlds and frames can be seen.

When we look at the six agents introduced in the documentary, unquestionably a certain "Americanisation" in the sense the call centre rhetoric is suggesting can be observed. To start with Glen, the only one who is very unhappy with his job, even he has taken over some ideas of the American dream—although this dream is most probably a universal dream today. Instead of wasting his time as a telephone operator he wants to become a model, modelling for Dolce and Gabana or Gucci. In his free time we see him hanging around with friends drinking beer in a bar or smoking drugs in the lonely places of Mumbai, sitting on the bonnet of the car and thinking about humiliating his boss by having a sexual affair with his wife. It appears that he has taken over some of the less wanted American habits and lifestyles. Glen is the only one who expresses very openly the feeling of being humiliated by the work in the call centre. Sydney also dislikes his job and thinks that he could do "something better." He loves to dance and dances for entertainment at parties and teaches other boys. Most certainly he thinks of himself as a professional dancer. The documentary shows Sydney strolling in a fancy shopping mall comparable to those in the pictures from America, looking for t-shirts and suits he cannot buy but flirting with the idea of doing so. He wants the shop assistant to believe that he could buy something, if he would like to, and of course he goes for American brands. Sydney describes the enormous effects of work in night shifts in a call centre: "All I can think about is work. All I do is work. All people I meet are working people, the same people as me" (i.e. call-centre agents). The consequences for his personality are obvious: even though Sydney does not like the job, the job has taken over and is dominating his thinking.

With Osmond, we meet a person who is dedicated to the American company Amway and the "American values" as taught in the call centre. He has organised every hour of his life in a time table, and everything in the present is subordinated to his future goal of becoming a millionaire. He listens to coaching tapes, reads self-help literature with titles like "The Magic of Believing" and has pictures of products on his walls such as a motorbike and a villa with dates on it: on the 25th October 2005, he will own the bike, and on the 26th October 2006 the villa. "No one can stop me," is his slogan. He and Naomi connected the call centre directly with America. America, in his view, "has always been ahead of all nations," in contrast to India, which he considers to be very uncivilised in some places. As everyone who goes to the US becomes rich in his view, his goal is to get there. Osmond expresses directly that his personality has completely changed through the call centre. Before he worked there, he was "very negative," "a minus," now he considers himself as a "plus." The call centre is his road to success and has taught him the necessary skills and experiences to become rich, the only goal he mentions.

Nikki, too, thinks that she has changed dramatically through the work in the call centre. She says that when she came to the call centre, she was introduced to a new person: herself. She excels there and has discovered an ability to be successful and at the same time useful for other people, as for her calling people means to help them: "You just want to give." For Nikki, the call center is a place of love and "like a family." Similar to Osmond, she is an orphan, what leads Osmond to say that Amway is like a mother to him: "A mother cares." "Everything I have missed in life (like family) I got in the call centre," states Nikki. She seems to be religious and express her belief that god will always look after her. In her free time, she goes to a Christian church, the praying led by white women.

From Nicholas we have already heard that he would prefer to live in the call centre to avoid the "hassle dazzle" outside and that through the English language, an American feeling was instilled into him. This culture has gone "into" him. Nicholas is the only one who expresses what seems to underlie the statements and feelings of many of them: "I don't want to be an Indian any more." He met his wife in a call centre, but now her shift has changed, so she works by day and Nicholas at night. In between they meet for 20 minutes in a mall next to her call centre, eating in a fast food restaurant.

Body in Transition: The Case of Naomi

With the case of Naomi, I want to point out the role the body has in these transitional processes. Until now aspects concerning the body have been only marginally touched. Although such aspects are implicit in the other cases, too, Naomi can be seen as a kind of cumulation of transformations and is as such appropriate for a more detailed analysis.

Naomi is the last agent we come to know in the documentary of Ahluwalia and embodies the ultimate of his picture about the alienated employees. She has transformed herself and her body nearly completely into a new, non-Indian being with blond curls, lightened skin and Midwest American accent. Even her eyelashes are bleached and she refuses mascara when advised by a make-up assistant in a shopping mall—it is obvious that she is very proud of this detail of her appearance. Of course Naomi also reports that she has changed completely after her training for the call centre. Now, she is "totally hip, totally different from all the other Indian girls," and the boys especially want to know her. When they see her, she reports, "they are like asking: Where do you come from?" Naomi enjoys this thought so much that she relishes it a second time. "Where do you come from?", expresses all her strangeness, her exoticness and difference, as the answer is certainly not "from India" but from America. "I am totally very Americanised," she states, and that she is "very much into today's world" which most probably means in the modern, Americanised world and not in the crowded Indian street we see her strolling, being ask something here and there by the boys hanging around as it is not possible to overlook her. Naomi is obviously enjoying the result of her efforts for her outfit very much. She expresses a great satisfaction with herself and loves to be "just me," "be myself" and "recall on myself," as she says. Together with Nikki, who has developed a deep belief in her god, Naomi is the only one who lives fully in the here and now and lives her life as it is with pleasure.

In consequence of the thoughts underlying the question "where do you come from?", Naomi declares and repeats seriously: "Don't mistake me for anything else, I am totally naturally blond. I want to make it officially right that I am totally naturally blond." The contradiction to what every one can see—her facial skin looked somehow burned—seems not to bother her. In her perspective, Naomi, as she has created herself, is obviously a naturally blond girl. The last shot with her makes unquestionably clear how serious she is with her statements. Standing in a discotheque, smoking a cigarette and drinking a beer she explains her philosophy: "I am looking for an ideal man. My ideal man should be just like me, a light guy. Blondes get attracted by blondes, I believe that. That's really natural. A natural tendency that happens." The camera then swings round and we see Naomi dancing, the only blonde in a crowd of black hair.

Person, body and consciousness—a theoretical differentiation

How could such a radical transformation of the identity, and in Naomi's case also of the body, be explained? And how can the dynamics and processes be described that result into self constructions like these of the call centre agents? Who are the "actors" in this interplay? To offer an interpretation, a theoretic framework is needed that takes the individuals and their perspectives and meaning constructions seriously on the one side and avoids pathologizing them on the other. I want to propose the theoretical differentiations between the concept of person, body and consciousness worked out by Niklas LUHMANN (2008) for a further analysis.

Luhmann's systems theory (LUHMANN 1987) conceptualises systems such as social (families, societies etc.) and psychic systems ("human beings") as autopoietic systems, which means that they are self-referential and link their operations only to their own earlier operations: they reproduce themselves by their own operations in consequence. This implies that they are closed systems, and nothing from outside can intervene. Changes are then always self-made changes; these systems can observe their environment of course and can also orientate their operations in accordance with these observations. But still these operations are based on the observations of the system itself and not on the "world outside." Social systems and psychic systems are structurally coupled during the course of evolution and as such are interdependent. Each of them provides necessary performances for the other. The basic system maintaining operations of social systems is communication—a social system has to link communications to earlier communications and communication must go on to maintain the system. The basic operation of psychic systems is thoughts: thoughts have to be linked to earlier thoughts and the consciousness can only continue through thoughts. As the focus here is on the self conceptions of the agents—the way they manage to oscillate between the different framed worlds they live in—and the changes of their conceptions due to the specific constellation of the work in the call centre, in the following I will focus first on psychic systems.

To generate an own unity and to maintain it, any system has to differentiate itself from its environment. It has to discriminate between itself and the rest of the world. Everything that is not conceptualised as part of the system belongs to its environment, like a baby has to learn that it is not identical to its mother. In the course of time, every system develops certain structures or patterns while observing and constructing itself and its environment to simplify the process of self constitution. The way a system differentiates itself from its environment constitutes its individuality, its uniqueness: that's me! For the psychic system, normally the body serves as a demarcation line between it and its environment. However in the systems theory approach, consciousness as a basic operation of human beings and the body is *not* a single entity, also consciousness cannot detach itself from its body. Whenever and wherever the body is moving, it has to follow. Because of this consciousness develops right from the beginning in identification with the body (Luhmann 2008). The human organism is a symbiosis of many autopoietic systems then, but consciousness constructs them as a unity and observes its own body as a priority. Only through this observation and through clues it gains from it, can it develop its own identity. The body therefore is existential for consciousness and its observations, but not identical to it. Identity as a consequence is an achievement of consciousness, a unity construction consisting of itself and the body. The term identity is consequently used with regard to this definition.

The difficulties start with any social situation. Consciousness cannot be communicated, and identity cannot be communicated, either. In addition very often it is not necessary to notice someone as a unique individual with all the resulting uncertainties in a communication, or on the contrary this would make certain communication and social processes (such as teaching or working) impossible. Therefore in communication the psychic system is often reduced to the form of a "person." Persons are a certain form to regulate social interactions and to observe individuals in a focused and reduced way.

Observing someone as a person means to attribute a specific behaviour and enable a set of expectations. It reduces the expected repertoire of behaviour and simplifies social interaction as one does not have to take into consideration the whole individual but only some specific aspects of it. Typically in any professional setting individuals are observed as persons: A teacher observes his students in their roles as students and reduces them accordingly to this role, from a colleague in the office one can aspect a certain behaviour, and when we meet our tax consultant he is not supposed to ask us about our eating habits like a physician probably is. All this makes social interaction easier and enables communication that does not have to take individual uniqueness into account. The observation as person therefore serves only the self organisation of social systems and not any psychical needs. But this in return does not mean that the person has no relevance for the psychic system.

Observing someone as a person helps the psychic systems to know which restrictions can be expected in social interactions and which restrictions they have to follow. They also make it possible for the psychic systems to experience these restrictions by themselves. "The consciousness to be a person gives the psychic system a social OK for normal situations" (LUHMANN 2008, p. 146, translation by I.C.), it knows how to act and behave. In cases of deviation the pattern of persons gives the psychic system a guideline of how much deviation can be absorbed as confusion. The psychic system "notices if it gets into trouble with itself as a person and has the possibility to search for ways out" (LUHMANN 2008, p. 146, translation by I.C.). In any case of trouble, in cases where the psychic system observes itself in deviation to itself as a person, many strategies to overcome the discrepancy are possible. An interesting perspective here includes the body into the relationship of psychic system (or consciousness) and person. A body can become a person or at least an important part of it, for example as a model or a professional sportsman. In case of confusion or trouble, if the body cannot fulfil the expectations for example, the psychic system can dissociate itself from the body: I have lost the match, but I am still a smart guy! Coming back to Naomi and the call centre agents the question here is now, whether in return a person can demand for a certain body and what happens if a deviation between consciousness, person and body or between different concepts of person occurs.

Getting into trouble with the identity construction: Strategies for overcoming paradoxical situations

After these short theoretical clarifications, the trio of consciousness, person and body now can be used to analyse the difficult identity construction by the call centre agents. The situation occurs that consciousness has to manage the fragile oscillation between very different frames of communicating and acting. There is the specific image of America, the virtual space-shuttle call-centre to sit and work in and India's every day world to sleep and live in.

As described, one goal of the training in the call centre is to change the habits and behaviour of the agents in a specific way to guarantee better selling results for the company. In accordance with the theoretical definition we can say that the agents are observed and addressed as persons in the call centre. The common shape of the person "call centre agent" has a specific set of competencies, behaviour, attitudes, language etc. This person is John and not Raju and Jane and not Gajatri. John or Jane should act and speak as much *like* an American on the phone as possible, should act as persons "as if" they would be Americans. But at the same time, he or she is definitely not supposed to *be* an American. Their working conditions and payment are Indian. The American values taught in the call centre like privacy, individualism and striving for happiness are not valid or intended for the Indian employees. Otherwise taking the image of America seriously, they obviously would not let them be exploited like they do, but would act individualistically and uncontrollably, and of course they would be much more expensive for the call-centre. In consequence, the expectations related to the person of a call centre agent are to be Indians who act professionally as if they are Americans, sitting with their bodies in the in-between space of the call centre.

Evidently this is not what the agents seem to experience. Their construction of their person deviates from that of the call centre. The possibilities of the new media to experience closeness apart from great geographical distance and intervene into processes thousands of kilometres away in real time supports the feeling of disconnection of the actual whereabouts or at least marginalizes the importance and relevance of the actual placement. Even more, consciousness is led by the experience of actually being in America. Instead of a passive reception of the offered contents and images as with TV, the agents interact many hours a day with Americans and intervene in their lives while changing certain conditions for them through the internet. Additionally, as the agents describe in the documentary, their consciousness is changing due to their work. Even when they are "back" in India after a nightshift like Sydney has said, their thoughts stay occupied with the calls, the centre and their image of America. They use their American names or at least the language outside the call centre. They are dressed as Westerners and behave in a manner that is adjusted to their image of America. All this can be interpreted in that way that, firstly their concept of their person is one other than that which is functional for the call centre and, secondly that the differentiation between the self as a person and their identity construction is vanishing. More and more the person has to be included and extensively recognised by their consciousness while creating its identity conception. Now, they *are* John and Jane.

The assumption here is, that the psychic systems have to handle a paradoxical situation when the differentiation between person and identity conception becomes more and more dissolved on the one side, but the expectations and demands regarding their person and their identity from their environment stay different: Be an American, but stay Indian. Act and speak according to a culture that is taught in the call centre, but live your daily life in another culture that is described as inferior. Talk about the snow in the morning in Colorado without knowing what snow feels like. Be Jane, but do not expect as Gayatri to live like Jane in her American world or to be treated like her. The identity conceptions of the consciousnesses have to cope with this paradox situation. As a consequence, the psychic system does not get in trouble with itself as a person as stated in the Luhmann citation, but has difficulties to dissociate the person from the identity conception and is additionally confronted with different concepts of person and identity by its environment.

How to live with a body in a transitional state?

In a certain way, the agents have to cope with these contradictory demands. But what, if consciousness is no longer coincident with the body? What, if the body is observed in a growing deviation to consciousness?

As stated, consciousness develops right from the beginning in identifying with the body and the body is existential for consciousness and its observations. Therefore it is consequent when the body gets involved in a solution for the paradoxical situation. Osmond and Naomi, most probably not by chance the two agents which identify the most with the call centre and especially with America, are seeking for a body-inclusive solution. Osmond actually wants to go to the U.S. If he were to live in the U.S., acting and behaving like an American would be the most normal thing of course. He would be one of them, and the discrepancy between feeling like an American in America and being one would disappear. He could reconcile his identity constructions with the observations and expectations of his environment. So going to the U.S. is his destiny and the here and now is only a waiting period which should be used best for preparation exercises.

Naomi however is using a different strategy instead of fleeing the now and here. She does not talk about migrating like Osmond, and she also does not want to live in the call centre, the proposed strategy of Nicholas to cope with the conflicting demands. Like Osmond Naomi no longer differentiates between herself as a person and her identity construction. The person has become an important part of her self concept or even the most important source for her identity. For doing the job in the call centre it would have been sufficient to adapt the consciousness to the American context while calling, as trained, and to change to the context of origin after leaving the centre. But Naomi has adopted everything to her call centre avatar, and in consequence her body has also been changed.

Naomi's strategy to reconcile the observations and experiences of her consciousness with the body is to adjust the body to the identity conception. With the blond hair and light skin her consciousness can harmonize its observations of the body with its conception of the self. In this perspective she is indeed "totally naturally blond," as it is most obvious that her identity as an Americanised, modern girl needs an expression, a sign visible for everyone, especially for herself. Otherwise, the difference between her consciousness and her body would have been much too big. No one would see who she is, would recognize her in the way she wants to be recognized, would ask: Where do you come from?

With this strategy she is an extraordinary example of what it means to live in a transitional state, using the body as means of transition, too. In times where the body can be created or recreated in many aspects due to new techniques or treatments, it has become nearly as available to changes and adoptions as anything else. After the death of god and that of man (Foucault), the body remains as a resource for creating meaning (WULF 2008). Sometimes even an obsession with regard to the thought of an improvement of the body is observable today (POSTER 2008). In consequence, the body can be adjusted to the demands of the consciousness. In the case analysed here, the consciousness, the body and the person have been harmonized to a unity, a kind of an artificial product named Naomi to overcome the paradoxical situation.

One last word about the framing. The stage for this artificial product is however Naomi's Indian whereabouts and not like in the case of Osmond, related to the future and another country. Naomi does not want to become someone else in an invented future. It is her Indian context that makes her something very special. It is there that the people ask her: Where are you from? Only within this Indian frame she can enjoy her efforts. She has made herself comfortable in the stage of transition.

References

AHLUWALIA, A. (Dir.) (2005): John and Jane. – India.

AHLUWALIA, A. (2006a): Filmmaker's Statement. – indianvibes.de: URL: http://www.indianvibes.de/projekt01/index.php?idcatside=29&sid=8ab8a4753b582e0bb67d710ea9a4b6ac – Download from 25.03.2009.

AHLUWALIA, A. (2006b): [Without title]. – Lecture given at First International Conference: Call Center India: Indian by Day—American by Night. – Museum of Communication. – Frankfurt a.M.

CHAKRAVORTY, B. (2007): Rights for the Third Gender: Problems of Identity and Recognition. In: BOSE, B./BHATTACHARYYA, S. (Eds.): The Phobic and the Erotic. – Calcutta, pp. 369–390.

DESHPANDE, S. (2003): Contemporary India: A Sociological View. – New Delhi.

FERNANDES, L. (2000): Restructuring the New Middleclass in Liberalizing India. In: Comparative Studies of South Asia, Africa and the Middle East, Vol. 20, No. 1–2, pp. 88–105.

LUHMANN, N. (1987): Soziale Systeme: Grundriß einer allgemeinen Theorie. – Frankfurt a.M.

LUHMANN, N. (2008): Soziologische Aufklärung. Vol. 6: Die Soziologie und der Mensch. – Wiesbaden.

MEHTA, S. (2004): Maximum City: Bombay Lost and Found. – New Delhi.

POSTER, M. (2008): Die Sorge um sich im Hyperrealen. In: Paragrana, Vol. 17, No. 1, pp. 201–227.

REDDY, G.(2007): Sexual Differences and their Discontents: Shifting Contexts of "Thirdness" in Hyderabad. In: BOSE, B./BHATTACHARYYA, S. (Eds.): The Phobic and the Erotic. – Calcutta, pp. 301–322.

SHETTY, V. (2006): [Without title]. – Lecture given at First International Conference: Call Center India: Indian by Day—American by Night. – Museum of Communication. – Frankfurt a.M.

VARMA, P. K. (1999): The Great Indian Middle Class. – New Delhi.

WULF, C. (2008): Anthropological Research in Education: Towards a Historical-Cultural Anthropology of Education. In: Critique & Humanism, Vol. 26, pp. 159–170.

About the Editors

AXEL MICHAELS is Professor of Classical Indology at the South Asia Institute, University of Heidelberg. In 2001 he was elected Spokesman of the Collaborative Research Centre SFB 619 "Ritual Dynamics", and since November 2007 he has been one of the Directors of the Cluster of Excellence "Asia and Europe in a Global Context — Shifting Asymmetries in Cultural Flows". His current fields of interest are social history and the history of Hinduism, theory of rituals, life-cycle rites of passage in Nepal, and the cultural and legal history of South India. His previous publications include *Hinduism: Past and Present* (2004) and *Śiva in Trouble: Rituals and Festivals at the Paśupatinātha Temple of Deopatan, Nepal* (2008).

CHRISTOPH WULF is Professor of Anthropology and Philosophy of Education, Interdisciplinary Centre for Historical Anthropology, Collaborative Research Centre "Cultures of Performance", Cluster of Excellence "Languages of Emotion" at Freie Universität Berlin. His research focuses on historical and educational anthropology, mimesis, aesthetics, and rituals and emotions. His previous publications include *Mimesis: Culture, Art, Society* (co-authored with Gunter Gebauer, 1995); *Logik und Leidenschaft* (co-edited with Dietmar Kampar, 2002); *Zur Genese des Sozialen* (2005); *Anthropologie Kultureller Vielfalt* (2006); *Anthropologie: Geschichte, Kultur, Philosophie* (2009); *Dynamics and Performativity of Imagination: The Image between the Visible and the Invisible* (co-edited with Bernd Hüppauf, Routledge, 2009); and *Der Mensch und seine Kultur* (2010).

Notes on Contributors

FABRIZIA BALDISSERA is Associate Professor of Sanskrit Language and Literature, and of Indian Cultural Traditions, Università degli Studi, Florence. She studied at Milan University, La Sorbonne, Oxford, and Pune and taught at the Universities of Milan, Venice, Orientale of Naples. Her research focuses on Kāvya, satire, drama (text and performance), dance, and goddess worship in ancient and contemporary ritual.

Univ. Doz. Dr. ARNO BOEHLER is Associate Professor of Philosophy at the University of Vienna and filmmaker. He was project leader of the FWF research project "Materiality and Temporality of Performative Speech-Acts" (2005–2007) and co-founded the Viennese cultural factory GRENZ-film (GRENZ-film (Ed.): *Philosophy On Stage* (2007). He has held fellowships at the Universities of Bangalore, Heidelberg, New York University, and University of Princeton.

CHRISTIANE BROSIUS is Professor of Visual and Media Anthropology at the Cluster of Excellence "Asia and Europe in a Global Context" (www.asia-europe.uni-heidelberg.de), University of Heidelberg. With a background in Cultural and Social Anthropology, Art History and Art Education, Brosius has published *Empowering Visions: A Study on Videos and the Politics of Cultural Nationalism in India* (2005) and *India's Middle Class: New Forms of Urban Leisure, Consumption and Prosperity* (Routledge, 2010).

IRIS CLEMENS received her PhD in Educational Science at the Goethe University, Frankfurt, and is a member of the faculty of educational science at the Interdisciplinary Centre for Historical Anthropology at the Freie Universität Berlin. Her main area of research interest is India and the general relationship between culture and education. Her publications include *Bildung – Semantik – Kultur: Zum Wandel der Bedeutung von Bildung und Erziehung in Indien* (Frankfurter Beiträge zur Erziehungswissenschaft).

GÉRARD COLAS, philologist and sanskritist, is Senior Fellow at the National Center for Scientific Research (CNRS). He has published on Sanskrit architectural, religious and philosophical works and on Indian palaeography. His major book publications include *Le Temple selon Marîci* (1986); *Vishnou, ses images et ses feux. Les métamorphoses du dieu chez les vaikhānasa* (1996); and, in collaboration with U. Chauhan, *A Descriptive Catalogue of the Sanskrit and Other Indian Manuscripts of the Chandra Shum Shere Collection in the Bodleian Library. Part V: Darçanas* (2007).

GAVIN FLOOD is Professor of Hindu Studies and Comparative Religion at the University of Oxford where he is also the Academic Director of the Oxford Centre for Hindu Studies. He has published five books including *The Tantric Body* (2006); *The Ascetic Self: Subjectivity, Memory and Tradition* (2004); and *An Introduction to Hinduism* (1996).

[JOHN] RICH[ARDSON] FREEMAN received his PhD in Cultural Anthropology from the University of Pennsylvania and teaches on the faculties of History and Religious Studies at Duke University. A specialist in Kerala, his fieldwork has focused on both lower-caste spirit possession and Brahmanical temple worship, while his textual research includes folklore, early and medieval Malayalam, Sanskrit, and comparative work with Tamil. He is currently engaged in a collaborative research project on the socio-cultural history of a major temple in central Kerala, and is writing a book on Teyyam.

UTE HÜSKEN, Professor for Sanskrit at Oslo University, lectured at Göttingen University and at the South Asia Institute, Heidelberg University (Department for Classical Indology). In Heidelberg, she was also a member of the executive committee of the "Dynamics of Ritual" collaborative research center. In 2007 she was appointed as a member of the steering committee of the Ritual Studies Group (American Academy of Religion), and since 2008 she has been serving as co-chair of the steering committee. Together with Ronald L. Grimes (Canada and the Netherlands) and Eric Venbrux (the Netherlands), she initiated the new Oxford University Press series entitled *Oxford Ritual Studies Series*, of which she is co-editor.

S. SIMON JOHN is Research Fellow at the Anthropological Survey of India. He did his Doctoral research on Children's Folklore, and has published four books and a number of research papers. He also specialises in audiovisual archiving on folk cultural heritage and has organised several exhibitions and folk festivals in various parts of India. He has published books in Tamil on children's folklore, oral myths, the Chennai Sangamam Folk Festival, and the history and trends of Tamil folkloristics.

MONICA JUNEJA is Professor of Global Art History at the Karl Jaspers Centre for Advanced Transcultural Studies, University of Heidelberg. She has taught at the universities of Delhi, Vienna, Hannover and at Emory University, Atlanta. Her research and writing focus on transculturality and visual representation, disciplinary practices in the art history of Western Europe and South Asia, and Christianisation and religious identities in early modern South Asia. She is Editor of the *Medieval History Journal*, a member of the editorial collective of *Werkstatt Geschichte*, and Editor of the series *Visual and Media Histories* (Routledge India).

CHARLES MALAMOUD was directeur d'études (professor) at the Ecole pratique des hautes études (Paris) up to his retirement. His field is Vedic India. His major publications include *Le svādhyāya, récitation personnelle du Veda* (1977); *Cuire le monde, rite et pensée dans l'Inde ancienne* (1989); *Le jumeau solaire* (2002); *La danse des pierres* (2005); and *Féminité de la parole* (2005).

PD Dr MARGRIT PERNAU is Senior Researcher at the Center for the History of Emotions at the Max Planck Institute for Human Development in Berlin. She studied History and Public Law at the University of Saarland and University of Heidelberg where she received her PhD in 1991. During 1997–2003 Margrit Pernau conducted research in Delhi on "Plural Identities of Muslims in Old-Delhi in the 19th century" and has been Research Fellow at the Social Science Research Center Berlin and at the Modern Orient Centre, also in Berlin. Besides the history of emotions, her areas of interest include modern Indian history, the history of modern Islam, historical semantics, comparative studies, and translation studies.

WILLIAM SAX is Professor and Head of the Department of Ethnology at the South Asia Institute, University of Heidelberg. He has previously studied and taught in Seattle, Chicago, Banaras, Harvard, and Christchurch, New Zealand. He has published extensively on Hinduism, pilgrimage, gender, ritual, performance, and healing. His major book publications include *Mountain Goddess: Gender and Politics in a Central Himalayan Pilgrimage* (1991); *The Gods at Play: Lila in South Asia* (1995; edited volume); *Dancing the Self: Personhood and Performance in the Pandav Lila of Garhwal* (2002); and *God of Justice: Ritual Healing in the Central Himalaya* (2008).

CORNELIA SCHNEPEL studied Social Anthropology and Romance Languages and Literature at the Johann Wolfgang Goethe-University in Frankfurt/Main. In her MA thesis (2003) she concentrated on the Indian dance Odissi with regard to regional traditions and cultural identity. Subsequent researches have led her to Mauritius in the Indian Ocean where she is focusing her research activities on the séga dance, francophone literature and tourism. She currently works at the Max Planck Institute for Social Anthropology as Editorial Assistant.

DAVID GORDON WHITE is Professor of Religious Studies at the University of California, Santa Barbara and Associate Research Fellow at the Centre d'Etudes de l'Inde et de l'Asie du Sud in Paris. He received his PhD in History of Religions from the University of Chicago in 1988. He is the author of *Myths of the Dog-Man* (1991); *The Alchemical Body: Siddha Traditions in Medieval India* (1996); *Kiss of the Yogini: "Tantric Sex" in its South Asian Contexts* (2003); and *Sinister Yogis* (2009), as well as of over seventy articles, chapters and reviews. He is also the editor of *Tantra in Practice* (2000) and *Yoga in*

Practice (2010). *Myths of the Dog-Man* was listed as one of the "Books of the Year" in the 1991 *Times Literary Supplement*.

Francis Zimmermann is Directeur d'études at the École des Hautes Études en Sciences Sociales (EHESS), Paris; Professor of Anthropology and History of Science of the Indian World, and responsible for the Divison de l'Informatique et des Systèmes de Communication (DISC) of the EHESS. Trained in classical philosophy, Sanskrit, social anthropology and traditional Indian medicine (Ayurveda), his research is based on continuing anthropological fieldwork in Kuttanad (South India), textual studies in the scholarly traditions of medicine, logic and philosophy in India, and explorations into the cognitive foundations of linguistic anthropology. Among his publications are *La jungle et le fumet des viandes* (1982; translated into English as *The Jungle and the Aroma of Meats: An Ecological Theme in Hindu Medicine*, 1987); *Le discours des remèdes au pays des épices. Enquête sur la médecine hindoue* (1989); *Enquête sur la parenté* (1993); and *La généalogie des médecines douces. De l'Inde à l'Occident* (1995).